The French Face of Nathaniel Hawthorne

The French Face of

Nathaniel Hawthorne

Monsieur de l'Aubépine and His Second Empire Critics

HISTORICAL INTRODUCTION AND TRANSLATIONS BY
Michael Anesko
AND
N. Christine Brookes

THE OHIO STATE UNIVERSITY PRESS / COLUMBUS

Copyright © 2011 by The Ohio State University.
All rights reserved.

Library of Congress Cataloging-in-Publication Data
Anesko, Michael.
The French face of Nathaniel Hawthorne : Monsieur de l'Aubépine and his Second Empire critics / Historical introduction and translations by Michael Anesko and N. Christine Brookes.
  p. cm.
Includes bibliographical references and index.
ISBN 978-0-8142-1143-4 (cloth : alk. paper)—ISBN 978-0-8142-9246-4 (cd)
1. Hawthorne, Nathaniel, 1804–1864—Criticism and interpretation—19th century.
2. Hawthorne, Nathaniel, 1804–1864—Appreciation—France. I. Brookes, N. Christine, 1974– II. Title.
PS1887.4.F7A54 2011
813'.3—dc22
                              2010036608

This book is available in the following editions:
Cloth (ISBN 978-0-8142-1143-4)
CD-ROM (ISBN 978-0-8142-9246-4)
Paper (ISBN: 978-0-8142-5607-7)
Cover design by Amelia Saul
Text design by Juliet Williams
Type set in Adobe Garamond Pro

This book is for
Matt
—in whose observant presence it was conceived—
and for
Christi's parents
—whose forethought made it possible.

There is a reflex of negation, of rejection, at the very root of the French character: an instinctive recoil from the new, the untasted, the untested, like the retracting of an insect's feelers at contact with an unfamiliar object; and no one can hope to understand the French without bearing in mind that his unquestioning respect for rules of which the meaning is forgotten acts as a perpetual necessary check to the idol-breaking instinct of the freest minds in the world.

—Edith Wharton, *French Ways and Their Meaning* (1919)

Contents

Preface		xi
Acknowledgments		xiii
Editorial Note		xv

Part 1   Historical Introduction

I.	The Problem of Recovery	3
II.	The Critical Foreground	7
III.	The Critics: A Biographical Overview	13
IV.	The French Face(s) of Nathaniel Hawthorne	21
V.	The Critical Legacy	71

**Part 2   Transatlantic Reflections:
The French Reception of Nathaniel Hawthorne**

VI.	Paul Émile-Daurand Forgues "American Poets and Novelists: Nathaniel Hawthorne" (1852)	99
VII.	Émile Montégut "A Socialist Novel in America" (1852)	129
VIII.	Louis Étienne "American Storytellers: Nathaniel Hawthorne" (1857)	164

IX. Émile Montégut
"A Pessimistic Novelist in America" (1860)   196

X. Louis Étienne
"The Transcendentalist Novel in America" (1860)   232

XI. Émile Montégut
"Nathaniel Hawthorne" (1864)   256

Biographical Register   291
Works Cited   295
Index   303

Preface

Quite unexpectedly, the idea for this book originated several years ago in an undergraduate honors seminar that I was teaching on Hawthorne and James. For the purpose of finding a suitable critical observation that might serve as the basis for an essay question on the students' midterm examination, I was rereading James's *Hawthorne* (for possibly the tenth time) and only then really noticed that he made repeated reference in his charming little study to an article by M. Émile Montégut, a writer for the *Revue des Deux Mondes*. Why, it suddenly struck me, did James feel compelled to address this critic? Who was he? What did he have to say about Hawthorne that provoked James to answer him? Why, after years of working on nineteenth-century American literature, had I not heard of Montégut or seen his work translated (particularly the essay to which James referred)? These were questions that compelled additional research.

Trying to answer them led to the surprising discovery of not just one but six major essays in French that were written about Hawthorne during that writer's lifetime. Montégut authored three of these; Paul Émile-Daurand Forgues had preceded him with one; and Louis Étienne wrote two more for journals that (importantly) rivaled the *Revue* for cultural prestige. Suddenly possessed of a considerable battery of unknown—or forgotten—criticism, I began the task of translation, in close and thankful cooperation with a fluent speaker, Professor N. Christine Brookes, the coauthor of this volume. The result has been the recuperation of a remarkable body of insights, work that can help us better understand the complexity of transatlantic cultural exchange in the nineteenth century. Literary scholarship in our own time calls more and more for the enlargement of perspective and the necessity for adapting our reading practices to dismantle the narrower limits of nationalist traditions. Knowing exactly what others have said and made of us has to be an important first step in making that progressive change possible.

In that spirit—and toward that end—we are proud to make available to English-speaking readers these six essays in criticism, revealing as they do the French face(s) of Nathaniel Hawthorne.

Michael Anesko

Acknowledgments

Compiling a volume of this kind entails many forms of indebtedness upon its authors. Because so many of the sources upon which we have depended are housed overseas, the courtesy of the interlibrary loan staffs at both the Pennsylvania State and Central Michigan universities has been crucial to our work. Without their efficient help, our access to important research materials would have been much more difficult. We are thankful, too, for the cooperative willingness of both libraries directly to acquire relevant sources that could not be obtained otherwise. Professor Burkhart Küster (Universität Stuttgart) generously clarified some of Montégut's more elliptical allusions for us; and the College of the Liberal Arts at Penn State has generously underwritten some of our expenses.

Portions of this book (in modified form) have been published in scholarly journals, and we are grateful to their editors for permission to reprint material that first appeared in their pages. *Resources for American Literary Study* has printed two of our translations: "A Socialist Novel in America" (under the title "Monsieur de l'Aubépine: The French Face of Nathaniel Hawthorne"), volume 31 (2007): 55–94; and "A Pessimistic Novelist in America" (under the title "Ancestral Footsteps: Montégut on Monte-Beni"), volume 32 (2008): 99–140. An important segment of "The Critical Legacy" appeared first in the *Henry James Review* ("Is James's Hawthorne Really James's Hawthorne?"), volume 29 (Winter 2008): 36–53.

Editorial Note

Throughout the notes and body text, references to Hawthorne's works are keyed to the *Centenary Edition of the Works of Nathaniel Hawthorne,* 23 volumes, edited by William Charvat, Thomas Woodson et al. (Columbus: The Ohio State University Press, 1962–97). The following abbreviations have been employed to simplify documentation:

- *BR*   *The Blithedale Romance*
- *HSG* *The House of the Seven Gables*
- *MF*   *The Marble Faun*
- *MM*   *Mosses from an Old Manse*
- *SI*   *The Snow-Image; Uncollected Tales*
- *SL*   *The Scarlet Letter*
- *TTT* *Twice-told Tales*

Where the critics translate Hawthorne, we have incorporated the corresponding excerpts from the Centenary texts. Passages appearing in square brackets were omitted in translation, but indicated there by ellipses; passages appearing in italics within square brackets were *silently* omitted. Incidental errors are enclosed in pointed brackets. Extended discussion of the critics' occasional deviations from Hawthorne's language is included in Part One, "Historical Introduction."

Historical Introduction

1

The Problem of Recovery

French appreciation of classic American literature is a subject about which we know relatively little. With the major exception of Edgar Allan Poe, who has always enjoyed "extravagant esteem" in France, the reception of other mid-nineteenth-century writers in that country remains undeservedly obscure.[1] Overshadowed by the enthusiasm shown for Poe by a distinguished lineage of French poets—Baudelaire, Mallarmé, Valéry—still, even the more modest transatlantic careers of other writers can deepen our understanding of them by inviting us to revisit their works from perspectives foreign to ours. Fully to appreciate that reorientation, however, requires greater familiarity with French criticism, almost none of which (again, apart from that devoted to Poe) has benefited from English translation.[2] Our purpose here, then, is really threefold: first, to make available to English readers the full texts of a number of contemporaneous French critical essays; second, to assess their significance in relation to their immediate historical context; and third, to examine their relevance to later critical trends and arguments.

Most students of American literature probably can recall the playful French *nom de plume* of Nathaniel Hawthorne. But very few will know that Monsieur de l'Aubépine enjoyed a surprisingly intelligent critical reception in France during his lifetime. As soon as publishers in New York and Boston made a serious effort (beginning in the 1840s) to claim some share of the British market by arranging for authorized reprints of their books in the United Kingdom, works by American authors increasingly found their way across the Channel and into the hands of serious literary journalists and intellectuals in France, an audience that was especially curious about the cultural manifestations of democracy. Tocqueville's provocative interrogation of that subject—and the turbulent upheavals of 1848—gave an immediate historical relevance to American books, a situation dutifully recognized by the leading instruments and agents of literary criticism in that violence-torn nation. Larry J. Reynolds has convincingly shown how political unrest in Europe affected American literature at mid-century, but as yet no one has tried to come at this subject in fully reciprocal terms.[3] Recovering even a portion of this criticism through translation can begin that useful task and help us to appreciate American literature from a more genuinely transatlantic perspective.

Several years after he was the first critic to introduce Poe to France, Paul Émile-Daurand Forgues (1813–83) performed a similar service for Hawthorne, bringing to readers of the *Revue des Deux Mondes* another new American talent. In 1846 Forgues had studied Poe not merely "as logician, as pursuer of abstract truth, as lover of the most eccentric hypotheses and the strictest calculations," but also as a writer intent on portraying "inner tortures, obsessions of the soul and diseases of the mind."[4] Six years later, an English friend prodded Forgues to consider another curious author from across the sea. "Have you noticed the American writer Nathaniel Hawthorne's works?" he wondered. "*The Scarlet Letter, The House with seven gables,* etc., etc.—they are full of power tinctured with a sort of gloomy mysticism."[5] Spurred by this prompt, within weeks Forgues had read both of those novels—and numerous short stories besides—in order to compose his inaugural essay on Hawthorne. With the appearance of *The Blithedale Romance* later in 1852, another distinguished writer for the *Revue,* Émile Montégut (1825–95), set his critical sights on Hawthorne and what he only half-seriously referred to as "the socialist novel in America." Before the decade was out, Louis Étienne (ca. 1820–75) would add two more essays to this growing bibliography, a list further supplemented by additional pieces from Montégut in 1860 and again in 1864. Altogether, these six essays comprise a unique (if undeservedly neglected) body of Hawthorne criticism. Their insights are remarkable not only for their time, but also to the extent that they anticipate many aspects of later trends in interpretation.

While the work of these three critics has not gone completely unremarked by Anglophone students of literary history, neither has its significance properly been measured. In her pathbreaking (and still quite useful) study of Hawthorne's contemporaneous reputation, Bertha Faust provided a one-paragraph précis of Forgues' "Poètes et romanciers américains: Nathaniel

Hawthorne"; but, while she found the essay "interesting," she dismissed it as "not strictly in keeping with our subject." (She briefly mentions Montégut's later essay, "Un romancier pessimiste en Amérique," in a footnote but seems unaware of Étienne altogether.)[6] Perhaps because he was the most prolific of the three, Montégut has attracted more sustained critical attention, but here again his occasionally moralistic limitations have tended to obscure the direct impact that his work had in shaping our modern understanding of Hawthorne—at least insofar as that understanding fundamentally has been influenced by Henry James's *Hawthorne* (1879), which drew rather surreptitiously from the Frenchman's essays. As far back as 1940, Ruth Brown rightly asserted that of all the French critics who engaged themselves with American intellectual history in the nineteenth century, Montégut was "the most outstanding and perhaps least known."[7] Her sympathetic view did not survive the onset of the Cold War. By 1948, Reino Virtanen complained that Montégut lacked "a broad sympathy for American life taken as a whole" and "was disheartened rather than encouraged by the spectacle of its energy and variety."[8] A generation later, James E. Rocks acknowledged that "French criticism of Hawthorne possessed moments of insight comparable to—in many instances, better than—critical writing done in America and England."[9] But even his survey—the most broadly informed that we have—aimed more to describe than to analyze and subordinated its sources to the theme of emerging literary nationalism in mid-nineteenth-century America.

Notes

1. Patrick F. Quinn, *The French Face of Edgar Poe* (Carbondale: Southern Illinois University Press, 1957), 4.

2. The best compilation of Poe criticism in translation is Jean Alexander, *Affidavits of Genius: Edgar Allan Poe and the French Critics, 1847–1924* (Port Washington, NY: Kennikat Press, 1971).

3. Larry J. Reynolds, *European Revolutions and the American Literary Renaissance* (New Haven: Yale University Press, 1988).

4. [Paul] É[mile]-D[aurand] Forgues, "Études sur le roman anglais et américain: les contes d'Edgar A. Poe," *Revue des Deux Mondes* (15 Oct. 1846). Translated in Alexander, *Affidavits of Genius*, 92, 95.

5. F. O. Ward to Forgues, 9 Feb. 1852, qtd. in Moira Anne (Curr) Helgesen, "Forgues: Nineteenth Century Anglophile," dissertation, University of Colorado, 1955, 113–14.

6. Bertha Faust, *Hawthorne's Contemporaneous Reputation: A Study of Literary Opinion in America and England 1828–1864* (1939; rpt. New York: Octagon Books, 1968), 96, 129n1.

7. Ruth Brown, "A French Interpreter of New England's Literature 1846–1865," *New England Quarterly* 13 (1940): 305.

8. Reino Virtanen, "Émile Montégut as a Critic of American Literature," *PMLA* 63.4 (Dec. 1948): 1275.

9. James E. Rocks, "Hawthorne and France: In Search of American Literary Nationalism," *Tulane Studies in English* 17 (1969): 157.

II
The Critical Foreground

It is no accident that French interest in American life and letters should have grown profoundly in the decade after the Revolution of 1848; but it is also important to recognize that men like Forgues, Montégut, and Étienne were insisting upon a fundamental redirection of that interest. For all of them, the pioneering work of Alexis de Tocqueville had established a vitally important (and inescapable) baseline for cultural inquiry into almost all aspects of American life. One of the earliest students of French literary history was hardly exaggerating when he observed that, before 1835 (the year in which the first volume of *De la démocratie en Amérique* appeared), "American literature can hardly be said to have had a real critic in France."[1] But, for all his significance, Tocqueville's probing intellect—so acute when dealing with social and political institutions—was less adept when, in the second volume of his treatise (published in 1840), he turned his attention to intellectual and cultural issues attendant to democratic societies. The second volume of *De la démocratie en Amérique* was, in fact, much less successful than its predecessor; besides being longer, its texture was denser, thus making it more difficult to read and comprehend. Especially problematic for the student of culture is the pervasive absence of documentation. In contrast to the earlier volume, in which Tocqueville could treat political questions "without specifically naming certain laws" and still analyze them "in relation to the democratic spirit," his speculative insights about literature in the second, advanced without a single reference to a specific author or literary work, are much more "confusing and unsatisfactory."[2] The next generation of French critics would be primed—perhaps even obliged—to redress those lacunae. Hawthorne's works, as we shall see, seemed to offer a particularly rich locus for assessing Tocqueville's more abstract hypotheses.

First and foremost, the new generation had to wrestle with Tocqueville's broad contention that "properly speaking . . . Americans still have no literature." Instead of *belles-lettres,* journalism dominated public discourse in the young republic: even the few literary authors America had produced were crudely imitative, their works "painted with colors borrowed from foreign mores."[3] In this, Tocqueville was reinforcing the viewpoint of Philarète Chasles (1798–1873), one of the great pioneers of comparative literature, who maintained that a polyglot population (like that of the United States) could never by definition produce cultural artifacts of truly national type. At a level of abstraction comparable to Tocqueville's, Chasles maintained that "colonies that have borrowed their dialect from a mother country enjoying a high degree of civilization have never been able to develop their own literature. Whether in a state of servitude, revolt, or emancipation, they are forever shackled to the former metropolis."[4] Since most French critics became aware of American writers only after deliberately immersing themselves in English literature and patterning their judgments after British authority, the discouraging implications of Chasles' elitist assumptions would prove stubborn. Still, in certain instances, the outlines of distinctively American originality arrested their attention. As Maurice Gonnaud recently has observed, despite their "principled scorn for a culture which had been branded, right from the beginning, as derivative and vulgar," the early French critics "harbor a curiosity for its expressions which can exceed a mere willingness to be entertained." If they are inclined to reject the notion of a truly superior literary culture emanating from the New World, "this rejection is balanced, and at times almost cancelled, by a surrender of the critic's self to qualities which he had simply not anticipated."[5] In various ways, Forgues, Montégut, and Étienne were guardedly open to that surrender, and it was Hawthorne who most consistently provoked it.

As the first to introduce Hawthorne to France, Forgues and Montégut confront the problem of derivative influence most directly. Rightly seeing Emerson as the harbinger of American newness, both critics affirm that, like him, Hawthorne has escaped (in Forgues' words) "the type of domination that old literatures, like old civilizations, exercise over new civilizations and literatures."[6] Even more bluntly, Montégut seeks to dispel the shadow that Tocqueville and Chasles had cast on postcolonial letters. With thinly veiled disdain, Montégut ridicules the "exaggerated" similarities that others have conjectured between American writers and their European forebears. "As soon as a new author appears," he laughs, "we hear it said, 'He is not an American, he's English, he's German.'" Emerson's debts to German Romanticism, Hawthorne's genial affinities with Charles Lamb: these, for Montégut, are trifling incidentals. "No one is formed on his own," he sanely argues: "every writer receives his education in a particular literature. This does not at all mean that he cannot be original. Our French writers all were educated by means of Latin literature. Are they less French because of it? To say that Emerson is German is no more accurate than to say, for example, that Montaigne is Roman." Once he has demolished the false analogy, Montégut proudly denominates Hawthorne as "the most American writer that the United States has produced since Emerson." By challenging opinions already entrenched in French intellectual culture, Montégut conferred on the United States a kind of "literary autonomy and dignity that no one had yet accorded to it."[7] Gradually, and haltingly, America began to emerge from the shadows of postcolonial prejudice and derogation.

The timing of these critics' enthusiasm—not to mention its venue, *La Revue des Deux Mondes*—was not coincidental. We should remember that the United States was the first nation to recognize the legitimacy of the short-lived Second Republic in 1848, and the leaders of that ill-fated government looked westward to America as a model for their revolutionary regime.[8] In the wake of the Revolution of 1848, François Buloz, the director of the *Revue,* determined that henceforth his journal would need to assess not merely the political and social aspects of democracy but also its literary consequences. He charged himself and his staff

> to look within, to defend sane ideas, something now more than ever necessary during these times in which everything is being overturned and utilitarianism is overflowing, to defend in particular sane literature and to provide guidance to enlightened and serious readers, . . . [and] to look at North America which continues that great experiment of democracy begun at the end of the eighteenth century with regularity and success.[9]

The *Revue* had as a new imperative the exploration and understanding of the events that had set France's middle class on edge. The official hostility of Napoleon III's government toward democratic America was often countered by liberal adversaries, for one of the few remaining weapons of the opposition "was to criticize indirectly the lack of freedom in France by casting longing glances at the political institutions of such countries as the United States."[10] While eager to keep democratic ideals alive, Buloz and the critics he employed were also skeptical of democratic excess. This creative tension between liberal aspiration and conservative instinct informs most of the journal's reviews and notices of American literature and social life, articles that became more frequent in the ensuing decade. Appreciating this dimension of the French cultural milieu also helps us understand why Hawthorne, in particular, should have been an inviting witness for these critics to interrogate.

He was hardly their sole subject, though, and we should first take note of the surprising catholicity displayed by these contributors to the Franco-American dialogue. Both Forgues and Étienne devoted substantial articles to Edgar Allan Poe (appreciative, but far from lionizing in the manner of Baudelaire); *Moby-Dick* and Maria Cummins also attracted their attention. But of the three, Montégut was most vigorously engaged with a surprisingly diverse array of American cultural phenomena. Besides writing about—and translating—Emerson, he contributed detailed essays on Longfellow, Melville, and Margaret Fuller to the pages of the *Revue*. But works of popular literature—*Uncle Tom's Cabin*, *The Lamplighter*, *Ruth Hall*—and other topics of historical and social interest also came within his purview. Travel writing by foreign visitors to the United States was a genre he relished, and he had a penchant for books dealing with American cultural idiosyncrasies: Maria Ward's *Female Life among the Mormons*, for example, and what he rightly designated *Le puffiste* (*The Life of P. T. Barnum, Written by Himself*). Slightly more than 10 percent of the astonishing 255 essays that Montégut published during his lifetime dealt with American subjects—twenty devoted to literature, the other eight focusing on social issues.[11] Their interest in America, then, was far from casual but, rather, historically deliberate. It also seems all the more remarkable when we remember that the greatest French critics of the period, Sainte-Beuve and Taine, showed almost no curiosity whatsoever for American materials. At least one historian has noted the disparity and considers the "meagerness of Sainte-Beuve's reading in American belles-lettres" as "nothing short of astonishing" in view of his wide knowledge of English literature and the fact that "in these middle years of the century there was a very considerable interest on the part of other French critics."[12]

If their fascination for American literature now seems eccentric, we must admit that they paid a heavy price for indulging it. By turning their attention so completely to works by foreign authors—British, Italian, and German, besides American—all three men suffered in the comparative esteem of their contemporaries and their successors. Considering the phenomenal range and scope of their combined output, it seems regrettable that so little is known about them as men of letters. All of them have been relegated to "a puzzling obscurity" (as one literary historian has called it), in part because of the suppleness of their intelligence and interests.[13] Eschewing a dictatorial theory (such as we find in Taine) or the tenacity of summary judgment (so characteristic of Sainte-Beuve), these men and their claims for posterity have always seemed modest. Shortly after Montégut's death, the redoubtable George Saintsbury suggested that the very catholicity of his intelligence (what Saintsbury called "horizontality") would work against him. "I am not sure that this 'horizontality'—this faculty of bringing himself in line with German, Italian, English, French subjects and interpreting them, has not done him some harm," Saintsbury prophetically reflected. "It is something so much out of the way, if not out of the reach, of most people that they suspect it."[14] Perhaps the same "horizontality" worked to eclipse the others? Of the three, only Montégut has had the benefit of a literary biographer's interest—and this almost a century ago. For information about Forgues we are largely indebted to an unpublished dissertation written in 1955, while next to nothing is known (or in print) about Étienne. While a recent monograph has called for a new collected edition of Montégut's best writings—a judgment with which knowledgeable reviewers have concurred—regrettably, most of his and the others' work remains relatively unknown.[15]

Notes

1. Harold Elmer Mantz, *French Criticism of American Literature before 1850* (New York: Columbia University Press, 1917), 155.
2. Mantz, *French Criticism of American Literature before 1850*, 89–90.
3. Alexis de Tocqueville, *Democracy in America*, translated by Arthur Goldhammer (New York: Library of America, 2004), 539. Hereafter cited parenthetically as *DA*.
4. Philarète Chasles, "De la littérature dans l'Amérique du Nord," *Revue des Deux Mondes* (1 Jul. 1835): 170. For a survey of Chasles' criticism of his French and English contemporaries see Abraham Levin, *The Legacy of Philarète Chasles* (Chapel Hill: University of North Carolina Studies in Comparative Literature, 1957).
5. Maurice Gonnaud, "Democratic Aesthetics," *Transatlantica* 1 (2007). http://www.transatlantica.org/, 5 Nov. 2007.
6. Throughout the Introduction, specific references to works in translation reprinted here are omitted to minimize clutter and redundancy. All other sources are fully documented in the Notes.
7. Barbara Antoniazzi, "The American Canon and the 'Revue des Deux Mondes,'" *Il bianco e il nero* (Udine [IT]: Campanotto editore, 1998), 110.
8. Sigmund Skard, *American Studies in Europe: Their History and Present Organization*, 2 vols. (Philadelphia: University of Pennsylvania Press, 1958), vol. 1, 133.
9. Qtd. in A[uguste]. Laborde-Milaà, *Un essayiste, Émile Montégut, 1825–1895* (Paris: M. Escoffier, 1922), 36.

10. Simon Jacob Copans, "French Opinion of American Democracy, 1852–1860," dissertation, Brown University, 1942, 203.

11. For a complete tabulation, see Pierre-Alexis Muenier, *Bibliographie méthodique et critique des œuvres d'Émile Montégut* (Paris: Librairie Garnier Frères, 1925), 3–6, 31–32.

12. Lander MacClintock, "Sainte-Beuve and America," *PMLA* 60.2 (June 1945): 430. Sidney Lamont McGee provides a descriptive survey of some of the most important criticism (notably that of Forgues and Montégut) in his published dissertation, *La littérature américaine dans la "Revue des Deux Mondes,"1831–1900* (Montpellier: Imprimerie de la Manufacture de la Charité, 1927), 84–101.

13. J. W. Skinner, "Some Aspects of Émile Montégut," *Revue de littérature comparée* 3 (1923): 283.

14. George Saintsbury, *A History of Criticism and Literary Taste in Europe from the Earliest Texts to the Present Day,* 3 vols. (Edinburgh: W. Blackwood and Sons, 1902–4), vol. 3, 447.

15. Gail Finney, reviewing Burkhart Küster's monograph, *Die Literatur des 19. Jahrhunderts im Urteil von Emile Montégut* (Tübingen: G. Narr, 1982), concludes by saying that this "informed and synthetic treatment of one of literary criticism's first comparatists more than justifies his call for a collected edition of Montégut's best writings." Her notice appeared in *Nineteenth-Century French Studies* 13 (Winter–Spring 1985): 177.

II

The Critics
A Biographical Overview

Paul Émile-Daurand Forgues was born in Paris, 20 April 1813. Like other parents influenced by Rousseau's *Émile,* his family sent him to the provinces, where he was schooled in the classics, and he received a law degree from Toulouse in 1833. Returning to the capital, he quickly joined the Liberal Party and became a confidante of Claude Alphonse Delangle (later Minister of the Interior and of Justice). Forgues' interest in politics was mixed, at best, and was soon outrivaled by a rising affection for *belles-lettres.* In the later years of the 1830s, he adopted the familiar pseudonym "Old Nick" and began writing essays and reviews of contemporary English literature for the *Revue de Paris,* the *Journal du Commerce, le Charivari,* and especially the *Revue britannique.* Impersonating an Englishman proved to be a turning point in his career, for "Old Nick" became a well-known literary figure. There was not only widespread speculation as to his true identity, but also informed appreciation of his work by no less a figure than Sainte-Beuve, who described him this way: "*Forgues, que la nature a fait distingué et que la politique a laissé esprit libre*" ["Forgues, made illustrious by nature and liberal by politics"].[1]

A visit to England in 1843 confirmed Forgues' Anglophile predilection and also helped him establish a network of friends who kept him abreast of new publications and books of special interest. While British literature, history, and social questions largely captivated his attention, he also found occasion to write seven major articles on American literature between 1846 and 1865, ranging from Poe, Hawthorne, and Melville to Susan B. Warner and Oliver Wendell Holmes. His rising popularity might also help to explain why the journal's founder, François Buloz, invited him to join the editorial ranks of the *Revue des Deux Mondes,* where all of his criticism on American literature first appeared. Like his great contemporary Sainte-Beuve, Forgues cultivated an impersonal and biographical approach to his subjects, doing "much the same thing for English literature as the former achieved for that of France."[2]

Besides publishing his own critical essays and reviews, Forgues also translated many English-language texts into French, including *La lettre rouge A* (1853) and *La maison aux sept pignons* (1865). Whatever their weaknesses, both of these translations went through multiple editions during Forgues' lifetime and certainly helped to create a French audience for Hawthorne's work. Altogether, there is no reason to gainsay the generous conclusion of Forgues' most serious student, who summarized his career this way:

> A pioneer, not only in thought but also in his particular field; a classic in style and taste; a realist in ideas; a humanitarian in criticism; a servant of international understanding; a sincere lover of literature—Forgues was all these, and served his ideals faithfully to the best of his ability and to the end of his active life.[3]

Illness forced Forgues to abandon writing in 1870, though he lived for another thirteen years. That long period of silence (from a writer previously so copious) may also have contributed to his "fall into oblivion," a fate not unlike that of the other French critics who commented on Hawthorne. In Forgues' case "this was doubly inevitable since he had concentrated on English literature to the exclusion of that of his own country—a fact which precluded him from consideration as a French critic, whilst the fact that he wrote in French excluded him from being counted among the English critics."[4] The same paradox would cripple the posthumous careers of Montégut and Étienne.

At the time of Hawthorne's death in 1864, Émile Montégut eulogized the author in strangely impassioned words:

> And somber Hawthorne, did he not endear himself to you at just the right moment? Isn't it true that he came to you in the bosom of happiness to present his casket wreaths and his funereal perfumes? Oh! What favorable hours, those, of black melancholy and sinister dreams, to have conversations with Hawthorne's visions, to read *The Scarlet Letter, The House of the Seven Gables, Mosses from an Old Manse!*

By this time, the critic was well acquainted with the American romancer, already having composed two extensive articles about him in 1852 and 1860. Throughout his long career at *La Revue des Deux Mondes,* he wrote many articles on American literature and culture, examining such diverse topics as the election of Franklin Pierce, Mormonism, the literary legacy of Margaret Fuller, and the poetry of Henry Wadsworth Longfellow. Beginning with his debut article on Ralph Waldo Emerson in 1847, Montégut's scrutiny of the United States coincided with a critical turn in that journal's literary and political objectives, much affected by the implications of the failed Revolution of 1848. A fluent speaker of English, an Anglophile, and a supporter of the constitutional monarchy of Louis-Philippe, Montégut was well suited to address issues and topics of timely interest to Second Empire France. Over the next three decades, he published twenty-eight articles on the United States and its literature for the journal. Despite this voluminous production (which also branched out well beyond Anglo-Saxon literary and cultural interests), and even though he was identified by a contemporary critic as "one of three or four great stockhouses of ideas of the nineteenth century," Montégut faded into obscurity after his death in 1895.[5]

This middle-class native of Limoges, born 23 June 1825, was a little younger than Jules Michelet and his illustrious colleague Charles Augustin de Sainte-Beuve, part of the same generation as Hippolyte Taine, Ernest Renan, Charles Baudelaire, Gustave Flaubert, and publisher Pierre-Jules Hetzel. He began his recognized and influential position at the *Revue* in 1847 as a darling of François Buloz during the first golden age of French criticism. He was a prolific writer, penning countless articles and just under thirty books on art, literature, and what we might now consider cultural criticism—for example, his analysis of French political and moral attitudes in *Libres opinions morales et historiques* (1858). His monumental ten-volume translation of Shakespeare's dramatic works won him the *Prix Langlois* from the Académie française in 1876. On a more personal level, friends and contemporaries anecdotally remarked upon Montégut's photographic memory, acute intelligence, peculiar work habits, and (in light of his vast productivity) unexpected humility. Unfortunately, this cluster of idiosyncrasies alienated him from others who wielded power within the cultural establishment of late-nineteenth-century France.

Even during his own lifetime, Montégut failed to receive adequate recognition. In an 1878 letter, Taine lamented that, despite thirty years of work as one of France's most prominent literary critics, Montégut had few accolades to show and suggested that he apply for the recently vacated chair at the prestigious Collège de France: "After writing so much and so well, I find it a shame that you have nothing. I've expressed this aloud this time, and I see that significant men—Renan, Gaston Paris, [Ernest] Legouvé, [Ernest] Bersot—are of the same mind."[6] Elme Marie Caro, a French philosopher and Académie française member, echoed Taine's feelings about the election: "I could not ask for better [for you] except for the Académie, but that will come in time. . . . I have already spoken with some of the most prominent professors and have made sure that your name will receive a very favorable welcome."[7] While Montégut turned down overtures for a chair at the Collège, he later stood twice for election to the Académie française, both times failing to win the votes needed. Though he had been the principal literary critic since 1857 at *La Revue des Deux Mondes,* he died in 1895 with little official recognition, even within his native France.

Overshadowed by Taine and Sainte-Beuve, he had partly himself to blame: although his productivity was by any measure enormous, he collected his critical writing in published volumes only infrequently, and even then restricted their scope to a relatively narrow range of topics. His noteworthy essays on American literature and culture have never been culled from back numbers of the *Revue des Deux Mondes* and other French periodicals. Instead, when he is remembered at all, literary historians have sniffed at his didacticism and dismissed him as a "moralizing critic."[8] Indeed he was. Montégut sought to trace the characteristics of literary genius and morality based on the individual author and the environment—national, religious, or other—in which that author's talent was cultivated. Writers from his native France, a country he deemed too fixed on abstractions and too committed to a literature in service of ideals, had never realized literary genius and had effectively missed out on what Romanticism had to offer. On the contrary, those countries that had allowed for a certain liberty from abstraction, valued the individual, and had a solid moral framework were able to produce the likes of Dante, Shakespeare, Gœthe, Carlyle, and Emerson.

His criticism touched on social mores in France, but also on political trends and tendencies. During a century of revolutions—both political and literary—he rarely, if ever, fell directly within republican, monarchist, or Bonapartist camps. Politically, he despised the emphasis on a selfish, divisive, and amoral individualism based on materialism that seemed to him to permeate post-1789 politics; yet he also abhorred growing currents of republicanism and socialism that denied the importance of the individual in relation to the whole of society. His political ideal was the July Monarchy of the Citizen-King Louis-Philippe in which a (quickly eroding) politics of *le juste milieu,* the "happy medium," tiptoed between some ideals of the Revolution and constitutional monarchy, and, ultimately, protection of France's *bour-*

geoisie. He minced no words in his criticism of the universal suffrage ushered in under the Second Republic. For him, this revolution for the masses had led to the debacle of the Second Empire. Montégut never sat firmly within any political camp during a century of much political upheaval. Repeatedly, his public seemed to demand that he be "democratic and anticlerical, *or* clerical and antidemocratic."[9] As a faithful, yet questioning, Catholic committed to Revolutionary ideals (but not as they had been implemented under any of the first formulations of the French Republic), Montégut could be neither.

Frustrated by both letters and politics in his native land, Montégut looked outward to Britain and America. His choice was not arbitrary, but rather ethically and politically motivated, and reinforced by the journal to which he dedicated the majority of his work. Small wonder, then, that (just four years after his arrival at the *Revue*) he reveled in his discovery of Nathaniel Hawthorne, an American writer whose work grappled with historical residues from Puritan austerity and displayed caustic disenchantment with half-baked political and social panaceas. Monsieur de l'Aubépine had something to say to contemporary France.

Any literary critic who, in 1857 (the same year as *Les fleurs du mal*), could launch an essay with this withering salvo—

> The poet who said that man is a flower whose roots reach down to hell should have been born in the United States—

deserves a better fate than oblivion. Yet the man who wrote that line, Louis Étienne, has all but vanished from chronicles of literary history.[10] In his time, however, Étienne stood among a distinguished group of French men of letters who felt a profound mission to make their countrymen better informed about the literature, politics, and culture of the English-speaking world. Étienne's active career was remarkably long, productive—and thankless: much like that of Forgues and Montégut. From the 1840s until his death, Étienne contributed dozens of articles on wide-ranging subjects to the most distinguished French periodicals of the day. Thackeray, Wordsworth, Tennyson, the Brontës, Poe—these and many other writers attracted his serious attention. Only rarely, however, did Étienne collect his work in published volumes, and almost none of it has been translated into English. Not surprisingly, then, almost all of his criticism has slipped into undeserved obscurity. To gauge the injustice, one need only glance at his penetrating critique of another contemporary, Nathaniel Hawthorne, which first appeared in the *Revue contemporaine* as part of a series ("Les conteurs américains") devoted to American authors.

Étienne's essay on Hawthorne was not the first in French to assess that writer, and it is important to see his piece as a significant contribution to an emerging critical dialogue in Second Empire France about the cultural work of fiction in democratic society. With the demise of the Second Republic and the *coup d'état* of Napoleon III, many French intellectuals and critics were anxious to ensure that certain Republican values and principles not be crushed or corrupted by imperial excess. Men of this persuasion gravitated toward the *Revue des Deux Mondes*, whose ebullient editor, François Buloz, had made it his journal's ambition to explore cultural, economic, and political innovations beyond France and Europe. This included a young United States, a fellow nation born of recent revolution. Even before Louis Napoléon came to power, Buloz had welcomed contributions that would expand French awareness of American literature, an impulse that happily coincided with the transatlantic publication of many of the works now recognized at the canonical center of the American Renaissance.[11] From the late 1840s on, the *Revue* took notice of Emerson, Poe, Melville, and Hawthorne (and many others less luminary), and French translations of some of their works quickly appeared. In every case, the *Revue des Deux Mondes* represented the cultural vanguard, exposing its readers to challenging new ideas and what often seemed like paradoxical efflorescences of Romantic sensibility from the land of materialistic Yankees.

Perhaps both to complement and to challenge the work of his rivals, Étienne aligned himself with the *Revue des Deux Mondes*' chief competitor, the *Revue contemporaine*. Founded in 1852, the *Revue contemporaine* was more closely aligned with the central government, which directly subsidized its publication as well as providing many subscriptions from administrative departments and ministries.[12] Despite—or possibly because of—these ties to the established regime, the *Revue contemporaine* never could shake off its underdog status; but that very cultural situation may have given its contributors a certain freedom or edge, at least when they turned their attention to matters external to France. With respect to Hawthorne, that distinction registers in the remarkable opening of Étienne's essay and is sustained to the closing line. While it is likely that some of Étienne's judgments were shaped or influenced by the earlier assessments of Forgues and Montégut (works that also shouldered the considerable burden of translating substantial excerpts from Hawthorne's texts to make him accessible to French readers), his analysis benefits from a presumption of familiarity and a consequent liberty to generalize. The results can be startling. "Nowhere is human nature more reviled than in this nation that believes itself called to renew humanity," Étienne asserts. "Those people like to think of themselves as God's elect; but, if you believe that, you also have to acknowledge that no other nation has a more unique relationship to the Devil." This is a critic who takes no prisoners.

Apart from the pleasure of his pointedly satiric viewpoint, Étienne provides insights about Hawthorne that have an almost prophetic quality. He didn't need Melville (or Harry Levin, for that matter) to instruct him about the power of blackness; he found it all by himself (and in just the same place):

> [W]e have not yet touched upon the principal trait of the Puritan spirit in Hawthorne. Here it is. He possesses a melancholy that comes not from life's suffering, painful experiences, or social disapproval, but rather from deep within the soul: a religious melancholy, borne from a vision of Evil. This is Calvinist melancholy, not René's, or Childe Harold's—Christian melancholy, almost disproportionate, occasioned by the ineffaceable shadow of sin.

Likewise, his contrast between the "old" American ethos and the "new" prefigures Van Wyck Brooks's classic formulation of Highbrow and Lowbrow (and possibly Richard Bushman's analysis of the transition *From Puritan to Yankee*). "With Hawthorne," Étienne carefully observes, "the marvelous always has a practical end. In the same way, the sectarians who peopled the shores of America had many visions, but they were never useless; every wonder had a moral lesson. . . . A truly American imagination, and such is that of our novelist, only admits the marvelous on the condition of proving something." A vivid capacity for epigram serves Étienne well: "One cannot know the meaning of ruthlessness unless one knows America." Even Jean Baudrillard could hardly have improved upon that.

Notes

1. Qtd. in Moira Anne (Curr) Helgesen, "Forgues: Nineteenth Century Anglophile," dissertation, University of Colorado, 1955, 18.
2. Helgesen, "Forgues: Nineteenth Century Anglophile," 133.
3. Helgesen, "Forgues: Nineteenth Century Anglophile," 144.
4. Helgesen, "Forgues: Nineteenth Century Anglophile," iv.
5. Arvède Barine, "Un critique contemporain: Émile Montégut," *Revue bleue* 37 (15 May 1886): 617. Montégut's obscurity has been reinforced even today by the lack of primary resources available to evaluate his role at the *Revue des Deux Mondes*. Assuming they survive, his papers remain uncollected or dispersed. At the Bibliothèque Nationale

de France (Paris), there are various letters written by Montégut, as well as some of his correspondence with the Hetzel publishing house. A miscellaneous collection of articles and letters surrounding the events leading up to the dedication of the writer's commemorative plaque at Limoges (collected by Henri Hugon, a member of the honorary committee) is housed at the Bibliothèque francophone multimédia de Limoges (Limoges, France). For more general information on the *Revue des Deux Mondes,* one may also consult the journal's archive at L'Institut Mémoires de l'édition contemporaine (Abbaye d'Ardenne, France).

6. Hippolyte Taine to Émile Montégut, 9 Apr. 1878, in Pierre-Alexis Muenier, *Bibliographie méthodique et critique des œuvres d'Émile Montégut* (Paris: Librairie Garnier Frères, 1925), 142–43.

7. Elme Marie Caro to Émile Montégut, 18 Apr. 1878, in Muenier, *Bibliographie méthodique,* 154–55.

8. Jean-Thomas Nordmann, *La critique littéraire au XIXe siècle, 1800–1914* (Paris: Librairie générale française, 2001), 138.

9. Émile Montégut to Elme Marie Caro, 3 May 1878, in Muenier, *Bibliographie méthodique* 157.

10. Very little is known of Étienne's life. Educated at Paris, he taught at Saint-Louis and later became Educational Rector of Besançon, where he died.

11. An important catalyst for this phenomenon was also the absence of international copyright. American titles were briskly pirated by British publishers (such as Richard Bentley, George Routledge, and Henry Bohn) who were just discovering an available mass market through their cheap reprint "libraries." See Clarence Gohdes, *American Literature in Nineteenth-Century England* (Carbondale: Southern Illinois University Press, 1944), 21–22.

12. Max Bach, "A Review of Second-Empire Reviews," *French Review* 35 (Jan. 1962): 297. In the last decade of his life, Étienne published critical essays on British poetry and history in the *Revue des Deux Mondes.* The *Revue contemporaine* folded in 1870 with the collapse of Napoleon III's regime.

IV

The French Face(s) of Nathaniel Hawthorne

Little in their inherited understanding of America prepared these later critics for Hawthorne, whose works seemed to defy the sweeping generalizations advanced by Chasles and Tocqueville when they considered "the literary aspect of democratic centuries."[1] If, as Tocqueville insisted, "democracy inspires in men a kind of instinctive distaste for all that is old" (*DA* 555), how to explain Hawthorne's retreat into the historical annals of New England for the source of so many of his works? If productions by earlier American writers—Brockden Brown, Irving, and Cooper—betrayed all the signs of what Forgues calls the "strange yoke" of postcolonial imitation (seen by Chasles and Tocqueville as inevitable), Hawthorne's fiction (like Emerson's philosophy) refuted their logic of restriction. Both Forgues and Montégut would agree that Poe's stories might confirm Tocqueville's prediction that literary style in the New World would "frequently seem bizarre, incorrect, exaggerated, or flaccid and almost always seem brazen and vehement" (*DA* 542). But both also recognized that Hawthorne, by contrast, was "more a master of his own mind, more strongly inspired by studies and thoughts of a higher order, swept away much less frequently by pure caprice or beguiled by vagabond fantasy." Hawthorne's psychological penetration of human nature was profound, his characters "true discoveries, native-born, and drawn with such sharply delineated individuality" that they seemed to appear in the world of fiction for the first time. In Poe's stories, on the other hand, these critics (Baudelaire notwithstanding) found "more bottles and laboratory apparatus . . . than men or women." To their way of thinking, Hawthorne was more genuinely American and more usefully representative of a nascent literary tradition.

No foolish consistency would be the hobgoblin of their critical minds, not least because these three men occupied different positions on the political spectrum. Their reactions to Hawthorne were not governed solely by ideology, but their country's disappointing experiments with republican institutions affected the inferences they drew from the American romancer's work. Even though Forgues had but a single occasion to comment on Hawthorne, it would seem as if he imagined him a kindred spirit in an ideal republic of letters. Much bruised by French political infighting (his own liberal aspirations having been "blighted" by Louis Napoléon's *coup d'état* in 1851),[2] Forgues was immediately captivated by Hawthorne's self-deprecating prefaces: "without them," he avers, "we might not have read a single one of his novels or tales." Learning from the "Custom-House" Introduction to *The Scarlet Letter* of Hawthorne's own political misfortunes, Forgues could only admire the American's determination to shake off disappointment and to resume his literary career. (The parallel with his own vocational situation must have seemed uncanny.) No less remarkable was the fact that Hawthorne represented the loss of his patronage job as if, metaphorically, he had been condemned to the guillotine, a figure of speech that was bound to strike a French imagination with particular force. Thus, Forgues takes inspiration from Hawthorne's dignified example of humble resignation. "All noble instincts are in him," he testifies: "Christian indulgence and graciousness, resistance to oppression, a thirst for what is right and truthful in all things." Forgues must have felt that he and his subject were comrades in the true party of humanity.

As the first to introduce Hawthorne to France, Forgues necessarily incorporates some lengthy passages in translation for the benefit of their new audience. The author's various prefaces—so genial and charming—were ideal for this purpose because they seemed to reveal Hawthorne's character and personal history in the absence of other biographical sources. Accordingly, Forgues offers substantial extracts from "The Old Manse" and "The Custom-House" to illustrate not just the felicities of Hawthorne's style but the republican virtue of his character, since they afford ample proof "of his unshakeable good-nature, of his philosophical moderation (allied nevertheless to deep-seated conviction), of that nobility of soul that we always want to believe is a privilege of intellectual superiority." Unlike other writers' "odious" prefaces—testaments of self-conceit—Hawthorne's beguile him with their modesty and balanced humor. In all the author's works, Forgues happily discovers an ethical imperative. Even the writer's most innocuous fables, ostensibly meant for children, convey deeper moral meanings. Forgues reads "The Snow-Image," for example, as an allegory of ideological intransigence, a powerful critique of bourgeois "common sense." "Hawthorne does not tell tales to tell tales," Forgues insists, "but rather to give material form to useful ideas, to popularize them, to make them sink in to distracted or rebellious minds." He is "a preacher to suit our frivolous temperaments, our limited spans of attention, our futile preoccupations, our aversion to serious things. He does not stand in the pulpit with an austere exterior or stiff-necked severity: to the contrary, his insinuating, pleasant, occasionally sarcastic chatter, his inoffensive and cautious taunting, his great gift for picturesque expression, his art of awakening curiosity and keeping it out of breath—all these combine supremely to disturb the imagination, to wrest it from its daily habits, to make it fly its highest flight, to take it to the land of chimeras."

What Forgues recognized as Hawthorne's essentially comic spirit was much less apparent to his French contemporaries. For Montégut, especially, the dark shadow of the Puritan past cast a pall over almost everything that came from Hawthorne's pen, and no nineteenth-century affectations—liberal democracy, socialism, or reforming zeal—could suppress it. "I do not know who could so blindly confuse the qualities of human genius and so completely lose the appreciation of nuance to say that Hawthorne is a humorist," he declares. "Hawthorne has wit and imagination; but to no degree does he possess that joyous opening up of the heart, that intellectual cordiality, that unexpected expansion of sympathy, the amicable jokes or complex fusion of high spirits and choler to which the English have awarded the name *humor*." Following a train of logic curiously akin to that of "Hawthorne and His *Mosses*" (1850), in which Melville (though perfectly aware of "the Indian-summer sunlight on the hither side of Hawthorne's soul") invites his readers to consider the other side ("shrouded in a blackness, ten times black"), Montégut quickly shifts the focus to the author's intellectual and moral genealogy.[3] "Only a descendant of the Puritans would be capable of devoting himself to the perpetual examination of conscience that one finds in Hawthorne's work," he recognizes. Only an artist who had inherited the Puritans' morbid instincts "would be capable of excavating the recesses of the soul to discover not treasure, but rather the repressed evidence of human frailty, finding subjects of horror, sleeping reptiles, witnesses to forgotten crimes." Somewhat more caustically, Étienne also attributes a want of humor in Hawthorne to his stubbornly dour ancestors. "The American storyteller would have refuted his Puritan filiation," he asserts, "if gay or even sweet or laughing apparitions ever appeared in his work. Puck, Ariel, Titania—gracious creations—are foreign to him. How could mid-summer nights' dreams be transplanted to the home of Reformed religion, the bivouac of Calvinism, on the borders of those immense forests where they thought they could hear the witches' sabbath every night?" Like most of Étienne's other insights, this one, too, exaggerates (or oversteps) the evidence on which it is based; yet there is a lurking rightness in the claim advanced, a sarcasm that teases out a latent truth.

The most thorough student of Hawthorne's French critics has suggested that their "most conspicuous misunderstanding" of the author stems directly from their skewed appreciation of the Puritan temperament and their exaggerated sense of the legacy it bestowed to him.[4] More recent investigations of Hawthorne's debts to his forbears help to redress this claim and should encourage us to reevaluate the cogency of earlier arguments. Michael Colacurcio, for example, compares Hawthorne to no less a figure than the great Harvard historian Perry Miller, whose erudite reconstruction of "the New England mind" reshaped modern understanding of America's seventeenth-century intellectual landscape.[5] Not least because they were (even if nominal) adherents to the Catholic faith, Forgues, Montégut, and Étienne were immediately struck by Puritanism's pervasive force in Hawthorne's writing—something again that only Melville seems to have appreciated with equal depth. "In spite of his fondness for tolerance, progress, and democracy, the old Puritan nature lives on in him," Montégut stubbornly asserts. "Hawthorne's talent marvelously explains the persistence of ancestral values that are perpetuated over time—the 'music of the blood,' as Calderón says, that (especially in provincial society) repeats in successive generations the same melody but with different variations."[6] Like Miller himself, Montégut also had a shrewd insight into the significance of the Puritans' removal to a wilderness setting, where the competing historical forces with which the Reformation in Europe had to contend were largely absent. "Do you not feel—you, children of the Latin race and of Catholic civilization—what a large gulf separates you from the society for which these tales were written?" Montégut ponders, as he tries to educate his French readers about Hawthorne's provincial milieu.

> It is a very peculiar world to which you have almost no connection and in which your disoriented imagination strays like a foreigner in an unknown land. Obviously, in the same way that you have none of the preoccupations of the author, he has never known any of yours. This kind of originality—where, if you will, singularities of thought and feeling are marked by such

excess—is such that our own European Protestant civilization can scarcely furnish us the means to understand it. We feel the presence of an incomparable moral element—exclusive and tyrannical, wholly unencumbered by the obstacles that restrained it in Europe—but there (in America) able to saturate the heart and soul of man.

Montégut may have been sitting on the quays of the Seine when he was inspired to this insight—while Miller, more exotically, discovered it atop oil drums on the banks of the Congo—but they share a deeply felt impulse to come to terms with American literature historically and comparatively.[7]

Montégut's most useful insights into the significance of Hawthorne's Puritan legacy evolve from his appreciation of the author's fixation on internal states of mind—what Henry James would call the "deeper psychology."[8] Hawthorne possesses, Montégut intuits, "an unparalleled feeling for impalpable things: fear, solitude, terror of annihilation—above all, the apprehension of those monstrous fancies that are spontaneously and unpredictably born in even the most moral and spotless minds." "After reading his work, we tremble to examine ourselves for fear of finding some latent madness," the critic maintains—"some thought of crime, some unsuspected depravity." Even though he himself lacks the precise vocabulary by which to express it, Montégut anticipates a remarkably modern psychological model of selfhood to describe the impact of his subject's work upon the reader. "Hawthorne's tales have made a bizarre vision pass before my eyes," he confides: "I see myself multiplied a hundred times in miniature, and everyone of me has just been caught in the filaments of a delicate web, at the center of which yet another me sits watching all the rest!"[9] Instinctively responding to (in F. O. Matthiessen's words) "the device of multiple choice" that Hawthorne employs to enrich the psychological complexity and dramatic intensity of his narrative situations, Montégut finds himself, like Dimmesdale, caught in a mental maze of (almost) his own making.[10] Hawthorne's fearful capacity to portray the mind in conflict with itself may trace its origins to the theological terrors of the seventeenth century, but its implications—to Montégut—are mercilessly up-to-date.

Just as remarkable is Hawthorne's uncanny power for delving into the mysterious recesses of the soul. "His eyes are as piercing as those of a lynx," Montégut affirms. "He can apprehend lurking evil. He can discover the devil in his many disguises, even those that appear honorable." As Montégut insists, only a true son of the Puritans could penetrate so deftly the shell of hypocrisy and pride behind which fallen Nature seeks to defend itself. "That subtle and profound analytical ability to see beneath exterior and visible motives, to perceive the heart of the root of evil, descends in a straight line from the pitiless scrutiny that the Puritans exercised upon themselves, that rigorous examination of conscience (interrupted only for prayer), that saintly espionage to which their souls subjected every action and thought." Even though he has abandoned his forebears' theological convictions, Hawthorne perpetuates their habits of mind. Taking his cue from "Sunday at Home," Montégut divines that Hawthorne "rarely goes to church," but, nonetheless (domestically sequestered), "the hymns of the faithful and the exhortations of the minister" reach his ears. His alienation from formal creeds and doctrinal observances is really superficial; a (not so little) lower layer of common feeling and temper runs deeper. "He no longer believes and lives the way" his ancestors did, Montégut alleges, "but he does have their intellectual outlook. He may no longer have their *soul,* but he does have their *spirit.* He follows their practice of strict investigation and pitiless analysis." That practice, in turn, profoundly affects the formal aesthetics of Hawthorne's work.

Long before Yvor Winters analyzed the Puritans' affinity for allegory, Montégut understood that symbolic mode as a generic extension of Reforming zeal, an "irresistible consequence," as he says, "of their examinations of conscience." His imaginative reconstruction of their frame of mind, if somewhat lurid, still suggestively illuminates the process of formal genesis, the compelling fusion of theology and aesthetics, that determined their preference:

> After long days of black reveries and painful interior confessions, those souls—starved for justice and vengeance, hardened by the persecution that they underwent and that likewise they inflicted—suddenly would see their solitude come alive and begin to converse with other strange characters: Sin, Death, Damnation, Grace, Salvation. These phantoms were not vain abstractions; they had recognizable human faces; they fated living creatures to death, to persecution, to hate, to love. Hallucination built a bridge between the abstract world of the soul and the concrete world of reality, and the Puritan passed from one to the other in a state of pious and terrifying somnambulism. For the Puritans, dream and reality formed a singularly close alliance, and from this came the tendency to express themselves through allegory.

Forgues had found Hawthorne's use of allegory "flagrant" (but "appealing"); Montégut's appreciation of the form is much richer and more nuanced. So different from its crude medieval antecedents (which "so baldly designate the symbol to be perceived and the dream to be discerned"), Puritan allegory, by contrast, "obscures the symbol altogether and just barely permits us to unravel the dream," because metaphysical abstractions assume more familiar guise and speak to us in voices we intimately recognize, the better to seduce or provoke us. "This gift for allegory," Montégut rightly insists, Hawthorne possesses "to the highest degree"; indeed, it "is an indispensable complement of his force of vision and psychological subtlety." "He knew how to animate and shed merciless light upon the hidden desires of the soul," Montégut continues, and how "to make the shadows of guilty thoughts tremble; he conversed with the facts of conscience as easily as we converse with real people; he knew how to create a body for the formless, a language for the mute; interior and moral history is played out in his pages with a lucidity and a precision that more than one historian of the exterior and concrete world might envy."

We should not be surprised, then, to discover that later criticism was obliged to consult 'historians of the exterior and concrete world' in order to perceive (as Winters was among the first to argue) that "the Puritan view of life was allegorical," and that "the allegorical vision" was "strongly impressed upon the New England literary mind."[11] At the same time that Perry Miller was delving much deeper into the intellectual underpinnings of Puritan theology (delineating its heretofore unrecognized indebtedness to the dualistic logic of Petrus Ramus),[12] Winters redacted its literary implications from other historical sources to arrive at a parallel conclusion. "Puritan theology," he summarized,

> rested primarily upon the doctrine of predestination and the inefficaciousness of good works; it separated men sharply and certainly into two groups, the saved and the damned, and, technically, at least, was not concerned with any subtler shadings. This in itself represents a long step toward the allegorization of experience, for a very broad abstraction is substituted for the patient study of the minutiae of moral behavior long encouraged by Catholic tradition.[13]

Precisely because they were educated in that Catholic tradition—and also schooled in the Republican reaction against it—Montégut and the other French critics more quickly could discern the relevance of the Puritan past to Hawthorne's mind and art. Their comparative frame of reference, though sometimes inviting embarrassing distortions, nevertheless gave them a vantage point to see Hawthorne's descent from the seventeenth-century founders without the trappings of Anglo-American literary nationalism, a strain that overwhelms so much other contemporaneous criticism.[14]

Whatever Hawthorne's genius for employing allegorical technique, his characters still seemed somewhat contrived and abstract to Montégut. "They are too metaphysical," he complains; "they have no blood, no entrails, no muscles—they rarely even have tears." The fault is not entirely theirs, he continues, because the author's detached relationship to his characters renders them "intellectual types" rather than fully realized human representations. Some contemporaneous English and American reviewers also spoke of this tendency in Hawthorne's works, but few supersede the French in pursuing its implications.[15] There is something too dispassionate about Hawthorne's psychological analysis, according to Montégut; his attitude is too cold and remote, as if (like Ethan Brand) he looked at his figures as subjects of an experiment, converting them into puppets and "pulling the wires that moved them to such degrees of crime as were demanded for his study." Their effect, then, on the reader is powerful, but partial. "Our minds shudder," Montégut shrewdly senses, "but not our entire being—when we contemplate these dramas that seem to take place between two or three ideas in one of the regions of the human brain." Finding numerous examples of the pitiless observer in Hawthorne's fiction (especially Holgrave in *The House of the Seven Gables* and Coverdale in *The Blithedale Romance*), Étienne arrives at a similar conclusion. Humorously suggesting that the novelist wears a pair of spectacles with the power of a microscope, Étienne notes that "by directing his magnifying glass at the fleeting expressions of the face, the mysterious relations of our physical attitude and our moral state, the timbre of our voice and the music of our soul, the storyteller comes to grasp the birth and torment of feelings, much as the biologist examines microbes in a drop of water." Hawthorne, to Étienne, "has all the curiosity of a physiognomist and all the patience of a psychologist," but his method is "too experimental not to cast a chilling pall over the drama." In this, perhaps Montégut and Étienne were simply taking a cue from Hawthorne himself (he says much the same thing in his self-deprecating 1851 Preface to Ticknor & Fields's edition of *Twice-told Tales*).[16] But it is just as likely that they arrived at their inferences independently, since earlier British piracies of *Twice-told Tales* (lacking the Preface) circulated widely.

When Montégut, at last, considers the overall effect of Hawthorne's technique, he describes the author's works as inducing a kind of moral paralysis in the reader, no less irresistible for being lethal. "One marvels," he confesses,

> at the tranquility with which he experiments with the soul's moral poisons—the poison of poverty, the poison of pride, the poison of regret—and the almost scientific precision with which he notes their progress. All the

great sentiments—love, hope, friendship, faith—waste away and trudge under watch like those touched by consumption. The effect is overwhelming, like witnessing a murder that justice is powerless to prevent or a gradual suicide that we cannot arrest.

For all its technical virtuosity—the cool precision of which Montégut speaks—Hawthorne's art seems almost perilously enticing, almost as if his stories were designed to entrap the reader, to seduce him with uncertainty, to undermine moral verities. Such qualities frankly worry Montégut (who sometimes sounds like a French Starbuck, desperately trying to cling to the remnants of a superannuated faith); but they also lead him to judgments that anticipate much more modern assessments. Even in his first essay, after surveying the author's shorter works, Montégut feels obliged to confess that Hawthorne likes "to play with a number of dangerous things." His social and political viewpoints seem ambiguous; he displays "a predilection for suspect notions"; here and there in his stories we might even perceive "the passing shadow of the taboo." These elements insinuate themselves into the reader's mind and cannot easily be dislodged. "Essentially," Montégut pregnantly concludes, "there is something unhealthy in his work that at first we do not discern, but that in the long run acts upon us like a very weak and very slow poison." The implicit conflation of Monsieur de l'Aubépine and Signor Giacomo Rappaccini suggested by Montégut's descriptive analysis is hardly accidental. Even though in the body of his criticism he addresses that tale only once (and then somewhat cursorily), the story's (im)moral implications seem to have permeated the critic's understanding of the author. From the start—consciously or not—Montégut employs imagery from "Rappaccini's Daughter" to characterize Hawthorne's oeuvre, a body of literature in which, he says, "the funereal dominates." Summarizing his first impression of the shorter fiction, Montégut suggests that while reading Hawthorne, "an odor similar to that which surrounds mortuary preparations—the pall, the boxwood branch that is placed in holy water, and the smell of those sadly everlasting flowers—rises to your nostrils and makes your head spin." Revisiting Hawthorne six years later, Montégut also resurrects the imagery, but now embellishes it with an even more emphatic Rappaccini touch. Observing that, previously, he had "examined with a fearful, antipathetic, yet real curiosity those funereal flowers" with which Hawthorne "loves to compose his literary bouquets," renewed acquaintance with them has only confirmed (and even intensified) his first impression. Again "inhaling their strange aroma," he feels "the same curiosity of mind, the same antipathy of heart, the same shudders of the soul, in front of these bizarre flowers, not one of which does not contain a hungry worm or a poisoned perfume." Only now they are even "more pungent, more acrid, more penetrating." One would almost think that Hawthorne had penned *Les fleurs du mal,* a work that, significantly, appeared just a few years before Montégut's second essay.

By suggestively describing Hawthorne's fictions as flowers of evil, Montégut was deliberately appropriating Baudelaire's central motif and, by reassigning it to the American writer, favorably associating the two artists. Given that poet's valorization of Edgar Allan Poe, whose works Baudelaire had begun to translate and champion, Montégut may also have been making rival claims, in a friendly way, for the American writer *he* felt was preeminent.[17] As we have seen, Étienne pursued the association more aggressively, since he opens his first essay on Hawthorne with a caustic allusion to Baudelaire (and in the same year that *Les fleurs du mal* was published). Not surprisingly, when Étienne continued his series *"Les conteurs américains"* with an essay on Poe (just two months later), he derided that writer's grotesque horrors and mysteries as the detritus of a diseased Romantic sensibility. "Poe's stories are the Chinese puzzles of literature," he jibed. "We do not fear the contagion of these difficult inanities in our country; we consider them very odd little exotic monsters."[18] Given the ultimate triumph of Baudelaire's campaign—possibly even aided by the reactionary responses of the French critical establishment—these backhanded compliments to Hawthorne might seem awkward gestures of endorsement. But at the time they first appeared, the contest was far from over—in fact, was just beginning; that Poe eventually would throw Hawthorne into relative eclipse in France should not prevent us from appreciating these early critical responses. As one recent literary historian has acknowledged, what Baudelaire saw in Poe was exactly what Montégut saw in Hawthorne: one of the most remarkable writers that America had yet produced.[19]

When Henry James had occasion to discuss the two writers in tandem, he played a subtle trick in Hawthorne's favor. "A good way to embrace Baudelaire at a glance," James suggested, "is to say that he was, in his treatment of evil, exactly what Hawthorne was not—Hawthorne, who felt the thing at its source, deep in the human consciousness. Baudelaire's infinitely slighter volume of genius apart, he was a sort of Hawthorne reversed."[20] In an analogous way, by seizing upon the principal topos of *Les fleurs du mal,* Montégut was suggesting that Hawthorne was a sort of Baudelaire reversed, and he certainly would have agreed that the American writer's apprehension of Evil originated deep within the recesses of the soul. For proof of that, one need only consider Hawthorne's earliest work, his youthful tales, in which one might have expected to find tender emblems of hopeful aspiration and love. After considering "The Wedding Knell," "The Minister's Black Veil," and other early sketches, Montégut marvels at their utter difference "from the romantic allegories with which we are so familiar, from hearts pierced by Cupid's arrows and souls held captive by martyred paramours for whom they will never die!" Instead we find a "long procession of people clothed in black, all mourning someone or something, come to tell us their invariably lugubrious stories, and, what is most poignant, perhaps, their eyes are dry as they confess. Hawthorne loves to speak for them when they have exhausted the wellspring of tears, when a surplus of misery has destroyed the magnetism of human sympathy." Characteristically, Étienne arrives at a similar conclusion, but even more stridently. In a passage (previously quoted) that vigorously echoes Melville's famous insight that Hawthorne's "great power of blackness . . . derives its force from its appeals to [a] Calvinistic sense of Innate Depravity and Original Sin," Étienne describes the weary burden of "Calvinist melancholy" that the American artist's imagination must bear.[21] No longer a Puritan by faith, Hawthorne "is still one in his heart and his imagination. Laws inscribed on tablets of stone are less durable than that those inscribed upon the fleshy tablet of the human heart, where they are written not with ink, but with the essence of the soul." Is it any wonder that Étienne thought Baudelaire should have been born in the United States?

As Patrick Quinn has demonstrated, the success of Baudelaire's translations of Poe owed much to the poet's complete identification with his subject and his typical willingness to accept Poe's language with almost literal frankness. By comparison, Hawthorne was never so well served in France. Unlike Poe, who had Baudelaire to render his prose into French with ardor and sympathy, Hawthorne "never found an alter ego who identified himself wholly with his works."[22] In Forgues' translation *La lettre rouge A* (1853), for example, the "richer dimensions of the romance" were "scrapped," according to one scholar, "reducing the masterpiece to a sentimental tale."[23] (Rather inexplicably, the same Preface ["The Custom-House"] that Forgues so much admired was omitted, perhaps for reasons of economy.) In 1854 the *New York Times* reported that a proposed translation of *The Blithedale Romance* had been abandoned because the "genius of the French tongue is opposed to the intelligent rendering of the style that Mr. Hawthorne has made his own."[24] Yet it is certainly worth noting that, imperfect as they were, Forgues' translations of *The Scarlet Letter* and *The House of the Seven Gables* (1865) ran through numerous editions in the nineteenth century. Throughout the 1850s, a range of French periodicals—*Le moniteur universel, Illustration, Mousquetaire, L'Athenaeum français*—published translations of some of Hawthorne's best tales (including "Young Goodman Brown" and "The

Birth-Mark").²⁵ The *Marble Faun* appeared serially (under the title *Miriam*) in the *Revue contemporaine* (1865); two editions of *Contes étranges* (*Strange Stories* [selections from *Twice-told Tales* and *Mosses from an Old Manse*], with Montégut's 1864 essay as an Introduction) were called for within a decade (1866–76); and a later popular edition of *Contes racontés deux fois* (*Twice-told Tales*) in 1888—priced at a mere 10 *centimes*—proudly announced that Hawthorne was "enjoying a great vogue" and "his writings today are viewed with keen interest."²⁶ At least one of the writer's early biographers acknowledged this,²⁷ but few scholars since have explored the subject seriously. The work of the men who created an audience for Hawthorne in France has been undeservedly shunted.

Important socioeconomic developments in France may also have contributed to Hawthorne's "vogue." The second half of the nineteenth-century saw the growth and diversification of the French literary market due to advancements in printing techniques and an ever-increasing French readership. Publishers such as Hachette and Hetzel were some of the most successful in this rapidly changing field. They recognized the need for new types of titles as they turned their attention to new modes of reading (as with Hachette's new series for train travel, the *Bibliothèque des chemins de fer*) and newly recognized genres, such as children's literature (for example, Jules Verne's popular *Voyages extraordinaires* series with Hetzel). At a time when international copyright was either nonexistent or unenforceable, foreign literatures in translation became an important part of these new product lines. Ivan Turgenev, Charles Dickens, and Nathaniel Hawthorne were just some of the foreign authors who were introduced via Hachette's *Meilleurs romans étrangers* and the children's series *La Bibliothèque rose/La Bibliothèque rose illustrée*. Just as important, through these new venues not only were Hawthorne's works more widely available to French readers, but they were also cheap: his *Trois contes* (*Three Stories* ["Dr. Higginbotham's Catastrophe," "Rappaccini's Daughter," and "David Swan"], 1853) was priced at 50 *centimes* in Hachette's railway library. The two-volume set of *Le livre des merveilles* (*A Wonderbook for Boys and Girls*, *Bibliothèque rose illustrée*) was somewhat more expensive because it was illustrated; still it cost but 4 *francs*.²⁸

Nathaniel Hawthorne's French critics also acted as his translators. Montégut, Forgues, and Étienne all rendered the American romancer's prose with varying translational strategies and degrees of skill. Not only do their choices tell us about their respective command of English: they also subtly reveal their critical predispositions. Were these translators faithful to Hawthorne's language and intention? Or did they purposefully change or suppress elements of the original work for a new, foreign audience? To what extent do their efforts at translation become implied acts of critical response?

Enterprising journalist that he was, Forgues (who was the first to tackle Hawthorne) seems always to have worked in great haste. Not surprisingly, then, his translations betray signs of carelessness, despite his obvious affinity for the American's writing. At first glance, Forgues seems to handle basic translation with skill, occasionally changing Hawthorne's syntax but retaining much of his original imagery intact. Compare the following passage from the Preface to *The Snow-Image*:

> I sat down by the wayside of life, like a man under enchantment, and a shrubbery sprung up around me, and the bushes grew to be saplings, and the saplings became trees, until no exit appeared possible, through the entangling depths of my obscurity. And there, perhaps, I should be sitting at this moment, with the moss on the imprisoning tree-trunks, and the yellow leaves of more than a score of autumns piled above me, if it had not been for you.

> [J'étais, comme un personnage enchanté, assis au bord du sentier de la vie, tout autour de moi grandissaient des centaines d'arbrisseaux, buissons d'abord, taillis ensuite, arbres enfin qui m'enveloppaient, me fermaient toute issue, m'entouraient de ténèbres inextricables. Ces arbres se seraient couverts de mousses, les feuilles sèches de vingt automnes m'auraient peu à peu enseveli, si vous ne fussiez venu à mon aide.]

Here, with slight modification of the order of Hawthorne's phrasing, Forgues has preserved the general sense of the passage he has excerpted. He translates "shrubbery" ("arbrisseaux" and "buissons") and "saplings" ("taillis") with accuracy into French. He skillfully handles the predicate "until no exit appeared," turning it into the French "me fermaient toute issue"—or, "closed off any exit to me." He also maintains the conditional sentence at the end of the passage. Upon closer inspection, however, we can see that Hawthorne's rather poetic English sentence becomes much duller in French, notably because of the use of the adjective "enseveli" ("shrouded" or "covered") in place of the original English notion of the author "sitting" and *then* slowly being covered up by the forest's detritus.

Other examples betray the same tendency to gloss over details and flatten the English original. For instance, Forgues reduces a richly nuanced passage from the "Custom-House" Introduction to *The Scarlet Letter* to very basic French.

But,	all this while,	I was giving myself very unnecessary alarm.	Providence
[M]ais		j'avais grand tort de m'inquiéter:	—la Providence
[But		I was really wrong to have worried.	Providence

had	meditated better things for me than I could possibly imagine for myself.
devait	pourvoir à mon avenir.
[had	to provide for my future.]

Another example from the Preface to *Twice-told Tales* illustrates the same sort of problem. Whereas Hawthorne confesses to the detachment of his method, acknowledging that "we have allegory, not always so warmly dressed in its habiliments of flesh and blood," Forgues erases the sartorial metaphor by writing that "nous y retrouvons l'allégorie si froidement incarnée" (*we meet allegory there so coldly incarnated*). He gets the temperature right, but sacrifices the original's modifying detail.

Forgues also makes some rather significant errors. He calls "blue-berries" "baies bleues" instead of the more appropriate "myrtilles." While Hawthorne describes a grave "marked by a small, moss-grown fragment of stone at the head and another at the foot," in Forgues' words the tomb is "marked by two big rocks, one at the head, the other at the feet" ("C'est le tombeau,—marqué par deux grosses pierres, l'une à la tête, l'autre aux pieds"). Not only does he change the size of the rocks, but he also omits the allusion to the passage of time—"moss-grown"—in the French. A more egregious (even comic) error can be found in his apparent confusion about adherents of Shakerism, whom he equates with (or mistakes for) Quakers. After a note describing Mother Ann, founder of the Shaker sect, he notes that Father Ephraim in "The Shaker Bridal" was "conquis au fanatisme des premiers quakers." Forgues does seem aware of the cultural pitfalls of translation, and sometimes we can see him doing his best to approximate cultural equivalents ("steel pens," for example, become more recognizable for his French readers by the inclusion of a brand-name: "plumes Perry"). But one has to admit that, all in all, Forgues seems rather clumsy and inconsistent in moving from the English to French.

Not so for Émile Montégut. Just eight months after Forgues wrote his premiere article on Hawthorne, the *Revue des Deux Mondes* also published Montégut's "A Socialist Novel in America," in which were included substantial extracts from *The Blithedale Romance*. Compared to Forgues, Montégut displays much more agility and precision in translating Hawthorne's English. (Already, we recall, he had worked through a considerable swath of Emerson's highly idiosyncratic prose; and he would go on to translate the complete works of Shakespeare [1868–73], a monumental task that earned him acclaim from the *Académie française* toward the end of his career.) In his first article dedicated to the new American writer, Montégut renders whole passages of *The Blithedale Romance* into French. More often than not, his method (more patient than Forgues') results in faithful, word-for-word transcription. Hawthorne's broad description of his modern arcadia—"It was gentility in tatters"—becomes "Nous étions une noblesse en haillons" (*We were a nobility in tatters*) in Montégut's French. To provide his readers with a better context for understanding Hawthorne, Montégut recalls the author's imaginary conversation with his ancestors in "The Custom-House" (and their presumed disdain for his artistic calling):

Such are	the compliments bandied	between my great grandsires and myself,
Tels sont	les compliments échangés	entre mes ancêtres et ma personne
[Such are	the compliments exchanged	between my ancestors and myself

across	the gulf of time!	
à travers	le gouffre du temps!	
across	the gulf of time!]	

Very little changes here; even the syntax remains the same in French. Montégut would follow this habit in his later work. Even Emerson's assessment of Hawthorne—"Hawthorne rides well his horse of night" (which, in Montégut's 1864 essay, he left for readers in the original English)—becomes "Hawthorne chevauche bien son cheval nocturne" (*Hawthorne rides well his nocturnal horse*). Such deliberate juxtaposition of the two languages must have helped assure Montégut's audience that his reading knowledge of English was consistently reliable.

Wanting to be faithful to Hawthorne's text, Montégut also tries to be conscientious about more idiosyncratic cultural details. For French readers unfamiliar with the phrase, he accurately defines "Grub Street" in a note: "A name that applies generally to poor writers—hacks—who eke out their living in garrets" (designation qu'on appliqué généralement aux auteurs pauvres et vivant dans des greniers). A more localized geographical detail trips him up just a bit, although he freely confesses a degree of uncertainty in his explanation. When Coverdale sneeringly alludes to "State Street" as an unlikely source of investment capital for Hollingsworth's model penitentiary, Montégut suggests (again in a footnote) that "undoubtedly" the author is referring to "a rich neighborhood in Boston," although more precisely the reference is to that city's financial district. Not surprisingly, other, more colloquial, expressions also prove difficult, and his instinct for the literal falls somewhat flat. When Hawthorne's characters forsake their town clothes for garments made of "homespun and linsey-woolsey," the best Montégut can do is to render the phrase as "étoffes de laine et de fil" (*woolen and woven fabrics*). He is still faithful to detail, but the French cannot capture the humble connotation of Hawthorne's words. We find another example in the passage from "The Masqueraders" in which a costumed Indian chief shouts, "Me take his scalp!" Montégut correctly uses the exact verb *scalper*, but he silently improves upon the diction of Hawthorne's cigar-store stereotype by permitting him the nominative case: "Je vais scalper sa chevelure" (*I am going to scalp him*). When Montégut recognizes that French has no worthy equivalent, he retains certain English words verbatim, perhaps assuming that his seasoned audience already will recognize them. Across the range of his three essays, certain linguistic peculiarities appear simply in italic font: *humbug* and *tomahawk*, for example, but also *gentlewoman, Yankees, lady,* and the phrase *at home*. The notion of informal domestic visitation could only be foreign to the French imagination.

All in all, this critic stays as closely as he can to the text. But when he does take liberties, he subtly reveals much about his qualities as a translator and as a critic of Hawthorne. In the following passage from "The Custom-House" Introduction to *The Scarlet Letter*, in which Hawthorne rather humorously describes his alienation from the unreality of his former Transcendentalist neighbors in Concord, Montégut more aggressively demonizes them by expanding upon the writer's use of the adjective "fastidious":

after growing		fastidious
après avoir fini par rendre	mon goût littéraire	extrêmement difficile et dédaigneux
[*after having made*	*my literary taste*	*extremely difficult and disdainful*

by sympathy	with the classic refinement of Hillard's culture
à force de sympathie	pour la culture classique et raffinée d'Hillard
by force of sympathy	*with Hillard's classic and refined culture*]

Likewise, when Hawthorne tartly concludes by saying that "Even the old Inspector [at the Custom-House] was desirable, as a change of diet, to a man who had known Alcott," Montégut sharpens the criticism by saying that the change the author experienced was not just of diet but "comme changement d'hygiène intellectuelle." Probably because he firmly believes Coverdale to be a stand-in for the author in *Blithedale*, Montégut is obliged to add weight to Hawthorne's rationale for distancing himself from his erstwhile companions. Conservative that he is, Montégut endorses what he takes to be Coverdale/Hawthorne's rational retreat from the corrupting influences of Hollingsworth and Zenobia/the more radical Transcendental reformers. In a passage from "A Village-Hall" in which Coverdale relates the perversions to which the practice of animal magnetism is prone, he cites as an example the possibility that "a mother with her babe's milk in her bosom," subject to such influence, "would thrust away her child." Montégut's translation melodramatically amplifies this affront against nature—"La mère qui serrait avec tendresse son enfant sur son sein et l'abreuvait de son lait était capable de l'abandonner" (*The mother who tenderly held her child to her breast and nursed with her milk was capable of abandoning him*)—making more powerful the suggestion of mesmerism's evil. Least surprisingly, perhaps, in a passage from Hawthorne that touches on the socialist philosopher Charles Fourier, Montégut can hardly disguise his acrimonious contempt for his radical compatriot. Hollingsworth's exclamation is severe enough, but Montégut literally turns up the heat:

[L]et him	make a Paradise,	if he can,	of Gehenna,	where,
Laissons Fourier	faire son paradis,	s'il veut,	de la géhenne,	où
[*Let us let Fourier*	*make his Paradise,*	*if he wants,*	*of Gehenna,*	*where*

	as I conscientiously believe,	he is floundering at this moment!
dans ce moment,	je l'espère bien,	il rôtit et se démène
right now,	*I truly hope,*	*he is roasting and struggling.*]

One can almost see Montégut stoking the coals under this hellish rotisserie!

Invariably, the same kind of inflection surfaces when Montégut wrestles with the questions of religious faith and morality that Hawthorne's texts invite. When, in "The Custom-House," Hawthorne imagines the disapproval his ancestors would feel for his choice of vocation, he employs the verb *scorn*: "[L]et them scorn me as they will...." Instead of using a French equivalent for "scorn" (such as "rejeter" or "mépriser"), Montégut chooses instead the verb "maudire," or "to damn," a predicate that connotes a much sterner rejection of Hawthorne's career as a writer. With this verb, the already sinister judgment by Hawthorne's spectral ancestors almost becomes an eschatological condemnation.[29] At another point, when Montégut is describing the characteristic mental habits of Hawthorne's characters, among them is a tendency "to dream lugubriously"—"rêver lugubrement"—used as a synonym for "brood" (an expression he leaves in English within parentheses).

In this instance, Montégut could have chosen a more neutral verb such as "ruminer"; instead, his preference makes even more ominous their representative mental state. Because of choices such as these, the universe in which Hawthorne's characters live, a world of Puritan exigencies and swift verdicts, becomes even more Manichean as Montégut represents it.

Louis Étienne, the one critic about whom almost nothing is known, still has left us with enough material in his two articles on Hawthorne to assess his qualities as a translator. This critic who pens such cavalier statements in his native tongue seems to approach transcribing Hawthorne's English into French with equal relish. Such bravado, as one might surmise, does not always do complete justice to the American originals.

As with the other critics, Étienne often chooses the path of least resistance and prefers to translate literally. Perhaps because the critic snipes chauvinistically about Zenobia's *bas-bleuisme*, he is only too happy to yield the floor to her tirade here:

"It is my belief [Zenobia says]— yes, and my prophecy,
"Ma conviction, dit Zenobia, "oui, ma prophétie,
[*"My belief,"* says Zenobia, *"yes, my prophecy,*

should I die before it happens —that, when my sex
si je dois mourir avant de le voir, c'est que le jour où notre sexe
if I should die before seeing it, is that the day when our sex

shall achieve its rights, there will be ten eloquent women, where there is now
entrera en possession de ses droits, il y aura dix femmes éloquentes pour
shall gain possession of its rights, there will be ten eloquent women for

one eloquent man. Thus far, no woman in the world
un homme éloquent. Jusqu'ici, pas une femme au monde
one eloquent man. Thus far, not a single woman in the world

has ever once spoken out her whole heart and her whole mind."
n'a jamais donné le dernier mot de son coeur et de son intelligence."
has ever given the last word of her heart and her mind."]

With respect to Coverdale, his literalism is rather a sign of sympathy for the point of view that Hawthorne's nonchalant character expresses:

IV. The French Face(s) of Nathaniel Hawthorne

I		by no means	wish to die.	Yet,	were
Je	ne souhaite	en aucune façon	de mourir;	cependant	si
[I	*do not wish*	*in any way*	*to die;*	*yet*	*if*

there any cause,	in this whole chaos of human struggle,		
	dans ce chaos des luttes humaines,	il y avait une cause	
	in this chaos of human struggles,	*there were a cause*	

worth	a sane	man's	dying for,
qui méritât	qu'un	homme	mourût pour elle,
that deserved	*that a*	*man*	*die for it,*

and which my death	would benefit,	then	—provided, however,
et que ma mort	pût servir	alors,	pourvu toutefois que
and that my death	*could benefit*	*then,*	*provided still that*

the effort	did not involve	an unreasonable amount of trouble	—methinks
cet effort	n'exigeât pas	trop de dérangement,	il me semble que
this effort	*did not require*	*too much trouble,*	*it seems to me that*

I might	be bold	to offer up my life.
j'aurais	encore le courage	d'offrir ma vie.
I might	*still have the courage*	*to offer my life.]*

Here, where French syntax calls for a rearrangement of terms (the adverbial phrase "en aucune façon" cannot precede the verb as it can in English), Étienne promptly reverts to simple transcription once he has cleared the grammatical hurdle.

Montégut and Étienne occasionally incorporate the same passages from Hawthorne into their analyses. Comparing them might suggest that the latter was quite familiar with his rival's work in the *Revue des Deux Mondes*. Consider this excerpt from *The Blithedale Romance*:

H:	In outward show,	I humbly conceive,	
M:	Au premier aspect,	je dois humblement l'avouer	
	[At first glance,	*I must humbly admit*	
É:	Par notre apparence,	j'imagine humblement	que
	[By our appearance,	*I humbly imagine*	*that*

H:	we looked	rather like	a gang of beggars or banditti,		than
M:	nous ressemblions	plutôt	à une bande de brigands ou de bandits		qu'
	we resembled	*more*	*a band of brigands or bandits*		*than*
E:	nous ressemblions	plutôt	à une troupe de mendiants ou de bandits,		qu'
	we resembled	*more*	*a troop of beggars or bandits,*		*than*

H:	either	a company	of honest laboring men,	or	a conclave
M:	à	une compagnie	d'honnêtes travailleurs	ou	à un conclave
		a company	*of honest working men*	*or*	*a conclave*
E:	à	une compagnie	d'honnêtes travailleurs	ou	à un conclave
	a	*company*	*of honest working men*	*or*	*a conclave*

H:	of philosophers.	Whatever	might be	our points of difference,
M:	de philosophes.	Quelles	que fussent	les différences qui nous séparent,
	of philosophers.	*Whatever*	*might be*	*the differences that separate us,*
E:	de philosophes.	Quelques	différentes que fussent nos vues personnelles,	
	of philosophers.	*However*	*different our personal views might be,*	

M: il y avait un point qui nous était commun à tous:
there was one point that was common to us all:

H:	we	all of us seemed to have come	to Blithedale
M:	nous	semblions tous être venus	à Blithedale
	we	*seemed all to have come*	*to Blithedale*
E:	Nous	semblions être venus	à Blithedale
	we	*seemed to have come*	*to Blithedale*

H:	with	the one	thrifty and laudable	idea of
M:	dans		la louable et économique	idée d'
	in		*the laudable and economical*	*idea of*
E:	avec	l'idée	utile et louable	d'
	with	*the idea*	*useful and laudable*	*of*

H:	wearing out	our old clothes.
M:	user	nos vieux habits.
	wearing out	*our old clothes.]*
E:	user	nos vieux vêtements.
	wearing out	*our old clothes.]*

As one can see here, Étienne's version mostly runs parallel to Montégut's. In some cases, Étienne keeps the same easy wording as Montégut ("nous ressemblions plutôt à une compagnie d'honnêtes travailleurs ou à un conclave de philosophes") or makes only minor changes (Montégut's slightly dusty "vieux habits" versus Étienne's more common "vieux vêtements"). While Étienne may have consulted the earlier translation, no one can accuse him of slavish copying; he is careful to stake his own ground. He avoids Montégut's glib additions to the original ("il y avait un point qui nous était commun à tous"). He more precisely uses the term "mendiants" for Hawthorne's "beggars" instead of Montégut's looser word, "brigands." Shortly after the passage cited, he is careful to include Coverdale's comic description of the banditti's clothing (ridiculously fashioned "with the waist at every point between the hip and arm-pit")—a detail that Montégut silently omits. In these particulars, at least, Étienne improves upon Montégut's translation.

Over all, though, Montégut's command of the translation enterprise still seems superior, not least because he is more inclined to be both faithful to Hawthorne's texts and also more patient in explaining his idioms and allusions. In the remainder of the paragraph that begins with the passage cited above, for example, Étienne makes no effort to gloss Hawthorne's use of "Grub Street," whereas Montégut does. Étienne also elides Hawthorne's telling allusion to *Henry IV* ("We might have been sworn comrades to Falstaff's ragged regiment"), something that the other critic—and Shakespeare translator—does not. In discussing *The Scarlet Letter,* Étienne silently omits significant phrases from Dimmesdale's imaginary confession to his faithful congregants:

"I,	whom	you behold	in these	black	garments	of the
Moi,	que	vous voyez	en		habits	de
[I,	*whom*	*you see*	*in*		*habits*	*of*

priesthood,—I, who ascend the sacred desk, [and turn my pale face heavenward,] taking upon myself to hold communion, in your behalf, with the Most High Omniscience

prêtre,	moi	qui monte à	cette tribune sacrée,
a priest,	*I*	*who climb to*	*that sacred platform,*

—I,	in whose daily life	you discern the sanctity of Enoch,
moi qui,	dans ma vie journalière,	vous parais aussi saint que le patriarche Enoch;
I who,	*in my daily life,*	*seem to you as saintly as Enoch the patriarch;*

—I,	whose footsteps,	as you suppose,	leave	a gleam
moi	dont les pas	vous semblent	laisser	un rayon lumineux
I	*whose footsteps*	*seem to you*	*to leave*	*a luminous ray*

Along my earthly track, [whereby the pilgrims that shall come after me may be guided to the regions of the blest,]—I, who have laid the hand of baptism upon your children

sur   la route de la terre au ciel,   moi qui ai donné le baptême à vos enfants,
along   the route from the earth to the sky,   I   who have given baptism to your children,

—I, who have breathed the parting prayer over your dying friends, [to whom the Amen sounded faintly from a world which they had quitted]
moi, qui ai exhorté les âmes de vos parents sur le seuil de l'éternité,
I, who have pleaded for the souls of your relatives on eternity's doorstep

—I, your pastor, whom you so reverence and trust, am utterly a pollution and a lie!"
Moi votre Pasteur, l'objet de votre respect et de votre confiance, je ne suis que souillure et
I,   your pastor, the object of your respect and trust,   I am only a stain and

mensonge!"
a lie!"

One doubts that Montégut, with his neo-Protestant sensibility and genuine regard for Hawthorne's Puritan heritage, would have silenced the author so recklessly. In *The House of the Seven Gables,* where Hawthorne darkly catalogues the hidden legacy of Colonel Pyncheon (a legacy that includes "a strange form of death, dark suspicion, unspeakable disgrace") Étienne collapses the suggestive appositives and renders this simply as "morts étranges" (*strange deaths*). The meaning and impact of Hawthorne's lugubrious enumeration are lost to the French reader. When Hawthorne elaborates the pathos Kenyon feels as he listens to Donatello's plaintive melody in *The Marble Faun,* he describes not only the sculptor's tears but the remarkable form of ecstasy they provoke in him: "They welled up slowly from his heart, which was thrilling with an emotion more delightful than he had often felt before, but which he forbore to analyze, lest, if he seized it, it should at once perish in his grasp." In Étienne's flatly abridged version, "They fell slowly from his heart, [which was] penetrated by one of the sweetest emotions he had known" (Elles [les larmes] tombaient lentement de son coeur, pénétré d'une de plus douces émotions qu'il eût connues). When Donatello loses his mysterious capacity for communicating with creatures of the forest, he laments the fact as a sign that, through him, Nature now recognizes "death." In Étienne's translation, however, that recognition is more pointedly criminal: "Murder, murder!" (*Le meurtre! C'est le meurtre!*), Donatello sobs.

We can justly see such casual disregard for Hawthorne's nuances as an extension of Étienne's caustic attitude toward America in general. Even with their occasionally erroneous idioms (even their possibly deliberate misreadings), Forgues and Montégut better grasp Hawthorne's subtleties when they render the American's delicate prose into French. Étienne, by comparison, displays little suppleness or patience for the intricacies of the task. Given his aggressive style as a critic, these lapses in translation should come as no surprise.

With varying degrees of emphasis, all of these French critics explore Hawthorne's affinities with Emerson, whose leading role in the vanguard of New England Transcendentalism they take for granted. Whenever they catch the note of moral Idealism in Hawthorne's work, his ties to the Concord sage seem most evident. Accordingly, what might be called Hawthorne's democratic fables of Republican virtue—"The Great Stone Face," for example, or "The Threefold Destiny"—give dramatic form (in their view) to Emerson's fundamental principle of self-reliance. Since Montégut was instrumental in bringing Emerson to his countrymen's awareness, having published the first French translations of the most important early essays in 1851,[30] he advances these claims most confidently. In various tales, he suggests, Hawthorne "has made numerous applications of Emerson's philosophical counsels and has rendered his abstractions into concrete, dramatic, and animated form." In both writers Forgues hears a voice of liberal prophecy railing against the petty materialism of the age. Étienne sees *Transformation* (the title by which the French knew *The Marble Faun*) as a fictional embodiment of the philosophical doctrine of Correspondence; he frankly labels Hawthorne Emerson's "disciple." "He does not write novels to spread philosophy," Étienne says of Hawthorne, "but he quarries philosophical ideas that give life and inspiration to his novels." Without Montégut's 1851 translations in hand, Étienne never would have arrived at that conclusion. The germ of Hawthorne's novel, he attests, "was hatched in one of the most abstruse and shadowy corners of Emerson's *Essays*" (and he shows convincingly which one).

Significantly, though, over time the clouds of history overshadow the tone of breezy optimism that we occasionally find in the first French readings of Hawthorne. By the 1860s, when the United States seemed to be disuniting itself in bloody catastrophe and France seemed absently complacent under Napoleon III, a tinge of nostalgia (if not desperation) creeps into Montégut's assessments of these same stories. Cleaving to his own tattered hopes for a meritocratic society, Montégut now declares that "The Great Stone Face" represents "the most noble page ever penned by Hawthorne." All of the author's philosophical allegories bring us back, he wistfully writes, "to those happy days, the happiest the American republic has ever known (*Halcyon Days*, in poetical English)"—the period from the "liberation" of Texas in 1836 to the outbreak of the Mexican-American War (1846–48). Harking back to the Revolution of 1848, when France looked across the Atlantic for inspiration and support, Montégut remembers that the confidence of the American republic in its destiny then was so great, and "so candid was its pride, that its illusions won other peoples who turned their attention to it as they would to a promised land where the redemption of humanity would be fulfilled." Even his choice of words betrays the conflation of American and French democratic aspirations. "*Les bons temps à venir*—'good times to come'": that was a motto shared by his countrymen and the "savants" of Massachusetts.

Such a climate of hope fostered utopian dreams in both countries, but America proved a more fertile laboratory for social experiment. In the three decades preceding the Civil War, the reform spirit unleashed by both the evangelical resurgence of the Second Great Awakening and the upwelling of Jacksonian democracy encouraged a bewildering array of communitarian enterprises and perfectionist schemes across the United States. Among the most famous of them was Brook Farm, at Roxbury, Massachusetts, in which Hawthorne invested one thousand dollars and about eight months of his life in 1841. Modeled upon the socialist theories of Charles Fourier (especially as they were more popularly formulated in works such as Albert Brisbane's *The Social Destiny of Man* [1840]), the "Association" was, in Montégut's opinion, "the only place in our times where a group of men has sought to live according to the philosophical doctrines they profess and to practice what they preach."[31] Less charitably—but with an almost deadly acumen—Étienne observes that in no other country but America are "projects for the renovation of the human race more frequent or less durable." The "group of empty dreamers" who surrounded Emerson "like moths around a flame" could not sustain their utopian enthusiasm because they could not be weaned from the bourgeois comforts they pretended to renounce. As is often the case, the sting of Étienne's sarcasm still serves as a vehicle for meaningful insight. "Attempts at communism in the Old World have had a different bearing," he notes, establishing an important contrast:

> Those who flirt with communism generally have had nothing to lose, and think that they have everything to gain. The masses are brought to it by

poverty and irresistible ambition. Those American communists were of a different order. They left their carpeted offices . . . forsook their tables covered with books and periodicals, their offices with their poems or articles just begun. They deprived themselves of capacious sideboards, covered with entrées, their entertainments, their teas. And why? To hoe, to reap, to sweat, and to tire themselves out. To serve as chambermaids to a pair of bulls and a dozen cows.

Long before Lionel Trilling began exploring the latent contradictions of the liberal imagination, Étienne was mapping them out with prophetic precision. The ideological conflict between what he terms the "Old" American Ethos—grounded in the covenant theology of the Puritans—and the "New"—based squarely on material self-interest—is a rather lopsided contest. "Competition is the life of modern peoples," he admits, "but to the American, it is the soul of his life, the blood of his heart, the marrow of his bones. One cannot know the meaning of ruthlessness unless one knows America." Contemplating the ruins of Blithedale, Étienne almost ruefully concludes, "The Yankees certainly got their revenge."

Étienne's reactionary instincts inspire him to bristling—sometimes outrageous—social commentary, but more often than not his criticism strikes a vulnerable spot and sounds a curiously modern note. If, on the one hand, he crudely dismisses the incipient feminism of Margaret Fuller (whom he identifies as Zenobia in *The Blithedale Romance*) as so much "petticoat charlatanism," his anxious thoughts on the disappearance of private life are not merely chauvinistic and can hardly be refuted in an age of ubiquitous "reality" TV programming and "communication" overload. In American society, he tellingly observes,

> public life invades everything: all citizens live under each other's eyes; no one hesitates to call attention to himself or his family. All aspects of private life are broadcast—even domestic matters of the hearth and table. They clamor for public notoriety by every means. . . . Every house is open to the public, invited by those who live in them: not even the birth chamber is off limits.

If the critic here is simply amplifying a concern implied by Hawthorne in his novel—especially at the moment when Hollingsworth rescues "The Veiled Lady" (Priscilla) from Westervelt's enslavement and public exploitation of her on the stage—Étienne's penchant for broad generalization is not radically misplaced. Like Tocqueville, he understood the "enormous power" of the press—and publicity—in America; its eyes are never shut, as that canny traveler reported: "ever vigilant, it regularly lays bare the secret springs of politics"; and, as the principal vehicle of public opinion, it already had begun to exercise unprecedented control over others (*DA* 212, 491).

Montégut's 1852 assessment of *Blithedale* also owes a debt to *Democracy in America*, because the critic prefers to see socialism in the United States as a form of resistance to the tyranny of the majority. "If you want to know which class sports the greatest number of socialists," he taunts, "the rich and educated would be a good bet."[32] Paradoxically, egalitarian ideals are advocated especially by the intellectual elite, "who grow weary more quickly than others of the multitude's yoke." For Montégut, however, the appeal of socialism also has a literary dimension, since he likens its doctrines to other forms of the fantastic, a genre to which Americans are particularly susceptible. Precisely because the vast majority of those living in the United States are "positive, practical, serious people, little disposed to reverie," American writers have no other recourse than to idealize and romanticize the most vulgar elements that surround them and to pander to an "appetite for the marvelous" that such starved imaginations crave. "Socialism," in Montégut's view, "has all the characteristics of the marvelous": the promise of "passionate attractions, a human race made for happiness, the prospect of joys without end, a new heaven and earth evoked by all-powerful formulas, the transformation of men into Olympian gods." No wonder, then, that writers of fiction should succumb to its allure. As Tocqueville had suggested, authors in democratic societies "will seek to astonish rather than to please and to engage the passions rather than beguile taste" (*DA* 542–43).

But Hawthorne, as Montégut knew quite well, was not just any author, and *The Blithedale Romance* was not really what he called it (a "socialist" novel). Certainly that adjective would catch the attention of French readers whose memories of the events of 1848 were still fresh; but, as the critic admits in his opening paragraphs, his real concern is the "moral malady" of ideological coercion, a theme he correctly finds at the center in Hawthorne's book. If *The Blithedale Romance* is not "socialist," neither is it even a "novel" in Montégut's eyes because the story privileges psychological analysis rather than the more overt drama of narrative action. Rather cleverly, he suggests that "Hawthorne has orchestrated a philosophico-humanitarian ballet, danced by four main characters." Coverdale, Hollingsworth, Priscilla, and Zenobia "make socialist *entrechats* and logical *faux pas;* and their footwork is not always confident. They cannot keep time with their system's music." The metaphor seems enchantingly apt to describe *Blithedale*, with its Arcadian masqueraders whirling through the woods to a fiddler's tune and leaving the stage in shambles.

Irresistibly drawn to the likelihood that *Blithedale* is a *roman à clef* (drawn from the author's experiences at Brook Farm), Montégut is tempted to read the novel as a chapter in the intellectual history of the United States: a cool dissection of Transcendental enthusiasm and reforming zeal. We should not be surprised to discover that in Miles Coverdale (the dilettante man of letters) Montégut finds a stand-in for the author—and even, for that matter, the voice of his own conservative temperament. Coverdale, he says, is the least "eccentric" of the four principal figures, "the one who does his best to keep his moral health intact and who fears losing it the most." The same touch of paranoia he discerns in Hawthorne's protagonist is almost embarrassingly evident in certain stretches of Montégut's essay, which awkwardly insists that a serious work of art have an overarching (and preferably Christian) moral intention. Hawthorne, he fears, is too detached, too skeptical, too agnostic: too much, that is, like Coverdale. Hardly an impediment, Montégut's inconsistencies, his vacillations of feeling, work to fuel his curiosity. Despite his rather flat-footed strictures, he allows his imagination to see and reach beyond them. Sensing that "there is something unhealthy" in Hawthorne's fiction, the critic still cannot put it down, even though it begins to affect him "like a very weak and very slow poison." He compares the American's work to "a spider's web, a seine that surprises a fish, a snare that holds a bird captive." To read him is "to be caught in a trap." Yet Montégut seems a willing victim.

Because of his need (and desire) to see Coverdale/Hawthorne sympathetically, Montégut occasionally is obliged to tinker with his extensive quotations from the novel in order to mute the author's broader satire, which in the original does not altogether exempt the first-person narrator. In a very long exchange between Coverdale and Hollingsworth, which Montégut includes to demonstrate the instinctive independence of the former's nature, by omitting the indirect transcription of the narrator's thoughts, he insulates Coverdale from the suggestions of prurience and jealousy that Hawthorne's text invites. Coverdale, we know, has good reason to resist Hollingsworth's monomaniacal scheme for the reformation of criminals. But when, during their conversation, his thoughts revert to Zenobia, he senses that Hollingsworth has appropriated her wealth to further his ambitions and cannot help wondering "on what conditions was it to be had? Did she fling it into the scheme with the uncalculating generosity that characterizes a woman when it is her impulse to be generous at all? And did she fling herself along with it?" Eliding these questions, Montégut enhances the impeccability of Coverdale's virtue. Likewise, when Coverdale later resolves to leave the Association in order to recover his mental balance, Montégut awards him full credit for his instinct to withdraw. "No sagacious man," he quotes, will long retain his sagacity, if he live exclusively among reformers and progressive people, without periodically returning into the settled system of things, to correct himself by a new observation from that old standpoint. It was now time for me, therefore, to go and hold a little talk with the conservatives, the writers of "The North American Review," the merchants, the politicians, the Cambridge men.

As represented by Montégut, Coverdale's choice is an indubitably sane alternative. But the last sentence that Hawthorne wrote goes on to qualify the conservative point of view by adding to the list an extended appositive—"all those respectable old blockheads who still, in this intangibility and mistiness of affairs, kept a death-grip on one or two ideas which had not come into vogue since yesterday morning." Silencing the comic tenor of the original disproportionately amplifies Coverdale's dignity.

These minor acts of misreading are understandable, given Montégut's impulse to identify with Hawthorne and his narrator. After quoting at length Coverdale's jeremiad at the village hall, a scene in which he inveighs against the "humbug" of contemporary culture and the degradation of orthodox religious sentiment, Montégut frankly says, "I share Hawthorne's opinion entirely," adding that "his book's characters are the clearest evidence of the fears he expresses." In his second (1860) essay on the American author, Montégut confesses that of all of Hawthorne's novels, *Blithedale* is his favorite, even though he feared that the book was too difficult to win enduring fame. "The audience for such a book necessarily must be limited," he regrets.

> *The Blithedale Romance* is made to be understood and felt only by a hundred or so people among the generation currently alive. It is a diamond, but a diamond whose value even lapidaries and connoisseurs of precious gems themselves cannot completely comprehend, and that is destined to be hidden again under a thick layer of oblivion in about twenty or so years.

A better critic than prophet, Montégut still has much of importance to say, and we should not be sidetracked by his more capricious judgments or idiosyncratic foibles. Anyone familiar with zealous reformers, he says more soundly, "will recognize the hand of a master in the portraits of Hollingsworth, Zenobia, and Miles Coverdale. There they are—just as you have met them—dreamers without poetry, philanthropists without love, politicians without a mind for innovation: all agitated, yet passionless hearts and cowering intellects. They have been captured and described with the artful finesse and suppleness of a truly admirable talent."

Étienne prefers to see *Blithedale* as an illustration of the larger cultural contest he sees at war in the United States between an older, communal ethos and the ascendant mercantile spirit of laissez-faire capitalism. With his characteristic brio, he conjectures an imaginary Republic in a remote wilderness of the Golden Age—a "Platonopolis," full of "dreams and poetry"—whose virtuous citizens, enticed by the prospect of a "Gold-rush of drachmas," are corrupted by dreams of avarice.[33] The analogy to modern America is comic but apt, and Étienne easily skewers the bourgeois Transcendentalists whose delusions lure them to the countryside—a dozen Yankees, he quips, playing at Arcadia. Unlike Montégut, who more perceptively gauges the interest of *Blithedale* to be altogether psychological, Étienne has no interest in the book's plot or characters; for him the romance is a political parable, perhaps even a kind of Conservative Manifesto. Certainly a chauvinist one, as he recoils from a social sphere in which women enjoy "all the virile liberties that decency will tolerate." Zenobia's fate, if tragic, is to him welcome because it has the advantage of shutting her up. "Eloquence—or, rather, let us say slickness," he savagely writes, "is the dominant character of the people of the United States. The gift of the nation is the gift of gab." How could women not be jealous of "the privilege of masculine loquacity?" If only (he laments) they had something to say. But Étienne is hardly eager to hear declamations from a "land of Bloomerism," a false utopia of "petticoat charlatanism and pedantry." Happily, he sides with Coverdale (or Hawthorne, whom he sees hiding behind that character's mask), whose removal from the community and rejection of reforming zeal he can only applaud. In Coverdale's closing confession, Étienne hears "the words of a democrat, but a democrat who needs some rest." "As with so many today," he acknowledges, "his faith is tepid, almost nonchalant." One senses that this Coverdale would make a perfect citizen of the Second Empire.

Differences of opinion make these critics worth reading, because their conflicting estimates of Hawthorne's value illuminate so many dimensions of his work. Drawn to (what he imagined were) Hawthorne's Locofoco politics, Forgues finds *The House of the Seven Gables* if not the author's best work then "at the very least the one in which he makes the best use of what constitutes his particular originality": affecting the reader powerfully through the exercise of his imagination. (We should remember that Hawthorne himself preferred the *Seven Gables* to all his other stories: another confirmation of Forgues' instinctive affinity.) Montégut, however, can "dismiss" this book "without regret." Only the opening chapters of the novel, recording Hepzibah's petty transformation from aristocratic gentlewoman to huckstress of a cent-shop, affect him deeply, because in them he feels that Hawthorne is altogether in his proper element: "unhappiness and destitution." "How Hawthorne's mind is at ease, at home, in the company of these painful sentiments!" Montégut exclaims, and with what "voluptuous and cruel curiosity" he traces the movements of this poor creature crushed under the burden of her misfortune. As soon as Phoebe's arrival "brings a glimmer of youth and Spring into the old house," he complains, "interest starts to wane, and the disappointed imagination of the reader would gladly say to the writer: 'Snuff out this sunbeam, chase away the Spring, give us solitude, and speak to us again of the tremors and terrors that grip the souls of the destitute!'" Many other critics also have regretted Phoebe's redemptive (and chronic) cheerfulness, but seldom for the same reasons. As Frederic Carpenter famously quipped, "Puritans preferred blondes"—and so, even against his innermost desire, did Nathaniel Hawthorne.[34]

Montégut does not want to be reminded—as the *Seven Gables* undeniably insists—that an invidious politics of class can permeate a social order presumably based upon egalitarian principles. He addresses this contradiction in his final essay on Hawthorne, confessing that the theme of declension he sees in the author's second romance comes as a painful shock. "It would seem that such a sentiment ought properly to belong to our own older civilization," he admits,

> much as ivy inseparably clings to ruins—and that it should be particularly painful in countries where gross inequities of condition transform all reversals of fortune into catastrophes, and where feudal family traditions implicate everyone in their consequences. In America, where that strict solidarity of the family and where inequities of condition do not exist, we have trouble understanding how such a sentiment has seen the light of day.

Whenever he faces this kind of problem, Montégut characteristically takes refuge in the comfortable abstractions of moral verity—or Tocqueville (equally convenient)—or both. Why should America be a stranger to class distinctions when "our psychological anatomy discovers in itself the roots of good and evil, a double harvest together, where hereditary virtues and the spirits of caste and inequality also sprout? In America, no more so than elsewhere," he continues, "man cannot escape this fate of his nature, both happy and sad at once, that pushes him to find stability in a world where all is fleeting, and to yearn for immortality in a world where nothing lasts."

Borrowing from Tocqueville's analysis instead of the catechism gives his own discussion perhaps more cogency. "It is a very interesting fact that equality renders all decline more painful," Montégut also claims, "because it leaves no resources to pride." In aristocratic countries, by contrast,

> condition is determined by moral realities that nothing can alter; it accompanies their possessor in ruin and unhappiness, is inseparable from that person and cannot even be undone by death. A ruined gentleman himself stays intact, and, except in the case of dishonor, decline affects only those circumstances external and contingent to his existence. But it is not so in democratic countries, because there rank and condition are determined only by riches. There, whoever loses his fortune loses his rank and condition, even his honor.

As Tocqueville shrewdly had observed, the most shameful smirch to a man's reputation in the United States was idleness; not even the wealthiest American democrat could escape its tarring brush. "Do you see this opulent citizen?" Tocqueville posits. "There is not a nobleman anywhere in Europe who is more exclusive in his pleasures than this man or more jealous of the least advantages conferred by a privileged position. Yet this same man leaves home to go work in a dusty hole in the business district downtown, where anyone is free to call on him" (*DA* 204). As Tocqueville understood so well, democratic institutions awakened a passion for equality that they could never entirely satisfy; but the majority would never demand the surrender of a rich man's wealth—only his pride (*DA* 593).

That excruciating psychological dimension of *The House of the Seven Gables* appealed most to Montégut. Comparing Hawthorne's romance to Sir Walter Scott's *The Bride of Lammermoor* (1819) allows him to make a key distinction. In Scott's historical romance, "decadence of nobility gives rise to nothing but savage despair and a proud taciturnity" among the Ravenswood clan. But "bourgeois decadence" for the Pyncheons "engenders the worst infirmity that can afflict the human soul: timidity." Hawthorne conducts his patient (and rather pitiless) analysis of Hepzibah's inner torture on the day she is obliged to stand behind the counter of her cent-shop with "lacerating delicacy." And his representations of the even more grievous afflictions of her deranged brother Clifford are similarly masterful. Unafraid of extravagance, Montégut describes Clifford as "a tortured soul in the manner of Torquato Tasso—a Torquato Tasso of the American middle class"—who, for that very reason, has none of the Italian's poetic gifts. If Hawthorne had confined himself to the dissection of their pain, Montégut would have been satisfied. Instead, he finds *The House of the Seven Gables* "long-winded," proof positive that Hawthorne's talent was better represented by his shorter tales.

Étienne, too, remarks upon the paucity of incident in Hawthorne's work and his seemingly natural bent for the short story. "Even his novels are tales," the critic pointedly says; "when celebrity and the assurance of having a readership permitted him broader scope," the author's imagination, "accustomed to this mold, did not want to change." (Years later, Hawthorne's American publisher, James T. Fields, famously confirmed this supposition when he related how strenuously he had had to push the author to transform *The Scarlet Letter* into a full-fledged novel, instead of just another contribution to a new volume of tales.)[35] Later critics—beginning with Henry James—would suggest that the meagerness of Hawthorne's cultural milieu, the thinness and provinciality of American society, necessarily worked to confine him to briefer narrative forms or, as a corollary, impelled him in his longer fictions to stray into domains of romantic and psychological abstraction. The novel—as the literary vehicle best suited for representing a dense and complex social field—could hardly prosper in a culture without one, as antebellum America was imagined to be. The "crude and simple society" that Hawthorne knew, in James's phrase, could only be detrimental to the development of a serious novelist.[36] Somewhat more generously, Montégut sees the short story as the vehicle best suited to describe the feelings of which Hawthorne is fondest—"solitude, destitution, meditative ennui"—because to indulge and explore these sentiments, his characters must protect themselves by the "barrier that sadness erects between those it has touched and the rest of men." Hawthorne's world, Montégut intuits, is the reverse of social: his "drama is entirely interior and remains, as it were, invisible. It cannot be translated by exterior acts, by passionate deeds, by adventures." Perhaps it is fitting that it would be James who could best fuse the two realms and transform the history of the novel in the process.

As we have seen, Montégut tended to discount the importance of *The House of the Seven Gables;* but for Étienne, that romance affords him the most crucial evidence to support his sweeping generalizations about the sorry triumph of the mercantile spirit in the United States. Consequently, he offers the most detailed French commentary on this novel and even proclaims it Hawthorne's best. Judge Pyncheon, of course, incarnates the Yankee fetish for busy-ness and money-making, and Étienne delights in tallying all the petty details that Hawthorne gives us about his overcrowded (and always self-serving) itinerary. Despite the wellspring of avarice from which his actions originate, his public carriage and credentials are impeccable; his social eminence is roundly accepted by church and state (as Hawthorne writes); his hypocrisies, if sometimes whispered about, are never exposed (except when Holgrave's daguerreotype brings to the surface the

Judge's latent affinity with his blood-stained ancestors). In all this he perfectly embodies a sentiment that Tocqueville first discerned among what he called the "vestiges of the aristocratic party" in America. Beneath their "conventional enthusiasm" and beyond their "obsequious politeness toward the dominant power," Tocqueville sensed that "the rich feel a deep disgust with their country's democratic institutions. The people are a power they fear and despise" (*DA* 204). Hawthorne powerfully captures this ugly dimension of the Judge's character, so carefully concealed behind the mask of civility he customarily displays. His smile becomes a metonym for his false public posture, and Étienne clearly relishes Hawthorne's satiric portrait of this "tyrannical hypocrite."

Like Montégut, Étienne recognizes the importance of Hawthorne's "psychological method," and his analysis of it richly complements that of his rival at the *Revue des Deux Mondes*. He appreciates the extent to which the author "does not simply disclose the private ruminations of his hero, but (what is more) how he perceives them." Appropriately, he likens the novelist to a scientist equipped with a powerful magnifier, intent upon examining "the fleeting expressions of the face, the mysterious relations of our physical attitude and our moral state, the timbre of our voice and the music of our soul"; by such means, he "comes to grasp the birth and torment of feelings." As does Montégut, Étienne feels that the artist "yields to commiseration less than to curiosity" and takes pleasure "in evoking touching dramas and looking on with a cold heart." But while Montégut worries about the moral ambiguities that Hawthorne's detached attitude suggests, Étienne focuses more on the aesthetic problems that it raises. Psychological scrutiny may be the author's forte, but as a consequence "the pace of the narrative slows to a crawl; every topic invites digression; the illusion of reality is suspended at every moment." Hawthorne is masterful in creating these psychological tableaux, but Étienne doubts that a well-constructed novel can be made up of a series of them: the critic compares the author to "a poet who conceives a drama in one act and then wants to spread it into three." His method invites a kind of narrative sprawl. (James would echo this criticism by saying that *The House of the Seven Gables* "has a sort of expansive quality which never wholly fructifies"; to him it remained "a magnificent fragment.")[37] The French analyst was more specific. Tabulating at most "two or three" incidents in the book ("just enough to construct a short story"), Étienne remarks that "by superadding philosophy, feeling, and humor, Hawthorne has made a novel out of it."

The psychological afflictions of Clifford affect Étienne profoundly. He sees the House of the Seven Gables weighing upon the half-crazed man "like one of those capes of lead that Dante placed upon the shoulders" of the damned in the Eighth Circle of Hell. The critic's imagination reaches out in sympathy to this character whose "whole life is a relentless study of the secret of suffering"; and he strongly suggests that, far from being a ridiculous aberration, Clifford's malady ominously reflects the dislocations of contemporary life. "Have you not met the man we have been describing?" he solemnly asks his readers; "do you not see all around you . . . (even, perhaps, in your own person) people who find only unhappiness and suffering in what, for others, would be a source of happiness and peace? They are forever fighting against the current: in whatever broad social channel fate has thrown them, inevitably they cannot go with the flow and the torrent passes over their body." Étienne even manages to perform an Emersonian somersault by denominating Clifford "the Representative Man of all souls devoted to unhappiness." He values in Hawthorne's narrative plan exactly what Montégut dismissed—the arrival of Phoebe and the gradual regeneration of Clifford's more fully human qualities.

Unlike so many other works of English and American fiction that obliged a French critic to discount their seriousness, in *The House of the Seven Gables* Étienne discovers what the others lack: "the expression of a society, the faithful mirror of a country, an epoch, and a people." Those desiderata are best conveyed by the character of Holgrave, in whom Étienne sees "the modern American type, the Representative Man of generations who will call themselves tomorrow the Republic of the United States." With all his robust energy and elastic aptitude for enterprises of all kinds, Holgrave embodies the democratic spirit with a vengeance. But this is precisely what Étienne mistrusts. His headstrong confidence in his own destiny (so like America's) is woefully misplaced. Holgrave's "mistake" (as Étienne calls it) "is to think that the time in which he is living is destined, by a flattering privilege, to strip off Antiquity's rags and to furnish itself in a brand new outfit, instead of replacing its garments (as our fathers did, bit by bit) by means of mending." Naturally, then, Étienne pricked up his ears at Holgrave's radical denunciation of the Past, his Jeffersonian appeal for the regeneration of society every twenty years, his regret that public buildings are made of stone and brick instead of materials that periodically might crumble to ruin. But after translating Holgrave's Jacobin fulminations at length, Étienne slyly undercuts them—in one terse paragraph—by revealing that, in the end, "the rich democrat becomes conservative" and yearns for a house built of masonry and mortar. His politics are just as pretentious as his claims to intellectual superiority. He is nothing more than a "Gil Blas in a Puritan and democratic country."[38]

Forgues' personal admiration for Hawthorne encouraged him to take the author at his word: "he is a democrat," he affirms, "an incorrigible democrat," opposed to all the "accomplices of political tyranny." If feelings of loyalty blinded Forgues to the American author's contradictory politics, Montégut and Étienne were more sensitive to the ideological implications of Hawthorne's textual maneuvers. As we have seen, Montégut believed that Hawthorne's liberalism was at best a veneer that overlay a deeper Puritan residue from the past. Hawthorne's ancestors may have been "capable of burning witches," he jibes, "but they never would have joined the communal experiment at Roxbury." Even though Montégut's knowledge of American colonial history is forgivably imprecise, his instincts—and style—are (occasionally) razor sharp. More than a century before Jonathan Arac posited an ideological link between *The Life of Franklin Pierce* and Hawthorne's fiction,[39] Étienne warned his readers that the question of slavery—"the Sphinx of American politics"—occupied a place "at the center of the Republic at a crossroads where all paths end," a path that Hawthorne, too, was treading. Étienne's conclusion—and the evidence upon which it is based—prefigures Arac's almost word for word. Calling attention to the same notorious passage in the Pierce biography (in which Hawthorne defers the question of abolition to the hands of Providence) that Arac uses to launch his critique, Étienne can only express the hope that slavery "will not be for the United States what the hereditary curse is in *The House of the Seven Gables,* an incurable evil to which the Puritan ethos resigns itself perhaps too easily." But the prospect of inaction was imminent, as Étienne well knew. "All in good time, Hawthorne urges; but would it not be wise and human to clear the path? Do not the partisans of the Compromise and all the other laws protecting slavery make the work of Providence that much more difficult?" Étienne had no difficulty linking the pattern of narrative "resolution" in Hawthorne's fiction with his political leanings. His transatlantic perspective allowed him insights that Anglophone criticism has needed much more time to uncover.[40]

As political consensus in the United States fatefully degenerated in the 1850s, a corresponding sense of malaise and disillusion surfaced in French criticism of American literature during the first decade of the Second Empire. Even Forgues, who found the political themes of Hawthorne's historical sketches so bracing, could not help glancing at the prospect. "Such a singular temperament, the American temperament!" he gladly reports, after surveying a series of tales ("The Legends of the Province-House") in which the historical agents of British tyranny are venomously remembered. "We can better understand how these uncouth citizens have remained free," he then goes on to say, "though we should refrain from asking how they might cease being so." Montégut and Étienne were neither so discreet nor so obliging. Alternately fascinated and repelled by popular democracy, they were more persuaded by Tocqueville's grimmer assessment of majoritarian tyranny and the social discord it might engender. Montégut's critique of "Earth's Holocaust" provides the best evidence for this, because he assigns a specific date to the events of Hawthorne's dystopian fable: the Fourth of August, the date in 1789 on which the French Constituent Assembly, successor to the legislative body formed in revolt against the meeting of the Estates General in Paris in May 1789, declared an end to long-held class privileges as a response to mob violence that had spread from Paris to the countryside in July of that same year. The literally inflamed imaginations of Hawthorne's spectators come to believe that the bonfire they have lit has consumed all the sources of evil and vice known to man, that they have purified the world in the name of Progress. But Hawthorne's cynical irony undercuts the illusion with a cold violence that leaves Montégut appalled:

> These men believed that they were obeying divine inspiration, the poor fools! Did they not see that they were playthings of the devil, who felt the need to renew his engines of damnation? The old machines of moral destruction were out of service—they clanked and were rusted—and what better occasion to renew the materiel of hell? All the equipment could now be replaced with the latest models, and, undoubtedly, all would go better. "Amen!" Hawthorne calmly replies in a tone that seems to say, "Just what I expected." You understand now the sort of dread—verging on terror—that Hawthorne's writings inspire, a dread all the more remarkable because the reader feels it without being able to do anything about it; it acts on him with a sort of displeasing fascination.

As Montégut (mis)reads it, the story seems to mock all aspirations for human betterment, and his conflation of it with a signal date in French history suggests the extent to which he has discovered in Hawthorne a resonant voice for his pessimistic disappointment with the course of events in his own country.[41]

Étienne's more conservative hauteur encourages him to read Hawthorne's "pessimism" as mere common sense, a rational instinct that he applauds. He is not surprised that the author's experience at Brook Farm "has soured him on utopias." How could it not? Without attribution, Étienne essentially rewrites "Earth's Holocaust" in his denunciation of Transcendental fallacies, reinscribing the fable with a more specifically American inflection.

In Concord, the group of empty dreamers who surrounded Emerson, like moths around a flame, alienated Hawthorne from philosophical and humanitarian speculation. We can see that rabble of bizarre men, with their dubious looks, their motley dress, who believe themselves, each and every one, called to regenerate the world—true nightmares to thought and common sense. Such has been the unfortunate influence of that original thinker: those who live too close to him have been besotted by his breath and saturated by false originality. Truth goes to their head like wine. Such is the vulgarity of innovation, the originality of bad taste that would make a man abhor all ideas that predate his own century.

With such a temperament, Étienne naturally would be attracted to Hawthorne's neo-orthodox satire, "The Celestial Railroad," patterned after Bunyan's *Pilgrim's Progress*. For the French critic, the declension of Calvinist rigor is even suggested by the circumstances that spawned these two narratives. Bunyan (as Étienne reminds us) "lived twelve-and-a-half years in Bedford prison with no other companions besides the Bible and Foxe's *Book of Martyrs*," forging "iron fetters by which to live by writing books of piety in which he scattered treasures of imagination and fanaticism." Hawthorne, on the other hand, "wrote 'The Celestial Railroad' in his Old Manse in Concord, in between a transcendental conversation with Emerson and a boat outing with the poet Ellery Channing." This comic contrast inspires Étienne to a brilliant redaction of Hawthorne's tale, from which he derives an appropriate moral: "Going to Hell," he concludes, "is so much harder than attaining salvation!" Sounding very much like a precursor to Ann Douglas, Étienne bemoans if not the feminization of American culture then the pitiful dilution of its first principles. "Oh, Bunyan, Foxe, Bellingham, Endicott!" he facetiously cries, "where are you? Persecutors and persecuted, what has happened to your great grandsons? Some, most of them, are lukewarm and sensual. Not only do they flee the straight and narrow path, but they also insist that it be convenient. They no longer want to go by foot, even to Heaven."[42] Even the small remnant of true believers nowadays comfort themselves with sentimental reforms—instead of scourging themselves, they join philanthropic leagues and temperance societies. Only a man who defies the stupid majority and flouts public opinion can win a martyr's honors in the relaxed times of today.

The climate, of course, was different in the seventeenth century, and all the French critics show a grim respect for Hawthorne's representation of that period in *The Scarlet Letter*. By 1852, Forgues seems already to take for granted French awareness of the novel, even though his own abridged translation of it would not appear for another year. Surprised by the title's popularity with Anglo-American readers (who typically have spurned any chronicle of marital infidelity or sexual license and reprimanded its author), Forgues welcomes *The Scarlet Letter* as "a true literary phenomenon, a sign of the times." For Montégut the book was a sign of something else—the epitome of Hawthorne's psychological method—for in it the "drama is entirely interior and remains, as it were, invisible." Because Hawthorne condemns Hester, Dimmesdale, and Chillingworth to exist in such radical isolation from each other and from their community, Montégut sees them performing the rituals of a kind of living death; irresistibly, the novel reveals "the slow destruction of three hearts, all differently, but all equally wounded." The spectacle, he avers, is "completely black, without precedent even in the somber literature of England." Henry James would borrow this opinion when he described the romance as "densely dark" and prophesied that it would "probably long remain the most consistently gloomy of English novels of the first order."[43] In this, too, he took a cue from Montégut, who assured his readers that there was "no second *Scarlet Letter* in all of literature" and, therefore, no "risk of encountering again such a distillation of misery." Étienne also recognized the singular significance of Hawthorne's first novel, for in his view its great success testified to "the vivacious power of Puritan thought." More profoundly than Forgues (who also invited the comparison between Hawthorne's work and that of George Sand), Étienne understood that to think of *The Scarlet Letter* as a novel of passion would be a gross mistake. "We might say that *The Scarlet Letter* is *Indiana,* that it is *Lélia,*" he quips. But he immediately insists upon a key distinction: "here (in its French incarnations) we have novels that reject human corruption, and there, one that exaggerates it. Here, vice does not exist; there, it is irreparable. Here, we flatter all that is in man; there, he is damned without mercy." Étienne's insistent logic of contrast illuminates the diabolical duplicity of *The Scarlet Letter* with a clarity unmatched until (at least) D. H. Lawrence's *Studies in Classic American Literature* (1923).

Étienne shares Montégut's conviction that Hawthorne's great power as a novelist derives from his implacable "vision of Evil" and his keenness for discerning "the ineffaceable shadow of sin." Already anticipating Montégut's assessment of Hawthorne's "pessimism," Étienne knew that if the author was no longer a Puritan by faith, he was still one "in his heart and imagination" and that his characters could not escape their enslavement to the corruptions of the soul. "They are born under evil stars," he writes, "predestinated by their passions, and the author resembles an astrologer who looks for proof in men's lives to justify his horoscopes." In France, where the Revolution had brought down not just the Monarchy but also the influence of the Church and its doctrines, writers conceived of human nature differently. "They can be fatalistic," Étienne admits, "but only by suppressing, as it were, the evil of human nature, and by displacing it on circumstances, on fate, on society." Hawthorne's fatalism inheres in the very nature of his art. Like D. H. Lawrence, Étienne knew that "you *must* look through the surface of American art, and see the inner diabolism of the symbolic meaning."[44] His telling gloss of Dimmesdale's mental scourge plumbs beneath that surface, and the paradoxical appositive he uses to describe the minister—"Prometheus' vulture" (but a vulture who gnaws at his own entrails)—brilliantly explains the clergyman's self-inflicted torture.

Étienne yearned to see Dimmesdale's anguish portrayed upon the stage, and Montégut apprehended the dramatic power of *The Scarlet Letter* in similar terms. "Only a lyric drama could furnish appropriate comparisons to express the intensity of pain contained within this book," he urges. The novel's lachrymose poetry would defy the talent of Gounod or Bizet. "Despite the resources of musical art," Montégut writes, "the most dramatic opera could not match the lugubrious trio that Hawthorne makes us hear." The book is a marvel of suffering: "it has no limits," by Étienne's measure, "but those of the human soul."

Even though he can appreciate the "Calvinist melancholy" that he finds in Hawthorne's best work, Étienne seems eager to mock America's Puritan antecedents and the "superstitious baggage" that the settlers of New England brought with them. Condensing the novelist's genealogy into a crude outline of the nation's history, Étienne devises a clever parody of the line of descent that Hawthorne traces in the "Custom-House" Introduction to *The Scarlet Letter*:

> Make the mystical sectarian go through two centuries of labor, pursue adventures, experience religious and philosophical decomposition; for a hundred years, make him penetrate the wilderness and clear the soil; for another hundred years, quarter him on a ship. Suppose that, having become in appearance the perfect Yankee (schooled by work, commerce, and Benjamin Franklin), one day he ceases from that drudgery and, just for a moment, has quenched his thirst for lucre. A hardy, yet generous philosophy makes him despise the commercial and materialist society that surrounds him. For the first time in two hundred years, he thinks. The old man quickly goes through changes of garb, habits, and opinions. He takes up a pen and writes Nathaniel Hawthorne's novels.

Montégut, on the other hand, approaches the question of Hawthorne's cultural inheritance with a deeper understanding of its artistic significance. Noticing that "whenever Hawthorne speaks of his terrible forebears, he speaks with respect, almost with fear," Montégut demonstrates a keener sensitivity to the historical nature of the author's imagination. Though he does not employ the vocabulary that Taine would make famous, Montégut nevertheless appreciates the importance of *la race, le milieu et le moment* in the genesis of the American romancer's art.[45] Instead of Taine's material determinism, however, Montégut preferred a poet's metaphor to suggest the relevance of these criteria. "Hawthorne's talent marvelously explains the persistence of ancestral values that are perpetuated over time," he insists— "the 'music of the blood' . . . that (especially in provincial society) repeats in successive generations the same melody but with different variations." For Montégut, Hawthorne's "sense of the past" has the power to evoke resonant echoes; to Étienne, the very notion of meaningful history in a land of money-grubbing Yankees seems absurd.

After the creative hiatus occasioned by Hawthorne's consular appointment at Liverpool (1853–57), the appearance of *The Marble Faun* (or *Transformation*, as the French knew it from the title preferred by the British publisher) in 1860 deepened this rift in critical opinion. To Montégut, the author's last romance confirmed his sense that a kind of Puritan misanthropy pervaded Hawthorne's outlook and kept him, as it were, a prisoner of the seventeenth century (but without a sustaining faith). Étienne, by contrast, seems more impressed with *The Marble Faun*'s Transcendental themes and origins, Romantic influences that ultimately triumph over the residues of Hawthorne's Puritan nature. Somewhat ironically, Étienne finds the best evidence for his interpretation in a work of Montégut's: the latter's 1851 French translation of Emerson's *Essays,* a text to which Étienne refers several times in the pages of his critique. Acknowledging that, in his prior assessment of Hawthorne, he had insisted upon the enduring relevance of the author's Puritan inheritance, Étienne now confesses that he "knew very well that this son of the Puritans was, at heart, a Transcendentalist." Only the occasion for proving it was wanting, and that occasion was now at hand with the publication of *The Marble Faun.* (Like Emerson himself, Étienne seems to have adopted the notion that a foolish consistency is merely the hobgoblin of little minds.) Significantly, though, Étienne openly regrets the extent to which Hawthorne has allowed Transcendental ideas—especially the heresy of Pantheism—to dominate his narrative. "At first glance," he admits, "we might easily be deceived about this": Hawthorne's last romance "might seem to be a new study of remorse in the human soul, a supplement to the powerful pages of *The Scarlet Letter* and *The House of the Seven Gables*." But the resolution of the plot—with the suggestion "that good might issue from the crime, that evil might be a means of progress"—would turn the tables on such an argument. "If the old Puritans were brought back to life," Étienne chuckles, they would find these ideas "a trifle unorthodox."

Reading Emerson would seem to have given Étienne the key to most if not all of Hawthorne's moral mythologies. The philosopher's aesthetic encounter with Rome, famously recorded in his essay "Art," prefigures Hawthorne's reactions to the Eternal City. His poetic incarnation of a forest seer (in "Woodnotes I") becomes the physical model for Donatello. His extended metaphors of metamorphosis (from "Compensation") collapse into the very theme and title of Hawthorne's work: *Transformation*. His rejection of theological absolutes (in "Circles") provides an apparent vehicle for the resolution of Hawthorne's plot. Étienne's astonished gloss on a passage from that essay—

> I own I am gladdened by seeing the predominance of the saccharine principle throughout vegetable nature, and not less by beholding in morals that unrestrained inundation of the principle of good into every chink and hole that selfishness has left open, yea, into selfishness and sin itself; so that no evil is pure, nor hell itself without its extreme satisfactions.[46]

—is humorously remarkable. "What a notion!" he exclaims: "This unfrocked Unitarian minister has almost affirmed that our crimes themselves might be the living stones that will serve to construct the temples of the true God!" Outwardly true to form, though, Hawthorne echoes this principle when Kenyon offers a type of moral closure to the parable of Donatello's fall from innocence. "'Sin has educated Donatello, and elevated him,'" he tells Hilda.

> "Is sin, then,—which we deem such a dreadful blackness in the universe,—is it, like sorrow, merely an element of human education, through which we struggle to a higher and purer state than we could otherwise have attained? Did Adam fall, that we might ultimately rise to a far loftier paradise than his?" (460)

Hilda, we know, strenuously rejects this view, and Kenyon apparently surrenders to the sterner logic of her puritanical orthodoxy; but Étienne brushes this aside as an irrelevance. The philosophical logic of the novel trumps the author's explicit intention. Literary pantheism is the "fashion" of the day, and Hawthorne's romance is perfectly *à la mode*.

With certain reservations, Montégut still is more forgiving of Hawthorne's moral ambiguity. If only because the novel's conclusion might offer some relief to the portrait of sin and suffering that Hawthorne has composed, Montégut seems eager to embrace the more hopeful of the two alternatives that the author presents in his final pages. From the grim survey of Hawthorne's oeuvre that the critic employs as a kind of extended preface to his specific commentary on *The Marble Faun*, we know that Montégut considers the author a frighteningly dispassionate anatomist of human frailty. Unlike other great moralists (whose strictures against humanity nevertheless inspire noble action and generous aspirations), Hawthorne's clinical dissections of the soul offer "nothing that makes the heart grow." "He is coldly cruel without knowing it," Montégut continues, "like the doctor who gives up hope on a patient and declares to his face that he has no chance of getting better. Our miseries appear irrevocable, our souls a realm of sin." What fascinates and repels Montégut at the same time is the curious way that Hawthorne's writing paralyzes the reader's ethical will. His tone is so neutral—even genial; and yet his meanings are insidious. Having "neither the ardor of a prayer nor the passion of a curse," Hawthorne's reflections on human nature are for that very reason terrifying. "Never will his aspirations for human betterment take flight," Montégut observes, for "they are missing warmth and wings." Death is the only escape from the metaphysical stasis that Hawthorne's work implies, and that implication drives Montégut to the verge of labeling him an "immoral" writer. But even though he is dismayed by Hawthorne's "pessimistic psychology," Montégut credits him for having made a truly important discovery—that "sensibility is the dominant function of the soul, the one that commands all the other functions and dominates the moral organs"—a discovery that has added "a new page to the moral annals of mankind" and, therefore, redeems him from that charge.

Less governed in his approach to the novel by an overarching thesis, Montégut can hence address its faults more squarely. Like some other contemporary English and American critics, Montégut complains about the bifurcated texture of *The Marble Faun* and its not wholly successful fusion of artistic and moral themes. "The novel is really two," he suggests: "it comprises both an aesthetic novel and a psychological novel that are at war with one another, and that, like two rivals, compete for the reader's attention." Instead of reinforcing each other, these two dimensions of the story frustrate the reader's desire for more complete disclosure of insight into the characters' interior states of mind. Montégut's assessment of this problem is hilariously on target. "I know no crueler disappointments than those that are reserved for us by stories with aesthetic pretensions," he admits. "We go out to accompany two lovers during their walk, surely counting that they will chat about their love and that they will acquaint us with their rapture. Not at all. Instead, they lead us in front of an arch of triumph and begin to take notes like British tourists." Montégut's descriptive parody of Hawthorne's narrative technique is almost worthy of his rival at the *Revue contemporaine*. Even more disappointing is what he terms the novel's willful obscurity. "From beginning to end," he complains, "the fates of the characters is [*sic*] crossed by a secret that it is impossible for us to explain to the reader, because the author has not explained it himself, and he is careful to warn us that even he does not know of what it consists. We know very well that such things can happen in real life, but we expect a novel to be more explicit than real life, and we have some trouble being satisfied by the excuses Hawthorne presents to the reader at the end of the book." Too much wrapped up in its own mysteries and its long-winded digressions on statuary and painting, *The Marble Faun* painfully reveals the exercise of an overextended imagination. Montégut is almost embarrassed to see an author he admires stretching awkwardly to fill up the pages of a Victorian triple-decker, and his reproach is fairly cutting. "Hawthorne could have given us one of his admirable psychological tales—to which he possesses the secret—but instead he offers us an inferior romance that will add little to his fame." In this instance, at least, Montégut's penchant for prophetical criticism seems justified. Henry James was among the first to repeat these judgments and cement them as a given in Anglo-American literary opinion. Also finding *The Marble Faun* the least successful of Hawthorne's longer fictions, James lamented that the "story struggles and wanders, is dropped and taken up again, and towards the close lapses into an almost fatal vagueness."[47] His last words on the novel were Montégut's first.

James was not the only Anglo-American critic to compliment Montégut by way of translation (or plagiarism!). Already in 1859 the venerable *North American Review* had referred to him as "the young and distinguished contributor to the *Revue des Deux Mondes*, with whose name readers on this side of the Atlantic are familiar, from the very excellently written pages he has more than once devoted to the contemporary productions of American literature."[48] Accordingly, the American art journal *The Crayon* published lengthy extracts from "Un romancier pessimiste en Amérique," just two months after it appeared in the *Revue des Deux Mondes* and applauded the author for his "admirable *critique*."[49] Especially significant for that audience was Montégut's shrewd analysis of the particular difficulties of appreciation that most nineteenth-century Americans encountered when they were confronted by works of fine art. The novelist's lengthy digressions on Italian painting and sculpture—betraying naïve judgment—prompt Montégut to an honest but sympathetic observation about Hawthorne's limitations. "We sense in his opinions, as in those of all of his compatriots in the arts, a certain intrinsic weakness that results from a fundamental deficiency in education, a deficiency that the historical circumstances of America have created, and that her best endowed minds will need much time to overcome." Somewhat surprisingly, perhaps, Étienne ignored this opportunity to skewer American provincialism, although his imaginary portrait of Hawthorne prowling through the galleries of the Vatican retains traces of his characteristic wit. And certainly there is some truth in his intimation that a New England artist like Hawthorne (craving for something beyond the utilitarian surfaces of his native land) would have been tempted to shout "Eureka!" when he found himself surrounded by a surplus of symbolic forms to which his imagination could respond.[50] Étienne's tableau goes beyond caricature to capture the same quality of naïveté that Montégut apologetically discerns:

> No doubt, one day, when he was strolling through those Vatican galleries (with his Poet's admiration and his American skepticism abreast and side to side), suddenly he stopped himself in front of that Faun of Praxiteles—so alive, so young, so handsome. He, the Puritan, the Transcendentalist, the citizen of a sad, mirthless nation, arrived in front of this beauty, this youth, this freshness, this childish laughter, and cried to himself, "I've found it!"

The truth of their insights compares favorably with Hawthorne's personal account, later published in *The French and Italian Notebooks*:

> We afterwards went into the sculpture-gallery, where I looked at the Faun of Praxiteles, and was sensible of a peculiar charm in it; a sylvan beauty and homeliness, friendly and wild at once. The lengthened, but not preposterous ears, and the little tail, which we infer, have an exquisite effect, and make the spectator smile in his very heart. This race of fauns was the most delightful of all that antiquity imagined. It seems to me that a story, with all sorts of fun and pathos in it, might be contrived on the idea of their species having become intermingled with the human race; a family with the faun blood in them, having prolonged itself from the classic era till our own days. The tail might have disappeared, by dint of constant intermarriages with ordinary mortals; but the pretty hairy ears should occasionally reappear in members of the family; and the moral instincts and intellectual characteristics of the faun might be most picturesquely brought out, without detriment to the human interest of the story.[51]

Eureka!—indeed.

Four years later—at the time of Hawthorne's death—Montégut would revise his estimate of *The Marble Faun,* feeling that he owed "a reparation to the author's memory." Still acknowledging the novel's defects, he now felt that "the beauty of the subject and the depth of psychological analysis" transcended all of them. A second reading had persuaded him that Hawthorne's treatment of the Augustinian doctrine of *felix culpa* (the Fortunate Fall) in some measure redeemed the troubling moral ambiguity of his work in general—a view accepted much later by many Anglo-American critics of neo-orthodox persuasion. Though not quite as effusive as Hyatt Waggoner (who treats the novel almost as the *summa theologica* of Hawthorne's career),[52] Montégut still needs to affirm that "in his own way, Hawthorne applies the revelation of truth that Christianity brought to the world: that the price of the soul is infinite and that, even in the sorriest conditions of existence, it cannot be bought with all the treasures of the earth." We should not be surprised (or even necessarily disappointed) to see that the critic's moral agenda has overtaken his more troubled apprehensions about the nature of Hawthorne's fiction. His compulsion to write a suitable epitaph for his favorite American author invariably would have led him to this orthodox, but debatable, conclusion. Indeed, it is hardly too much to say that Montégut's interest in American culture died with Hawthorne. His 1864 essay was the last work of criticism he wrote about American literature. After that date, the changing nature of American social life attracted his attention only twice. The French face of Nathaniel Hawthorne was limned.

Notes

1. Alexis de Tocqueville, *Democracy in America,* translated by Arthur Goldhammer (New York: Library of America, 2004), 538. Hereafter cited parenthetically as *DA.*

2. Moira Anne (Curr) Helgesen, "Forgues: Nineteenth Century Anglophile," dissertation, University of Colorado, 1955, 116.

3. Herman Melville, "Hawthorne and His *Mosses,*" *The Writings of Herman Melville,* vol. 9: *The Piazza Tales and Other Prose Pieces 1839–1860,* edited by Harrison Hayford et al. (Evanston and Chicago: Northwestern University Press and The Newberry Library, 1987), 243.

4. James E. Rocks, "Hawthorne and France: In Search of American Literary Nationalism," *Tulane Studies in English* 17 (1969): 151.

5. Michael Colacurcio, *The Province of Piety: Moral History in Hawthorne's Early Tales* (Cambridge, MA: Harvard University Press, 1984), 1–3.

6. Montégut's allusion to Spanish poet and playwright Pedro Calderón de la Barca

(1600–1681) is incorrect. The phrase *música de la sangre* is instead found in not one but two other dramatic works by Calderón's contemporaries: the opening scene of *Los amantes de Teruel* (1635) by Juan Pérez de Montalbán (1602–38) and Act II of *El más impropio verdugo* (1645) by Francisco de Rojas Zorrilla (1607–48). We are grateful to Professors Don Cruickshank (University College, Dublin) and Germán Vega García-Luengos (University of Valladolid) for confirming this misattribution.

7. Perry Miller, *Errand into the Wilderness* (Cambridge, MA: Harvard University Press, 1956), vii–viii.

8. Henry James, *Hawthorne* (1879), in *Literary Criticism: Essays on Literature; American Writers; English Writers,* edited by Leon Edel (New York: Library of America, 1984), 368.

9. In his *Study of Hawthorne* (1876; rpt. New York: AMS Press, 1969), George Parsons Lathrop describes an interview with Hawthorne's sister-in-law, Elizabeth Peabody, who told him that the author once recounted to her a dream "by which he was beset, that he was walking abroad, and that all the houses were mirrors which reflected him a thousand times and overwhelmed him with mortification" (155). The parallel with Montégut's "bizarre vision" is suggestively uncanny.

10. F. O. Matthiessen, *American Renaissance: Art and Expression in the Age of Emerson and Whitman* (New York: Oxford University Press, 1941), 276.

11. Yvor Winters, *Maule's Curse: Seven Studies in the History of American Obscurantism* [1937], in *In Defense of Reason* (Chicago: Swallow Press, 1947), 158.

12. Perry Miller, *The New England Mind: The Seventeenth Century* (New York: Macmillan, 1939), esp. 111–53.

13. Winters, *Maule's Curse,* 158. Almost all of Winters's citations refer to (then standard) works of colonial American history and Puritan thought.

14. Perhaps most spectacularly in Melville's, in which he asserts that the difference between Shakespeare and Hawthorne "is by no means immeasurable. Not a very great deal more, and Nathaniel were verily William." See "Hawthorne and His *Mosses,*" 246.

15. Reversing an earlier enthusiasm for Hawthorne's tales, Edgar Allan Poe famously denounced the writer's allegories, in defense of which he found "scarcely one respectable word to be said." More temperate—and judicious—was the judgment of Edwin P. Whipple, who (in 1860) echoed Montégut's assessment almost line by line. "The defect of the serious stories," he noted

> is, that character is introduced, not as thinking, but as the illustration of thought. The persons are ghostly, with a sad lack of flesh and blood. They are phantasmal symbols of a reflective and imaginative analysis of human passions and aspirations. The dialogue, especially, is bookish, as though the personages knew their speech was to be printed, and were careful of the collocation and cadence of their words. . . . [The author] cannot contract his mind to the patient delineation of a moral individual, but attempts to use individuals in order to express the last results of patient moral perception.

Edgar Allan Poe, rev. of *Twice-told Tales* and *Mosses from an Old Manse* [1847], in *Essays and Reviews* (New York: Library of America, 1984), 582; Edwin P. Whipple, "Nathaniel Hawthorne" [1860], in *Character and Characteristic Men* (Boston: Ticknor & Fields, 1867), 226. Poe's earlier, more generous, assessments of Hawthorne are also reprinted in *Essays and Reviews,* 568–77.

16. "[T]here can be no harm in the Author's remarking," Hawthorne admits, that his stories

> have the pale tint of flowers that blossomed in too retired a shade—the coolness of a meditative habit, which diffuses itself through the feeling and observation of every sketch. Instead of passion, there is sentiment; and, even in what purport to be pictures of actual life, we have allegory, not always so warmly dressed in its habiliments of flesh and blood, as to be taken into the reader's mind without a shiver. (*TTT* 5)

17. Baudelaire's translations of individual stories and poems began to appear in French periodicals as early as 1848. In volume form, *Histoires extraordinaires* was published by Michel Lévy in 1856 (with an important Preface by Baudelaire, "*Edgar Poe: sa vie et ses œuvres*") and followed up the next year by *Nouvelle histoires extraordinaires*. It is surely worth noting that in his Preface to the second volume ("*Notes nouvelles sur Edgar Poe*"), Baudelaire plagiarized Poe's criticism of *Twice-told Tales*, lifting generalizations about the "unity of effect" that only shorter fiction could evoke and then applying such praiseworthy criteria to Poe himself. See Melvin Zimmerman, "Baudelaire, Poe and Hawthorne," *Revue de littérature comparée* 39 (Jul./Sept. 1965): 448–50. For detailed bibliographical information about Baudelaire's translations, see Célestin Pierre Cambiaire, *The Influence of Edgar Allan Poe in France* (New York: G. E. Stechert & Co., 1927), 13–41, 95–119; and Patrick F. Quinn, *The French Face of Edgar Poe* (Carbondale: Southern Illinois University Press, 1957), 70–108.

18. Louis Étienne, "The American Storytellers—Edgar Allan Poe," in *Affidavits of Genius,* edited by Jean Alexander (Port Washington, NY: Kennikat Press), 143. The essay was first published in the *Revue contemporaine* 32 (15 Jul. 1857): 492–524.

19. "*Ein Gutteil dessen, was Baudelaire in Edgar Allan Poe fand, erfaßte Montégut in Hawthorne, 'un des plus remarquables conteurs d'Amérique.'*" Burkhart Küster, *Die Literatur des 19. Jahrhunderts im Urteil von Emile Montégut* (Tübingen: G. Narr, 1982), 128.

20. "Charles Baudelaire" [1876], *Literary Criticism: French Writers; Other European Writers; The Prefaces to the New York Edition,* edited by Leon Edel (New York: Library of America, 1984), 155.

21. Melville, "Hawthorne and His *Mosses,*" 243.

22. Roger Asselineau, "Hawthorne Abroad," in *Hawthorne Centenary Essays,* edited by Roy Harvey Pearce (Columbus: The Ohio State University Press, 1964), 381.

23. Hugh J. Dawson, "Discovered in Paris: An Earlier First Illustrated Edition of *The Scarlet Letter,*" in *Studies in the American Renaissance,* edited by Joel Myerson (Woodbridge, CT: Twayne Publishers, 1988), 278.

24. [Frank B. Goodrich], "France," *New York Times* (11 Sept. 1854) 2: 2.

25. Simon Jacob Copans, "French Opinion of American Democracy, 1852–1860," dissertation, Brown University, 1942, 178–79.

26. Nathaniel Hawthorne, *Contes racontés deux fois* [*Twice-told Tales*], Nouvelle bibliothèque populaire (Paris: Henri Gautier, 1888), back cover: "*Très populaire en Amérique, connu par de nombreuses traductions dans toute l'Europe, Nathaniel Hawthorne a eu de son vivant une grande vogue et se lit encore aujourd'hui avec les plus vi' intérêt.*" Information about French editions of Hawthorne's work can be found in Nina E. Browne, *A Bibliography of Nathaniel Hawthorne* (Boston: Houghton, Mifflin & Co., 1905), 96–99, supplemented by additional entries in the Bibliothèque Nationale (http://www.bnf.fr/).

27. In his *Life of Nathaniel Hawthorne* (New York: Scribner & Welford, 1890), Moncure D. Conway suggests that the writer's French *nom de plume*—Monsieur de l'Aubépine—"was one cause of the interest of French writers in Hawthorne" (40). He also refers explicitly to Montégut's 1860 essay, most of the translations noted in the text, as well as those by Paul Masson ("La Fiancée du Shaker"—"The Shaker Bridal"—in *Revue bleue* [16 Nov. 1889]: 627–30) and Léonce Rabillon, who translated *Le livre des merveilles* (*A Wonderbook for Boys and Girls*) for Hachette in 1858.

28. For more on nineteenth-century French publishing and readership, see Roger Chartier and Henri-Jean Martin (eds.), *Histoire de l'édition française*, vol. 3 (Paris: Promodis, 1985); Eileen S. DeMarco, *Reading and Riding: Hachette's Railroad Bookstore Network in Nineteenth-Century France* (Bethlehem, PA: Lehigh University Press, 2006); Martyn Lyons, *Le triomphe du livre: histoire sociologique de la lecture dans la France du XIXe siècle* (Paris: Promodis, 1987); and Jean-Yves Mollier, *Louis Hachette, 1800–1864: fondateur d'un empire* (Paris: Fayard, 1999).

29. This instance is from his 1860 essay. Curiously, in both 1852 and later in 1864, Montégut preferred forms of the more literally correct "*mépriser*" in citing this passage.

30. *Essais de philosophie américaine, de R. W. Emerson, traduits de l'anglais par É. Montégut, avec une introduction et des notes* (Paris: Charpentier, 1851).

31. Émile Montegut, "Scènes de la vie et de la littérature américaine," *Revue des Deux Mondes* (1 Dec. 1854): 881.

32. Montégut's jibe can be seen as a snide anticipation of Lionel Trilling's deeper recognition (speaking of the title character in James's *The Princess Casamassima* [1886]) that, in her purblind quest for social justice, the Princess "constitutes a striking symbol of that powerful part of modern culture that exists by means of its claim to political innocence and by its false seriousness—the political awareness that is not aware, the social consciousness which hates full consciousness, the moral earnestness which is moral luxury." Hawthorne's exploration of the profound psychological limitations of his fictional reformers hints at all these dimensions of troubled modernity. *The Liberal Imagination: Essays on Literature and Society* (1950; rpt. New York: Anchor Books, 1953), 88.

33. Some years earlier, Chasles had confirmed the stereotype of Yankee materialism, echoed here by Étienne. Americans "wish to push conquest in every direction," Chasles bristled, "to experiment, to try every chance. At the age of fifteen, the man learns that he is to be the architect of his own fortune. The ties of family are so elastic, and virility begins so early, that it is a hard matter to tell where youth ends or minority ceases. . . . Each hopes to get rich, to make one leap from deepest poverty to opulence. The national morality suffers from this; activity and energy are developed at the expense of the calmer virtues. . . . Impatience to acquire, and love of lucre, prevent the culture of art, and that happy disposition which is content to give and receive enjoyment. Nothing but money and the enterprize which wins it are respected." Philarète Chasles, *Anglo-American Literature and Manners*, translated by Donald MacLeod (New York: C. Scribner, 1852), 294–95.

34. Carpenter does not discuss *The House of the Seven Gables* in his classic essay ("Puritans Preferred Blondes: The Heroines of Melville and Hawthorne," *New England Quarterly* 9 [1936]: 253–72), but Hawthorne displays the same preference in that novel, too. Phoebe sports the same "light-brown ringlets" as that other daughter of the Puritans, Hilda, in *The Marble Faun*.

35. James T. Fields, *Yesterdays with Authors* (Boston: J. R. Osgood & Co., 1871), 50–52.

36. Henry James, *Hawthorne*, 351.

37. Henry James, *Hawthorne*, 412.

38. Hawthorne himself was aware of the contradiction. "A romance on the plan of Gil Blas," he wrote, "adapted to American society and Manners, would cease to be a romance" (*The House of the Seven Gables*, 176).

39. Arac's essay, "The Politics of *The Scarlet Letter*" (first published in *Ideology and Classic American Literature*, edited by Sacvan Bercovitch and Myra Jehlen [New York: Cambridge University Press, 1986], 247–66), is generally acknowledged to have initiated the contemporary reinvestigation of Hawthorne's ideological complicities, also explored in Bercovitch's later work, *The Office of the Scarlet Letter* (Baltimore: Johns Hopkins University Press, 1991).

40. Étienne's rhetorical questions anticipate Arac's broadest conclusion—that "the organization of (in)action" in both the Pierce biography and Hawthorne's novels "works through a structure of conflicting values related to the political impasse of the 1850s"— as well as his implicit call to action for contemporary readers ("The Politics of *The Scarlet Letter*," 259).

41. As an earlier student of Montégut has observed, his faith in France was unshakeable; but whenever he approaches the events of 1848 or 1871, "he shows the profoundest pessimism; everywhere there is 'la disparition de la tradition, disparition du lien religieux, disparition de l'homme éclairé'; all is corrupted by the new forces of industry; and the ultimate cause of nineteenth century *malaise* was the Revolution." See J. W. Skinner, "Some Aspects of Émile Montégut," *Revue de littérature comparée* 3 (1923): 284.

42. Cf. Ann Douglas, *The Feminization of American Culture* (New York: Knopf, 1977), *passim*.

43. James, *Hawthorne*, 401.

44. D. H. Lawrence, *Studies in Classic American Literature* (1923; rpt. New York: Viking Press, 1964), 83.

45. Taine elaborated the significance of these factors in the Preface to his *History of English Literature* (1863).

46. Ralph Waldo Emerson, "Circles," *The Collected Works of Ralph Waldo Emerson*, edited by Alfred R. Ferguson et al., 7 vols. to date (Cambridge, MA: Belknap Press of Harvard University Press, 1971–), vol. 2, 188.

47. James, *Hawthorne*, 447.

48. Anon., "Contemporary French Literature," *North American Review* 88 (Jan. 1859): 225.

49. Anon., "Sketchings: Hawthorne in Relation to Art," *The Crayon* 7 (Oct. 1860): 299.

50. Harry Levin makes a similar observation in *The Power of Blackness: Hawthorne, Poe, Melville* (1958; rpt. New York: Vintage Books, 1960), 91.

51. The *Centenary Edition of the Works of Nathaniel Hawthorne*, 23 vols., edited by William Charvat, Thomas Woodson et al. (Columbus: The Ohio State University Press, 1962–97), vol. XIV, *The French and Italian Notebooks*, edited by Thomas Woodson, entry for 22 Apr. 1858, 178–79.

52. As Wagonner writes, "Hawthorne's whole career had prepared him to write *The Marble Faun*, his 'story of the fall of man'" (*Hawthorne: A Critical Study*, [Cambridge,

MA: Harvard University Press, 1955], 209). Other theological interpretations of the novel include Richard Harter Fogle, *Hawthorne's Fiction: The Light & the Dark* (Norman: University of Oklahoma Press, 1952); Roy R. Male, *Hawthorne's Tragic Vision* (Austin: University of Texas Press, 1957); and Edward Wagenkknecht, *Nathaniel Hawthorne: Man and Writer* (New York: Oxford University Press, 1961).

V

The Critical Legacy

By now, we have disclosed many latent connections between Anglo-American criticism of Hawthorne and the early French responses to his work. Significantly, a vital—and quite direct—link exists between at least one of them (Montégut) and Henry James, whose remarkable contribution, *Hawthorne,* to Macmillan's English Men of Letters Series in 1879 has been a touchstone for Hawthorne criticism ever since. "It is generally recognized as the first American literary biography of permanent artistic value," Elsa Nettels rightly affirms, "and it remains one of the best biographical and critical studies in English."[1] Precisely because James's biography has secured that stature, however, it seems surprising that scholars have failed to subject the author's methods and sources to more careful scrutiny. Closer analysis will suggest that, when it came to writing literary criticism, James occasionally poached on others' territory and opinions. Even if one admits that contemporary standards for the protection of intellectual property or academic integrity should not be applied, retroactively, with a vengeance, neither should one shrink from calling a spade a spade. In composing his critical biography, Henry James was, if not an outright plagiarist, then at the least a transparently deceptive appropriator of another distinguished critic's work.

When British critic and editor John Morley invited Henry James to contribute a volume to his rapidly expanding English Men of Letters Series of literary biographies, the American author was both flattered and diffident. Having only recently established himself in London (and having just published his first book of literary criticism with the prestigious House of Macmillan [*French Poets and Novelists*, 1878]), James received Morley's proposal as a welcome sign of his rapid assimilation to English literary life. Certainly he would not have wanted to jeopardize his budding relationship with such a great publishing empire; still, he did not accept the invitation at once. To broaden not only his base of subjects but also his potential audience, in early October 1878 Morley had offered James a choice of American authors—Washington Irving? Hawthorne?[2]—but for weeks the writer shuffled his feet. Given the option, he knew that Hawthorne would be more to his liking, but he questioned his desire to take on such a job. All the same, he didn't want to be disobliging, and so he told Frederick Macmillan a few days later that he had written a letter to Morley assenting to the proposal, but had kept the envelope on his desk, "hesitating to send it."[3] Within a week, however, James changed his mind altogether and decided to pull out. Recounting his latest social and professional news for his family back in America, James boasted that he had received an offer from Macmillan for a biography of Hawthorne but had declined because he despaired of finding adequate material: the circumference of Hawthorne's life was too small and its substance without incident. "One can't write a volume about H[awthorne]," he confided, knowing that the proposal still would please the folks at home "& attest my growing fame."[4] Of course, one *could* write a volume about Hawthorne, and Henry James eventually did; but his reluctance to undertake the project invites us to revisit the biography and to interrogate James's methods and sources, about which he expressed explicit concern.

Hawthorne is not in any sense a work of modern scholarship, and it might seem inappropriate to assess it according to contemporary standards of academic rigor. But even if one accepts the book as a kind of dilettante's (not to say amateur's) exercise, the method of its composition is still worth investigating, especially because it was written by an author whom we now regard as The Master of late-nineteenth-century narrative. Indulging, for a moment, in unjust comparison, we might observe, for example, that in the entirety of James's text the reader will encounter but a single footnote, worth quoting in its entirety. "It is proper that before I go further," James notes on his fifth printed page,

> I should acknowledge my large obligations to the only biography of our author, of any considerable length, that has been written—the little volume entitled *A Study of Hawthorne*, by Mr. George Parsons Lathrop [1851–98], the son-in-law of the subject of the work. (Boston, 1876.) To this ingenious and sympathetic sketch, in which the author has taken great pains to collect

the more interesting facts of Hawthorne's life, I am greatly indebted. Mr. Lathrop's work is not pitched in the key which many another writer would have chosen, and his tone is not to my sense the truly critical one; but without the help afforded by his elaborate essay the present little volume could not have been prepared.[5]

At various points further on, James acknowledges Lathrop by attribution and, less frequently, through direct quotation. Apart from this earlier biography, James seems to have relied for information almost exclusively upon Hawthorne's published works (the autobiographical prefaces, especially) and the volumes of his *Notebooks* brought out posthumously by the author's widow. These and one other contemporaneous source (*The Memoirs of Margaret Fuller Ossoli* [1860]) make up his absent Bibliography or list of Works Not Cited.

Apart from this handful of routine biographical sources, James alludes in *Hawthorne* to the work of only one other literary critic, Émile Montégut, whose 1860 essay on *The Marble Faun* ("Un romancier pessimiste en Amérique") provokes him to challenge what he claims are mistaken judgments about Hawthorne's fundamental nature. Given this earlier essay's centrality to James's arguments, that it has lapsed into obscurity seems both undeserved and unwarranted—especially since *Hawthorne* has gone on to become a canonical point of reference for almost all modern scholarship touching the author. Careful scrutiny of James's use of Montégut's work—his selective (and sometimes misleading) quotations, his misrepresentation of the critic's conclusions, his silent appropriation of critical ideas—invariably suggests that James's *Hawthorne* is not altogether his own but rather a plagiaristic amalgam of insights.

In one of his late autobiographical volumes, James had occasion to recall a number of gloomy events traceable to the early spring of 1864. The Civil War, of course, was dragging on in its bloodstained way; and then came the hideous shock from Washington of Lincoln's assassination. Just as significant to James, however, was the news of another's death—the passing of Nathaniel Hawthorne—an event that he preferred to remember in the present tense:

> I sit once more, half-dressed, late of a summer morning and in a bedimmed light which is somehow at once that of dear old green American shutters drawn to against openest windows and that of a moral shadow projected as with violence—I sit on my belated bed, I say, and yield to the pang that made me positively and loyally cry.

James's tears came to him so readily because, as he tells us, he had just that preceding winter taken it upon himself to read Hawthorne "for the first time and at one straight draught," a saturation that confirmed for him "that an American could be an artist, one of the finest, without 'going outside' about it . . . quite in fact as if Hawthorne had become one just by being American *enough*."[6]

On the other side of the Atlantic, another distinguished man of letters was also deeply affected by Hawthorne's death, a critic who had some justification for feeling that he had discovered this American writer, had brought him to an audience that could only rub its eyes in wonder at his curious stories and tales. Anticipating James's much later conclusion, the French critic Émile Montégut had already affirmed (in 1852) that Hawthorne was "the most American writer that the United States has produced since Emerson" (c'est l'écrivain le plus américain que les États-Unis aient produit après Emerson).[7] Having read all of Hawthorne (though not all at once), Montégut was also privileged to tender summary judgments, assessments that have a curiously indirect—or, quite possibly, direct—bearing on later Anglophone criticism. "Somber Hawthorne," this critic lamented,

> did he not endear himself to us at just the right moment? Isn't it true that he came to us in the bosom of happiness to present his casket wreaths and his funeral perfumes? Oh! What favorable hours, those, of black melancholy and sinister dreams, to have conversations with Hawthorne's visions, to read *The Scarlet Letter, The House of the Seven Gables, Mosses from an Old Manse!* How the nascent celebrity of this lugubrious talent went hand in hand with melancholy preoccupations that were new, perhaps, for us as well! How the sentiments he expressed with so much depth—solitude, superstition, fear, despondency—lived and breathed in us!
>
> [Et le sombre Hawthorne n'est-il pas venu, vous cher—cher au moment propice? n'est-il pas vrai que ce n'est pas au sein du bonheur qu'il est venu vous présenter ses bouquets de fleurs de cimetière eet ses parfums funèbres? Oh! les favorables heures, celles, de la mélancolie noire et des rêveries sinistres, pour s'entretenir avec les visions d'Hawthorne, pour lire *La lettre rouge, La maison aux sept pignons, Les mousses du vieux presbytère!* Comme la célébrité naissante de ce talent lugubre s'associait bien avec les préoccupations, nouvelles aussi pour vous peut-être, du malheur! Comme les sentiments qu'il exprime avec tant de profondeur, la solitude, la superstition, la peur, l'accablement, vivaient alors et respiraient en vous!]

For Montégut, there could forever be only one Hawthorne: his genius was too singular, too morbid, too intense, ever to be replicated. "No other writer will arrange those funereal bouquets he excelled at making" (Aucun écrivain ne composera désormais ces bouquets funèbres qu'il excellait à former), this astute Frenchman averred. "The cypress and the willows of that abandoned cemetery that he has made his literary domain will no longer have a caretaker. That somber and profound psychology lived only once" (Les cyprès et les saules de ce cimetière abandonné dont il avait fait son domaine littéraire ne trouveront plus qui en prenne soin. Cette sombre et profonde psychologie a vécu une fois et pour toujours).[8]

Already we have documented this critic's deliberate curiosity about American life and letters. Taking his cue from Tocqueville, Montégut was particularly interested in the problematic nature of democratic individualism. Not surprisingly, then, Emerson was the first American writer to attract his attention. Besides offering his public two affirmative appraisals of the American philosopher, Montégut also translated his most central essays to afford the Sage of Concord a better foothold in France.[9] But if Emerson was an early favorite, Montégut's discovery of Hawthorne (and the puzzling ambiguity of his work) significantly complicated his views about the promise of American life. Having made his literary acquaintance, Montégut was struck by the apparent paradox of such a lugubrious talent finding its voice in the Transcendentalist milieu of New England. Clearly fascinated by Hawthorne, Montégut wrote about him at length on three separate occasions. It cannot be coincidental that the appearance of his final "obituary" essay would be the last time he would comment on an American writer. With Hawthorne's death, Montégut's sustained interest in the literature of the United States came to an end.

To read Montégut (and the handful of other contemporaneous French critics of Hawthorne) is to invite, from time to time, the experience of *déjà vu* all over again, for many of his insights have silently permeated the Anglophone critical tradition. Montégut's perceptions about the significance of Hawthorne's Puritan heritage are especially suggestive, not least because in tracing its roots he found justification for the kind of historical conservatism that served as the ideological basis of his own critical perspective. One should not be fooled, Montégut wrote in 1852, by Hawthorne's flirtation with socialism at Brook Farm. "In spite of his fondness for tolerance, progress, and democracy, the old Puritan nature lives on in him," Montégut affirms:

> Hawthorne's talent marvelously explains the persistence of ancestral values

that are perpetuated over time—the "music of the blood," as Calderón says,[10] that (especially in provincial society) repeats in successive generations the same melody but with different variations. Hawthorne betrays the symptoms: he rarely goes to church, but even at home can hear the hymns of the faithful and the exhortations of the minister. His ideas would have been anathema to his forebears and his profession would have been detested. He no longer believes and lives the way they did, but he does have their intellectual outlook. He may no longer have their *soul*, but he does have their *spirit*.

[En dépit de toutes ses idées de tolérance, de progrès et de démocratie, la vieille nature puritaine existe en lui. Le talent de M. Hawthorne explique merveilleusement cette persistance de la race, cette force de l'éducation première qui se perpétue à travers les temps, cette *musique du sang*, comme dit Calderon, qui chante les mêmes airs sur toutes sortes de variations dans les générations successives d'une même famille et d'un même pays. M. Hawthorne l'avoue quelque part: il va rarement au temple, et se contente d'écouter de sa maison les cantiques des fidèles et les exhortations du ministre; ses idées eussent été anathématisées par ses ancêtres, et sa profession détestée par eux; il n'a plus ni leurs croyances ni leur manière de vivre, mais il a encore leurs qualités intellectuelles; il n'a plus leur *âme*, mais il a leur *esprit*. . . .]

Comparing this passage with a more famous one from the *Hawthorne* biography will reveal the first of many uncanny parallels. "It is interesting to see," James writes,

> how the imagination, in this capital son of the old Puritans, reflected the hue of the more purely moral part, of the dusky, overshadowed conscience. The conscience, by no fault of its own, in every genuine offshoot of that sombre lineage, lay under the shadow of the sense of *sin*. This darkening cloud was no essential part of the nature of the individual; it stood fixed in the general moral heaven, under which he grew up and looked at life. . . . Nothing is more curious and interesting than this almost exclusively *imported* character of the sense of sin in Hawthorne's mind; it seems to exist there merely for an artistic or literary purpose. He had ample cognizance of the Puritan conscience; it was his natural heritage; it was reproduced in him; looking into his soul, he found it there. But his relation to it was only, as one may say, intellectual; it was not moral and theological. (362–63)

Making fair allowance for the differing aims of these two critics, their perceptions about the role of history in the formation of Hawthorne's aesthetic essentially are parallel. Montégut, after all, was trying not only to explain the American writer to his French audience but—much more heroically—to persuade that audience of Hawthorne's immediate cultural relevance; and he was writing during Hawthorne's lifetime. Still caught in the shadow of 1848, Montégut feels obliged to analyze the ideological attractions of socialism reflected in *The Blithedale Romance,* especially because he sees them undercut (or overmastered) by competing historical forces. Further removed from the utopian spirit of the times, James necessarily views Hawthorne's naïve dalliance at Brook Farm differently, enveloped instead by the haze of innocent American provincialism. James, coming later, does not have to shoulder any political burden, which only makes the fundamental similarities between their viewpoints that much more striking.

Because James's biography of Hawthorne has had such profound influence on later criticism, resonances and echoes from Montégut do not always stop there. A key transitional figure, of course, is T. S. Eliot, whose brief reflections on what he called "The Hawthorne Aspect" of James would go on—disproportionately—to inform almost all of F. O. Matthiessen's monumental scholarship and, from there, to an even later generation of critics such as Richard Brodhead. A recently expatriated Eliot composed his observations (in 1918) with a kind of reverent sarcasm, but he clearly wanted to feel that, somewhere, there was a remnant that could be saved from the historical residue of New England culture. Thus, for Eliot,

> James is positively a continuator of the New England genius . . . which has discovered itself only in a very small number of people in the middle of the nineteenth century. . . . I mean whatever we associate with certain purlieus of Boston, with Concord, Salem, and Cambridge, Mass.: notably Emerson, Thoreau, Hawthorne, and Lowell . . . pleasantly shaded by the Harvard elms. One distinguishing mark of this distinguished world was very certainly leisure; and importantly not in all cases a leisure given by money, but insisted upon. . . . Of course leisure in a metropolis, with a civilized society (the society of Boston was and is quite uncivilized but refined beyond the point of civilization), with exchange of ideas and critical standards, would have been better; but these men could not provide the metropolis, and were right in taking the leisure under possible conditions.[11]

Eliot's incisive phrasing is memorable precisely because his evocation of New England is so genial—until he plants the sting; but, again, his rhetoric takes on an almost borrowed hue when we consider that Montégut much earlier had observed that Hawthorne's genius could have come to fruition only in a milieu where "culture" had reached its apogee: where leisure, refinement, and (consequently) boredom were overlain upon a substrate of lingering Puritan scruples. "Hawthorne's talent at first presents an indecipherable enigma," he suggested (in 1860),

> but on closer inspection, it can be solved rather easily. All the characteristics of this talent are found whenever culture reaches its apogee. He has the morbid love of abnormalities that distinguishes blasé minds, the intelligent taste for rarities that distinguishes connoisseurs of human nature. He has the same fancies and caprice that we find in societies consumed with boredom and eager to experience new sensations. He is a casuist, a collector of curiosities, a horticulturalist of exotic plants. He translates only the feelings of souls in ruin, the scruples of consciences that have been refined beyond the point of civilization.
>
> [Le talent d'Hawthorne présente une énigme indéchiffrable en apparence, mais qui, avec un peu d'attention, peut se résoudre assez facilement. Tous les caractères de ce talent sont ceux des époques les plus avancées. Il a l'amour morbide des singularités qui distingue les esprits blasés, le goût intelligent des raretés qui distingue les collectionneurs de race. Il a les bizarreries et les caprices de tous ces types des sociétés ennuyées en quête de sensations nouvelles. C'est un casuiste, un amateur de curiosités, un horticulteur de plantes excentriques. Il ne traduit que les sentiments des âmes en ruines, les scrupules des consciences raffinées qui ont depassé les limites les plus extrêmes de la civilisation.]

Comparing the two passages, we find the mirrored reflection of a particular phrase, but it is the most pregnant one in Eliot's critique; and, as with James, it is embedded within a context of remarkably similar critical generalization. Unlike later readers of *Hawthorne,* Eliot traced his way back to Montégut and (like James) made good—but camouflaged—use of him. Again and again, one hears phrases, finds opinions and judgments, in these contemporaneous French essays that have infiltrated Anglophone criticism and yet have gone unnoticed and, just as important, unacknowledged.

It is doubly ironic that we can trace at least some responsibility for Montégut's obscurity to Henry James. In his sole review of Montégut's work, James regretted the French critic's "inflexible modesty," his apparent unwillingness to assemble a more voluminous career for himself, a judgment repeated by almost all subsequent Anglophone historians of literary criticism. Compared to his other great French contemporaries in the world of letters, Montégut also was less inclined to push his judgments aggressively. According to James, Montégut had "neither the weight and mass and emphasis" of Taine, "nor the bristling malice—the critical *scratch,* as one may call it—of Sainte-Beuve. Many readers," he went on to say, would find Montégut "tame and dull, and his best friends must be those contemplative minds who care more for the journey than for the goal—more to look out of the window than to arrive." From George Saintsbury to René Wellek, James's rather sweeping formulation has worked to confine Montégut's reputation among Anglophone critics and served to relegate him to the fringe.[12]

In the 1870s, however, Montégut was at the very center of the Parisian literary world. For decades, his columns had been appearing in the *Revue des Deux Mondes* (where he had succeeded Sainte-Beuve as principal critic of literature); and his monumental ten-volume translation of Shakespeare already was achieving canonical status in France. As we have seen, Henry James had become familiar with the shape of Montégut's career as a man of letters and was generally sympathetic to his admittedly conservative critical viewpoint. "Both as connoisseur and as moralist, M. Montégut is equally ingenious and penetrating," James observed; his "rare originality" could be traced to a combination of exquisitely developed qualities: "the sense of the artist, the joy in material forms, and the conscience of the moralist, the care for spiritual meanings."[13] Small wonder, then, that when James arrived in Paris in the early winter of 1876 as a reporter on culture and the arts for the *New York Tribune,* he looked forward to sizing up this Frenchman face to face. The American found Parisian hospitality difficult, however, and he would have to wait several months before encountering Montégut at the salon of Auguste Laugel, a French historian to whom James had been given a letter of introduction by his colleagues on the staff of *The Nation.* The meeting was not auspicious, however, and James took an immediate dislike to the man. To his sister James described Montégut as "a little black man, with an abnormally shaped head and a crooked face—a Frenchman of the intense, unhumorous type, *abondant dans son propre sens* and spinning out his shallow ingeniosities with a complacency to make the angels howl. He is a case of the writer in the flesh killing one's mental image of him."[14] Eager to maintain his presence in Parisian literary circles, James nevertheless was obliged to encounter the little black man with the crooked face more than once; and, eventually, he began to soften his tone. To his father James later admitted that he liked Montégut, the man, less than his criticism, and would find it hard to forgive him "for having, *à l'avenir,* spoiled his writing a little for me."[15]

All the same, Montégut was a formidable critical voice—and the only one, we should remember, whom James felt obliged to answer when he undertook his own analytical biography of Hawthorne later in the decade. Besides Hawthorne's son-in-law, George Parsons Lathrop, upon whose more conventional life history (*A Study of Hawthorne,* 1876) James depended for basic facts, Montégut stands alone as the sole literary critic to whom he makes reference in that volume. Because James's *Hawthorne* has been so enormously influential (its reach extends down to the present day), it seems all the more remarkable that the author's methods and sources have not been rigorously investigated.[16] More careful scrutiny of James's work—and of others, in turn, influenced by it—will not only help us recover a more accurate genealogy of insight but also require us to rethink the relationship between French and Anglo-American criticism of a major author.

In the critical biography, we find four specific allusions to Montégut, always with reference to his 1860 essay about *The Marble Faun,* "Un romancier pessimiste en Amérique," a title—and a characterization—from which James begs to differ. "Pessimism consists in having morbid and bitter views and theories about human nature," James insists, "not in indulging in shadowy fancies and conceits." Having the benefit of Hawthorne's newly published notebooks and diaries from which to conclude (materials not available to Montégut), James goes on to say, perhaps somewhat remarkably,

> These volumes contain the record of very few convictions or theories of any kind; they move with curious evenness, with a charming, graceful flow, on a level which lies above that of a man's philosophy. They adhere with such persistence to this upper level that they prompt the reader to believe that Hawthorne had no appreciable philosophy at all—no general views that were in the least uncomfortable. (340)

While it seems easy for James to make the claim that Montégut has exaggerated Hawthorne's morbidity, he does not take into consideration the possibility that the "curious evenness" of the writer's diaries might have resulted from editorial punctiliousness and a calculated effort to present Hawthorne to the world as a harmless, healthy-minded American democrat. James alleges that Montégut's assessment is clever but superficial, but his own willingness to take this supposedly documentary evidence at face value is problematically flawed. Modern scholars have long since taken note of Sophia Peabody's bowdlerizations—the wholesale erasure of her husband's references to alcohol, sex, and the body—in the texts of his American, English, and French & Italian Notebooks; but James, though conceding that he cannot know "what passages of gloom and melancholy may have been suppressed," confidently asserts that these volumes exhibit the placid record of an "unperplexed intellect" (339, 340).[17]

Having set himself in deliberate opposition to Montégut, James must take pains to distinguish his point of view as a necessary corrective to his predecessor's presumably hasty judgments and misreadings. To accomplish this, however, James is obliged to resort to a certain degree of subterfuge—which, by any other name, might just as well be labeled plagiarism. His principal dispute with Montégut centers on the real meaning of Hawthorne's Puritan heritage, and this is how James sets up the discussion:

> "This marked love of cases of conscience," says M. Montégut, "this taciturn, scornful cast of mind, this habit of seeing sin everywhere and hell always gaping open, this dusky gaze bent always upon a damned world and a nature draped in mourning, these lonely conversations of the imagination with the conscience, this pitiless analysis resulting from a perpetual examination of one's self, and from the tortures of a heart closed before men and open to God—all these elements of the Puritan character have passed into Mr. Hawthorne, or to speak more justly, have *filtered* into him, through a long succession of generations." This is a very pretty and very vivid account of Hawthorne, superficially considered; and it is just such a view of the case as would commend itself most easily and most naturally to a hasty critic. It is all true indeed, with a difference; Hawthorne was all that M. Montégut says, *minus* the conviction. The old Puritan moral sense, the consciousness of sin and hell, of the fearful nature of our responsibilities and the savage character of our Taskmaster—these things had been lodged in the mind of a man of Fancy, whose fancy had straightway begun to take liberties and play tricks with them—to judge them (Heaven forgive him!) from the poetic and aesthetic point of view, the point of view of entertainment and irony. This absence of conviction makes the difference; but the difference is great. (364–65)

If we give the original source its due priority, however, and read Montégut first, we can see to what extent James has misrepresented his predecessor's conclusions and, in fact, appropriated his crucial insights. James's translation of this passage from Montégut's essay is very fine, indeed, but he carefully terminates it to create the impression of a distinction that cannot survive comparison with the primary text. What follows immediately in Montégut's analysis is precisely the penetrating elucidation that James then claims (with gratuitous *italic* emphasis) for himself. "If we do not recognize [these elements of the Puritan character] all at once," Montégut continues,

> we should not be surprised; the soul of the Hawthorne family necessarily was modified in each *avatar* that it sent forth, but the substance has remained the same. With each generation, something has been lost: first, religious ardor; next, political readiness; and, then again, the fervor of hate. Everything owing to spiritual conviction has disappeared, all that was from nature has stayed. The visions that haunt Hawthorne's mind are the same that his ancestors knew; but these phantoms have kept up with the fashion of the times and have renewed their sinister costumes. Long ago, they wore a Christian shroud, now they don philosophical togas. Hawthorne's ancestors knew where these visions were coming from because they knew that they had been besieged by two enemy powers, Satan and Christ, who battled for their hearts like a fortress. They were skilled in distinguishing the visions that came from heaven and those that came from hell. Hawthorne's vision comes neither from heaven nor hell; these two words have lost all meaning for him. Heaven has been replaced by the black room of the imagination, and hell by the cavern of the heart.

> [Cet amour morbide des cas de conscience, cette tournure d'esprit taciturne et méprisante, cette habitude de voir le péché partout et l'enfer toujours béant, ce regard sombre promené sur un monde damné et sur une nature vêtue de deuil, ces conversations solitaires de l'imagination avec la conscience, cette analyse impitoyable résultant d'un perpétuel examen de soi-même et des tortures d'un cœur fermé devant les hommes, toujours ouvert devant Dieu, tous ces traits de la nature puritaine ont passé dans M. Hawthorne, ou, pour mieux dire, ont *filtré* en lui à travers une longue série de générations. Si nous ne les reconnaissons pas tout d'abord, il ne faut pas s'en étonner, l'âme de Hawthorne s'est nécessairement modifiée avec chacun des *avatars* qu'elle a traversés, mais la substance est restée la même. A chaque génération, elle a perdu quelque chose: une fois l'ardeur religieuse, une autre fois l'âpreté politique, une autre fois encore la ferveur de la haine. Tout ce qui était de la grâce a disparu, tout ce qui était de la nature est resté. Les visions qui hantent l'esprit d'Hawthorne sont les mêmes que ses ancêtres ont connues; seulement les fantômes ont suivi les modes du temps et renouvelé leur garde-robe sinistre. Jadis ils avaient un suaire chrétien, maintenant ils ont des toges philosophiques. Les ancêtres de Hawthorne savaient d'où sortaient ces visions, car ils savaient qu'ils étaient assiégés par deux puissances ennemies, Satan et le Christ, qui se disputaient leurs cœurs comme

une forteresse; ils étaient habiles à distinguer les visions qui venaient du ciel et celles qui venaient de l'enfer. Les visions de Hawthorne ne viennent au contraire ni du ciel ni de l'enfer; ces deux mots ont perdu pour lui toute signification: le ciel est remplacé par la chambre noire de l'imagination et l'enfer par la caverne du cœur.]

James's manipulation of the evidence here does justice neither to the reach of Montégut's vivid historical imagination nor to the distinctively suggestive language in which he gives it concrete form. In effect, James continues to translate (or paraphrase) but without the acknowledging punctuation of quotation marks. "I take possession of the Old World," he once richly intoned: "I inhale it, I appropriate it!"[18] At least on this occasion, he did.

Calling attention to James's academic infractions need not diminish our sense of his critical accomplishment—such practices surely were not uncommon then (if now); and, besides, he made no particular claims to scholarly rigor.[19] Like the goals of other contributors to Macmillan's English Men of Letters Series, James's goal as a biographer was synthetic, not pedantic.[20] Still, evidence gleaned from informed comparison should complicate and enrich our understanding of James's more genuine indebtedness and thus, by implication, that of others (such as T. S. Eliot) whose profoundly influential assessments of Hawthorne use the 1879 biography as a touchstone. Even when making specific reference to a critic like Montégut, James was capable simultaneously of concealing the extent of his dependence, a tactic amply repaid by the silence of intervening decades.

We can measure the immediate success of this strategy in contemporaneous reviews, many of which register a certain patriotic pride in James's supposed dressing down of the French critic. *The Nation*, for example, felt that James really had the field to himself, alleging that "no serious criticism" of Hawthorne had been written "heretofore to any purpose, unless Mr. James would have us except Poe's." With that presumed advantage, it is irresistible to repeat the author's own formulations. "Hawthorne appears in this portrait a very different figure from the fiction conceived by M. Emile Montégut," the notice continues, "who represents him, as he would perhaps be likely to appear to the Gallic imagination, as a *romancier pessimiste*. All that can be said in support of this Mr. James says is true 'with a difference.' Hawthorne was a *romancier pessimiste*, 'minus the conviction.'"[21] *Voilà!* The *Literary World* made just the same point, once again quoting James's selective translation of Montégut (glossing the Frenchman's assessment as "brilliant, but . . . extravagant"), and then congratulating the biographer presumably for refuting it.[22] By emphasizing a distinction more apparent than real, James could reinvent many of Montégut's insights as his own.

The felicity of James's style and the refined nature of his critical intelligence impressed even French readers. Applauding "the shrewdness of its insights and the sustained elegance of its execution," Arvède Barine also felt obliged to square *Hawthorne* with the insights of Montégut, for he was a critic she greatly admired. If James's biography was a signal accomplishment, so, too, had been her countryman's essays: Barine commended them as the work of "a penetrating critic of refined psychology and political philosophy" that "no other living author, in France or elsewhere, would be capable of writing." James, she contends, has had the benefit of documents denied to Montégut—his notebooks, and Lathrop's sympathetic biography—and so arrives at more cheerful conclusions about Hawthorne's personality. But she also suggests that, through a fault of semantics, both critics have confused an important issue by conflating Puritanism with pessimism. "If James takes great pains to persuade us that Hawthorne, far from being Puritan, was more or less lukewarm towards religion, it is in order to excuse him from the crime of pessimism. On the other hand, and with the same reasoning, Montégut intertwines Hawthorne's Puritanism and his morose philosophy (seeing them as two inseparable traits), as if they were mutually corroborating forms of testimony." Barine's attempt to reconcile these differences through an appeal to Christian moralism is not very satisfactory, but she at least recognized some of the problems that James's (mis)use of Montégut generated.[23]

When James first attempts to dismantle Montégut's allegation of pessimism, he again uses the technique of deceptive quotation to make his point. "To speak of Hawthorne, as M. Emile Montégut does, as a *romancier pessimiste,* seems to me very much beside the mark," James says. Rather, he insists, Hawthorne cannot be accused of having any kind of philosophy at all. "'His bitterness,' says M. Montégut, 'is without abatement, and his bad opinion of man is without compensation. . . . . His little tales have the air of confessions which the soul makes to itself; they are so many little slaps which the author applies to our face'" (363–64). Apart from the fact that these two statements in Montégut's essay are separated by six pages of print, James also silently elides the context in which the French critic is careful to frame his argument. James presents Montégut's opinion as if it were an overarching generality, a simplistic formulation, rather than a targeted insight, developed, as it is in context, from close inspection of a particular Hawthorne work ("Earth's Holocaust"). More pointedly, since Montégut reads that tale as an allegorical repudiation of all revolutionary ideals (significantly, he dates the event of the story as the 4th of August—the day in 1789 when the French Constituent Assembly abolished the regime of class privilege), we should not be surprised by his conclusion that the "impression of cold and sadness is even more powerful because Hawthorne's bitterness is undiluted, because his bad opinion of mankind affords no compensation" (Cette impression de froid et de tristesse est d'autant plus puissante, que l'amertume d'Hawthorne est sans mélange, et que sa mauvaise opinion de l'homme est sans compensation). Distorting Montégut's more complex perspective makes it much easier to dispose of, which James seems eager to do.

Moreover, the second part of James's (mis)quotation derives not from any discussion of "pessimism," but rather from Montégut's analysis of Hawthorne's preference for allegory, another topic on which James follows his lead. "For a long time, allegory has been labeled and classed in books on rhetoric as suiting the needs of the lazy and pedantic," Montégut acknowledges, but "the Puritans found it where we find all the great things, in nature or in the contemplation of the world, and recreated it for the needs of their hearts" (Elle était étiquetée et classée depuis longtemps dans les livres de rhétorique pour les besoins des oisifs et des pédans; ils la retrouvèrent là où l'on trouve toutes les grandes choses, dans la nature et dans la contemplation du monde, et la recréèrent pour les besoins de leur cœur). Likewise, James dismisses the form as "one of the lighter exercises of the imagination" and suggests that "the taste for it is responsible for a large part of the forcible feeble writing that has been inflicted upon the world" (366). In making significant exception for Hawthorne, Montégut understands the way in which the allegorical form was perfectly suited to the writer's psychological obsessions. True descendant of the Puritans, he has "inherited the same gift" and knows,

> as they did, how to give life to abstraction and how to creep up on the most hidden secrets of interior life. Any psychologist is necessarily an egoist. But we can say in all truth that the egoism of Hawthorne is heroic and disinterested. Not one of the movements of the self eludes him, even in such moments when . . . it has wanted to escape and not be observed. This method of extreme egoism, this procedure of excessive *personality*, detracts nothing, however, from the *impersonality* of the characters he draws and the protagonists that he puts into his work. By expressing his individuality, Hawthorne expresses general human nature. His short stories above all have the air of confessions that your soul makes to itself. They are so many small slaps that the author applies to your face. You would swear that they apply

personally to you, so much so that you want to say to the author, "How do you know that and who told you so?"

[Leur maladif et mélancolique descendant a hérité du même don. Il sait, comme eux, animer les abstractions et surprendre les secrets les plus cachés de la vie intérieure. Tout psychologue est forcément un égoïste; mais on peut dire en toute vérité que l'égoïsme d'Hawthorne est héroïque et désintéressé. Aucun des mouvemens de son *moi* ne lui échappe, même dans ces momens où . . . ce *moi* désirerait fuir et n'être pas observé auparavant. Cette méthode d'extrême égoïsme, ce procédé d'excessive *personnalité*, ne nuisent en rien cependant à l'*impersonnalité* des caractères qu'il dessine et des héros qu'il met en scène. En exprimant son individualité, Hawthorne exprime la nature humaine générale. Ses petites nouvelles surtout ont l'air de confessions que notre âme se fait à elle-même: ce sont autant de petits soufflets que l'auteur nous applique sur le visage. Vous jureriez qu'elles se rapportent toutes personnellement à vous, si bien que vous auriez envie de dire à l'auteur: "Comment savez-vous cela, et de qui le tenez-vous?"]

After discussing the limitations of Hawthorne's allegorical technique, James famously concludes by offering an analogous summary judgment. "The fine thing in Hawthorne," he memorably says,

is that he cared for the deeper psychology, and that, in his way, he tried to become familiar with it. This natural, yet fanciful familiarity with it, this air, on the author's part, of being a confirmed *habitué* of a region of mysteries and subtleties, constitutes the originality of his tales. And then they have the further merit of seeming, for what they are, to spring up so freely and lightly. The author has all the ease, indeed, of a regular dweller in the moral, psychological realm; he goes to and fro in it, as a man who knows his way. (368)

When T. S. Eliot pointed to this passage as confirmation of the fundamental link between Hawthorne and James, he suggested that their kinship was established because the two writers shared "a kind of sense, a receptive medium, which is not of sight. . . . They perceive by antennae; and the 'deeper psychology' is here." Through this mechanism, Hawthorne could "grasp character through the relation of two or more persons to each other; and this is what no one else, except James, has done."[24] This is exactly what Montégut affirms when he tells us that the "characteristic element of Hawthorne's talent is his dramatic power. He has what I will call a feeling for impalpable things to the utmost degree: fear, solitude, terror of annihilation—above all, the apprehension of those monstrous fancies that are spontaneously and unpredictably born in even the most moral and spotless minds" (L'élément caractéristique du talent de M. Hawthorne, c'est la puissance dramatique. Il a au plus haut degré ce que j'appellerai le sentiment des *choses insaisissables,* la peur, la solitude, la terreur des ruines, et surtout le sentiment de ces imaginations monstrueuses qui naissent spontanément et tout à coup dans l'esprit même le plus moral et le plus candide). The tautology comes full circle (almost becomes laughable) when Eliot tried to explain himself more clearly—in French: "*L'intérêt de ce passage réside dans sa double application: il est vrai en ce qui concerne Hawthorne, il est vrai ou plus vrai encore en ce qui concern James lui-même.*"[25] As Alan Holder has suggested, with the publication of Eliot's later assessment in this venue, "a curious repetition of literary history seems to have taken place": James had tried to "correct" Montégut's interpretation of Hawthorne, and now Eliot was trying to remand an erroneous French interpretation of James.[26] In my end is my beginning.

What embroiled James in greatest controversy were, of course, the repeated allegations of American provincialism and cultural backwardness that he laid at Hawthorne's feet. Although he hardly needed cues from Montégut to appreciate the differences between an older and an ever-so-much-younger civilization, still he could have found them in the Frenchman's work. All the same, if anything Montégut is seemingly more tolerant than James of Hawthorne's cultural limitations, even when he is obliged to point them out. Any discussion of *The Marble Faun* would have to address this topic, and Montégut tackles it quite honestly. "Hawthorne's observations and thoughts on Italy, Italian arts, art in general, are such as we would expect from his sharp and subtle mind," the critic begins. "He penetrates beneath the surface and goes to look for the hidden soul of things, but somewhat at random and with a degree of hesitation that indicates that the author is not absolutely sure of himself. He speaks self-consciously, proposes his opinions without conviction, in a muffled voice, and suddenly interrupts himself as if he were afraid that he had gone too far and dreaded the judgment of those whom he is addressing." But Montégut understands this fallibility as an inevitable consequence of Hawthorne's limited experience:

> We sense in his opinions, as in those of all of his compatriots in the arts, a certain intrinsic weakness that results from a fundamental deficiency in education, a deficiency that the historical circumstances of America have created, and that her best endowed minds will need much time to overcome.

Hawthorne lacks neither the depth nor the subtlety of mind to understand exactly certain great things; what he needs is practice. Neither mind nor even genius can take the place of educational familiarity in understanding the value of great works of art. Nothing can substitute for this primary schooling, not even the most exquisite sensitivity. Any European of ordinary judgment, even with a soul lacking elevation and only moderate sensibility, will surpass Hawthorne in this arena. I do not want to say that he will better comprehend than Hawthorne the essence and the aim of art; he might not comprehend them at all; but he will be less deceived as to the productions of art, and will not fall into the same errors of detail.

[Les observations et les pensées d'Hawthorne sur l'Italie, les arts italiens, l'art en général, sont telles qu'on pouvait les attendre de son esprit fin et subtil. Il pénètre les surfaces et va chercher l'âme cachée des choses, mais un peu à l'aventure et avec une hésitation qui indique que l'auteur n'est pas absolument sûr de lui-même. Il s'écoute parler, propose ses opinions sans hardiesse, à demi-voix, et tout à coup s'interrompt comme s'il craignait de s'être trop avancé, et qu'il redoutât le jugement de ceux auxquels il s'adresse. On sent dans ses opinions, comme dans celles de tous ses compatriotes sur les arts, une certaine faiblesse intrinsèque qui résulte d'une lacune première dans l'éducation, lacune que les circonstances historiques de l'Amérique ont creusée, et que les esprits les mieux doués de ce pays auront longtemps de la peine à combler. Ce n'est ni la profondeur ni la finesse d'esprit qui manquent à Hawthorne pour comprendre exactement certaines grandes choses, c'est l'habitude. Ni l'esprit, ni même le génie, ne valent l'habitude que donne l'éducation pour connaître la valeur des grandes œuvres d'art. Rien ne peut remplacer cette éducation première, pas même la sensibilité la plus exquise. Un enfant de l'Europe, d'un jugement ordinaire, d'une âme sans grande portée, d'une sensibilité sans finesse, battra Hawthorne sur ce terrain. Je ne veux pas dire qu'il comprendra mieux que lui l'essence et le but de l'art; il ne les comprendra pas du tout peut-être, mais il se trompera moins sur les produits de l'art, et ne tombera pas dans les mêmes erreurs de détail.]

One can only imagine that James (already so widely traveled and long since expatriated) read this passage with a certain degree of cosmopolitan self-congratulation. At any rate, it surely would have strengthened his confidence in describing Hawthorne as "the last of the old-fashioned Americans." James's immediate qualification of the term looks as much to Montégut as it does in the mirror. "I do not mean by this," he goes on to say,

V. The Critical Legacy   89

> that there are not still many of his fellow-countrymen (as there are many natives of every land under the sun,) who are more susceptible of being irritated than of being soothed by the influences of the Eternal City. What I mean is that an American of equal value with Hawthorne, an American of equal genius, imagination, and, as our forefathers said, sensibility, would at present inevitably accommodate himself more easily to the idiosyncrasies of foreign lands. An American as cultivated as Hawthorne, is now almost inevitably more cultivated, and, as a matter of course, more Europeanised in advance, more cosmopolitan. (441–42)

Montégut's hypothetical European could almost be James himself: "from childhood he has been raised with a familiarity with the arts. He has spent his youth in museums, in the shadow of palaces; at every moment, he has seen, felt, and been moved by the most beautiful works of art in every possible form." Gently, he concludes by way of apology:

> Would that Hawthorne not feel wounded by our observations, because the customs that encourage conviction in matters of taste do not necessarily imply a great understanding of art, any more than an ease in manipulating the instruments of modern science implies a deep understanding of science. If Roger Bacon or Albert the Great came back to the world, they would fumble around in any modern laboratory: even beginning chemistry students would laugh at their clumsiness. Hawthorne's sojourn in Europe was not long enough to insure him the security of taste that only familiarity creates, that is all.

> [. . . cet enfant a été élevé dans la familiarité des arts, il a passé sa jeunesse dans les musées, à l'ombre des palais, il a vu, senti, touché à toute heure, sous toutes les formes possibles, les plus belles œuvres de l'art. Que M. Hawthorne ne se sente pas blessé par nos observations, car cette habitude qui crée la sûreté du goût n'implique en rien une intelligence profonde de l'art, pas plus que l'habileté à manier les instrumens de la science moderne n'implique une intelligence profonde de la science. Si Roger Bacon ou Albert le Grand revenaient au monde, ils manieraient gauchement les instrumens de la science moderne, et prêteraient probablement à rire par leur maladresse au dernier préparateur des cours de chimie. Le séjour de M. Hawthorne en Europe n'a pas été assez long pour lui donner cette sûreté de goût que crée l'habitude, et voilà tout.]

James's taste was nothing if not secure, and it was formed precisely in the fashion that Montégut describes. Other Americans bristled at the condescension they felt in the biography (even James's friend Howells, who was inclined to be sympathetic, waited "with the patience and security of a spectator at an *auto da fé*");[27] few were inclined to forgive James as Montégut had forgiven Hawthorne.

Even though the biography makes specific reference only to Montégut's 1860 essay, it is not unreasonable to assume that James also knew that critic's other commentary on Hawthorne. "Un romancier pessimiste en Amérique" makes its particular claims as an extension of the author's previous encounter with the novelist, for the publication of *The Marble Faun* (or, rather, *Transformation,* as he had access to the British edition of the romance) offered Montégut "the pretext," as he says, "to verify and test" his former impressions. "On that occasion," he reminds us (and a footnote clearly directs us to the source),[28] he discovered the American writer's fiction to be a "literary bouquet" composed of strange "funereal flowers." Contemplating them—"and inhaling their strange aroma"—produced in him "a nervous shudder or even more so a moral shudder, a presentiment." Hawthorne's new novel only confirmed the validity of this initial judgment. Reading *The Marble Faun,* Montégut again felt

> the same curiosity of mind, the same antipathy of heart, the same shudders of the soul, in front of these bizarre flowers, not one of which does not contain a hungry worm or a poisoned perfume. It is only that in smelling these flowers a second time I find them more pungent, more acrid, more penetrating. Far from diminishing after a second go-round, my esteem for Hawthorne has grown and gotten stronger. Thanks to the interval that has passed between reading these two books, the experience has permitted me to recognize as true what up to now I only had felt, confirming exactly what I had all along suspected. I had not said too much and I must admit to the contrary that I had not said enough. Hawthorne is certainly the least lovable man of genius; however, in many ways he merits this illustrious title, and we shall give it to him without his asking.

> [J'avais examiné alors avec une curiosité craintive, antipathique, mais réelle, ces fleurs de cimetière dont il aime à composer ses bouquets littéraires, et j'avais noté les impressions, assez semblables à un frisson nerveux ou mieux encore à ce frisson moral qui s'appelle pressentiment, que j'avais éprouvées en les respirant et en les contemplant. . . . J'ai ressenti la même curiosité d'esprit, la même antipathie de cœur, les mêmes frissons de l'âme, devant ces

fleurs bizarres dont il n'est aucune qui ne contienne un ver rongeur ou un parfum empoisonné. Seulement, en ressentant pour la seconde fois ces anciennes sensations, je les ai trouvées plus vives, plus âcres, plus pénétrantes. Loin de s'affaiblir après cette seconde lecture, mon estime pour Hawthorne a grandi et s'est fortifiée. Grâce à l'intervalle qui s'est écoulé entre les deux lectures, l'expérience m'a permis de reconnaître pour vrai ce que j'avais pressenti, et pour exact ce que j'avais soupçonné. Je n'avais pas trop dit, et je suis contraint d'avouer au contraire que je n'avais pas dit assez. Hawthorne est certainement le moins aimable des hommes de génie; cependant il mérite à beaucoup d'égards ce titre illustre, et nous le lui accordons sans nous faire prier.]

The 1852 back numbers of the *Revue* were probably shelved within arm's reach of the 1860 volume that James consulted (at the British Museum or, just as likely, in the private library of the Reform Club), and we know from other sources that he was hungry—even desperate—for material to fulfill his contract with Macmillan. If James took the trouble to track down Hawthorne's son in the provincial town of Hastings in the winter of 1879 (obviously wanting to "pump" him for the biography of his father), he certainly would have availed himself of resources closer to hand.[29] Montégut's 1864 memorial essay, though less accessible in periodical form, still might have been available to James, since it was reprinted both independently and as an Introduction to an 1866 translation of Hawthorne's short stories—volumes that surely would have attracted a cosmopolitan's attention had he discovered them in the bookstalls along the Seine during either his first grand tour of the continent (1869–70) or his later residence in the French capital.[30] Having procrastinated for months, James finally buckled down to a task all the more "difficult," as he said, for "the want of material and (as I think) slenderness of the subject." Appropriately enough, it was in Paris that he finished his manuscript in the first weeks of autumn 1879.[31]

When we think of the impact of nineteenth-century American literature in France, naturally we think of Poe and the heroic welcome extended to him by Charles Baudelaire. Yet everywhere in Montégut's criticism we find the same telling image: again and again he describes Hawthorne's tales and stories as flowers of evil—blossoms that are gorgeous in appearance but also possessed of a fragrance that is fatal to inhale. By now we are quite familiar with the French face of Edgar Poe, but we are only just beginning to discern the outline of another American writer whose significance was also appreciated there: the French face of Nathaniel Hawthorne.

Notes

1. Elsa Nettels, "Henry James and the Art of Biography," *South Atlantic Bulletin* 43 (1978): 115.

2. John Morley to Henry James, 9 Oct. 1878, *The Correspondence of Henry James and the House of Macmillan, 1877–1914: "All the Links in the Chain,"* edited by Rayburn S. Moore (Baton Rouge: Louisiana State University Press, 1993), 17.

3. Henry James to Frederick Macmillan, 11 Oct. [1878], *The Correspondence of Henry James and the House of Macmillan*, 18. Part of James's ambivalence may have stemmed from the fact that Macmillan and Morley had first wanted James Russell Lowell to write *Hawthorne* (he declined), but it is unclear whether James was aware of his runner-up status. See John J. Kijinski, "Professionalism, Authority, and the Late-Victorian Man of Letters: A View from the Macmillan Archive," *Victorian Literature and Culture* 24 (1996): 234.

4. Henry James to Henry James, Sr., 18 Oct. [1878] (bMS Am 1094 [1873] Houghton Library, Harvard).

5. Henry James, *Hawthorne*, in *Literary Criticism: Essays on Literature; American Writers, English Writers*, edited by Leon Edel (New York: Library of America, 1984), 322n1; hereafter, the Library of America edition will be cited parenthetically in the text. Lathrop's book was published by J. R. Osgood & Company, the successors to Hawthorne's publisher, Ticknor & Fields. Despite this gesture of acknowledgment, after finishing the biography James anticipated that Lathrop would "*hate* it, and me for writing it; though I couldn't have done so without the aid (for dates and facts) of his own singularly foolish pretentious little volume. The amount of a certain sort of emasculate twaddle produced in the United States is not encouraging." Henry James to Thomas Sergeant Perry, 14 Sept. 1879, *Henry James Letters*, 4 vols., edited by Leon Edel (Cambridge, MA: Belknap Press of Harvard University Press, 1974–84), vol. 2, 255. Even if he didn't "hate it" (as James prophesied), Lathrop did respond to James's biography by publishing a satiric counterattack in the *New York Tribune* (9 Feb. 1880), lampooning *Hawthorne*'s notorious list of the items of "high civilization" presumably absent from American life. See George Monteiro, "'The Items of High Civilization': Hawthorne, Henry James, and George Parsons Lathrop," in *The Nathaniel Hawthorne Journal 1975*, edited by C. E. Frazer Clark, Jr. (Englewood, CO: Microcard Edition Books, 1975), 146–55.

6. Henry James, *Notes of a Son and Brother* (1914), in *Autobiography*, edited by Frederick W. Dupee (New York: Criterion Books, 1956), 478, 480.

7. Because of the nature of the argument that follows, translations from Montégut will be followed by corresponding passages in his original French.

8. In *Notes of a Son and Brother* James testifies to a remarkably similar reading experience:

> The joy of recognition was to know at the time no lapse—was in fact through the years never to know one, and this by some rare action of a principle or a sentiment, I scarce know whether to call it a clinging consistency or a singular silliness, that placed the Seven Gables, the Blithedale Romance and the story of Donatello and Miriam . . . somewhere on a shelf unvisited by harsh inquiry. (478)

9. "Un penseur et poète américain: Ralph Waldo Emerson," *Revue des Deux Mondes* (1 Aug. 1847): 462–93; and "Carlyle et Emerson" [review essay on *Representative Men*],

Revue des Deux Mondes (15 Aug. 1850): 722–37. Montégut's pivotal role in securing Emerson's reputation in France is best documented by Hans Keller, *Emerson in Frankreich: Wirkungen und Parallelen* (Diss. Hessischen Ludwigs-Universität zu Giessen, 1932), esp. 87–105.

10. See chapter IV, note 6, for Montégut's misattribution of this allusion.

11. T. S. Eliot, "The Hawthorne Aspect," *The Little Review* 5 (1918): 48–49.

12. James also suggested that Montégut's "characteristic fault" was a "tendency to prolixity" (although he immediately qualified this judgment by saying that "this prolixity is so sincere, so suggestive, so charged with information and reflection, that we rarely desire to abridge it"). Henry James, rev. of *Souvenirs de Bourgogne* by Émile Montégut [1874], in *Literary Criticism: French Writers; Other European Writers; The Prefaces to the New York Edition*, edited by Leon Edel (New York: Library of America, 1984), 588–89. Most critical assessments in English run directly parallel to James's. According to Saintsbury, "Montégut's delicate, intricate reflection and sympathy, especially at the length at which they are given, can hardly, by the most attentive and sensitive of readers, be taken in all at once; there are always gleanings of the grapes, always second mowings of the grass to be made." J. W. Skinner echoed this in 1923, when he wrote that Montégut's "retiring personality, the extent of his erudition, the over-shadowing fame of Sainte-Beuve and Taine, his methods of work and publication, all that has helped to relegate him into a puzzling obscurity." Two generations later, Richard Chadbourne arrived at the same conclusion. It comes as no surprise, then, to hear Wellek say that Montégut "is in danger of being forgotten, not only because his books have not been reprinted and are all only collections of articles that he wrote for the *Revue des Deux Mondes*, with their accepted prolixity and leisurely approaches, but also because he lacks the strong individuality, either as a theorist or a judge, which alone conveys a name to posterity." See George Saintsbury, *A History of Criticism and Literary Taste in Europe from the Earliest Texts to the Present Day*, 3 vols. (Edinburgh: W. Blackwood and Sons, 1902–4), vol. 3, 445; J. W. Skinner, "Some Aspects of Émile Montégut," *Revue de littérature comparée* 3 (1923): 283; Richard M. Chadbourne, "The Essay World of Émile Montégut," *PMLA* 76.1 (Mar. 1961): 99; and René Wellek, *A History of Modern Criticism, 1750–1950*. 7 vols. [vol. 4] *The Later Nineteenth Century* (New Haven, CT: Yale University Press, 1965), 8

13. Henry James, rev. of *Souvenirs de Bourgogne* [1874], 590.

14. Henry James to Alice James, 22 Feb. [1876], *Henry James Letters*, vol. 2, 30.

15. Henry James to Henry James, Sr., 11 Apr. [1876], *Henry James Letters*, vol. 2, 38.

16. Charles Caramello provides a useful overview of the critical tradition in *Henry James, Gertrude Stein, and the Biographical Act* (Chapel Hill: University of North Carolina Press, 1996), 21–56. Other recent contributions are Dan McCall, *Citizens of Somewhere Else: Nathaniel Hawthorne and Henry James* (Ithaca, NY: Cornell University Press, 1999), 1–10; and Willie Tolliver, *Henry James as a Biographer: A Self among Others* (New York: Garland, 2000).

17. In his earlier 1872 review of *Passages from the French and Italian Note-Books*, James had already concluded that these volumes ("judged with any real critical rigor") represented their author "as superficial, uninformed, incurious, inappreciative" (*Literary Criticism: Essays on Literature; American Writers; English Writers*, 307–8). For descriptive analysis of Sophia Peabody Hawthorne's editorial scruples, see "Historical Commentary," in Centenary Edition, vol. VIII, *The American Notebooks*, edited by Claude M. Simpson,

677–98. Professor Randall Stewart spent most of his career promoting critical awareness of the editorial complexity surrounding Hawthorne's published texts. Besides preparing restored editions of the American and English Notebooks (in 1932 and 1941, respectively), Stewart also investigated the fate of Hawthorne's manuscripts in the crucial period following the novelist's death. See, for example, "Editing Hawthorne's Notebooks: Selections from Mrs. Hawthorne's Letters to Mr. and Mrs. Fields, 1864–1868," *More Books, Being the Bulletin of the Boston Public Library* 20 (1945): 299–315.

18. Henry James to the James family, 1 Nov. [1875], *Henry James Letters*, vol. 1, 484.

19. While some scholars have claimed that James also took interesting liberties with Hawthorne's texts, particularly when he chose to "quote" from the author's notebooks, such inferences are bibliographically naïve. Willie Tolliver, for example, makes the mistake of assuming that James had available to him the unexpurgated texts of Hawthorne's notebooks and letters when, in fact, he was faithfully dependent upon the more limited primary sources in print at the time he composed *Hawthorne*. (See *Henry James as a Biographer*, 86–89.) Still, we do know that James did tamper with primary evidence when he compiled other biographical narratives. See, for example, Alfred Habegger, "Henry James's Rewriting of Minny Temple's Letters," *American Literature* 58.2 (May 1986): 159–80.

20. Ira B. Nadel provides an informed overview of the Series as an exemplary Victorian cultural practice in *Biography: Fiction, Fact and Form* (London: Macmillan, 1984), 31–47.

21. Rev. of *Hawthorne* by Henry James, *The Nation* 30 (29 Jan. 1880): 80, 81.

22. Rev. of *Hawthorne* by Henry James, *Literary World* 11 (14 Feb. 1880): 52.

23. Arvède Barine, "Puritain ou pessimiste," *Revue bleue* 19 (31 Jul. 1880): 99, 104, 106. In the winter of 1881, James took pleasure in reporting to his family that M. Guillaume Guizot, professor of English literature at the Sorbonne, had greatly admired his critical study. "He had desired much to meet me," James immodestly reported,

> owing to a perusal of my little book on Hawthorne, for whom, in his quality of French protestant or "puritan," he has a great admiration. He was most effusive & fraternizing, repeated whole passages of my book to me, with the most extraordinary accent, &c. He had a phrase which I should have liked my critics to hear: he was speaking of the beauty of Hawthorne's genius in comparison with the provinciality of his training & circumstances. "*Il sortait de toute espèce de petits trous—de Boston, de—comment appelez-vous ça?—de Salem, &c!*"

Henry James to Henry James, Sr., 24 Feb. 1881, *Henry James Letters*, vol. 2, 345.

24. Eliot, "The Hawthorne Aspect," 50–51.

25. T. S. Eliot, "Les lettres anglaises: le roman anglais contemporain," *La Nouvelle Revue Française* 28 (1 May 1927): 669.

26. Alan Holder, "T. S. Eliot on Henry James," *PMLA* 79.4 (Sept. 1964): 492.

27. William Dean Howells, rev. of *Hawthorne* [1880], in Michael Anesko, *Letters, Fictions, Lives: Henry James and William Dean Howells* (New York: Oxford University Press, 1997), 143.

28. "*Voyez* Un Roman socialiste en Amérique, Revue *du 1er décembre 1852*."

29. The impression was Julian Hawthorne's, who recorded it in his journal on 14 Jan. 1879. See David W. Pancost, "Henry James and Julian Hawthorne," *American Literature* 50.3 (Nov. 1978): 461.

30. Émile Montégut, *Nathaniel Hawthorne* (Paris: J. Laisné, 1866); and *Contes étranges imités d' Hawthorne*, translated by E. A. Spoll, with an Introduction by Émile Montégut (Paris: Librairie contemporaine, 1866). These republish (with slight modifications) the obituary essay that Montégut published in four installments of the *Moniteur universel* in the summer of 1864.

31. Henry James to Thomas Sergeant Perry, 14 Sept. 1879, and James to Frederick Macmillan, 28 Sept. [1879], *Henry James Letters*, vol. 2, 255, 257.

2

Transatlantic Reflections
The French Reception of Nathaniel Hawthorne

VI

Paul Émile-Daurand Forgues

"American Poets and Novelists: Nathaniel Hawthorne" (1852)

I know authors—the number is large—whose prefaces are odious, odious like the *I,* and perhaps for the same reasons. For others, on the contrary, the preface is worthy of the book, sometimes even more. A preface by Walter Scott, a preface by Charles Nodier—what literary delicacy! Henceforth one must add to these the prefaces by Nathaniel Hawthorne. They have made him known to us and loved above all others; without them we might not have read a single one of his novels or tales.

All the same, America is proud of Nathaniel Hawthorne. He is counted, and counted by many, in that literary phalanx, already numerous, for whom Brockden Brown, Washington Irving, and Fenimore Cooper cleared the path, and who have furnished the contents of a large biographical dictionary, adorned with portraits, compiled by Mr. Rufus Wilmot Griswold. In this imposing volume, where there are so many names crowded together (unknown to us but famous over there), you can look up an entry on Nathaniel Hawthorne, and you will find the elements of a biography like so many we see, where the order of the dates is observed, the catalog of works is complete, the chronology irreproachable. You will learn there that Hawthorne was born in Salem, Massachusetts; that his ancestors were seafarers from father to son for generations; that one of them, "Bold" Hawthorne, was the hero of a ballad composed during the Revolutionary War, and in which his exploits on the *Fair American*—no doubt some frigate—were celebrated.[1]

You will also learn that, having graduated in 1825 from Bowdoin College (Maine), Hawthorne found himself there a school companion of the poet Longfellow; that in 1837 and 1842 his first two works came out—the two series of *Twice-told Tales*—published under a French pseudonym of the so-called Monsieur de l'Aubépine;[2] that the romancer was, for a while, part of a Fourierist community, Brook Farm, in West Roxbury; that he lived for the next three years in Concord, the village famous for having been the theater of the first battle when the American Minutemen pushed back General Gage's soldiers;[3] that after this time of retreat, he filled the function of a customs house officer in Boston until Taylor's presidency;[4] that the Whig administration, no longer needing his services, left him to the laborious pleasures of a literary life; and, finally, born around 1807, Nathaniel Hawthorne is about forty-five years old.

This is the series of facts that the conscientious biographer has compiled in his two-columned quarto. If only a very mediocre interest is attached to it, it is not Mr. Rufus Wilmot Griswold's fault. Hawthorne's prefaces, it must be said, add not one salient fact to what we can glean from the entry in *Prose Writers of America;* on the other hand, they reveal to us a charming mind, an exclusive nature.

From these prefaces, we clearly see that Hawthorne belongs to the class of humorists, humorists like Sterne and Lamb, and his books confirm it. Overexcited by solitary habits, inclined to mysticism in forest depths and given to fireside visions, nourished with strange doses of German metaphysics, his imagination has escaped (through its frequent communion with nature) the type of domination that old literatures, like old civilizations, exercise over new civilizations and literatures. (In this he is like that original thinker, [Ralph] Waldo Emerson, whose brilliant essays have awakened both the Old and New Worlds.) It is a strange yoke, this one, from which America will have great pains to free herself. From the beginning, it has been noticeable. Just as the inhabitants of New England, perpetuating the traditions of the old country across the sea, celebrated the New Year with a ceremony that mimicked the procession of the Lord-Mayor in London, so too has Brockden Brown been condemned to copy Godwin, Washington Irving to write like Addison and Mackenzie, Cooper to walk in the steps of Walter Scott. The same is true for the poets. It would be easy to find, for example, the godfathers of Bryant and Longfellow. Students of literary influence could link Emerson to Thomas Carlyle, and Nathaniel Hawthorne to Charles Lamb, the English Nodier. But to our mind, this would be, overstepping the bounds of genealogical criticism. Emerson, with his pantheistic tendencies, his ardent admiration of originality, no more resembles Carlyle (imbued with German skepticism and the enthusiasm of denial), than does Hawthorne, so obviously absorbed in the concentrated study of the most ardent moral problems, resemble Lamb. Admittedly, they share certain external qualities—a fondness for analyzing old dramas, reproducing a pastiche of Shakespearean language and archaic forms. For the poor erudite poet, this was a sovereign preoccupation, but for Hawthorne it is secondary. Lamb's great originality was to remind us of the ideals and style of Jeremy Burton or Samuel Pepys[5]—with more wit than either of them, it goes without saying—but with far less conviction.

There is one American storyteller whom we have already had the chance to appreciate and whose relation to Hawthorne seems less doubtful: we are speaking of Edgar Poe.[6] But who would profit from this comparison? It would really be difficult for us to say. Poe's stories possess a fascination, a very special sting, that we can most likely attribute to a deep-seated mental disorder. Even a pearl, so they say, is nothing more than a morbid excrescence of the oyster. Hawthorne, by contrast, is more a master of his own mind, more strongly inspired by studies and thoughts of a higher order, swept away much less frequently by pure caprice or beguiled by vagabond fantasy. Therefore, he reaches his reader much better. He has a gift, a rare one for an egoist, for making himself loveable, and an even rarer gift, for a storyteller, for inspiring a certain respect. With Edgar Poe, we live in an unhealthy place; his work induces the feeling of vertigo. The shock he causes you, which is real, puts you defiantly on guard. His method seems illegitimate; you do not really know if his love potion is just an innocently modified form of alcohol or a poison in disguise, deceptively similar in color and taste. The alchemist, on the other hand, is not so well hidden behind his curtain that you do not see his mocking glance or hear his sardonic laugh. What does it matter that he has intoxicated himself before intoxicating you? Does that excuse suffice to justify your predicament? Do you not harbor some secret remorse—you, a thoughtful man!—for letting yourself be taken in by a taunting and perfidious folly that mocks you when you, too, have fallen into the same trap? By contrast, even in his most fantastic inventions, when he most deftly employs his mysterious power to transform before your very eyes the realities of this world into strange specters and marvelous apparitions, Hawthorne still obeys the wish to make you better by showing you, through appealing allegory, the stern truth. A fairy tale that would otherwise make you sleep standing up is all he needs to make you reflect deeply about some hidden vice in your nature, about some iniquity of human judgment, about some long-lived preconception the root of which philosophical revolutions have exposed to decay. All noble instincts are in him: Christian indulgence and graciousness, resistance to oppression, a thirst for what is right and truthful in all things, and, to speak like his friend Emerson, "a love of love, a hatred of hate."[7]

To give evidence of what Hawthorne is saying to us here, we can cite him directly, by reproducing the numerous passages in which he speaks of his youth and the many active, zealous friendships for which he is grateful. From them Hawthorne has received self-knowledge, encouragement, and support. Without them, he would still be unknown: they acted as heralds of his nascent fame, assiduous propagators of a talent that was too delicate and discrete to win for itself the honors of popularity.

> If anybody is responsible for my being at this day an author, it is yourself. I know not whence your faith came; but, while we were lads together at a country college,—gathering blue-berries, in study-hours, under those tall academic pines; or watching the great logs, as they tumbled along the current of the Androscoggin; or shooting pigeons and gray squirrels in the woods; or bat-fowling in the summer twilight; or catching trout in that shadowy little stream which, I suppose, is still wandering river-ward through the forest,[—*though you and I will never cast a line in it again,*—] two idle lads, in short (as we need not fear to acknowledge now), doing a hundred things that the Faculty never heard of, or else it had been the worse for us,—it was your prognostic of your friend's destiny, that he was to be a writer of fiction.
>
> And a fiction-monger, in due season, he became. But, was there ever such a weary delay in obtaining the slightest recognition from the public, as in my case? I sat down by the wayside of life, like a man under enchantment, and a shrubbery sprung up around me, and the bushes grew to be saplings, and the saplings became trees, until no exit appeared possible, through the entangling depths of my obscurity. And there, perhaps, I should be sitting at this moment, with the moss on the imprisoning tree-trunks, and the yellow leaves of more than a score of autumns piled above me, if it had not been for you.[8]

The discouragement that followed the failure of his literary debut can account, no doubt, for some of the intellectual sparring in which Hawthorne was engaged with his "brothers in harmony" at the Roxbury community. About his Fourierist past, regretfully he says little, and what he says betrays a certain unhappiness. He calls his stay at Brook Farm "a fellowship of toil and impracticable schemes" (*SL* 25). Happily, these years of trial and error, of worried and contradictory aspirations, would be followed by three more fulfilling years, the best of his life, three long years full of dreams and the sort of engaged idleness that sits so well with poetic temperaments. Those are the years he spent in the Old Manse, situated at the end of Concord's bridge. Waldo Emerson, who had lived in the house before him, stayed as his neighbor, and Concord became the center of many a poetic or philosophical pilgrimage of which Hawthorne speaks in his preface to *Mosses from an Old Manse*. The portrait he traces of this old dilapidated abode is worth reproducing in some of its details: they reveal to us how, under its mellow influences and as a site of profound contemplation, it developed this American storyteller's instincts as a moralist romancer.

More frequently than even the deserted houses of little German villages, the old and sparse dwellings of the New England countryside are haunted by traditional ghosts, and their oak-paneled drawing rooms lend themselves to popular legend. We find in these stories (affectionately told and avidly received) the residue of German superstitions and the background color (if we may put it this way) of those bizarre rhymed chronicles that were the chief literary product of the German Middle Ages. So too, then, did the Old Manse of Concord have its familiar ghost. In a certain corner of the living room, from time to time, one heard a sigh. Sometimes, in the long hallway of the upper floor, the ghost seemed to be turning pieces of paper, as if he were rereading a handwritten sermon. Still, he remained invisible, even though moonbeams abundantly poured through the east window of the haunted hallway.

> Not improbably, [writes the romancer], he wished me to edit and publish a selection from a chest full of manuscript discourses that stood in the garret. Once, [*while Hillard and other*] friends sat talking with us in the twilight, there came a rustling noise as of a minister's silk gown, sweeping through the very midst of the company, so closely as almost to brush against the chairs. Still, there was nothing visible. A yet stranger business was that of a ghostly servant-maid, who used to be heard in the kitchen at deepest midnight, grinding coffee, cooking, ironing—performing, in short, all kinds of domestic labor—although no traces of anything accomplished could be detected the next morning. Some neglected duty of her servitude, some ill-starched ministerial band, disturbed the poor damsel in her grave and kept her at work without any wages.
>
> (*MM* 17–18)

Of course, these plainly are jokes, but with an accent of good faith that singularly augments their value. Do you want a more realistic description, a Dutch landscape, worthy of Kuyp or Van de Velde? You will find one a couple pages further on.

> We stand now on the river's brink. It may well be called the Concord—the river of peace and quietness—for it is certainly the most unexcitable and sluggish stream that ever loitered, imperceptibly, towards its eternity, the sea. Positively, I had lived three weeks beside it, before it grew quite clear to my perception which way the current flowed. It never has a vivacious aspect, except when a north-western breeze is vexing its surface, on a sunshiny day. From the incurable indolence of its nature, the stream is happily incapable of becoming the slave of human ingenuity, as is the fate of so many a wild, free mountain-torrent. While all things else are compelled to subserve some useful purpose, it idles its sluggish life away, in lazy liberty, without turning a solitary spindle or affording even waterpower enough to grind the corn that grows upon its banks. The torpor of its movement allows it nowhere a bright pebbly shore, nor so much as a narrow strip of glistening sand, in any part of its course. It slumbers between broad prairies, kissing the long meadow-grass, and bathes the overhanging boughs of elder-bushes and willows, or the roots of elms and ash-trees, and clumps of maples. Flags and rushes grow along its plashy shore; the yellow water-lily spreads its broad, flat leaves on the margin; and the fragrant white pond-lily abounds, generally selecting a position just so far from the river's brink, that it cannot be grasped, save at the hazard of plunging in.
>
> It is a marvel whence this perfect flower derives its loveliness and perfume, springing, as it does, from the black mud over which the river sleeps, and where lurk the slimy eel, and speckled frog, and the mud turtle, whom continual washing cannot cleanse. It is the very same black mud out of which the yellow lily sucks its obscene life and noisome odor. Thus we see, too, in the world, that some persons assimilate only what is ugly and evil from the same moral circumstances which supply good and beautiful results—the fragrance of celestial flowers—to [*the daily life of*] others.
>
> (*MM* 6–7)

The Concord River had its historic day, and Hawthorne tells it this way:

> Come; we have pursued a somewhat devious track, in our walk to the battle-ground. Here we are, at the point where the river was crossed by the old bridge, the possession of which was the immediate object of the contest. On the hither side, grow two or three elms, throwing a wide circumference of shade, but which must have been planted at some period within the three-

score years and ten, that have passed since the battle-day. On the farther shore, overhung by a clump of elder-bushes, we discern the stone abutment of the bridge. Looking down into the river, I once discovered some heavy fragments of the timbers, all green with half-a-century's growth of water-moss; for, during that length of time, the tramp of horses and human footsteps have ceased, along this ancient highway. The stream has here about the breadth of twenty strokes of a swimmer's arm; a space not too wide, when the bullets were whistling across. Old people, who dwell hereabouts, will point out, the very spots, on the western bank, where our countrymen fell down and died; and, on this side of the river, an obelisk of granite has grown up from the soil that was fertilized with British blood. The monument, not more than twenty feet in height, is such as it befitted the inhabitants of a village to erect, in illustration of a matter of local interest, rather than what was suitable to commemorate an epoch of national history. Still, by the fathers of the village this famous deed was done; and their descendants might rightfully claim the privilege of building a memorial.

A humbler token of the fight, yet a more interesting one than the granite obelisk, may be seen close under the stone-wall which separates the battle-ground from the precincts of the parsonage. It is the grave—marked by a small, moss-grown fragment of stone at the head and another at the foot—the grave of two British soldiers, who were slain in the skirmish, and have ever since slept peacefully where Zechariah Brown and Thomas Davis buried them. Soon was their warfare ended;—a weary night-march from Boston—a rattling volley of musketry across the river;—and then these many years of rest! In the long procession of slain invaders, who passed into eternity from the battle-fields of the Revolution, these two nameless soldiers led the way.

Lowell, the poet, as we were once standing over this grave, told me a tradition in reference to one of the inhabitants below. The story has something deeply impressive, though its circumstances cannot altogether be reconciled with probability. A youth, in the service of the clergyman, happened to be chopping wood, that April morning, at the back door of the Manse; and when the noise of battle rang from side to side of the bridge, he hastened across the intervening field, to see what might be going forward. It is rather strange, by the way, that this lad should have been so diligently at work, when the whole population of town and country were startled out of their customary business, by the advance of the British troops. Be that as it might, the tradition says that the lad now left his task, and hurried to the battle-field, with the axe still in his hand. The British had by this time retreated—the Americans were in pursuit—and the late scene of strife was thus deserted by both parties. Two soldiers lay on the ground; one was a corpse; but, as the young New-Englander drew nigh, the other Briton raised himself painfully upon his hands and knees, and gave a ghastly stare into his face. The boy—it must have been a nervous impulse, without purpose, without thought[, *and betokening a sensitive and impressible nature, rather than a hardened one*]—the boy uplifted his axe, and dealt the wounded soldier a fierce and fatal blow upon the head.

    I could wish that the grave might be opened; for I would fain know whether either of the skeleton soldiers have the mark of an axe in his skull. The story comes home to me like truth. Oftentimes, as an intellectual and moral exercise, I have sought to follow that poor youth through his subsequent career, and observe how his soul was tortured by the blood-stain, contracted, as it had been, before the long custom of war had robbed human life of its sanctity, and while it still seemed murderous to slay a brother man. This one circumstance has borne more fruit for me, than all that history tells us of the fight.

(*MM* 8–10)

The same human feeling, philanthropic sentiment, and fraternal instinct that are revealed in these last lines we find again, and no less amiably or sympathetically, in another passage of Hawthorne's writings where he recounts his administrative misadventures. The romancer was obliged, we know, to leave his peaceable retreat in Concord and go to Boston to perform the duties of a custom house inspector. After having spent three years in his administrative career, he was brusquely removed from office when the Whigs came to power.[9] Even though he was linked to the Democratic Party by his antecedents and his affinities, Hawthorne nevertheless carefully kept out of his writings anything that might have appeared as a direct attack on an administration that did little to accommodate him. In one of his prefaces, he mentions the fact, and you shall see if it is with bitterness:

[*To confess the truth,*] it was my greatest apprehension,—as it would never be a measure of policy to turn out so quiet an individual as myself; and it being hardly in the nature of a public officer to resign,—it was my chief trouble, therefore, that I was likely to grow grey and decrepit in the Surveyorship, and become much such another animal as the old Inspector. Might it not, in the tedious lapse of official life that lay before me, finally be with me as it was with this venerable friend,—to make the dinner-hour the nucleus of the day, and to spend the rest of it, as an old dog spends it, asleep in the sunshine or in the shade? A dreary look-forward, this, for a man who felt it to be the best definition of happiness to live throughout the whole range of his faculties and sensibilities! But, all this while, I was giving myself very unnecessary alarm. Providence had meditated better things for me than I could possibly imagine for myself.

A remarkable event of the third year of my Surveyorship[—*to adopt the tone of "P.P."*—]was the election of General Taylor to the Presidency. It is essential, in order to form a complete estimate of the advantages of official life, to view the incumbent at the in-coming of a hostile administration. His position is then one of the most singularly irksome, and, in every contingency, disagreeable, that a wretched mortal can possibly occupy; with seldom an alternative of good, on either hand, although what presents itself to him as the worst event may very probably be the best. But it is a strange experience, to a man of pride and sensibility, to know that his interests are within the control of individuals who neither love nor understand him, and by whom, since one or the other must needs happen, he would rather be injured than obliged. Strange, too, for one who has kept his calmness throughout the contest, to observe the bloodthirstiness that is developed in the hour of triumph, and to be conscious that he is himself among its objects! There are few uglier traits of human nature than this tendency—which I now witnessed in men no worse than their neighbours—to grow cruel, merely because they possessed the power of inflicting harm. If the guillotine, as applied to office-holders, were a literal fact, instead of one of the most apt of metaphors, it is my sincere belief, that the active members of the victorious party were sufficiently excited to have chopped off all our heads, and have thanked Heaven for the opportunity! It appears to me—who have been a calm and curious observer, as well in victory as defeat—that this fierce and bitter spirit of malice and revenge has never distinguished the many triumphs of my own party as it now did that of the Whigs. The Democrats take the offices, as a general rule, because they need them, and because the practice of many years has made it the law of political warfare, which, unless a different system be proclaimed, it were weakness and cowardice to murmur at. But the long habit of victory has made them generous. They know how to spare, when they see occasion; and when they strike, the axe may be sharp, indeed, but its edge is seldom poisoned with ill-will; nor is it their custom ignominiously to kick the head which they have just struck off.

In short, unpleasant as was my predicament, at best, I saw much reason to congratulate myself that I was on the losing side, rather than the triumphant one. If, heretofore, I had been none of the warmest of partisans, I began now, at this season of peril and adversity, to be pretty acutely sensible with which party my predilections lay; nor was it without something like regret and shame, that, according to a reasonable calculation of chances, I saw my own prospect of retaining office to be better than those of my Democratic brethren. But who can see an inch into futurity, beyond his nose? My own head was the first that fell!

The moment when a man's head drops off is seldom or never, I am inclined to think, precisely the most agreeable of his life. Nevertheless, like the greater part of our misfortunes, even so serious a contingency brings its remedy and consolation with it, if the sufferer will but make the best, rather than the worst, of the accident which has befallen him.

(*SL* 40–41)

These lines, whose value lies in their ability to throw a relatively new light on one aspect of political life in the United States, at the same time give a very accurate idea of the writer who traced them, of his unshakeable good-nature, of his philosophical moderation (allied nevertheless to deep-seated conviction), of that nobility of soul that we always want to believe is a privilege of intellectual superiority. This is the man of wit and of heart whom circumstances have pushed into the sad melee of material interests and political infighting. To this arena he brought his calm, his reason, his habitual generosity. No crazed inebriation or cruel instinct made him deviate from this. In his humble sphere, vested with a certain power, he exercised it with infinite circumspection, a rare indulgence. More than once he regretted the independence of his hours and his thoughts. He feared becoming accustomed to the daily grind and succumbing to the deleterious influence of complacent security (the price of a routine job). His enemies win out and strike him, poor unknown soldier, in the obscurity that was supposed to save him. Well! With the classic grace of an immolated gladiator, he falls as a man of heart, still with a smile on his lips, lamenting these fevered aggressors more than he laments himself. How can one deny him sympathy and respect?

American newspapers raised a cry about his brutal dismissal. Hawthorne, who knew the press, and who never courted that noisy accomplice of false reputations, did not thank them very warmly for it:

Meanwhile, the press had taken up my affair, and kept me, for a week or two careering through the public prints, in my decapitated state, like Irving's Headless Horseman; ghastly and grim, and longing to be buried, as a political dead man ought. So much for my figurative self. The real human being all this time, with his head safely on his shoulders, had brought himself to the comfortable conclusion that everything was for the best; and, making an investment in ink, paper, and steel pens, had opened his long-disused writing desk, and was again a literary man.

(*SL* 42–43)

If we listen carefully to this little lecture, we can discover not only the intimate details of a dreamy existence, but also, and more significantly, the process of deliberate and untroubled thought, of serene and profound observation, that a love of solitude, innate good taste, the study and practice of a largely speculative philosophy, and frequent commerce with metaphysicians and poets, has gradually nurtured and matured. Hawthorne does not tell tales to tell tales, but rather to give material form to useful ideas, to popularize them, to make them sink in to distracted or rebellious minds. His stories have all the attractive form and interest of the well-made tale. Yet dig, and you arrive at an apologue, a figurative reality, a symbolic drama, filled with teachings but also saturated with emotion. Hawthorne is a preacher to suit our frivolous temperaments, our limited spans of attention, our futile preoccupations, our aversion to serious things. He does not stand in the pulpit with an austere exterior or stiff-necked severity: to the contrary, his insinuating, pleasant, occasionally sarcastic chatter, his inoffensive and cautious taunting, his great gift for picturesque expression, his art of awakening curiosity and keeping it out of breath—all these combine supremely to disturb the imagination, to wrest it from its daily habits, to make it fly its highest flight, to take it to the land of chimeras.

That Hawthorne wrote these strange tales for children might be cause for alarm, considering the formidable power of his style, yet we know of no allegory to equal his "Snow-Image." One glacial afternoon, two beautiful children, Peony and Violet, leave their mother's hearth (bundled up with gloves and scarves) to play in the garden—a small merchant's garden, separated from the street by a white fence and dotted with bare shrubs, newly blanketed with snow. Their mother, seated at the window, has her eye on them while she carefully sews new clothes for her dear children. Left to themselves and eager for diversion, what do they imagine? Violet suggests to her brother that he work with her to create a beautiful little sister made of snow. Peony accepts. He brings the materials, and little by little Violet marks out the contours of the statue. A formless mound at first, the snow-image is gradually refined by the agile hands of these improvised sculptors, and their mother—completely surprised, but delighted to no end to see their success thus far—commends herself inwardly for having recognized in them such remarkable artistic talents. Not able otherwise to explain the beauty of the image crafted by their hands, she wonders if, by chance, Peony's and Violet's guardian angels have not come down from on high to frolic with them, invisible accomplices and collaborators. The image grows more and more complete. A fistful of snow, thrown as if by chance, gives its hair the last chiseling. Two small blocks of ice sparkle in its open eyes. Before long, the children themselves, delighted with their work, loudly call their mother, who wants to humor them by admiring their creation of a new order. To her own surprise, however (and momentarily blinded by the setting sun whose dazzling rays glance from the statue), she truly believes that she sees a blonde-haired girl, with sparkling eyes, fallen from heaven in the middle of the garden. The children's illusion is even stronger. They have a sister, a sister who is going to live, whose eyes are alight with the fire of the West, whose slightly pale cheeks and almost purple lips will be warmed by their kisses.

The miracle is accomplished; the little image comes to life (as Galatea did once upon a time). Excellent Mistress Lindsey, Violet's and Peony's mother, comes to ask herself what thoughtless neighbor let such a charming child outside during an arctic chill, clad in nothing more than a simple white dress. She is surprised as well to see her children's new friend running and jumping, but never saying a word. Just as astonishing, a flock of birds swoops down familiarly, lighting on the neck, arms, and shoulders of the new companion Violet has created for herself. While the mother does not know what to do, think, or make of all this, her husband appears at the garden gate.

Mr. Lindsey is a hardware merchant, brusque and benevolent, going straight to the facts on every occasion, knowing and valuing only one thing in the world: good sense, common sense. The presence of this little white stranger in his garden at this hour, in such light dress, greatly perplexes him. His perplexity, so natural, is only augmented when his excellent wife tries to persuade him that she saw, with her own eyes, the miraculous transformation of the snow-image into an agile and playful child. Still, she dares only tell him this as a secret and as a joke. The children affirm it more seriously, but the stolid bourgeois (why should we be surprised?) persists in his unbelief. In his opinion, the child cannot stay outside; she will get sick with so little protection against the cold. She must come inside as quickly as possible; they must go from house to house asking to whom she belongs; she must be announced to the town.

Violet and Peony, nevertheless, in their childlike wisdom, oppose this unsound charity. Their little snow sister does not like fire. One must be careful not to make her come near the stove. Bah! The man of common sense has already grabbed the little stranger by the hand, even though she protests, even though she escapes from him, even though he is forced to run after this white sylph, who drifts like one of those swirls of crystalline flakes that the wind forms on new-fallen snow. The obstinate Lindsey catches up to her, corners her against a wall, and grabs hold of her, in spite of her protests, in spite of his wife's charitable warnings, in spite Violet's pleas, in spite of Peony's anger. The snow child must be cold; she must go inside and stand next to the coal stove that gives off almost tropical heat. Alas! In front of this magnificent contraption, the industry's work of art filled with glowing anthracite, the little white girl, far from warming up, droops, staggers, and sinks. However, as this seems to him to be contrary to the laws of nature, the man of good sense pays no heed. His work is not yet finished. He promised himself to find the family of this young stranger and to chide the mother who let her stray without a shawl or a coat. Fearing that his family will spoil his good intentions, he leaves on his errand, taking the key to the room, which is now transformed into a hothouse. When he returns after a fruitless search, we easily surmise that he finds no trace of the pallid girl he has "saved." Yet no: all that remains of her, in front of the red, gaping mouth of the splendid coal stove (of Belgian manufacture) is a puddle of water spread out on the floor. The children cry for their little sister with frozen hands; Mistress Lindsey is saddened by their desperation, which she understands, and by this involuntary assassination to which she would never have been a willing accomplice. As for Mr. Lindsey, he is shocked, genuinely shocked; but he remains convinced that he was doing his duty not to leave a little girl out in the cold, even if she were made of snow: she would catch her death! The moral of the story is lost upon him. Let it not be so for us. It must teach all men, but in particular certain so-called *friends of man*, that, prior to yielding to their philanthropic impulses, they must be sure, completely sure, that they understand fully the nature of the beings whose betterment they pursue and their relationships of all kinds with the general order of humanity. For what might seem to be very good and salutary—robust heat, for example, from a Belgian stove—can, in a particular case, serve no end or even become instead something very harmful—especially if it involves, as in Hawthorne's tale, a snow child.

But, after all, there is no teaching anything to wise men of good Mr. Lindsey's stamp. They know everything—oh, to be sure!—everything that has been, and everything that is, and everything that, by any future possibility, can be. And, should some phenomenon of nature or providence transcend their system, they will not recognize it, even if it comes to pass under their very noses.

"Wife," said Mr. Lindsey, after a fit of silence, "see what a quantity of snow the children have brought in on their feet! It has made quite a puddle here before the stove. Pray tell Dora to bring some towels and sop it up!"

(*SI* 25)

This lovely tale appears at the head of a collection that should not be considered merely as juvenile literature. We find here the little story of Silvia Etheredge (who falls in love with a miniature, and dies when she has to marry the original of this deceitful portrait) and that of Ethan Brand, who searches the world over for the Unpardonable Sin.[10] This search prodigiously develops his intelligence, but it atrophies and hardens his heart. He no longer belongs to humanity; he has isolated himself from the magnetic chain that ties together the innumerable beings placed here below to live a common life. At last, having abused his overpowering influence by forcing others to submit to his psychological experiments like so many inert elements (men are perverted by him, women become his toys), Ethan finds the Unpardonable Sin, the one that God himself, in his infinite mercy, will never punish. Universal hate shadows him, and, despite the pride he feels in his rare discovery, he grows weary of himself and throws himself into a lime kiln whose fire he has promised to stoke. This prosaic suicide is very peculiarly underscored by the vividness of description, the verisimilitude of the rural setting, the energy of the details. The night when he takes his life is stormy and loud. Strange laughter troubles the sleep of the poor lime-burner whose place at the kiln Ethan Brand has coveted. But morning comes, radiant and pure. The honest Bertram and his son Joe leave their little cottage together and happily take the path to the marble-sided mountain, its peaks gilded by the rising sun. As they near the kiln, little Joe exclaims,

"Dear father," cried he, skipping cheerily to and fro, "that strange man is gone, and the sky and the mountains all seem glad of it!"

"Yes," growled the lime-burner, with an oath, "but he has let the fire go down, and no thanks to him if five hundred bushels of lime are not spoilt. If I catch the fellow hereabouts again, I shall feel like tossing him into the furnace!"

With his long pole in his hand, he ascended to the top of the kiln. After a moment's pause, he called to his son.

"Come up here, Joe!" said he.

So little Joe ran up the hillock, and stood by his father's side. The marble was all burnt into perfect, snow-white lime. But on its surface, in the midst of the circle—snow-white too, and thoroughly converted into lime—lay a human skeleton, in the attitude of a person who, after long toil, lies down to long repose. Within the ribs—strange to say—was the shape of a human heart.

"Was the fellow's heart made of marble?" cried Bartram, in some perplexity at this phenomenon. "At any rate, it is burnt into what looks like special good lime; and, taking all the bones together, my kiln is half a bushel the richer for him."

So saying, the rude lime-burner lifted his pole, and, letting it fall upon the skeleton, the relics of Ethan Brand were crumbled into fragments.

(*SI* 101–2)

Here, as before, as in twenty other tales of Hawthorne that we could choose at random, allegory is flagrant. It is better disguised in his two long-winded novels, *The House of the Seven Gables* and *The Scarlet Letter,* but it is there all the same but does not worry about being recognized. Hawthorne is not at all a convert to the doctrines of art for art's sake (which often means art for the artists')—far from it! He moralizes without a mask. As he tells us himself, he is a democrat, an incorrigible democrat. Even destitution has not cured him. So we are not surprised to encounter in his tales a good number of local legends that relate to the revolutionary history of Massachusetts. In the annals of New England, there is a whole gallery of Rembrandt-like portraits—grave Puritans dressed in black, with high ruffled collars and pointed, wide-brimmed hats—that exercise an irresistible attraction on the novelist. In this collection of indigenous art, we see representations of elected governors, who, with the blessing of the Crown, assiduously worked to maintain and to extend the rights and privileges of the American colonists. One might think oneself among the Flemish and Dutch bürgermeisters, whose stubborn resistance blunted the Spanish executioners and irritated the omnipotence of Louis XIV. Hawthorne loves these old Puritans, and their names, unknown in France, recur on every page of his tales. He even has a whole historical series (*Legends of the Province House*) where, one by one, he evokes, so to speak, the ancestors of democracy in New England: Endicott, Winthrop, Vane, Bellingham, Bradstreet. Opposing them, he always places the agents and accomplices of English tyranny, as if to revive the popular execration to which the latter were subjected: the Androses, the Bellamonts, the dignified predecessors of the Gages and the Howes. Among these appears Edward Randolph, whose abhorred memory still lives in Massachusetts: Edward Randolph, who drank the bitter cup of unpopularity to the dregs; Edward Randolph, guilty of having secured the retraction of the first charter under which the province enjoyed more or less democratic privileges. The name, the descendants, the tomb, even the portrait of Randolph are still chased by popular anathema. Liberated from the yoke, the following generations keep an immortal rancor for whoever wanted to subjugate them ages ago, and it flatters them in their lively hatred to repeat the traditional malediction against departed tyrants. Such a singular temperament, the American temperament! We can better understand how these uncouth citizens have remained free, though we should refrain from asking how they might cease being so. Their obtuse and rigid nature has not learned, as ours has, how to bend to circumstances and to accept what has passed.

Apart from the political, there is also a moral and philosophical dimension in Hawthorne's tales, no less deserving our interest. Orthodox religions, their rites, their formulas, their strict rules do not at all comport with his independent nature. Instead, the democratic romancer willingly sees them as accomplices of political tyranny. This is the dominant idea of one of his tales, "Endicott and the Red Cross." Hawthorne resists their austere dogmas, that only stifle legitimate desires and the necessary growth of our moral nature. This latter point of view is the basis for the short story "The Shaker Bridal," a tale that seems worthy of rapid analysis.

Father Ephraim, president of the elders, the Goshen Shakers' spiritual and temporal director, has been ill for some time and now senses death approaching. He summons the leading men of the group, who respond to him from Lebanon, Canterbury, Harvard, Alfred, and twenty other districts fertilized by the work of these rigid pioneers. They take part in the crude ceremonies dictated by this encounter, emptying many a jug of Shaker cider (that enjoys such a widespread reputation) and joining together in sacred dances, each step of which, separates their enthusiasts from worldly things and transports them towards supernal regions of purity and eternal bliss. The time has come for Father Ephraim to relinquish the most worthy symbol of his authority, the patriarchal staff that he has bravely carried for forty years, but which soon will leave his failing hands. Before him, in his sick chair, stand a man and woman, who have been called to appear. Ephraim engages the elders, his colleagues, to study their faces, to unravel (with the keen perspicacity characteristic of the sect) the good and bad sides of their nature, because it is to this man, to this woman that he wants to yield the authority invested in him. It is they whom the inner spirit has singled out. By any chance, could his choice be mistaken?

The man, Adam Colburn, is in the prime of manhood. His tan face carries the imprint of rustic work—long worries have carved ineffaceable traces. His face is cold and severe, his attitude imposing and rigid. At first glance, one is tempted to take him for a schoolmaster; and, so it is: he has practiced that profession for a long time. The woman, Martha Pierson, has just reached her thirtieth year. She is thin and pale (as are all sisters of Shaker communities), and her white clothing, reminiscent of the folds of a shroud, contributes to her cadaverous air.

Even so, some elders, with a suspicious look, insinuate that the autumn frost has not yet whitened the heads of brother Adam and sister Martha. They fear the return of juvenile ardor that the couple felt for one another in years gone by, because they know that long ago the two had expressed their carnal desires. Indeed, raised next to one another and arriving at adolescence together, Adam and Martha were to have been united as soon as their ages permitted this union, a marriage much desired by their families. But, just when they were going to crown their long and pure loves, disasters of fortune obstructed the realization of their vows. Martha, as it happens, has already resigned herself to a poverty that the affection of her spouse would have rendered light. But Adam, more calm and prudent, even at that age when one seldom calculates, thinks he can afford to wait. He travels far, he works, he tries different trades, he learns about the world and life. Martha, for her part, is a seamstress, a nurse, a school mistress, barely earning her keep, always waiting for her fiancé to return. Months follow months, years follow years, but fortune does not soften the first hardships; still, the two young people do not forget their sworn faith. Each of them could have profited from a marriage of convenience, but they only want happiness and wealth on the condition that they share them with one another.

Adam is the first to grow weary of such a long wait. A kind of despair grabs hold of him. He comes to find Martha, and suggests that they find refuge in a community of Shakers. Unhappiness pushes as many proselytes as fanaticism into that sect, and the doors of its society open without any inquiry about the motivations of those who knock there. Martha had sworn to follow the fiancé of her youth wherever he went. She faithfully keeps her word. Over time, each of them, in that community where intelligence is rarer than zeal, comes to be noticed: Adam for his aptitude for managing the temporal affairs of the community, Martha for fulfilling the duties proper to her sex.

These are the successors Ephraim has chosen. The moribund old man wants to entrust them with the direction of the community. He wants Adam to become the Father and Martha the Mother of the Goshen Shakers.

> "Son Adam, and daughter Martha," said the venerable Father Ephraim, fixing his aged eyes piercingly upon them, "if ye can conscientiously undertake this charge, speak, that the brethren may not doubt of your fitness."

"Father," replied Adam, speaking with the calmness of his character, "I came to your village a disappointed man, weary of the world, worn out with continual trouble, seeking only a security against evil fortune, as I had no hope of good. Even my wishes of worldly success were almost dead within me. I came hither as a man might come to a tomb, willing to lie down in its gloom and coldness, for the sake of its peace and quiet. There was but one earthly affection in my breast, and it had grown calmer since my youth; so that I was satisfied to bring Martha to be my sister, in our new abode. We are brother and sister; nor would I have it otherwise. And in this peaceful village I have found all that I hoped for,—all that I desire. I will strive, with my best strength, for the spiritual and temporal good of our community. My conscience is not doubtful in this matter. I am ready to receive the trust."

"Thou hast spoken well, son Adam," said the Father. "God will bless thee in the office which I am about to resign."

"But our sister!" observed the elder [*from Harvard*], "hath she not likewise a gift to declare her sentiments?"

Martha started, and moved her lips, as if she would have made a formal reply to this appeal. But, had she attempted it, perhaps the old recollections, the long-repressed feelings of childhood, youth, and womanhood, might have gushed from her heart, in words that it would have been profanation to utter there.

"Adam has spoken," said she hurriedly; "his sentiments are likewise mine."

But while speaking these few words, Martha grew so pale that she looked fitter to be laid in her coffin than to stand in the presence of Father Ephraim and the elders; she shuddered, also, as if there were something awful or horrible in her situation and destiny. It required, indeed, a more than feminine strength of nerve, to sustain the fixed observance of men so exalted and famous throughout the sect as these were. They had overcome their natural sympathy with human frailties and affections. One, when he joined the Society, had brought with him his wife and children, but never, from that hour, had spoken a fond word to the former, or taken his best-loved child upon his knee. Another, whose family refused to follow him, had been enabled—such was his gift of holy fortitude—to leave them to the mercy of the world. The youngest of the elders, a man of about fifty, had been bred from infancy in a Shaker village, and was said never to have clasped a woman's hand in his own, and to have no conception of a closer tie than the cold fraternal one of the sect. Old Father Ephraim was the most awful character of all. In his youth he had been a dissolute libertine, but was converted by Mother Ann herself,[11] and had partaken of the wild fanaticism of the early Shakers. Tradition whispered, at the firesides of the village, that Mother Ann had been compelled to sear his heart of flesh with a red-hot iron before it could be purified from earthly passions.

However that might be, poor Martha had a woman's heart, and a tender one, and it quailed within her, as she looked round at those strange old men, and from them to the calm features of Adam Colburn. But perceiving that the elders eyed her doubtfully, she gasped for breath, and again spoke.

"With what strength is left me by my many troubles," said she, "I am ready to undertake this charge, and to do my best in it."

"My children, join your hands," said Father Ephraim.

They did so. The elders stood up around, and the Father feebly raised himself to a more erect position, but continued sitting in his great chair.

"I have bidden you to join your hands," said he, "not in earthly affection, for ye have cast off its chains forever; but as brother and sister in spiritual love, and helpers of one another in your allotted task. Teach unto others the faith which ye have received. Open wide your gates,—I deliver you the keys thereof,—open them wide to all who will give up the iniquities of the world, and come hither to lead lives of purity and peace. Receive the weary ones, who have known the vanity of earth,—receive the little children, that they may never learn that miserable lesson. And a blessing be upon your labors; so that the time may hasten on, when the mission of Mother Ann shall have wrought its full effect,—when children shall no more be born and die, and the last survivor of mortal race, some old and weary man like me, shall see the sun go down, nevermore to rise on a world of sin and sorrow!"

The aged Father sank back exhausted, and the surrounding elders deemed, with good reason, that the hour was come when the new heads of the village must enter on their patriarchal duties. In their attention to Father Ephraim, their eyes were turned from Martha Pierson, who grew paler and paler, unnoticed even by Adam Colburn. He, indeed, had withdrawn his hand from hers, and folded his arms with a sense of satisfied ambition. But paler and paler grew Martha by his side, till, like a corpse in its burial clothes, she sank down at the feet of her early lover; for, after many trials firmly borne, her heart could endure the weight of its desolate agony no longer.
(*TTT* 422–25)

In this simplest of scenes (the outline of which we have sought here to trace) can we not find the noble hallmarks of austere poetry, a fairly high moral ideal and a beautiful and serene structure, not to mention the philosophical idea (in no way vulgar) that these elements express? A similar idea, but even more daring, governs one of Hawthorne's most important compositions, the novel entitled *The Scarlet Letter*. Most fanciful in design, but utterly serious in content, this story touches the very heart of the problem of marriage, and treats this theme with a freedom seldom encountered among other Anglo-American writers. The immense popularity of this book across the Atlantic and with cousins across the Channel has made it a true literary phenomenon, a sign of the times. Anathemas recently hurled against *Lélia* by the chorus of British reviews and magazines did not prepare us in the least for understanding how a novel—a saucy one at that, much more so even than that of George Sand—miraculously could receive such a different welcome, win so much acclaim, encounter so few detractors.[12] It is true that if anyone has the right to change its mind, it is the public. *Flat spiritus ubi vult*—"the spirit moves where it wishes." Like the wind, its opinion is ever-shifting but all-powerful: its inconsistency is the privilege of its infallibility.

Besides *The Scarlet Letter*, Hawthorne can count only one other full-length novel among his various works. *The House of Seven Gables* is, in our opinion, if not the best work of the American novelist, then at the very least the one in which he makes the best use of what constitutes his particular originality: the gift of acting powerfully, by the force of his own imagination, upon the imagination of his readers. The story he tells rehearses a time-worn theme: the chronicle of two warring families. There is a lost document the possession of which will guarantee an immense fortune. There is a hereditary fatality that pits four or five generations of these two clans against each other. There is a house peopled with tragic memories. There is an old portrait recessed in ancient paneling that a bizarre will has fixed there forever. This portrait happens to be involved in the plot, where it plays the role reserved for ghosts before the invention of oil painting. It hides the long-lost document. It holds in suspense and then unravels the chain of events. In short, here are all the hackneyed elements of the kind of ghost story that Walter Scott, Lewis, Radcliffe, and Washington Irving (not to mention Maturin, Hoffmann and many others) have made familiar. But if the basis of the story is outdated, Hawthorne nevertheless displays unquestionable talent in the choice of dim colors, of mysterious harmonies, of half-seen forms, of strange intuitions that have allowed him to give new vigor to this over-worked theme, to embellish it with new figures, and to give the prosaic details of contemporary life the poetic coloring of the past.

At the beginning of the book, the intelligent reader is soon made aware that he should not look for more than what can be found; he should not look for originality of plot, but rather for an irresistible charm of detail and an acute sensitivity to the relationship between the outer world and the inner one that lives in each of us. From that moment on, he will surrender to the powerful influence of a meticulously and intelligently finished work of art. He will admire, in the gradually increasing intensity of effects, so sparingly felt at the beginning, a sustained progression. He will sense how much the contrast of the rather ironical forms of the modern novelist adds to the fantastic effects with which he is gradually surrounded. Most of all, he will recognize the mastery of an author whose characters are true discoveries, native-born and drawn with such sharply delineated individuality that they appear in the world of fiction for the first time. He will see this in the character of Hepzibah Pyncheon, the old spinster with an aristocratic lineage, whom poverty reduces to opening a cent-shop, and whose moral sufferings, in the midst of this decline, awaken, as much as the most poignant tragedy, our melancholy sympathies. He will recognize this, too, in the analysis of a strange form of madness that afflicts Hepzibah's brother, born with all the instincts of highly refined sensibility, and whose youth, as a result of infernal scheming, has wasted away in a dungeon (where in truth he has lost his reason). He will recognize this above all in the delicacy of execution and perfection of finish that Hawthorne combines with a rare breadth of composition and an astonishing liberty in the disposition of groups, light and color. His philosophical and poetic instincts (for, incontestably, he is both a philosopher and a poet) are always sufficiently predominant to keep him at a certain height, and safeguard him from the trivial details and futile prolixity of the modern novel.

Hawthorne himself has described his tales with a modesty both overstated and rare:

> They have the pale tint of flowers that blossomed in too retired a shade—the coolness of a meditative habit, which diffuses itself through the feeling and observation of every sketch. Instead of passion, there is sentiment; and, even in what purport to be pictures of actual life, we have allegory, not always so warmly dressed in its habiliments of flesh and blood, as to be taken into the reader's mind without a shiver. Whether from lack of power, or an unconquerable reserve, the Author's touches have often an effect of tameness; the merriest man can hardly contrive to laugh at his broadest humor; the tenderest woman, one would suppose, will hardly shed warm tears at his deepest pathos. The book, if you would see anything in it, requires to be read in the clear, brown, twilight atmosphere in which it was written; if opened in the sunshine, it is apt to look exceedingly like a volume of blank pages.
>
> (*TTT* 5)

After this honest criticism of his own works, he recognizes a merit that they indeed have: a clarity which, given their origins and the solitude in which they were conceived, might have been absent. Making no pretense to profundity, Hawthorne does not risk being misunderstood: he is mysterious without being obscure; his thinking veils, but does not undress itself. Justifiably, he says his tales "are not the talk of a secluded man with his own mind and heart, (had it been so, they could hardly have failed to be more deeply and permanently valuable,) but his attempts, and very imperfectly successful ones, to open an intercourse with the world" (*TTT* 6).

We have arrived at the decisive feature of the literary physiognomy we have been trying to reproduce just as we have seen it: Hawthorne is a dreamer and an observer. His moral nature is reflective, meditative, generalizing; his physical impressions are lively, and he places great importance upon the minute particulars of incidents that befall his characters, the scenes they cross, and the individuals they meet or with whom life puts them into contact. His imagination avidly takes possession of situations that no one else perceives; it assimilates them and gives them a moral dimension; he alone can claim the honor or the responsibility for comprehending their philosophical reach. In understanding these situations, his mind transforms them, bends them to its needs. As Hawthorne has said, it furnishes them with "habiliments of flesh and blood," without which certain abstract ideas and theorems cannot do when a solitary man wishes to impart them to the world. And from this combination (sometimes happy and sometimes sad) have come stories (more or less interesting) that replicate the duality that produced them—they are half dreamt and half real, true chimeras joining a lion's chest and mane to a goat's torso.

While out for an evening stroll, you have seen passing by in her coach a beautiful, young woman, slightly disfigured by a birthmark—a microscopic imprint of a bloody hand, barely visible on her sweet, rosy cheek. To all appearances it would seem a trifle, and yet you become fixated by it. In a country like America, where individual liberty is practiced as widely as possible and where eccentricity is given free rein, you hear of a priest, a minister of God, who suddenly appeared in front of his congregation dressed in a black veil, and that he has vowed never to remove this veil, even after his death, even in his casket. You have heard tell about such strange things, and after the moment passes, you do not attach great importance to them. Finally, you might read in a newspaper that an upstanding married bourgeois, weary of family life, suddenly quits his home, and, under a false name, disguising his face as best he can, prefers to live on a different street in the same city after his disappearance. Meanwhile, his wife thinks herself a widow, but stays true to him; and he, too, despite his strangely recovered liberty, never abuses her by forming other bonds. Twenty years pass in this manner, and, at the end of this interval, one beautiful evening, this peculiar man comes back home as if he were at the end of a stroll, and takes possession once more of his household. At the most, this new Belphégor would make you think of the quaint tale of La Fontaine.[13]

With Hawthorne, nothing goes away quickly, and that is the subject of three of his most interesting tales. In the first ("The Birth-Mark"), he tries to symbolize the egoism of science in contrast to the devotion of love. The "marked" woman has as a husband a chemist, or rather an alchemist, who is used to struggling with nature's caprices. The ecstasies of matrimony having subsided, he begins to hate the mark that disturbs the perfect harmony of his wife's features. At first this feeling betrays itself unawares in his demeanor, but before long he no longer has scruples about expressing it aloud, which throws his unfortunate companion into a sort of desperation. In order to erase this odious mark that alienates her from her husband's affections, she is willing to suffer all, to risk all. For his part, he believes that by pushing beyond the frontiers of known science, he will discover the means to get rid of the stigma, the sight of which obsesses him. Before this terrible combat that the chemist wages against God himself, we stand in attendance. We anticipate a resolution that will be fatal to someone. At last, the noble and courageous wife perishes in this ultimate ordeal, without lamenting life too much, willingly surrendering herself, a devoted victim, to the insatiable curiosity of the savant. Almost happy to die if she does not achieve the perfection he wishes to give her, she leaves him without reproach, regretting only the happiness she might have been able to give him, if, with more genuine wisdom, he would have been content to accept her, a veritable angel of heaven, with that indelible mark of terrestrial origin.

The story of the "Minister's Black Veil" is yet another veritable parable. A note tells us that the tale is based on a true fact, that during the last years of the eighteenth century, a man of the cloth in New England, having accidentally killed one of his dearest friends, hid his face from all human view, and persisted in his bizarre resolution until his death. Hawthorne gives an altogether different meaning to this stubbornly-worn black veil. Mr. Hooper, the protagonist, has killed no one, and no one among his parishioners, frightened by this strange decision, can figure out his motivation. Their conjectures, their suspicions, the malaise that their minister throws upon them, the horror and the fear he ends up inspiring in them, the type of repulsion that the worthy minister himself feels over the long run for the sinister barrier he has thrown up between himself and the world; the tentative desperation that his poor, alarmed, intended wife risks to penetrate this mystery; the terror that she feels when she sees Mr. Hooper determined to wear the fatal crepe to the tomb; the separation of the two lovers, brought on only by the reason of conjugal incompatibility; the isolation that gradually surrounds the unfortunate minister, and, at the same time, the terrible prestige he owes to his black veil; the power of conversion that this black funereal mask gives him; at last, after a long and praiseworthy existence, his agony, his death—still veiled—form a very surprising, very riveting story, whose strange fascination Hoffmann would envy. We discover the knot of the enigma in the last words of the dying minister, when one of his brethren commands him to reveal the horrendous crime for which he has mourned his entire life.

> "Why do you tremble at me alone?" cried he, turning his veiled face round the circle of pale spectators. "Tremble also at each other! Have men avoided me, and women shown no pity, and children screamed and fled, only for my black veil? What, but the mystery which it obscurely typifies, has made this piece of crape so awful? When the friend shows his inmost heart to his friend; the lover to his best beloved; when man does not vainly shrink from the eye of his Creator, loathsomely treasuring up the secret of his sin; then deem me a monster, for the symbol beneath which I have lived, and die! I look around me, and, lo! on every visage a Black Veil!"
>
> (*TTT* 52)

We now turn to the curious escapade of the honest bourgeois of whom we were speaking. First, is it really true that a man by the name of Wakefield ever left his wife? It matters little to us, and even less so to the author. He read this anecdote in some tattered old newspaper, and that is all he needed to believe it. Once it had entered into his mind, this bizarre story tormented him. He wanted to understand it, he wanted to get to the bottom of this mysterious eccentricity. Wakefield has left his wife for twenty years, and during those twenty years, he has lived just a few steps from her; at the end of twenty years, with not a single reason to justify his brusque return, no more so than when he first took leave, here he is returning to his abode. What is one to think of this? How should one interpret these two contradictory resolutions and the persistence of what, in theory, should only have been a caprice pure and simple? These are the questions that our dreamer asks himself, and it is hard to imagine how this narrow subject expanded in his restless mind. This Wakefield—what sort of man is he? How did he love his wife? From what reserve of stubbornness did he draw that such behavior could erupt? Was it routine?—false shame?—pure indolence? The answer to these questions is the portrait of this bold man, an ideal portrait—hypothetical, but excellent. Wakefield has arrived at the mid-point of his life. His conjugal tenderness, which has never been very lively, has been tempered by habit. He has—and will—be faithful to his wife: that is how his eminently peaceable nature would want it. His disposition of mind is completely intellectual, incapable of a single action, given up to endless daydreams that rarely tire themselves out striving for some sort of expression. He has none of the hotheadedness that pushes certain people to distinguish themselves from others through remarkable determination. If we were to ask ourselves which Londoner would be the most certain to do nothing one day that we would remember the next, Wakefield would be the unanimous choice. Only his wife, knowing him better, would have been able to apprehend the peaceful egoism that characterizes him and that has rusted the surface of his truly immobile soul. She could have sounded the alarm on a certain latent vanity, the signs of which she crept up on, from a penchant for trickery that betrays itself in him as a mania for petty secrets, to what, at last, she recognizes as a particle of almost indefinable strangeness, but which she writes off as one of the elements common to the indolent nature of an honest bourgeois.

Following this masterful portrait, we have Wakefield's escape, leaving home under the pretext of travel and promising to return after eight days. We have his last handshake with mistress Wakefield. We see the door gently reopen that he had slammed behind him, and we are surprised by the equivocal smile he extends, like a Parthian arrow, to his mistreated wife. We follow him afterwards to the hideout he has made for himself in the middle of London. He is happy with the success of his ruse! How he lauds himself for having escaped detection! What delicious titillations are felt in the depths of this perfidious soul when the abstract idea of desertion is realized in the form of a headless household, and in the face of that inconsolable widow who struggles in vain, asking repeatedly for news of her Wakefield! Sometimes the fugitive feels vague remorse, sometimes he anxiously asks himself about the possible consequences of his indefinable mischief, sometimes his solitude weighs upon him. But when he must decide whether to return to the burden of the yoke, hesitation returns—a strange combination of vanity, laziness, and curiosity—that comes from an equally strange situation. Very often Wakefield, having gone out for air, finds himself, without knowing why, in his old neighborhood and almost at his door. Is it chance? One day, in a throng occasioned by the overcrowded street, does he not find himself face to face with mistress Wakefield! What terror that day! What a speedy getaway! How he gallops home, climbs the stairs four steps at a time, and jumps into bed fully clothed and pulls the covers up over his head! Meanwhile, mistress Wakefield, her prayer book in her hand, continues peacefully on her way to church. It is only when she arrives there that, stopping on the steps, she looks behind her to see if, by chance, that unknown man, whose traits reminded her of her husband, has not been following her.

Here we cannot, as Hawthorne does in his story, explore the minutiae of this personality and the details of this situation; but we have already explained what the work of the novelist consists of, and how masterfully his insights capture our interest in a tale otherwise so barren and stripped of surface charms. The way in which he brings Wakefield back home after twenty years is not the least felicitous aspect of the story.

> One evening, in the twentieth year since he vanished, Wakefield is taking his customary walk towards the dwelling which he still calls his own. It is a gusty night of autumn, with frequent showers that patter down upon the pavement, and are gone before a man can put up his umbrella. Pausing near the house, Wakefield discerns, through the parlor windows of the second floor, the red glow and the glimmer and fitful flash of a comfortable fire. On the ceiling appears a grotesque shadow of good Mrs. Wakefield. The cap, the nose and chin, and the broad waist, form an admirable caricature, which dances, moreover, with the up-flickering and down-sinking blaze, almost too merrily for the shade of an elderly widow. At this instant a shower chances to fall, and is driven, by the unmannerly gust, full into Wakefield's face and bosom. He is quite penetrated with its autumnal chill. Shall he stand, wet and shivering here, when his own hearth has a good fire to warm him, and his own wife will run to fetch the gray coat and small-clothes, which, doubtless, she has kept carefully in the closet of their bed chamber? No! Wakefield is no such fool.
>
> (*TTT* 139)

We shall let him go back peacefully, with that same sardonic smile on his lips, to the home where he has craftily snared his better half. Their happiness does not concern us; but, without impertinent curiosity, we can ask ourselves what philosophical teaching (in the eyes of the romancer) there might be, in this bourgeois adventure, whose hypothetical contrivance has not, far from it, vulgarly disguised it. The author charges himself to reveal it to us: "Amid the seeming confusion of our mysterious world, individuals are so nicely adjusted to a system, and systems to one another and to a whole, that, by stepping aside for a moment, a man exposes himself to a fearful risk of losing his place forever. Like Wakefield, he may become, as it were, the Outcast of the Universe" (*TTT* 140). Who would have expected to find such a solemn line at the end of a whimsical, almost ridiculous story? Surely no one, and the narrator even less so than anyone else. But he could not have been a friend of Waldo Emerson without retaining some reflection of that man's amazing facility for enlarging the small incidents of life, for reducing the great facts of humanity, for switching their relative importance and shattering generally accepted ideas by new modes of appreciation, by virtue of a completely independent—and absolutely individual—critical method.

It is in the renewal of what we would gladly call "the metaphysical process," in the originality of certain perspectives (none altogether reliable) that we locate the interest of those scattered chapters in Hawthorne's work that are simple essays, discussions of a given topic. "Sunday at Home," "The Vision of the Fountain," "Sights from a Steeple," "Buds and Bird-Voices," and "Snow-Flakes" belong to this category, in which we also find two noteworthy chapters that seem to have contributed more than the others to popularize Hawthorne's name. In one, he animates a public fountain and makes it speak. This free translation of the murmur of water is full of charming and poetic motifs. It has thus become a classic, as it were, of American literature. "A Rill from the Town-Pump" is as well known in the United States as one of Merimée's best sketches is in France. The other essay, which one finds cited almost as often in American *Elegant Extracts,* is entitled "The Celestial Railroad."[14] A rewriting of John Bunyan's parable-novel, *The Pilgrim's Progress,* this work satirizes the religion of convenience that we have substituted for the rigors of primitive Christianity, but it will only be half intelligible for French readers, who take no interest in lukewarm Protestants. "The Procession of Life," another of Hawthorne's philosophical visions, suits our temperament better and lacks neither truth nor grandeur. From his moss-covered manse, the lone thinker looks on humanity and observes the current classifications that make the rich live with the rich, the nobles with the nobles, and the workers to themselves, according to which profession they belong. He supposes himself charged with rearranging this imposing cortege according to less common criteria that have sprung up in his imagination. His herald, armed with a trumpet that looks a lot like that of the Last Judgment, calls one by one to the four corners of the globe, summoning all who suffer from the same diseases, the afflicted who are consumed by the same chagrins, the guilty who have dirtied themselves with the same crimes, and so forth. Young or old, rich or powerful—from now on they are jumbled together, forming successive fragments of an endless column, the categories of a great cortege guided by death to the doors of eternity. What a happy and beautiful idea, in that vast human procession, to have reserved a special rank for all those that life's fortunes have displaced, and who, disinherited by chance, have failed to reach the rank or perform the functions for which they would have been useful, honored, happy! Here they are together, in the same group, united by the same vague worry, by the same vague hope. Here we see

> the members of the learned professions, whom Providence endowed with special gifts for the plough, the forge, and the wheelbarrow, or for the routine of unintellectual business. We will assign to them, as partners in the march, those lowly laborers and handicraftsmen, who have pined, as with a dying thirst, after the unattainable fountains of knowledge. The latter have lost less than their companions; yet more, because they deem it infinite. Perchance the two species of unfortunates may comfort one another.
> (*MM* 219)

Next come the Quakers in whom the instinct of war foments, and soldiers who were born to be Quakers; writers to whom nature has given, along with a crazy opinion of their genius, the passionate wish for celebrity but no means by which to acquire it; others still who, strong in thought, do not have one of the indispensable conditions to manifest the force with which they are entrusted: silent orators, singers without a voice, great captains without armies; yet again the victims of eminent success that they cannot possibly justify, those who by chance attain celebrity, but who have not one of the indispensable qualities to keep it and to make it grow; writers, actors, painters who see their laurels shrivel for the rest of their lives as their heads turn gray; politicians whom a mischievous fate has put at the head of affairs, and who, pierced by the recognition of their worthlessness, curse (while the world looks on, dumbstruck) both fortune that has served them so poorly and even the day they were born; finally, amid these social climbers, we see the man with exceptional talent, to whom only a revolution might give his due, ensconced at the heart of a peaceful, inert, and lethargic society.

We now know Nathaniel Hawthorne's work. All we have left to do is to look one last time at the physiognomy of his style. Among the storytellers to whom we can compare him, Charles Nodier and the Genevan novelist Töpffer head the list. Yet, we must remember differences of place and literary education. We must remember, for example, that if there is more philosophical sincerity in Hawthorne, in Nodier there is a more curious study of the effects of style, a grammatical chiseling more painstaking and knowing, as well as more delicate satire, more exquisite taste. Töpffer moves in a more restricted horizon than the American romancer. His imagination cuts closer to earth. It does not have to the same degree the gift to make poetic all the agents it employs, be it a rooster or a cat, like the "Chanticleer" or

"Grimalkin" of *The House of the Seven Gables,* or a town pump, like the one in Salem at the corner of Essex and Washington, and whose chatty monologue, translated by Hawthorne, rang out to all America. Above all, his work does not achieve the same degree of terror that the American author can always produce, nor does it exercise the remarkable fascination that even the most rebellious reader feels towards Hawthorne's work.

Hawthorne's tales are interesting not merely because they reveal an original and bold talent: for us they are also a remarkable witness to the efforts that current American literature is making to rid itself of the industrialism that is suffocating it. Today, that society—only dedicated (so they say) to the development of its material greatness—is producing for itself thinkers and poets, accepted at home and abroad, as popular in London and Edinburgh as they are in Philadelphia and Boston. The jealous pride of the Old World is forced to applaud this tentative emancipation, and instead of dismissing—or ignoring—anything with American provenance (as we have done in the past), we now recognize feelings of goodwill and habits of international courtesy whose secret will be found nowhere else than in the progress of purely literary sympathies. Indeed, one of the most characteristic signs of the rapprochement to which we are drawing attention was Thomas Carlyle's patronage of Emerson. Hawthorne's rapid success is another symptom of the same sort. Now Carlyle, Emerson, and Hawthorne all possess the same sort of mind: all are freethinkers in philosophy and in politics. Doesn't this coincidence merit attention?

Revue des Deux Mondes (15 Apr. 1852)

Notes

1. Griswold alludes to Hawthorne's maritime genealogy in the headnote to his entry in *Prose Writers of America*. Daniel Hathorne (1731–96), the author's grandfather, was a privateersman who ran British blockades to get cargo to Salem's wharves during the American Revolution. His exploits were celebrated in a war-time ballad:

> Bold Hathorne was commander,
> A man of real worth,
> Old England's cruel tyranny
> Induced him to go forth;
> She, with relentless fury,
> Was plundering our coast.

The actual surname of the writer's ancestors was "Hathorne." He amended the spelling after leaving Bowdoin. Major William Hathorne (ca. 1606/7–1681) arrived in the New

World with John Winthrop aboard the *Arbella* in 1630 and settled in Salem around 1636. His third son, John Hathorne (1641–1717), was a magistrate and chief interrogator of the accused in the Salem witchcraft hysteria of 1692. Later descendants were ship owners and merchant seamen, including Hawthorne's father (1775/6–1808), for whom he was named.

2. Forgues was misled by Hawthorne's facetious prefatory remarks to "Rappaccini's Daughter" (first published in *Mosses from an Old Manse*), in which he affects the French *nom de plume* as the author of *Contes deux fois racontées* [sic]. Both the first and second editions of *Twice-told Tales* appeared with Hawthorne's name on the title page.

3. Forgues refers to the famous battle at the beginning of the Revolutionary War, in anticipation of which the colonists had been warned by Paul Revere, whose horse ride from Boston alerted them to the advance of General Gage's troops. As Forgues himself notes, "[The British] were sent to Concord (twenty miles from Boston) to destroy any military preparations for the next battle. The goal of their mission was accomplished, but they had to draw back, faced with an insurrection taking hold of the whole country."

4. Hawthorne's tenure at the Boston Customs House lasted from 1839 to 1841. Zachary Taylor (1784–1850) was the successful Whig candidate for the presidency in 1848. Forgues has conflated Hawthorne's term as a customs official in Boston with his later appointment at Salem (1846–49), from which he was terminated because of Taylor's election.

5. Most likely, Forgues intended an allusion to Robert Burton (1577–1640), author of *The Anatomy of Melancholy*. Samuel Pepys (1633–1703), an English politician, whose posthumously published diary is celebrated for its accounts of daily life in seventeenth-century London.

6. Forgues' essay in the *Revue des Deux Mondes* (15 Oct. 1846: 341–66) was the first critical discussion of Poe to be published in France.

7. The phrase is not a literal quotation from Emerson, but corresponds in sentiment to his essay "Love," in *Essays: First Series* (1841).

8. The Preface to *The Snow-Image* is addressed as a letter to Horatio Bridge (1806–93), who had encouraged Hawthorne's literary career at least since their days together as classmates at Bowdoin. The quotation is from Centenary Edition, vol. VIII, *The Snow-Image and Uncollected Tales*, edited by Fredson Bowers et al., 1972, 4–5.

9. See note 4, above, for a more accurate chronology of Hawthorne's career.

10. "Sylph Etherege" and "Ethan Brand," first published in *The Snow-Image and Other Twice-told Tales* (1852).

11. Forgues' note: "Mother Ann, the female apostle and founder of the Shaker sect."

12. The London *Athenaeum*, for example, considered George Sand's 1833 novel "an unreal mockery . . . a bold, brazen paradox born, fostered and nourished in the very hot-bed of scepticism, in the whirl and turbulence of Parisian politics, manners and questionable morality" (Sept. 1833: 646).

13. Forgues refers here to a tale about a minor demon, "Belphégor," from Jean de la Fontaine's 1668 *Fables*.

14. In the first half of the nineteenth century, many anthologies of American writing made claims in their subtitles that they comprised "elegant extracts in prose and poetry."

VII

Émile Montégut

"A Socialist Novel in America" (1852)

Decidedly to its credit, modern literature is moving closer to certain sciences that, up until now, art and poetry have carefully avoided: indeed, contemporary writing has become a veritable course in moral medicine. The other day, *Uncle Tom's Cabin* put before our eyes the evidence in the great debate over the question of slavery.[1] Besides that, other recent novels and literary works frequently have called attention to the condition of the English working or rural classes. In Miss Fuller's *Memoirs* we had an opportunity to analyze moral aberrations, dangerous subtleties, and the ravages of pride.[2] A study of this latter class of maladies is what America now sends us in *The Blithedale Romance* by Nathaniel Hawthorne. This time the question is not about the miseries and sorrows wrought by slavery and its injustices; instead we are presented with the philosophical foolishness and social deviance of the literati. With scientific superstitions and animal magnetism supplanting religion and the supernatural world, with a belief in electrical currents replacing a belief in eternal ideas, with the laws of the material world substituting for the laws of the moral world, with Fourier's passionate attraction replacing the sacrament of marriage, with the idea of obligation replaced by the idea of happiness and the vague impulse of devotion toward one's peers founded on the self-centered desire for individual well-being, we see the refined, the subtle, the quintessential illustration of the moral principle articulated by Molière's Sganarelle: "When I have drunk and eaten well, I want everyone else in my house to be intoxicated."³ A different kind of social exploitation has not been sufficiently analyzed—namely, the exploitation of an individual by his peers, not to achieve material gains, but to satisfy an abstract *idée fixe,* a systematic mania, a philosophical hobbyhorse. These are the beautiful things that the subtle and ingenious Mr. Hawthorne offers us in his latest work.

Before beginning an analysis of this book—a book that takes us back six years and makes us daydream of a time filled with intellectual debate, intellectual frivolity, naive philosophical musings, and ambiguous aspirations for human betterment—we would like to sketch briefly the general character of Hawthorne's talent. We know that even in this journal the author of *The Scarlet Letter* has found a spiritual admirer.⁴ All the same, *The Blithedale Romance* will be an indecipherable enigma unless the reader knows something of the author and his mental disposition.

Nathaniel Hawthorne is a true American, descended from the first settlers of New England. In certain Walter Scott novels, we remember those dreadful characters, walking alone in the countryside, who read the Bible aloud with sword in hand.⁵ We recognize those invincible men who dominate seventeenth-century English history—Scottish Presbyterians, Anglican dissenters who were shorn of their ears and put in the stocks, Cromwell's martial saints, the *Mayflower* emigrants. These zealous and somber characters—"grim and earnest" as the English would say—resemble Hawthorne's ancestors. It has been two hundred and twenty-five years since the first Hawthorne arrived in America, one of the colonists who built the small town of Salem, Massachusetts, and who, as his descendant has said, struck the family's roots deep into the soil of New England.⁶ The first Hawthorne was a terrible man. "He was a soldier, legislator, judge; he was a ruler in the Church; he had all the Puritanic traits, both good and evil" (*SL* 9).

Tolerance was not exactly his defining trait. The Quakers have immortalized his name in their histories as a reminder of the persecution and injustice to which he subjected them. His son, who inherited both his virtues and his bigotry, made his mark by branding agents of the devil in the village of Salem, notorious for its witch trials. This is the stock from which Nathaniel Hawthorne comes. Humbly and obscurely perpetuated by shopkeepers and seafarers, this family at last produced an artist and a novelist. Whenever Hawthorne speaks of his terrible forebears, he speaks with respect, almost with fear. He asks this century's forgiveness for their intolerance and zeal, because he is liberal and a democrat, a would-be socialist and humanitarian. In this he is mistaken. His ancestors were capable of burning witches, but they never would have joined the communal experiment at Roxbury.⁷

In the most remarkable preface to his novel entitled *The Scarlet Letter,* Hawthorne imagines some of his ancestors discussing and judging the behavior of the latest descendant of their family. What would they say about him? Certainly, they would not approve of his ambitions nor would they applaud his literary successes. "'What is he?' murmurs one grey shadow of my forefathers to the other. 'A writer of story books! What kind of business in life—what mode of glorifying God, or being serviceable to mankind in his day and generation—may that be? Why, the degenerate fellow might as well have been a fiddler!' Such are the compliments bandied between my great grandsires and myself, across the gulf of time! And yet, let them scorn me as they will, strong traits of their nature have intertwined themselves with mine" (*SL* 10).

In this, Hawthorne is not mistaken. In spite of his fondness for tolerance, progress, and democracy, the old Puritan nature lives on in him. Hawthorne's talent marvelously explains the persistence of ancestral values that are perpetuated over time—the "music of the blood," as Calderón says, that (especially in provincial society) repeats in successive generations the same melody but with different variations.[8] Hawthorne betrays the symptoms: he rarely goes to church, but even at home can hear the hymns of the faithful and the exhortations of the minister. His ideas would have been anathema to his forebears and his profession would have been detested. He no longer believes and lives the way they did, but he does have their intellectual outlook. He may no longer have their *soul,* but he does have their *spirit.* He follows their practice of strict investigation and pitiless analysis. Only a descendant of the Puritans would be capable of devoting himself to the perpetual examination of conscience that one finds in Hawthorne's work. He alone would be capable of excavating the recesses of the soul to discover not treasure, but rather the repressed evidence of human frailty, finding subjects of horror, sleeping reptiles, witnesses to forgotten crimes. The very agreeable and useful ability to deceive oneself does not belong to the present-day Hawthorne any more than it did to his ancestors. His eyes are as piercing as those of a lynx. He can apprehend lurking evil. He can discover the devil in his many disguises, even those that appear honorable. He can say with John Bunyan: "I have seen that there are roads that leave from heaven and go straight to hell."[9] His true foundation lies in his Puritanical nature. Upon that foundation, the nineteenth century has overlaid the ideas of liberalism, democracy, and socialism. Our times have also given Hawthorne his literary manner: his love of color, his romanticism, his facility in handling his material. He also has another quality that sets our century apart from all others in matters of literature: a willingness to extrapolate meaning from a first encounter—a strange face, the color of someone's hair, a mysterious event—with as much passionate conviction as if it were the absolute truth.

In the life of Hawthorne, there are three principal events. All three are related in his books: his participation in the Fourierist Roxbury community that has resulted in *The Blithedale Romance;* his time spent at Concord in the old venerable domicile that brought us *Mosses from an Old Manse;* and his stint as an employee at Salem's custom house that enabled him to form the idea and collect the materials for *The Scarlet Letter*. In Massachusetts he was a part of a small group of intellectuals and also the close friend of Miss Fuller. "In 1842," wrote Emerson, "Nathaniel Hawthorne, already then known to the world by his Twice-Told Tales, came to live in Concord, in the 'Old Manse,' with his wife, who was herself an artist. With these welcomed persons Margaret formed a strict and happy acquaintance. She liked their old house, and the taste which had filled it with new articles of beautiful form, yet harmonized with the antique furniture left by the former proprietors."[10] Hawthorne has been influenced by many different philosophies and genres, but they have not marked him indelibly. He is a man with a sharp mind who knew how to escape the despotism (something that is not always easy) of the men with whom he has lived. Hawthorne has lived among utopians, reformers, sectaries, and *philosophes*. Never did he give in to them. While he was attracted to some of these secular religions, he never became a convert to any of them. There is a very curious passage in the preface to *The Scarlet Letter*. The author recounts that, when he became a humble customs inspector, he felt no dismay with the practical work he had to do and that he even found great charm in his duties. Tired of philosophy and abstraction, he escaped the yoke of ideas and his friends.

> After my fellowship of toil and impracticable schemes with the dreamy brethren of Brook Farm; after living for three years within the subtle influence of an intellect like Emerson's; after those wild, free days on the Assabeth, indulging fantastic speculations, beside our fire of fallen boughs, with Ellery Channing; after talking with Thoreau about [*pine-trees and*] Indian relics in his hermitage at Walden; after growing fastidious by sympathy with the classic refinement of Hillard's culture; after becoming imbued with poetic sentiment at Longfellow's hearthstone—it was time, at length, that I should exercise other faculties of my nature, and nourish myself with food for which I had hitherto had little appetite. Even the old Inspector was desirable, as a change of diet, to a man who had known Alcott.
>
> (*SL* 10)

This passage is important, and the impetus behind these lines circulates in all of Hawthorne's work. He is mistrustful. He is afraid of being the fool. He uses his wits to maintain his intellectual independence. He refuses to accept the domination of ideas; he fears that this would compromise his originality. He wants to put his talent above moral ideas. All of this is in vain and possibly even criminal! At the end of *The Blithedale Romance*, Hawthorne puts these remarkable words into the mouth of Miles Coverdale (who is a stand-in for the author himself): "I have no goal. . . . I am disoriented; my life has become completely sterile, and I have arrived at an impasse."[11] Hawthorne's work, for all its perfection, suggests an analogous kind of incompleteness. It does not have an overriding purpose; it is not held together by a unifying principle. His works are artistic fantasies, insightful but inconsistent. A certain skepticism dominates them all. Clearly, the author is disillusioned with many things and sure of nothing. This defiance, this fear of the domination of ideas that is very common among artists and writers, always produces the same deplorable results. The writer must have a purpose, just like a politician or a general. He must be the servant of an idea, and not allow it to become an auxiliary vehicle for his talent. If he falls into this sin of pride and of rebellion against morality, he will be punished. His skepticism will not keep him from being a fool. He will fall into all the excesses of the systems of thought that he has visited out of curiosity and while looking for inspiration. He will only attain the ridiculous instead of finding the real, and, at the end of thirty years of a life of literature, he will find himself to be a great *dilettante*, an author of admirable fragments that have no common aim, admirable essays that answer no need. This observation does not apply to Hawthorne exclusively—there are more examples of this elsewhere than in America.

We have said that Nathaniel Hawthorne is a quintessential American. In this regard, we shall see that similarities drawn thus far between American and European literatures perhaps have been exaggerated: as soon as a new author appears, we hear it said, "He is not an American, he's English, he's German." I often hear people say that Emerson is a German. Some people have spoken of Lamb in relation to Hawthorne; I have even heard Godwin's name mentioned! Nothing is more certain than that Emerson has studied German literature. But the application he makes of it is essentially American: his morality, style, eloquence—all are entirely original and American. No one is formed on his own; every writer receives his education in a particular literature. This does not at all mean that he cannot be original. Our French writers all were educated by means of Latin literature. Are they less French because of it? To say that Emerson is German is no more accurate than to say, for example, that Montaigne is Roman. The resemblance that has been supposed between Hawthorne and Lamb is no better founded. Here and there in Hawthorne's work, there are little essays that resemble Lamb's; in general, however, nothing less resembles Lamb's delicate pages (that delicious writer's quaintness, his little passions and small bachelor disappointments, the small egotisms of his excellent heart and the small sensualities of his exquisite soul) than the lugubrious stories, the merciless and almost perverse analysis of the supersubtle American storyteller. Neither does Hawthorne resemble Godwin because he strikes an entirely different chord. Godwin has only one deep and overriding sentiment—justice. He is violent, passionate, like a man who has only one love and one hate. It is not at all for pleasure that he speaks to us of terrible things and shows us frightening scenes. Hawthorne, on the contrary, loves the funereal and terrible; he looks for it, he has a taste for it as some people have a taste for cemeteries. Whereas Godwin's gothic tales foment anger, Hawthorne's remain cool and dispassionate. Once again, this indeed is the author of *The Blithedale Romance*. He is certainly an original. He is the most American writer that the United States has produced since Emerson.

The characteristic element of Hawthorne's talent is his dramatic power. He has what I will call a feeling for impalpable things to the utmost degree: fear, solitude, terror of annihilation—above all, the apprehension of those monstrous fancies that are spontaneously and unpredictably born in even the most moral and spotless minds. After reading his work, we tremble to examine ourselves for fear of finding some latent madness, some thought of crime, some unsuspected depravity. His characters are truly mad philosophers who reason with a desperate logic and who abandon themselves to enormous eccentricities. Here is a minister who puts a black veil over his face and who dies without taking it off, a symbol of human egoism and man's mistrust of his peers.[12] There is an old man who, at sixty, marries a woman to whom he had been engaged in his youth, but whose arrival at the wedding chapel is marked by the sound of a death knell; the groom is covered in a funeral shroud, to be joined with his bride no longer for life, but instead for the eternity of the tomb.[13] Elsewhere there is a character who sets out to find the Unpardonable Sin and who, after a thousand pilgrimages, finds it in himself. This Unforgivable Sin was to put affection at the mercy of reason, to break the hearts of those who love us in order to feel the rapture of immoral pride—in a word, to trample the human race like the idolatrous chariots of India that careen over the bodies of the faithful—in order to satiate a perverse intellectual ambition.[14] The funereal dominates. An odor similar to that which surrounds mortuary preparations—the pall, the boxwood branch that is placed in holy water, and the smell of those sadly everlasting flowers[15]—rises to your nostrils and makes your head spin. The religious terror of Protestantism, the fear of eternal damnation, circulates in these tales without the author's knowledge. And yet, in spite of this dramatic talent, Hawthorne's works are cold. A certain transcendental skepticism permeates his stories. He judges and explains human actions. He does not allow us to arrive at our own interpretations or to make judgments of our own free will. His characters are all intellectual abstractions: they are too metaphysical, they have no blood, no entrails, no muscles—they rarely even have tears.

Hawthorne's tales have made a bizarre vision pass before my eyes: I see myself multiplied a hundred times in miniature, and everyone of me has just been caught in the filaments of a delicate web, at the center of which yet another me sits watching all the rest! The American romancer's talent makes us think of a spider's web, a seine that surprises a fish, a snare that holds a bird captive, the insect held under the microscope of a scientist or pinned in the herbarium of a naturalist—of all the ways to be caught in a trap. In a word, we cannot help attributing to him an egoism that is peculiar to an artistic nature that is afraid of nothing, that profits from everything and most innocently amasses little treasures of observation and anecdote without emotion, without hate, without sympathy. All the artists and poets who have had this capacity for cold, impartial, lucid, and indifferent analysis have produced finely tooled, accomplished, well composed, often profound works, but from which passion is lacking, sometimes even absent. This is the case for Hawthorne: his dramatic effects and the very real terror that they invoke are equally abstract. Our minds shudder—but not our entire being—when we contemplate these dramas that seem to take place between two or three ideas in one of the regions of the human brain.

With Hawthorne there is also a very delicate point that we will not insist upon, but which we are obliged to note: his writings are ambiguous and display many different mannerisms. At first it is impossible to know what to think about the author's general philosophy: What does he think? What does he believe? What doctrines does he support? If the author wanted simply to entertain us, why then this profusion of philosophical ideas? Why such profound depth beneath the details? To what end does he employ his powers of analysis? If he wants to instruct us, why can we never perceive his general idea, his explicit intention? His mind seems like an intricate timepiece, chiming minutes, but not hours. The details of his work are admirable—the first thought is almost always imperceptible. Yet these writings are ambiguous because the author loves to play with a number of dangerous things.

He has a predilection for suspect notions; we even perceive here and there the passing shadow of the taboo. Essentially there is something unhealthy in his work that at first we do not discern, but that in the long run acts upon us like a very weak and very slow poison. Such reading is difficult to bear: it leaves us chagrined and morose, uncertain of what to think about a host of ideas important to man and society.

Let us drop this unpleasant subject. Hawthorne is an analyst and he constructs his society out of intellectual types—this is more or less obvious in his writings. Among the different influences that have affected him, Emerson's has been the most significant. In many short sketches, in a number of passages in his novels, this influence is easily noted. He has made numerous applications of Emerson's philosophical counsels and has rendered his abstractions into concrete, dramatic, and animated form. We know that Emerson's thought is epitomized in the essay "Self-Reliance": spiritual excellence comes only when it acts upon instinct itself, when man's depraved will does not overexcite it or impel it to diseased modes of action. Self-reliance has its sole worth insofar as it joins a man's activity with a child's innocence and naïveté. Let childlike simplicity and tranquility be the law of your nature, Emerson instructs his fellow Americans, and you will again see an age of miracles, prophets, and saints; your life will be surrounded by new forms, new colors—fresh and original.[16] Hawthorne has transported this idea to a tale called "The Great Stone Face."[17] Somewhere in New England, there lies an outcropping of rocks arranged in such a way that, from a distance, it offers the viewer a profile of a gigantic human face.[18] A prophetic tradition, which embodies American pride (and which recalls the legend of the severed head found beneath Rome's Capitol),[19] says that there will appear in America a man whose traits will resemble those of the Great Stone Face. This man will be the greatest figure on earth, he will dominate America, and through him America will dominate the universe. From childhood, a young American who has heard this legend looks everywhere for the man whose visage is similar to the Stone Face; others around him do the same and think they have found him: first they gather around a rich merchant whose vessels are sailing the seas and who holds in his hands tremendous capital; next they flock to a general who has won many battles; then they cleave to an eloquent orator. "He is the very image of the Great Stone Face!" they cry, but they are always let down and the great man never appears. Meanwhile, the young child becomes an innocent devoted man. With quiet modesty, he accomplishes the work that, little by little, is put before him by obligation or necessity. He earns his keep, helps his neighbors—even with the smallest of jobs—and over time he finds that by excelling in life he has earned a fine reputation without even thinking about it. His neighbors, his city, then the state, and then the entire Nation, perceive that they have among them a man who grew up inconspicuously, like a solitary oak in the forest, simple, but full of strength all at once. And the traits of this man resemble those of the Great Stone Face. Another tale, "The Threefold Destiny,"[20] contains Emerson's idea that our most infinite wishes can be realized in the most limited space and that we should be content to stay there without chasing after fate. A young man dreams of three things: that he will discover treasure; that the most beautiful woman in the world will love him; that he will be named king and rule over all mankind. He leaves to search for all of these things, and, after many long years of sojourning, returns without finding anything, weary and sad. Upon his return, he discovers the treasure at home, at the base of a tree in his garden: a young girl, a companion from childhood, gives him her heart. And, with regard to temporal power, the responsibilities of a village schoolmaster compensate him amply: he who forms human character and instructs a child to embrace virtue—is not he a veritable king more than a dictator or czar?

We now know the writer's characteristics and influences. His latest book will shed light on the writer himself and on certain facets of an intellectual movement in the United States. Around 1840, a group of dreamers formed a Fourierist association in Roxbury, Massachusetts, under the direction of George Ripley. A crowd of young enthusiasts made up this association, some of whom Hawthorne names in the preface to his new novel: Mr. Channing (Junior), Mr. Parker, the poet Dana, utopians, philanthropists, and several young women.[21] From the memory of his stay with the association at Brook Farm, Hawthorne has selected the elements of his new novel. He has not written a history, nor does he chronicle the association's activities. He gives us the novel and says less about what *did* happen there than about what *might have* happened. If this tale has a moral, it is incontestably the following: utopian societies are more impossible for intellectuals than for the rest of humanity for the simple reason that the most educated, more quickly prone to fantasizing than others, also recognize their mistakes more promptly and find living in the absurd intolerable.

What is socialism in the United States? We have spoken about this question—a question that is raised out of necessity by Nathaniel Hawthorne's novel—many times here. Socialism has awakened interest in the United States and still captivates certain types of demagogues. If you wanted to know which class sports the greatest number of socialists, the rich and educated would be a good bet. There are two reasons for this: one is literary, the other clearly political.

The political reason is unique: socialism has the allure of science; it speaks of political harmony, hierarchy, and remuneration according to deeds of merit. Where are these things most lacking? Quite possibly in the American Union. There, the multitude is an absolute master: it rules, governs, makes laws, and makes the state in its own image. The United States present the aspect of a large multitude of people who are only ephemerally linked together, forming groups that are broken as quickly as created, joining together on one issue, disbanding because of another. This is the image that comes to mind when thinking of this country. Minorities count for nothing and have no power, no matter how cultivated or moral they may be. Thus, the idea that there are higher laws than those of the Constitution has entered many minds. It has been said that there have been men who are more righteous than entire nations and that they have claims over and above the majority. The abolitionists of the North, for example, a great majority of whom are Whigs, have taken this idea from the socialists and have made it a weapon against the South. When they are accused of attacking the Compromise of 1850, they protest that there is a law more fundamental than political law. This is the famous theory of the higher law that the abolitionists, the Syracuse convention, Seward, Hale, Gerritt [sic] Smith, and many others have used so much in recent years.[22] Socialist doctrines are more favorable to a strong central government than to the original ideals of democracy. There are even highbrow Whig newspapers—the New York *Tribune,* for example—composed with talent, that are drenched with socialism. Additionally, the democrats, partisans of government by the masses, arm themselves with all the socialist ideas that appear favorable to the progress of the multitude. There is also a sort of agrarian law—The Homestead Act—that has been under discussion for the last two years a law that would give one-hundred-sixty acres of land for free to any family who agrees to cultivate it for five years. This project, rejected so far by the Whigs, has given rise to speeches where socialist ideas naturally find their place.[23] The thinkers and well-educated, who grow weary more quickly than others of the multitude's yoke, have asked in turn, like certain socialists, that the state be better managed by the laws of intelligence and reason. In a word, American socialism almost resembles the battle of the books in Boileau's *Le lutrin* where the different parties throw doctrines at each others' heads.[24] In behaving this way, the parties are true to their role: they can make arrows out of any kind of wood. This may not be entirely sound, but this is the way things are.

The literary reason for socialism's success can be found in the American appetite for the marvelous. American poets and novelists have nothing to sustain the magic of memories that can exist only among nations with long histories. All around them they see a new, positive, practical, serious people, little disposed to reverie, whose minds and manners are devoid of the marvelous. What then are American novelists to do? They idealize everything at all costs, they *romanticize* the most vulgar and ordinary things. The noises of the street become the music heard in dreams; the lights that illuminate the merchants' shop windows at night transform them into palaces from *The Arabian Nights;* a little girl is a fairy, a woman a sorceress; an old man with white hair and deep wrinkles is a wise man; every country bumpkin a being in touch with nature's hidden forces; a young gentleman has the stature of a Walter Raleigh or a Sir Philip Sidney; a bourgeois who, at first glance, is only a character with a vulgar sense of humor, becomes a clown, the likes of which Shakespeare never invented. What is more, Americans idealize even things that are not animate, even the scientific: an experiment with electricity, a séance of animal magnetism, a combination of numbers, a magnetized needle, astral gravitation, planetary laws—all become elements of poetry. Anyone who has read Edgar Poe's tales—"The Gold-Bug," "A Descent into the Maelström," "The Unparalleled Adventure of One Hans Pfaall"—knows this. A Poe story employs the calculation of probabilities and transforms mathematical axioms into natural and supernatural agents. There are more bottles and laboratory apparatus in his tales than men or women. Americans share the tendencies of their writers: they have superstitions that are scientific in character. This is easily conceivable: the imagination, while looking for fodder and no longer able to believe in old superstitions, turns to the first thing that can astound it. It does not believe in witches any more, but instead in magnetizers. It no longer finds the devil frightening, but is amused by electric lights and hot-air balloons. The so-called Spiritualist sect that chats with dead spirits through a sleep-walking intermediary is based on animal magnetism. Socialism has much in common with the marvels of science and magnetic experiments. Socialism has all the characteristics of the marvelous: passionate attractions, a human race made for happiness, the prospect of joys without end, a new heaven and earth evoked by all-powerful formulas, the transformation of men into Olympian gods, and Hell itself becoming a sufficiently comfortable place to live. All of this is genuinely seductive. The socialists can transform themselves very easily into more or less marvelous characters, magicians and alchemists. It should not be surprising, then, that socialist doctrines have seized the minds of novelists, for whom these ideas offer the marvelous. All these superstitions—all the bizarre beliefs of the well-educated (made of the most artificial, the most charlatanesque stuff), the rage of animal magnetism that has reigned for a long time in the United States and that has not yet completely disappeared—all of this is reflected in Hawthorne's novel and his conception of the fantastic.

Socialism's marvelous uniqueness has always attracted certain writers. Well-educated Americans never speak of the doctrine's moral implications except with repugnance. We did not descend from the Puritans, we were not formed by their harsh discipline and by two centuries of positive energy only to be corrupted by the first depraved reverie. Thus we must see in Hawthorne's novel the efforts that these honest believers often make to reject the morality of modern reformers. However much they are socialists, they cannot consent to be unprincipled men, when "unprincipled" is the most offensive word in the English language. Here is the conversation between two of Hawthorne's characters about Fourier's doctrine:

> "Let me hear no more of it!" cried he, in utter disgust. "I never will forgive this fellow! He has committed the unpardonable sin; for what more monstrous iniquity could the Devil himself contrive than to choose the selfish principle—the principle of all human wrong, the very blackness of man's heart, the portion of ourselves which we shudder at, and which it is the whole aim of spiritual discipline to eradicate—to choose it as the master workman of his system? To seize upon and foster whatever vile, petty, sordid, filthy, bestial, and abominable corruptions have cankered into our nature, to be the efficient instruments of his infernal regeneration! And his consummated Paradise, as he pictures it, would be worthy of the agency which he counts upon for establishing it. The nauseous villain!"
>
> "Nevertheless," remarked I, "in consideration of the promised delights of his system—so very proper, as they certainly are, to be appreciated by Fourier's countrymen—I cannot but wonder that universal France did not adopt his theory at a moment's warning. But is there not something very characteristic of his nation in Fourier's manner of putting forth his views? He makes no claim to inspiration. He has not persuaded himself—as Swedenborg did, and as any other than a Frenchman would, with a mission of like importance to communicate—that he speaks with authority from above. He promulgates his system, so far as I can perceive, entirely on his own responsibility. He has searched out and discovered the whole counsel of the Almighty in respect to mankind, past, present, and for exactly seventy thousand years to come, by the mere force and cunning of his individual intellect!"
>
> "Take the book out of my sight," said Hollingsworth with great virulence of expression, "or, I tell you fairly, I shall fling it in the fire! And as

for Fourier, let him make a Paradise, if he can, of Gehenna, where, as I conscientiously believe, he is floundering at this moment!"

"And bellowing, I suppose," said I—[*not that I felt any ill-will towards Fourier,* but] merely want[ing] to give the finishing touch to Hollingsworth's image—"bellowing for the least drop of his beloved *limonade à cèdre!*"

(*BR* 53–54)

It is fairly difficult to explain the merits of Nathaniel Hawthorne's last book through simple analysis. The plot is extremely subtle and light. Its characters speak a language and express feelings that are not the language or the feelings of the ordinary world. These characters are cultivated, but (happily) the world does not yet know that every man who has raised himself to a certain level of literary culture possesses certain qualities—delicacy, subtlety, acute sensibility. Such minds eventually become susceptible to perceptions of an almost supersubtle kind. The necessary notions of morality, all the eternal and indestructible social commonplaces, are viewed differently and by optical instruments that modify their character. The mind no longer submits absolutely to eternal laws; but, almost by way of compensation, conscience becomes less forgiving. Why not establish a new moral system in advance, based upon principles no matter how absurd? Why not give one's desires the force of a law of nature, as Descartes said?[25] In practice, however, contradictions surface everywhere. So it is for the inhabitants of Blithedale. Their plans for social reformation are absurd, but they soon recognize the obstacles they face. On the one hand, there are two characters who butt heads and whose stubbornness makes one doubt the possibility of establishing a genuine community. On the other, there is a free-thinking woman who demands equal rights for her own sex, but whose will is less strong than her passion. In chasing an uncertain goal, we sometimes neglect the better portion of our nature; instead of working to found another Eden, we work simply to exhaustion. The poet makes no verses, the philosopher conceives not a single idea, the enthusiastic woman loses her vigor—this is the inevitable result of a life sacrificed for an unattainable goal. The one lesson that comes from this book is that if a priori systems of reform are stillborn in the hands of ordinary folk, they are even less suited to the educated classes. Of no use for the people in general (who act according to their instincts, and not through reflection or perseverance of will), these systems are even more useless to analytical minds, proudly defiant and always on guard against stupidity.

This novel is not, properly speaking, a novel. Analysis, not the storyline, takes precedence. If we were obliged to define it absolutely, we would say that Hawthorne has orchestrated a philosophico-humanitarian ballet, danced by four main characters. The characters make socialist *entrechats* and logical *faux pas;* and their footwork is not always confident. They cannot keep time with their system's music. They mock one another or explode in each other's faces. That is a quick summary of *The Blithedale Romance.* What happens and is said there is very peculiar, but this book's peculiarity is completely psychological, as we shall see.

As we have already mentioned, four characters dominate the whole novel: a poet, Miles Coverdale; a utopian, Hollingsworth; a free-thinking woman, Zenobia; and a victim of all the evil spells of modern-day charlatans, Priscilla. The poet Miles Coverdale—in other words, Hawthorne—is the least eccentric of the four. He is the one who does his best to keep his moral health intact and who fears losing it the most. The other three are dreams incarnate. By all appearances, they live, they eat, they sleep, they speak like the rest of us. But they are clothed chimeras. They each have arrived at that particular perversion where the soul collapses. It does so when, having conversed only with abstractions and dreamy formulas, it loses a feeling for real things and believes utterly in impossibilities. All of them have, as the Scriptures say, emptied their heart and soul of all natural feelings and of all commonly accepted ideas that come from experience and, instead, have filled them with feelings and ideas of their own making and they gorge themselves on this empty meat.[26] They appear eloquent, poetic. And, indeed, they are: eloquent as a gust of wind on an arid plain, upon which there is neither tree to uproot nor leaf to blow; poetic like the lone sound one hears at night, audible only because of the absence of all other sounds. They are as profound and vast as nothingness or the three dimensions of space. Miles Coverdale is not like this. Conscientious and defiant, he analyzes everything, he meditates on everything, he lets nothing escape him. Before leaving for Blithedale, he procrastinates. En route there, he regrets having abandoned the comforts of town. Meeting a traveler along the way, Coverdale's companions greet him like a brother, saying to him enthusiastically, "We are going to regenerate the world!" The man looks flabbergasted as if he doesn't understand. We will have trouble regenerating the human race, thinks Miles Coverdale.[27] At the end of a three-month stay at the farm, he is no more convinced of the community's success than on the first day. Hour by hour he notes the faults of the system: his literary habit of analyzing everything that he perceives bothers him enormously, because there is nothing like the faculty of analysis to reduce to dust the fantasies and chimeras begotten by pride. Every system that springs from human will, every synthesis based upon abstract and a priori ideas that is not a simple generalization of fact, cannot survive analysis. The Baconian method is unassailable on this point. This is Miles Coverdale, then: the skeptical utopian, the would-be socialist.

Hollingsworth is the simple opposite of Miles Coverdale. Where Coverdale is timid, Hollingsworth is daring. Heroically, he marches off into the realm of the absurd. Courageously, he resists the facts. He exerts enormous will power to realize his illusions. Yet it is not for the greater glory and success of Blithedale that he summons this heroism and will power. (He is just as skeptical as Coverdale with regard to the community.) For his own personal ideas, for his *own* philosophical hobbyhorse—what he calls the "moral regeneration of criminals"—he would sacrifice the entire universe. Hollingsworth also displays a frightening mark that utopia imprints on its lovers—egoism. The man believes himself to be devoted because he commits his life to the service of a private idea. He cannot see that this idea is nothing more than the reflection and extension of himself; that he loves his shadow; that he falls to his knees before his own thinking; that he commits an act of fetishism and pride worse than that of Pygmalion. Like every egoist, inebriated with himself, Hollingsworth ossifies his capacity for sympathy. He will trample you underfoot; he will break your heart; he will forsake you after having drawn you to him; he will sacrifice all his feelings to his monstrous conceptions. The love of this philanthropist is not reserved for the virtuous or the good. In fact, he prefers the guilty. He cannot love you unless you are triflingly criminal, innocuously poisonous, slightly murderous. As for the rest, quick as many of the utopians are in general, he will stop at nothing to make allies and partisans for himself until the day when, his army formed, he (an incurable despot) can command as a sovereign. While waiting for this army to fall into its ranks, he abandons himself to the design of a future palace—a penitentiary—drawing up architectural plans and constructing the imaginary edifice where one day his illusory project can be realized.

Zenobia is what used to be called a "free" woman. She is the queen of the association, a prideful monarch, incurably disdainful. When she smiles at you, her smile seems to say that she pities you. When she speaks to you with words of affection, she is indulging in an act of charity. Modest appearances are not at all for her; silk and velvet are her favorite fabrics, and her hair is always adorned with a rare and precious flower from the tropics, expensively renewed every morning. Her beauty has nothing of fleeting modernity. Through her physical traits, the shape of her body, the outline of her physiognomy, Zenobia recalls a type of beauty that has virtually disappeared today: solid beauty—*substantial,* precise, strong, and proud—that has been dethroned by the pale English ideal. Our conceptions of beauty suffer revolutions and vicissitudes just as do empires and the planets themselves.

Seeing Zenobia pass with her head held high and a regal sureness in her step, we cannot help noticing that she confronts us with a strange dilemma: is she really a queen or merely an actress? Clearly, she is a dangerous woman. Whenever we think of her, our thoughts turn to dramatic scenes: her natural accoutrements would seem to be the classic dagger or the romantic vial of poison. Miles Coverdale, who watches her with trepidation, who glances at her furtively, who even (in his mind's eye) undresses her, discovers something remarkable: he is convinced that she has been someone's wife. No one has ever heard of her marriage, yet no one would mistake her for a virgin. Zenobia has none of the freshness or the dewy atmosphere that surrounds young girls. She is a rose whose petals are all blown and whose calyx retains not the smallest dewdrop. Whether marriage or seduction, therein lies the secret of Zenobia's story.

Priscilla, the young girl brought to the farm by Hollingsworth and placed by him under the protection of Zenobia, is an ethereal, sickly creature, always falling prey to a slight nervous trembling. She walks with the lightness of a somnambulist; her eyes seem magnetically transfixed by something far away; her spirit is timid like that of a human being who has been tutored by the despotism of necessity or an imperial nature. She has neither character nor will. She can only obey. She is a fragile and charming toy, free to be taken up even by the hand of a child. A poor, pale flower who is lacking air and sun to grow, she is taken to the farm by Hollingsworth in order that her health might improve; but, in fact, he has intervened to wrest her from the hands of a tyrant and charlatan. But is there not something strange about these four characters? It is obvious that they will never reform the world. All four of them are going to find themselves face to face with one another. Their personal intrigues will occupy us more than the history of the community. Let us stop, then, for a moment to contemplate the spectacle of this fraternal society.

Nothing is more important than the first evening our reformers spend together at Blithedale after supper. Their society is made up of two very distinct types of people: those who are accustomed to work and those who prefer to dream. Once the table is cleared, what can they do with one another? Silas Foster, the old Yankee who is in charge of making the farm work and keeping an eye on the practical needs of the establishment, sets about fixing an old pair of boots. His wife, already half asleep, pulls a stocking from her pocket and begins to knit. One of her servants hems a hand towel. Another labors over a pair of sleeves to embellish her Sunday best. And our dreamers, what are they doing? Sitting on a stool, as if in a sort of ecstasy, Priscilla watches the beautiful Zenobia, who turns from time to time, with eyes full of disdain, to look at the young girl. Hollingsworth, dismayed by this hauteur, looks angrily at Zenobia. And the observer Miles Coverdale contemplates all three. While the others work with their hands, the more refined characters prefer to employ only their thoughts and perceptions. Then arises a great and very important question: what name shall they call their community? The word *Blithedale* means nothing. Extraordinarily, the old name that the Indians gave to the place seems now irrelevant. Zenobia proposes the name of "Sunny Glimpse." The skeptic Coverdale pronounces the name "Utopia." Others put forward the name "Oasis." This important discussion might have continued for a good part of the night if not for the practical Silas Foster, who interrupts and ends it with these words: "'Take my advice, brother-farmers, [*said he, with a great, broad, bottomless yawn,*] and get to bed as soon as you can. I shall sound the horn at day-break; and we've got the cattle to fodder, and nine cows to milk, and a dozen other things to do, before breakfast'" (*BR* 37).

This is how things begin. And, here, several months later is the spectacle presented by this Arcadia when it is in full bloom, before the characters start to offend each other, before hopes begin to fade, while they are still working toward the regeneration of the world:

> On the whole, it was a society such as has seldom met together; nor, perhaps, could it reasonably be expected to hold together long. Persons of marked individuality—crooked sticks, as some of us might be called—are not exactly the easiest to bind up into a fagot. But, so long as our union should subsist, a man of intellect and feeling, with a free nature in him, might have sought far and near without finding so many points of attraction as would allure him hitherward. We were of all creeds and opinions, and generally tolerant of all, on every imaginable subject. Our bond, it seems to me, was not affirmative, but negative. We had individually found one thing or another to quarrel with in our past life, and were pretty well agreed as to the inexpediency of lumbering along with the old system any further. As to what should be substituted, there was much less unanimity. We did not greatly care—at least, I never did—for the written constitution under which our millennium had commenced. My hope was, that, between theory and practice, a true and available mode of life might be struck out; and that, even should we ultimately fail, the months or years spent in the trial would not have been wasted, either as regarded passing enjoyment, or the experience which makes men wise.
>
> Arcadians though we were, our costume bore no resemblance to the beribboned doublets, silk breeches and stockings, and slippers fastened with

artificial roses, that distinguish the pastoral people of poetry and the stage. In outward show, I humbly conceive, we looked rather like a gang of beggars, or banditti, than either a company of honest laboring-men, or a conclave of philosophers. Whatever might be our points of difference, we all of us seemed to have come to Blithedale with the one thrifty and laudable idea of wearing out our old clothes. Such garments as had an airing, whenever we strode afield! Coats with high collars and with no collars, broad-skirted or swallow-tailed[, *and with the waist at every point between the hip and arm-pit*]; pantaloons of a dozen successive epochs, and greatly defaced at the knees by the humiliations of the wearer before his lady-love—in short, we were a living epitome of defunct fashions, and the very raggedest presentment of men who had seen better days. It was gentility in tatters. Often retaining a scholarlike or clerical air, you might have taken us for the denizens of Grub Street,[28] intent on getting a comfortable livelihood by agricultural labor; or Coleridge's projected Pantisocracy in full experiment; or Candide and his motley associates at work in their cabbage garden[*; or anything else that was miserably out at elbows, and most clumsily patched in the rear*]. We might have been sworn comrades to Falstaff's ragged regiment. Little skill as we boasted in other points of husbandry, every mother's son of us would have served admirably to stick up for a scarecrow. And the worst of the matter was, that the first energetic movement essential to one downright stroke of real labor was sure to put a finish to these poor habiliments. So we gradually flung them all aside, and took to honest homespun and linsey-woolsey, as preferable, on the whole, to the plan recommended, I think, by Virgil—"Ara nudus; sere nudus,"—which as Silas Foster remarked, when I translated the maxim, would be apt to astonish the women-folks.

After a reasonable training, the yeoman life throve well with us. Our faces took the sunburn kindly; our chests gained in compass, and our shoulders in breadth and squareness; our great brown fists looked as if they had never been capable of kid gloves. The plough, the hoe, the scythe, and the hay-fork grew familiar to our grasp. The oxen responded to our voices. We could do almost as fair a day's work as Silas Foster himself, sleep dreamlessly after it, and awake at daybreak with only a little stiffness of the joints, which was usually quite gone by breakfast-time.

To be sure, our next neighbors pretended to be incredulous as to our real proficiency in the business which we had taken in hand. They told slanderous fables about our inability to yoke our own oxen, or to drive them afield when yoked, or to release the poor brutes from their conjugal bond at nightfall. They had the face to say, too, that the cows laughed at our awkwardness at milking-time, and invariably kicked over the pails; partly in consequence of our putting the stool on the wrong side, and partly because, taking offence at the whisking of their tails, we were in the habit of holding these natural fly-flappers with one hand and milking with the other. They further averred that we hoed up whole acres of Indian corn and other crops, and drew the earth carefully about the weeds; [and that by dint of unskilful planting few of our seeds ever came up at all, or, if they did come up, it was stern-foremost; and that we spent the better part of the month of June in reversing a field of beans, which had thrust themselves out of the ground in this unseemly way. They quoted it as nothing more than an ordinary occurrence for one or other of us to crop off two or three fingers, of a morning, by our clumsy use of the hay-cutter.] Finally, and as an ultimate catastrophe, these mendacious rogues circulated a report that we communitarians were exterminated, to the last man, by severing ourselves asunder with the sweep of our own scythes! and that the world had lost nothing by this little accident.

But this was pure envy and malice on the part of the neighboring farmers. The peril of our new way of life was not lest we should fail in becoming practical agriculturists, but that we should probably cease to be anything else. While our enterprise lay all in theory, we had pleased ourselves with delectable visions of the spiritualization of labor. It was to be our form of prayer and ceremonial of worship. Each stroke of the hoe was to uncover some aromatic root of wisdom, heretofore hidden from the sun. Pausing in the field, to let the wind exhale the moisture from our foreheads, we were to look upward, and catch glimpses into the far-off soul of truth. In this point of view, matters did not turn out quite so well as we anticipated. It is very true that, sometimes, gazing casually around me, out of the midst of my toil, I used to discern a richer picturesqueness in the visible scene of earth and sky. There was, at such moments, a novelty, an unwonted aspect, on the face of Nature, as if she had been taken by surprise and seen at unawares, with no opportunity to put off her real look, and assume the mask with which she mysteriously hides herself from mortals. But this was all. The clods of earth, which we so constantly belabored and turned over and over, were never etherealized into thought. Our thoughts, on the contrary, were fast becoming cloddish. Our labor symbolized nothing, and left us mentally sluggish in the dusk of the evening. Intellectual activity is incompatible with any large amount of bodily exercise. The yeoman and the scholar—the yeoman and the man of finest moral culture, though not the man of sturdiest sense and integrity—are two distinct individuals, and can never be melted or welded into one substance.

Zenobia soon saw this truth, and gibed me about it, one evening, as Hollingsworth and I lay on the grass, after a hard day's work.

"I am afraid you did not make a song today, while loading the hay-cart," said she, "as Burns did, when he was reaping barley."

"Burns never made a song in haying-time," I answered very positively. "He was no poet while a farmer, and no farmer while a poet."

"And on the whole, which of the two characters do you like best?" asked Zenobia. "For I have an idea that you cannot combine them any better than Burns did. Ah, I see, in my mind's eye, what sort of an individual you are to be, two or three years hence. Grim Silas Foster is your prototype, with his palm of sole-leather, and his joints of rusty iron (which all through summer keep the stiffness of what he calls his winter's rheumatize), and his brain of—I don't know what his brain is made of, unless it be a Savoy cabbage; but yours may be cauliflower, as a rather more delicate variety. Your physical man will be transmuted into salt beef and fried pork, at the rate, I should imagine, of a pound and a half a day; [*that being about the average which we find necessary in the kitchen*]. You will make your toilet for the day (still like this delightful Silas Foster) by rinsing your fingers and the front part of your face in a little tin pan of water at the doorstep, and teasing your hair with a wooden pocket-comb before a seven-by-nine-inch looking-glass. Your only pastime will be to smoke some very vile tobacco in the black stump of a pipe."

"Pray, spare me!" cried I. "But the pipe is not Silas's only mode of solacing himself with the weed."

"Your literature," continued Zenobia, apparently delighted with her description, "will be the 'Farmer's Almanac;' for I observe our friend Foster never gets so far as the newspaper. When you happen to sit down, at odd moments, you will fall asleep, and make nasal proclamation of the fact, as he does; and invariably you must be jogged out of a nap, after supper, by the future Mrs. Coverdale, and persuaded to go regularly to bed. And on Sundays, when you put on a blue coat with brass buttons, you will think of nothing else to do but to go and lounge over the stone walls and rail fences, and stare at the corn growing. And you will look with a knowing eye at oxen, and will have a tendency to clamber over into pigsties, and feel of the hogs, and give a guess how much they will weigh after you shall have stuck and dressed them. Already I have noticed you begin to speak through your nose, and with a drawl. Pray, if you really did make any poetry to-day, let us hear it in that kind of utterance!"

"Coverdale has given up making verses now," said Hollingsworth, who never had the slightest appreciation of my poetry. "Just think of him penning a sonnet with a fist like that! There is at least this good in a life of toil, that it takes the nonsense and fancy-work out of a man, and leaves nothing but what truly belongs to him. If a farmer can make poetry at the plough-tail, it must be because his nature insists on it; and if that be the case, let him make it, in Heaven's name!"

(*BR* 62–68)

In this Arcadia, undertaken for the cause of progress (and where each individual's nature, instead of developing itself, shrinks)—in this Arcadia founded on false principles, we can expect that all feelings and all affections will also be false and artificial. Love—the passion *par excellence*—does not wait to gain entrance to this community. By assimilating their language and demeanor, love can blend in with the members of this eccentric society. Our four dreamers love—or, more precisely, three of them love and one is loved: Hollingsworth. This egotistical man, this dry and obstinate philanthropist, this walking utopia, conquers the hearts of the two young women, Zenobia and Priscilla, because Hollingsworth possesses that kind of magnetic fascination which usually distinguishes the more intellectual bird of prey from others of his species, and very often acts upon women like Zenobia: gifted with intelligence, but deprived of wisdom, incapable of justifying their passions, incapable of finding a being who really deserves to be loved, incapable of distinguishing a rascal from his imposing appearance or discovering the madman concealed beneath the guise of genius. Zenobia is one of these creatures. Once upon a time, she loved a monstrous, cynical, immoral being whose shameful soul wore a mask of great exterior beauty; and she was fooled. Now she turns to Hollingsworth, a man whose heart is completely dried up, whose affections have been melted by the ardent fire of Utopia just like a piece of candy brought too close to the blacksmith's forge. She will be fooled again, except that this time, she will die because of it. These two mistakes—impossible to forgive—deserve an exemplary punishment. Proud Zenobia, the promoter of women's rights, bows her head before this utopian. He scoffs at her, he criticizes her ideas, he condemns her projects to emancipate women, he tramples on all of which she is proud, but Zenobia's passion for him only grows larger. She begs for this dreamer's pity and lowers herself until she comes to accept her own inferiority. One day Coverdale surprises Zenobia, who, after a violent dispute about women's rights, is effusively shaking Hollingsworth's hand. This creature, who rebels against the whole world, finds herself crushed by the limits that nature has assigned to her sex, and the passions of her heart repudiate the theories of her intelligence. As for Priscilla, she is attached to Hollingsworth like ground ivy to an oak. She falls for him like a bird enchanted by a snake. The most equivocal situation is that of Miles Coverdale. He would not dare fall in love with Zenobia; he secretly loves Priscilla yet says nothing of it. Through all this imbroglio of intrigue, of overheard conversations and suggestive handshakes, in the end Miles Coverdale plays the role of the star-struck lover familiar to comedies and novels.

The characters of Zenobia and Hollingsworth, perfectly false in nature, are entirely real in the times in which we live. They are two contemporaries. Haven't you met a Zenobia? Haven't you chatted with a Hollingsworth? Haven't you been witness to the horrible exploitation of one person by another, to the moral servitude imposed upon a weak and passionate creature by some despotic dreamer or some audacious charlatan? Hollingsworth calmly allows himself to be loved. He achieves his goals by any means, even by the feelings he inspires. Zenobia will be of great help to him in the realization of his plans. When she is no longer of use, he will know well how to break this fragile instrument. Zenobia will be sacrificed to *the reformation of criminals*. However, Hollingsworth does not restrict himself to the conquest of Zenobia. He is on the lookout for supporters and attempts to convert Coverdale. Hesitating and timid though he may be, the latter has the strength to say no. What a curious scene! The day when Coverdale voices certain apprehensions about the success of their socialist enterprise, Hollingsworth takes him at his word and seeks his discipleship in order to realize his own utopias.

> "But," said I, "whence can you, having no means of your own, derive the enormous capital which is essential to this experiment? State Street, I imagine, would not draw its purse-strings very liberally in aid of such a speculation."[29]
>
> "I have the funds—as much, at least, as is needed for a commencement—at command," he answered. "They can be produced within a month, if necessary."
>
> My thoughts reverted to Zenobia. It could only be her wealth which Hollingsworth was appropriating so lavishly. [And on what conditions was it to be had? Did she fling it into the scheme with the uncalculating generosity that characterizes a woman when it is her impulse to be generous at all? And did she fling herself along with it? But Hollingsworth did not volunteer an explanation.]
>
> "And have you no regrets," I inquired, "in overthrowing this fair system of our new life, which has been planned so deeply, and is now beginning to flourish so hopefully around us? How beautiful it is, and, so far as we can yet see, how practicable! The ages have waited for us, and here we are, the very first that have essayed to carry on our mortal existence in love and mutual

help! Hollingsworth, I would be loath to take the ruin of this enterprise upon my conscience."

"Then let it rest wholly upon mine!" he answered, knitting his black brows. "I see through the system. It is full of defects—irremediable and damning ones!—from first to last, there is nothing else! I grasp it in my hand, and find no substance whatever. There is not human nature in it."

["Why are you so secret in your operations?" I asked. "God forbid that I should accuse you of intentional wrong; but the besetting sin of a philanthropist, it appears to me, is apt to be a moral obliquity. His sense of honor ceases to be the sense of other honorable men. At some point of his course—I know not exactly when or where—he is tempted to palter with the right, and can scarcely forbear persuading himself that the importance of his public ends renders it allowable to throw aside his private conscience. Oh, my dear friend, beware this error! If you meditate the overthrow of this establishment, call together our companions, state your design, support it with all your eloquence, but allow them an opportunity of defending themselves."

"It does not suit me," said Hollingsworth. "Nor is it my duty to do so."

"I think it is," replied I.

Hollingsworth frowned; not in passion, but, like Fate, inexorably.

"I will not argue the point," said he.]

"What I desire to know of you is—and you can tell me in one word—whether I am to look for your cooperation in this great scheme of good? Take it up with me! Be my brother in it! It offers you (what you have told me, over and over again, that you most need) a purpose in life, worthy of the extremest self-devotion—worthy of martyrdom, should God so order it! In this view, I present it to you. You can greatly benefit mankind. Your peculiar faculties, as I shall direct them, are capable of being so wrought into this enterprise that not one of them need lie idle. Strike hands with me, and from this moment you shall never again feel the languor and vague wretchedness of an indolent or half-occupied man. There may be no more aimless beauty in your life; but, in its stead, there shall be strength, courage, immitigable will—everything that a manly and generous nature should desire! We shall succeed! We shall have done our best for this miserable world; and happiness (which never comes but incidentally) will come to us unawares."

It seemed his intention to say no more. But, after he had quite broken off, his deep eyes filled with tears, and he held out both his hands to me.

"Coverdale," he murmured, "there is not the man in this wide world whom I can love as I could you. Do not forsake me!"

(*BR* 131–33)

The conversation continues for a long time. Coverdale hesitates and Hollingsworth cries out all of a sudden:

> "I must have your answer! Will you devote yourself, and sacrifice all to this great end, and be my friend of friends forever?"
>
> "In Heaven's name, Hollingsworth," cried I, getting angry, and glad to be angry, because so only was it possible to oppose his tremendous concentrativeness and indomitable will, "cannot you conceive that a man may wish well to the world, and struggle for its good, on some other plan than precisely that which you have laid down? And will you cast off a friend for no unworthiness, but merely because he stands upon his right as an individual being, and looks at matters through his own optics, instead of yours?"
>
> "Be with me," said Hollingsworth, "or be against me! There is no third choice for you."
>
> "Take this, then, as my decision," I answered. "I doubt the wisdom of your scheme. Furthermore, I greatly fear that the methods by which you allow yourself to pursue it are such as cannot stand the scrutiny of an unbiassed conscience."
>
> "And you will not join me?"
>
> "No!"
>
> I never said the word—and certainly can never have it to say hereafter—that cost me a thousandth part so hard an effort as did that one syllable.
>
> (*BR* 135)

Coverdale, after this rupture, decides to leave the farm for a little while. This argument gives him a pretext to separate himself from a society that has begun to oppress him like a nightmare. In the company of these dreamers, his faculties lose their balance, his feelings their strength. Reality loses its salutary sway over the empire of his mind. "No sagacious man will long retain his sagacity, if he live exclusively among reformers and progressive people, without periodically returning into the settled system of things, to correct himself by a new observation from that old standpoint. It was now time for me, therefore, to go and hold a little talk with the conservatives, the writers of 'The North American Review,' the merchants, the politicians, the Cambridge men [*and all those respectable old blockheads who still, in this intangibility and mistiness of affairs, kept a death-grip on one or two ideas which had not come into vogue since yesterday morning*]."[30] Almost daily, then, he discovers a new fault with the community. One day, he remarks that they have neglected to make provision for a cemetery; on another, he notes the absence of a plan for matrimony: as if these forgetful utopians were never supposed to die and were going to regenerate the world by eternal celibacy! Furthermore, perhaps he will find clues to certain mysteries that have bothered his mind and piqued his curiosity for some time now. Disgust, boredom, and mental restlessness urge him, all at once, to leave the farm.

This bizarre story, very complicated under its apparent simplicity, now becomes more ambiguous than ever. The conscience of all these characters is not healthy, as we have seen. Notions of good and evil, of honor and virtue, having gone into their minds, are deformed there. How can one begin (like Zenobia, for example) to pledge one's heart to unreal passions? How does one get to the point of loving, like Priscilla, without being aware of one's addiction to loving? A mystery envelops the existence of these two women. While he is at the farm, Coverdale receives two singular visits—the first from a poor old man named Moodie, who inquires about Zenobia and Priscilla. "Does Zenobia love Priscilla?" the old man asks. Then, hidden behind the trees, he watches Zenobia's face with rapture, as only a father or a lover can. On another occasion a stranger approaches Coverdale and, with insulting familiarity, interrogates him about Zenobia and Priscilla, wanting to know certain particulars about their current life. Coverdale rebuffs his interlocutor, who seems outwardly handsome but from whose pores, as it were, licentiousness and knavery ooze. "His beauty," says Hawthorne, "seems like a mask. It might be easily removed, and, once the mask was taken off, one would find underneath his true face: that of a deformed elf or the fearful grimace of a dead man."[31] This evil genius betrays all the customary signs of vulgarity and, as is common with his sort, his charm seems like an imitation. This character gives his card to Coverdale, who discerns these words on it: "Westervelt, doctor of medicine." Evidently this Westervelt is an adventurer or a charlatan. Now, do you remember Priscilla's nervous trembling? Do you remember that her whole being renders her vulnerable to magnetic influence, that her weak character makes her prey to the will of the first comer? Then you will understand why Mr. Westervelt, M.D., inquires about her with such zeal; why Hollingsworth takes her to the farm while recommending that Zenobia keep an eye on her; why old Moodie comes to ask if Zenobia loves the poor girl and if she is really safe.

Coverdale takes leave of Zenobia and Priscilla and he goes into town. During the first days of his arrival, he is preoccupied in his character as a poet with observing the little incidents of the neighborhood and all the little movements of life that demonstrate, even in the most solitary and cramped place, nature's activity—children playing in the window, cats wandering in the gutters, turtledoves cooing in their dovecote. He notices precisely the same Westervelt in a window facing his own. Westervelt motions and soon

Zenobia appears, the same Zenobia whom Coverdale had left behind at the farm a couple of days before and who had demonstrated then no desire to leave. Coverdale fears some catastrophe. He goes to visit Zenobia and finds her in the company of Priscilla and Westervelt. The awful truth begins to shine into his eyes. Priscilla is the victim of this charlatan. Priscilla is the veiled lady whose magnetic clairvoyance everyone (several months earlier) had gone to admire. He urges her to leave for Blithedale in order to escape the tyranny of this miserable charlatan. But the influence of Westervelt on Priscilla is such that—with one single word—he forces her to reject Coverdale's admonition. What role, then, does Zenobia play? (Who, though present at this scene, cannot speak a single word in favor of Priscilla?) What influence does Westervelt exercise on her as well? Just now, Coverdale recollects old Moodie, who earns his living by selling purses and other little fancy goods in public markets and taverns. Coverdale the poet has always been struck by his timid and mysterious habits. He has loved to see him walking on tip-toe in the most public of places, going by without being seen, suddenly appearing in front of you to offer you his wares while whispering in your ear, then disappearing like a rat who scurries back into its hole. Where does this strange reclusiveness come from? Is it the cause of his long miseries? Can it explain his tattered clothes? Or his helplessness before the mockery and rudeness of customers upon whom his earthly existence depends? Coverdale sets off to find this vagabond, and he locates him in one of those taverns in which, even as a young man, he has been accustomed to spend his nights. "So, he's neither temperate nor wise," Coverdale says. Here, he takes old Moodie aside and, not without some pain, extracts his story.

Old Moodie has seen better days. In those days, he went by the name Fauntleroy. He was a man of despicable character who derived all his happiness from superficial luxury. Ruined in turn by prodigal self-indulgence, he commits a crime—a theft or a forgery—and departs, leaving behind a young girl who is taken up by her relatives. The child he abandons in this manner was precisely the beautiful Zenobia, a veritable portrait of his first existence, proud and superb on the outside—inside, artificial. After his disasters, Fauntleroy fled to the North and, suddenly, his character changed. He becomes as timid, as servile, as fearful as (previously) he had been sumptuous and arrogant. From a second marriage with a poor common woman, he had a small daughter, Priscilla, a living replica this time around of his second existence. Timid, without will, without character, this child—with every passing year—betrays all the symptoms of excessive nervous susceptibility. This trait earns her the nickname "Little Prophetess" among their neighbors and attracts the attention of one of those fakirs who are so common in the

United States, where medical charlatanism reigns supreme. You know the rest. The charlatan is Westervelt. He makes a fortune from Priscilla. In order to maintain this lucrative income, he goes to look for her at Blithedale where she has found refuge. And if Zenobia cannot protect her sister, it is because Westervelt has, in fact, seduced Zenobia (and, by some accounts, secretly married her): she is bound to him by who-knows-what shameful ties that she cannot break.

Having been apprised of this sad and ugly story (haven't we read its familiar parallels in our own *Gazette des Tribunaux,* redolent of modern crime fiction and characterized, too, by a certain scientific charlatanism and the philosophical exploitation of the stupidity of others?),[32] Coverdale, in the midst of an excursion, stops in a small Massachusetts village and enters a room where the Yankee country folk have come to witness a séance of magnetism's miracles and marvels. Here the author takes us to watch a spectacle of modern superstitions—one that might make us regret the supersession of witches and their sabbath. In the crowd, Coverdale discovers Hollingsworth; both of them are plagued by a sinister foreboding in which neither is mistaken. The magician is Westervelt and the veiled woman is Priscilla. Hollingsworth throws himself up on the stage, wrests Priscilla from her tyrant's domination, and takes her back to Blithedale as if to a safe harbor.

Coverdale does not tarry either in going back to Blithedale. While approaching the farm, he hears joyous voices. He conceals himself to observe the source of this glad commotion. And what does he see? All of our reformers in fantastic costumes, masquerading through the woods. This scene is only an incident, but it is very curious and gives rise to too many reflections for us not to take notice of it.

> Skirting farther round the pasture, I heard voices and much laughter proceeding from the interior of the wood. Voices, male and feminine; laughter, not only of fresh young throats, but the bass of grown people, as if solemn organ-pipes should pour out airs of merriment. Not a voice spoke, but I knew it better than my own; not a laugh, but its cadences were familiar. The wood, in this portion of it, seemed as full of jollity as if Comus and his crew were holding their revels in one of its usually lonesome glades. Stealing onward as far as I durst, without hazard of discovery, I saw a concourse of strange figures beneath the overshadowing branches. They appeared, and vanished, and came again, confusedly with the streaks of sunlight glimmering down upon them.
>
> Among them was an Indian chief, with blanket, feathers, and war-paint, and uplifted tomahawk; and near him, looking fit to be his woodland bride,

the goddess Diana, with the crescent on her head, and attended by our big lazy dog, in lack of any fleeter hound. Drawing an arrow from her quiver, she let it fly at a venture, and hit the very tree behind which I happened to be lurking. Another group consisted of a Bavarian broom-girl, a negro of the Jim Crow[33] order, one or two foresters of the Middle Ages, a Kentucky woodsman in his trimmed hunting-shirt and deerskin leggings, and a Shaker elder, quaint, demure, broad-brimmed, and square-skirted. Shepherds of Arcadia, and allegoric figures from the Faerie Queen, were oddly mixed up with these. Arm in arm, or otherwise huddled together in strange discrepancy, stood grim Puritans, gay Cavaliers, and Revolutionary officers with three-cornered cocked-hats, and queues longer than their swords. A bright-complexioned, dark-haired, vivacious little gypsy, with a red shawl over her head, went from one group to another, telling fortunes by palmistry; and Moll Pitcher, the renowned old witch of Lynn, broomstick in hand, showed herself prominently in the midst, as if announcing all these apparitions to be the offspring of her necromantic art. But Silas Foster, who leaned against a tree near by, in his customary blue frock and smoking a short pipe, did more to disenchant the scene, with his look of shrewd, acrid, Yankee observation, than twenty witches and necromancers could have done in the way of rendering it weird and fantastic.

A little farther off, some old-fashioned skinkers and drawers, all with portentously red noses, were spreading a banquet on the leaf-strewn earth; while a horned and long-tailed gentleman (in whom I recognized the fiendish musician erst seen by Tam O'Shanter) tuned his fiddle, and summoned the whole motley rout to a dance, before partaking of the festal cheer. So they joined hands in a circle, whirling round so swiftly, so madly, and so merrily, in time and tune with the Satanic music, that their separate incongruities were blended all together, and they became a kind of entanglement that went nigh to turn one's brain with merely looking at it. Anon they stopt all of a sudden, and staring at one another's figures, set up a roar of laughter; whereat a shower of the September leaves (which, all day long, had been hesitating whether to fall or no) were shaken off by the movement of the air, and came eddying down upon the revellers.

Then, for lack of breath, ensued a silence, at the deepest point of which, tickled by the oddity of surprising my grave associates in this masquerading trim, I could not possibly refrain from a burst of laughter on my own separate account.

"Hush!" I heard the pretty gypsy fortuneteller say. "Who is that laughing?"

"Some profane intruder!" said the goddess Diana. "I shall send an arrow through his heart, or change him into a stag, as I did Actaeon, if he peeps from behind the trees!"

"Me take his scalp!" cried the Indian chief, brandishing his tomahawk, and cutting a great caper in the air.

"I'll root him in the earth with a spell that I have at my tongue's end!" squeaked Moll Pitcher. "And the green moss shall grow all over him, before he gets free again!"

"The voice was Miles Coverdale's," said the fiendish fiddler, with a whisk of his tail and a toss of his horns. "My music has brought him hither. He is always ready to dance to the Devil's tune!"

Thus put on the right track, they all recognized the voice at once, and set up a simultaneous shout.

"Miles! Miles! Miles Coverdale, where are you?" they cried. "Zenobia! Queen Zenobia! here is one of your vassals lurking in the wood. Command him to approach and pay his duty!"

The whole fantastic rabble forthwith streamed off in pursuit of me, so that I was like a mad poet hunted by chimeras.

(*BR* 209–11)

The scene is truly charming—but what singular reformers! Poor children who have tried to remake the world! This masquerade is a scene from *The Decameron,* a scene from an Italian comedy, a scene from Shakespeare's *Merry Wives of Windsor.* It is one of those diversions that the author's ancestors would have called pagan, one of those scandalous rituals (so they still say) that they outlawed, and which the severe John Endicott had stopped as soon as he arrived in New England, as Hawthorne himself recounts.[34] Decidedly, Blithedale's joyous association will never stretch to the far reaches of the globe.

The dénouement of this strange story is tragic. With Zenobia's and Hollingsworth's first words, Coverdale perceives that the friendship that brought them together is now dead and, henceforth, that everything is finished between them. Hollingsworth uses Zenobia's conduct toward Priscilla and the destitution in which she leaves her as a pretext for his rupture. He almost accuses her of connivance with Westervelt. That is only the apparent reason. The true reason is the likelihood that Zenobia's fortune has been compromised, and that she can no longer be of any help to him in realizing his plans. Faithful to his cold abstractions, Hollingsworth breaks the heart of the woman he has never really loved, but whose love he has tolerated as long as it could be of use to him. The split occurs—full of bitter reproaches, accusations, tears—one of those rifts in which long-standing friends (soon to become enemies of or indifferent to each other) mutually discover all of the other's evil instincts, the criminal thoughts, and shockingly egotistical designs that have permeated their intercourse. After this rupture, Zenobia confides in Coverdale her intention to quit the community forever, and she says her farewells. Coverdale, worried and full of terrible suspicions, wanders the whole night until the moment when the imagined possibility of Zenobia's suicide utterly consumes him. Obeying a mysterious inspiration, he wakes Hollingsworth and Silas Foster to share his premonitions and makes them come with him to search for the body. The scene is a beautiful one: the hushed conversation between Coverdale and Hollingsworth through the raised farmhouse window; the appearance of old Silas Foster in his nightcap, thrusting out his head to find out what all the commotion is about; his astonishment when he is asked to join the two friends in their search; his disbelief when he learns that Zenobia has drowned (not to mention all his out-of-season pleasantries—so rustic and incongruous); discovering the body; Hollingsworth's and Coverdale's overwrought anxiety; Silas's lugubrious raking of the streambed (as if he were merely fishing for salmon); the description of the body as it is pulled from the water, under the clear white moonlight. All these brushstrokes make up a sinister nocturnal painting. In this manner, *The Blithedale Romance* comes to a close. All these romantic passions, all this chimerical ardor, culminate in a larger (the largest) reality—death. Suicide is the natural end to the book, because a crime against humanity is the inevitable punishment for false existences and artificial passions. When life is founded on false principles and, as a consequence, cannot continue, suicide is the logical resolution to the crisis. In such a way, then, Providence has found a punishment for passions that transcend—and transgress—natural limits: a retribution equally contrary to nature.

We have tried to give an idea of this subtle book, one that recommends itself to careful analysis. *The Blithedale Romance* has excellent moments, but as a whole it is too metaphysical, and the dramatic element of the novel is taken up in a world that is too exceptional. For this reason, we prefer certain other books by Hawthorne.[35] His style, however, is what deserves praise. From one end of the story to the other, he sometimes runs quickly, sometimes capriciously, sometimes voluptuously, sometimes ethereally. Never has Hawthorne exhibited so many descriptive qualities and such strength of expression. Among the marvelous descriptions contained in *The Blithedale Romance,* we cite those of Coverdale's hermitage at Blithedale, the tavern where he meets old Moodie, the village lecture hall where he watches the magnetic séance. All of these places, vulgar in and of themselves, take on— from Hawthorne's pen—the appearance of a palace, with aspects resembling those that Puck's and Ariel's retreats could have had. His style is, so to speak, *impersonal*. He cloaks his thoughts, but not in an arbitrary way. He is mysterious when the thought is mysterious, subtle when the thought is subtle, solid when it is solid.

What conclusions should be drawn from such a book? Let us listen to Hawthorne himself. He describes his impressions while watching the magnetic séance:

> I heard, from a pale man in blue spectacles, some stranger stories than ever were written in a romance; told, too, with a simple, unimaginative steadfastness, which was terribly efficacious in compelling the auditor to receive them into the category of established facts. He cited instances of the miraculous power of one human being over the will and passions of another; insomuch that settled grief was but a shadow beneath the influence of a man possessing this potency, and the strong love of years melted away like a vapor. At the bidding of one of these wizards, the maiden, with her lover's kiss still burning on her lips, would turn from him with icy indifference; the newly made widow would dig up her buried heart out of her young husband's grave before the sods had taken root upon it; a mother with her babe's milk in her bosom would thrust away her child. Human character was but soft wax in his hands; and guilt, or virtue, only the forms into which he should see fit to mould it. The religious sentiment was a flame which he could blow up with his breath, or a spark that he could utterly extinguish. It is unutterable, the horror and disgust with which I listened, and saw that, if these things were to be believed, the individual soul was virtually annihilated, and all that is sweet and pure in our present life debased, and that the idea of man's eternal responsibility was made ridiculous, and immortality rendered at once impossible, and not worth acceptance. But I would have perished on the spot sooner than believe it.
>
> The epoch of rapping spirits, and all the wonders that have followed in their train—such as tables upset by invisible agencies, bells self-tolled at funerals, and ghostly music performed on jew's-harps—had not yet arrived. Alas, my countrymen, methinks we have fallen on an evil age! If these phenomena have not humbug at the bottom, so much the worse for us. What can they indicate, in a spiritual way, except that the soul of man is descending to a lower point than it has ever before reached while incarnate? We are pursuing a downward course in the eternal march, and thus bring ourselves into the same range with beings whom death, in requital of their gross and evil lives, has degraded below humanity! To hold intercourse with spirits of this order, we must stoop and grovel in some element more vile

than earthly dust. These goblins, if they exist at all, are but the shadows of past mortality, outcasts, mere refuse stuff, adjudged unworthy of the eternal world, and, on the most favorable supposition, dwindling gradually into nothingness. The less we have to say to them the better, lest we share their fate!

(*BR* 198–99)

Here, I share Hawthorne's opinion entirely: his book's characters are the clearest evidence of the fears he expresses. Yes, the human soul is turning perverse. Human life, in all countries, tends to regress. The clearest proof of this fact is that man's actions are no longer judged according to everlasting rules of what is just and what is unjust, nor weighed in the eternal balance: and there can be no going back. Human actions have a vague and equivocal character that defies precise and simple understanding. In which times, in what era, did beings like Hollingsworth and Zenobia exist? How should one understand their acts? Are they criminal? No one wants or dares to say this. Are they honest people in the strictest sense of the word and according to long-standing morals? Certainly not. What are they, then? Human tongues have not yet found a word to express what they are, but they must find one because the family to which these characters belong is becoming more numerous every day. In the absence of a better word, we will say that they are ambiguous characters. They possess virtues, but these are ineffectual and remain in a state of abstraction; and they entertain thoughts such as the truly guilty have never imagined. They are neither perverted nor virtuous, neither corrupt nor innocent. They defy men's judgment. They are beyond God's laws, yet they are not ruled by the Devil's laws. Today, the number of men who are like Dante's damned—rejected by Heaven and refused by Hell—is large. Their affections, their feelings, their thoughts, even their superstitions—all of these lack humanity. They are feelings, affections, and superstitions that are outside of nature and that demand other conditions for existence, other moral rules, another atmosphere, another planet. All of this is not simply extra-human, but, as Hawthorne aptly puts it, it is beneath humanity. We cannot do any better in explaining our thoughts than to cite the famous Muslim legend that our favorite philosopher has employed with such eloquence.[36] Once upon a time, on the edge of the Dead Sea, there were a singularly impious and corrupt people. God sent Moses to convert them. God's envoy lost his nerve. The impious laughed at him and his sermons. So, to punish them, Moses transformed all of them into simian creatures. Ever since, this unhappy lot leap about, run, climb trees, grimace, and screech like monkeys. Only from time to time do they remember that they were once human beings. When they do, they interrupt their lascivious acts, their obscene gesturing, and, for several moments, become dreamy and sad. Let us meditate on this legend. It holds a terrible meaning, from which we can benefit.

Revue des Deux Mondes (1 Dec. 1852)

Notes

1. Montégut wrote an extensive review of *Uncle Tom's Cabin* for the *Revue des Deux Mondes* (1 Oct. 1852): 155–85.
2. See Montégut's notice of *Memoirs of Margaret Fuller Ossoli,* edited by Ralph Waldo Emerson and W. H. Channing, *Revue des Deux Mondes* (1 Apr. 1852): 37–73.
3. The line is spoken by Sganarelle in Act I, Scene 1, of *Le médecin malgré lui* (1666), by Molière (Jean-Baptiste Poquelin [1622–73]).
4. See E.-D. Forgues, "Poètes et romanciers américains: Nathaniel Hawthorne," *Revue des Deux Mondes* (15 Apr. 1852): 337–65, translated in chapter VI of this volume.
5. Perhaps the most memorable being John Balfour o'Burley in *Old Mortality* (1816).
6. Montégut loosely paraphrases this passage from the "Custom-House" Introduction to *The Scarlet Letter:* "It is now nearly two centuries and a quarter since the original Briton, the earliest emigrant of my name, made his appearance in the wild and forest-bordered settlement, which has since become a city. And here his descendants have been born and died, and have mingled their earthy substance with the soil; until no small portion of it must necessarily be akin to the mortal frame wherewith, for a little while, I walk the streets" (Centenary Edition, vol. I, 8–9). For the author's genealogy, see chapter VI, note 1.
7. Altogether, twenty men and women were executed at Salem: nineteen were hanged and one pressed to death—none was burned alive.
8. For the correct attribution of this phrase, see chapter IV, note 6.
9. The correct quotation from *The Pilgrim's Progress* is "Then I saw that there was a way to Hell, even from the Gates of Heaven, as well as from the City of Destruction" ([1678; rpt. Baltimore: Penguin Books, 1965], 205).
10. *Memoirs of Margaret Fuller Ossoli,* 2 vols. (Boston: Phillips, Sampson and Co., 1852), vol. 1, 218.
11. Montégut paraphrases from a series of passages at the novel's conclusion as Coverdale reflects, "I have made but a poor and dim figure in my own narrative, establishing no separate interest, and suffering my colorless life to take its hue from other lives . . . my own life has been all an emptiness. . . . Life, however, it must be owned, has come to rather an idle pass with me" (*BR* 245, 246, 247).
12. "The Minister's Black Veil," first published in *Twice-told Tales* (1837).
13. "The Wedding Knell," first published in *Twice-told Tales* (1837).
14. "Ethan Brand," first collected in *The Snow-Image, and Other Twice-told Tales* (1851). Montégut alludes to the chariot festival at the Indian temple of Jagannath—from which we get the English word *juggernaut.*

15. Various species of flowering plants (*Helichrysum, Xeranthemum,* and *Erythrina*)—*immortelles* in French—that keep their shape and color when dried. In France, a wreath of *immortelles* was customary at funerals.

16. Montégut's concise paraphrase of Emerson's "Self-Reliance" does not correspond to any particular passage from that essay, but the following excerpt may be taken as representative:

> Trust thyself: every heart vibrates to that iron string. Accept the place the divine providence has found for you, the society of your contemporaries, the connection of events. Great men have always done so, and confided themselves childlike to the genius of their age, betraying their perception that the absolutely trustworthy was seated at their heart, working through their hands, predominating in all their being. And we are now men, and must accept in the highest mind the same transcendent destiny; and not minors and invalids in a protected corner, not cowards fleeing before a revolution, but guides, redeemers, and benefactors, obeying the Almighty effort, and advancing on Chaos and the Dark.
>
> (*Collected Works* 2: 28)

17. First published in *The Snow-Image, and Other Twice-told Tales* (1851).

18. Montégut refers, of course, to the monumental granite outcropping known as the "Old Man of the Mountains," which has long been the state symbol of New Hampshire, but which collapsed in May 2003 owing to the eroding powers of snow, wind, and rain.

19. "Hard upon this happy augury came another strange event, which seemed to foretell the grandeur of our empire: a man's head with the features intact was discovered by the workmen who were digging the foundations of the temple. This meant without any doubt that on this spot would stand the imperial citadel of the capital city of the world." Livy, *The Early History of Rome: Books I–V of the History of Rome from its Foundations,* translated by Aubrey de Sélincourt (Baltimore: Penguin, 1960), book 1:55.79.

20. First published in *Twice-told Tales,* 2nd ed. (1842).

21. The women most often remembered for their activities at Brook Farm include Margaret Fuller and Elizabeth Peabody (1804–94), a pioneer in children's education who was soon to become Hawthorne's sister-in-law.

22. Montégut refers to the 1848 gatherings of woman's rights advocates at Seneca Falls, New York (and other upstate cities), where the now famous Declaration of Sentiments, listing the many discriminations against women, was first read. William Henry Seward (1801–72), a zealous Whig politician and future Secretary of State under Lincoln, threw down the gauntlet in a famous speech of 11 March 1850, in which he attacked the slave system as being contrary to "a higher law than the Constitution." John Parker Hale (1806–73) was a Democratic legislator from Maine who was exiled from his own party because of his antislavery views. He ran as the Free Soil Party candidate for the presidency in 1852. Gerrit Smith (1797–1874) was a reformer and philanthropist, later notorious for his support of John Brown and the use of force against proslavery adherents in Kansas.

23. This legislation eventually was enacted in 1862.

24. Nicolas Boileau (1636–1711) published his mock-epic, *Le lutrin,* in 1674. With sustained humor and literary parody, the story details a furious ecclesiastical quarrel over the placing of a lectern.

25. Perhaps somewhat freely, Montégut draws this inference from Descartes' *Dis-*

course on Method, Part Three (1637), in which the philosopher attempts to justify a system of morality based upon reason, not faith.

26. Montégut may be thinking of a text from Jesus' sermon on the shores of the Sea of Galilee (John 6:27): "Labour not for the meat which perisheth, but for the meat which endureth unto everlasting life, which the Son of man shall give unto you: for him hath God the Father sealed."

27. Using a technique common to French literary criticism of this period, Montégut puts into quotation marks phrases that do not literally appear in *The Blithedale Romance*. He has accurately paraphrased a scene from chapter II of the novel, however. Compare the Centenary Edition, vol. III, 12.

28. Montégut's note: "A name that applies generally to poor writers—hacks—who eke out their living in garrets."

29. While Montégut advises his readers that State Street is "undoubtedly a rich neighborhood in Boston," the phrase more accurately serves as a metonym for the city's financial district.

30. Founded in 1815, the *North American Review* deliberately modeled itself after the great British journals of the period and was long associated with the scholarly traditions of Harvard and Boston Unitarianism.

31. In the original text, Hawthorne writes: "I felt as if the whole man were a moral and physical humbug; his wonderful beauty of face, for aught I knew, might be removable like a mask; and, tall and comely as his figure looked, he was perhaps but a wizened little elf, gray and decrepit, with nothing genuine about him, save the wicked expression of his grin. The fantasy of his spectral character so wrought upon me, together with the contagion of his strange mirth on my sympathies, that I soon began to laugh as loudly as himself" (Centenary Edition, vol. III, 95).

32. *La Gazette des Tribunaux* documented important changes and decisions in legislation and jurisprudence in France and also covered important, or at least sensational, trials.

33. Montégut's note: "Jim Crow, an emblematic term for the negro race, used in the same way that John Bull is to refer to the English nation and Brother Jonathan in reference to the American."

34. In "The May-Pole of Merry Mount," first published in *Twice-told Tales* (1837).

35. Hawthorne's shorter tales were an object of fascination for Montégut, as this and his later articles confirm.

36. Montégut paraphrases the concluding paragraphs of Book III, chapter 3, from Carlyle's *Past and Present* (1843), ostensibly drawn from the Koran.

VIII

Louis Étienne

"American Storytellers: Nathaniel Hawthorne" (1857)

I. The Old American Ethos

The poet who said that man is a flower whose roots reach down to hell should have been born in the United States.[1] The wicked nature of man, the evil spirit of our species—oh, we might as well cut to the chase!—the Devil himself has no larger dominion than the literature of America. He is not always named: sometimes he is called human perversity, corruption without remedy; sometimes the power of evil, the fatality of crime. But who is the mysterious being hidden behind these names if not the Satan of the old Puritans? But now he appears in a different form. Instead of being a supernatural character, half man and half animal, he is a philosophical and religious principle—abstract, no doubt, but always standing at the forefront of consciousness. He is the only demon in which the nineteenth century feigns belief, but he is indeed real and present in the American imagination. Beelzebub, reduced to an abstraction, might seem to mean nothing. On the contrary, he is everything. Suppose that in all souls there is a deep belief in the principle of evil that shackles them and now and then pulls them down, much like those unfortunates who always drag around an iron leash, bolted to their ankles for crimes they do not remember; the ball and chain of human misery cruelly warns them of their weakness. They want to throw themselves joyously into life and feel—just at that moment—the drag of damnation pulling behind them. Who can ever measure the weight of evil? How little is needed to counterbalance an infinite measure of good! Alter imperceptibly the proportions of their mixture; add a few drops of vice and criminal intent to the dose. What a heavy burden for the soul! Under this oppression it can hardly breathe! All its joys grow dim, its lightness vanishes, and even its laughter becomes sad.

The idea of the mysterious power of evil has been dismissed in Europe for some time, but it has never left Puritan America. One might even say that the Devil emigrated to the New World with all his infernal cortege. There a new Chosen People, Bible in hand, have continued warring against Asmodeus, Astaroth, and Belphegor. One could even say that the evil spirits of folktales have resurrected themselves in that country. We do not want to ridicule turning tables, rapping spirits, and self-winding clocks, nor to reproach America for the hundredth time for all the bizarre superstitions from which she seems to have recovered. But it is useful to observe that these terrors of the mind, the only possible ones these days, come to us from across the water. Puritan nonsense has spawned a serious belief in the Fiend. Nowhere is human nature more reviled than in this nation that believes itself called to renew humanity. Those people like to think of themselves as God's elect; but, if you believe that, you also have to acknowledge that no other nation has a more unique relationship to the Devil.

What sort of literature comes from such a country? A constant, relentless depiction of man's battle with evil. The writers will have piercing vision (especially for perceiving evil tendencies), a rare sagacity for discovering our corrupted fiber, an insatiable appetite for revealing vice hideously worming its way through the heart of all human virtues, an incomparable talent for sorrowful moral anatomy. Among all the beautiful and great things that the human soul keeps to itself, American writers will seek out its horrors. Their portraits will not only be severe, but desperate. Evil has no remedy. When it seizes the heart, nothing can get rid of it: it is a spirit of darkness for which there is no exorcism. Try as you might to hunt it down, once it has entered the soul it will abide forever. There shall be no reconciliation: the man who has sinned is one of Hell's elect. If the author is Christian, he will nevertheless be a fatalist; if he is not religious, he will be even more of one. He might not believe in God, but he certainly believes in the Devil. His impiety resembles that of the Old World, where we believe in the goodness of man but can do without God, persuaded that we no longer need Him. He, on the other hand, is convinced of the power of evil, the attraction of crime, the prestige of perversity. He has a mystic belief in evil, even when he no longer believes in good. Neither class of writers has remained simply

Puritan. The religious have gravitated to Transcendentalism, an American philosophy penetrated completely by German thought; the irreligious (there are few, but they exist) have borrowed from England and France. Both of these groups, maturing into schools and keeping up with the times, have always remembered the lessons of their ancestors. At the risk of making a grand generalization, we would define American literature as the literature of a people reared by Puritan tutors.

No one believes more firmly than Nathaniel Hawthorne in the permanence of inherited moral types. A reformed socialist, he pushes the principle of transmission to such extremes that he makes us stand back, modest conservatives that we are. It seems sufficient to us that the son inherit the family fortune: for better or worse, Hawthorne wants him to inherit the heart, the temperament, and the paternal passions. All of his characters reproduce in a fatal way the virtues and vices of the forebears who gave them life, not just the traits of their physiognomy. Little Pearl, born out of wedlock, has the follies and audacity of a nature that rebels against all rules; Zenobia, daughter of an opulent Fauntleroy, has the pride and ambition of a queen; Priscilla, daughter of a ruined Fauntleroy, has the sickly docility of a magnetic subject. It would not be unjust or arbitrary to follow the author's example and to apply to him the laws he applies to all of his heroes. *Patere legem quam [ipse] fecisti*—follow the laws you have made. Hawthorne the novelist, who has made himself known through his stories and longer fictions written between 1840 and 1852, is indeed the son of Hawthorne the Puritan who came to Salem two hundred years ago. Make the mystical sectarian go through two centuries of labor, pursue adventures, experience religious and philosophical decomposition; for a hundred years, make him penetrate the wilderness and clear the soil; for another hundred years, quarter him on a ship. Suppose that, having become in appearance the perfect Yankee (schooled by work, commerce, and Benjamin Franklin), one day he ceases from that drudgery and, just for a moment, has quenched his thirst for lucre. A hardy, yet generous philosophy makes him despise the commercial and materialist society that surrounds him. For the first time in two hundred years, he thinks. The old man quickly goes through changes of garb, habits, and opinions. He takes up a pen and writes Nathaniel Hawthorne's novels. We would not understand the novelist well if we saw, in those sad and fantastical conceptions, only caprice or calculation. We would even be unjust if we turned their occasionally ambiguous morality against him. Simply put, he is a Puritan who has changed with the times. Permit me to treat the author as he treats his characters. I will strive to compare him to his forefathers.

Hawthorne's ancestors brought a lot of superstitious baggage to America, which they cherished almost as much as Aeneus loved his Di Penates.[2] They lived surrounded by spirits, and the supernatural world was in daily contact with the world around them. Is the novelist truly sure that he does not believe in spirits? In his *Old Manse,* he hears the ghost of a clergyman who comes and goes, who sighs in a certain corner of the hall, who riffles through the pages of an invisible sermon. The author and his friends, meeting at twilight, make out in intervals of silence the fluttering of a minister's silk robe as he traverses the meditative circle and brushes the chair of a poet or philosopher while passing by. In the kitchen, strange noises emerge at the hour of midnight: the shadow of a cook, with the shadow of an iron, irons the shadow of a minister's collar, or, with the phantom of a grinder grinds the phantom of coffee of which there is no trace the next day. The author jokes with his visions: the ghostly minister wants his manuscript discourses published; that specter of a cook has regrets about a poorly-starched cravat, scruples that bring the poor girl back from her tomb and that make her work every night without wages. These reflections prove that the author has imagination; but his visions are not just pure chatter. Everything that touches him becomes a phantom: his imagination could not take flight without being carried away by the supernatural.

Does he want to paint a contrast between the practical mind and fantasy? He imagines the story "The Snow-Image."[3] The fantasy is a charming little girl of snow who some children shape with their own hands, and who—suddenly coming to life—sets off running in the garden. The practical mind is Mr. Lindsey, who catches the little, light phantom, moralizes on the thoughtless parents who have let the girl run around all alone, and locks her in front of a Heidenberg stove. Two minutes later, there is nothing left of the poetic and sprightly apparition besides a small puddle of cloudy water on the floor. Does he want to capture that moment of brusque transition that happens to a woman, the first accident that reveals her true character through the inalterable sweetness of a honeymoon? He invents the little story of "Mrs. Bullfrog."[4] Two young newlyweds are traveling, poetically, in a coach. What chariot does Love not transform into an elegant carriage? If a man who is riding in a carriage with his paramour is not a little bit of a poet, one must give up hope on his imagination. Just think with what sort of eyes he must see this young bride who belongs to him! Those caring looks that fix upon him, those lovely curls that he has not yet seen in disarray! All of the sudden, the carriage flips. What a sad turn of events! In the midst of cries and confusion, there is a diabolical apparition. They cannot find the beautiful, young, amiable girl. Is she hidden under some trunk? Amid the chaos of packages and baggage tossed from the overturned carriage, the young husband sees a sort of demon dressed as a woman, swearing, storming about, abusing the coachman—God have mercy: she even lands two or three punches on the poor soul's head! Where is his fiancée? Where has this odious vision, with a scarlet, contorted face and a screeching voice, come from? Just like his carriage, the new husband's reason has turned upside down. Little by little everything returns to order: the coach is back on its four wheels and the young man's mind on its normal footing. A sweet voice calls to him: God be praised! His beautiful bride has been found. The journey resumes, but what has happened to that ugly little diabolical being? She is left behind on the highway.

With Hawthorne the marvelous always has a practical end. In the same way, the sectarians who peopled the shores of America had many visions, but they were never useless; every wonder had a moral lesson. If signs appeared in the sky, it was to announce the punishment of crimes; it was a sermon given to preachers by meteors. There we find none of the purely naïve wonder that abounds in pagan religions: everything has a meaning and a moral. Ann Radcliffe piles up phantoms, specters, and wonders that are then easily explained: amusing and frivolous phantasmagoria that have nothing in common with the marvels of a people accustomed to nourishing themselves with the Bible. Hoffmann believes in his visions, but they are only food for his sickly imagination. He feels sincere fright, but this same fright is an end in itself. He takes harsh pleasure in his horrors, and when he has made his hair stand on end, he is content. A truly American imagination, and such is that of our novelist, only admits the marvelous on the condition of proving something.

The American storyteller would have refuted his Puritan filiation, if gay or even sweet or laughing apparitions ever appeared in his work. Puck, Ariel, Titania—gracious creations—are foreign to him. How could mid-summer nights' dreams be transplanted to the home of Reformed religion, the bivouac of Calvinism, on the borders of those immense forests where they thought they could hear the witches' sabbath every night? It is not Shakespeare, but the Bible that supplied the fairy tales of mothers and nurses; and from the Bible, they chose the terrible miracles of the Old Testament. Readers of Hawthorne, then, will never want for sad and menacing legends, a fantastical world destined to take the real world to task, visions sent by an irritated or jealous God. What pleasure they will get, for example, spending the night with the cadaver of Judge Pyncheon in one long chapter of *The House of Seven Gables!* Every night, at midnight, all the deceased members of the family meet in the lower room of that mansion where the portrait of their forefather hangs, the head of their house and the author of the original sin that has weighed on them for two centuries. The procession begins with the subject of the portrait himself, the phantom of a Calvinist of the first years of the seventeenth century, wearing a black coat, breeches held in place by a leather strap, and carrying a large sword with a steel hilt. He looks at the painting, which has been kept in this place as a condition of his last will and testament. All is well; he is always obeyed; and yet a cruel thought deepens the furrowed creases of his forehead. He goes away with a sad nod of the head. Then his descendants arrive, hurrying and elbowing one another to get to that faded portrait. All the generations of the family that the novel parades before our eyes follow one another: ancestors of all ages, in their different costumes—ministers in starched Puritan garb, officers in red uniform, a shopkeeper with rolled-up sleeves, wrinkled grandmothers, young and pensive women, powdered gentlemen dressed in brocade—one by one they come to look at and to touch the portrait. A mother lifts her child in her arms so that he might feel it with his small hands. What are these specters seeking? A parchment concealed behind the painted likeness that proves the right of the Pyncheon family to vast lands, to a more than princely property. An enemy fatality, chastisement for their avarice, has deprived them of their title for two hundred years. Judge Pyncheon has vaguely known of the existence of this treasure. In order to acquire it for himself, he comes to threaten his poor cousin Clifford, but just at the moment of committing this crime, the hereditary crime of the family, a hideous death takes him by the throat. His blood suffocates him as it did his uncle, and all of his lineage, even the first of his ancestors. Keeping watch the whole of a long night next to his cadaver, the novelist attends this meeting of the Pyncheon specters.

Hawthorne is a philosopher. His reason is no longer Puritan, but his imagination still is. If his ancestors occasionally come back at night (why shouldn't they, in a country where the dead are not used to leave the living alone?), if they visit his study to flip through his manuscripts, they certainly will not be surprised to find there fat treatises on theology, twenty-volume commentaries (in quarto) on one chapter of the Apocalypse, books (in folio) on the invisible world, learned manuals on the procedures for battling witches. Least surprising of all, they will utter deep groans when they discover that their unworthy grandson writes novels! But I am sure that they will recognize themselves despite all that separates them from their prodigal son. Only hear their regret that he does not turn this precious knowledge of the invisible world to better use!

Let us pursue this comparison of the novelist with the ancient founders of New England. If anything might delight them in their tombs, it would no doubt be that their spirit still reigns in the country that they settled. Which of Hawthorne's tales is the most popular? Perhaps "The Celestial Railroad," that allegorical satire of the laxity of the latter-day Puritans, a parody of old Bunyan, the author of *Pilgrim's Progress*. The famous Anabaptist ironmonger, who lived twelve-and-a-half years in Bedford prison with no other companions besides the Bible and Foxe's *Book of Martyrs*,[5] forged iron fetters by which to live by writing books of piety in which he scattered treasures of imagination and fanaticism. Hawthorne wrote "The Celestial Railroad" in his old manse in Concord, in between a transcendental conversation with Emerson and a boat outing with the poet Ellery Channing. This connection says everything about the two eras.

Since Bunyan, civilization's progress has rendered life incomparably easier, even for a Christian. It has done away with distances, even between heaven and earth. No longer is the City of Destruction the point of departure for Bunyan's arduous pilgrimage—a railway has been laid that leads to the Celestial City. The directors of the Company have thrown up an admirably daring (but flimsy) bridge over the Slough of Despond, into which (according to Bunyan) over twenty thousand cartloads of wholesome instructions had been thrown without making the ground solid. Now one can cross over in an omnibus and with lots of excess baggage. The Evangelist who, in Bunyan's time, gave each pilgrim a mystic scroll is now charged with giving out passes through a window of the ticket-office. One must be grateful to the Company for having perfected these tickets: they are so much more convenient and now fit in one's pockets, and they have secured a promotion for the Evangelist. The most remarkable service that this railway has rendered to religion has been making it fashionable: now the world's rich and carefree can run—what am I saying?—they can fly on the route of salvation in first-class coaches. In other times, few voyagers, almost all of them poor and covered in rags, carrying their heavy burdens, trod the demanding pathway between heaven and earth. Today the most respectable men—men of State, magistrates, financiers, great landowners—now serve as examples. The best of society is on the road. They chatter about everything: the news of the day, business, politics, pleasure. They even have the good taste not to talk about religion. Even the most susceptible unbeliever would not find the slightest pretext to be shocked. Going to Hell is so much harder than attaining salvation! Even more admirable in this arrangement of the new railway is that the directors have gone into partnership with a prince named Beelzebub, whose minions once directed their arrows ceaselessly against the poor pilgrims. Thanks to mutual concessions, a friendly treaty was signed, and the agents of that former enemy are now employed by the Company—

carrying luggage, stoking the firebox, or offering a thousand friendly services to the passengers. We were wrong about them: they are proving themselves to be, as they say, relatively good devils. Oh, Bunyan, Foxe, Bellingham, Endicott!—some martyrs, others tyrants, where are you? Persecutors and persecuted, what has happened to your great grandsons? Some, most of them, are lukewarm and sensual. Not only do they flee the straight and narrow path, but they also insist that it be convenient. They no longer want to go by foot, even to Heaven. They must be carried there as if by enchantment. As long as the names remain the same, they worry little that things have changed. As long as the railway's tickets carry the Puritan stamp, they are happy and do not worry whether the tickets can be redeemed at the end of the trip. In the other descendants (and how few there are!), the flame of religious ardor still burns—but for what? For a philanthropic league or for a temperance society. Today there is no shortage of goodwill; but how hard it is to be persecuted! One has to libel someone to have a martyr's honors. A minister, a partisan of the temperance movement, paints a verbal picture of Hell and the Devil: Hell resembles a known distillery, and the Devil, a certain maker of whisky. The minister is condemned to a month in prison. From his comfortable cell, he lectures on Bunyan and makes his reputation and his fortune. That is today's Puritanism.

But we have not yet touched upon the principal trait of the Puritan spirit in Hawthorne. Here it is. He possesses a melancholy that comes not from life's suffering, painful experiences, or social disapproval, but rather from deep within the soul: a religious melancholy, borne from a vision of Evil. This is Calvinist melancholy, not René's[6] or Childe Harold's[7]—Christian melancholy, almost disproportionate, occasioned by the ineffaceable shadow of sin. To embrace it was a sign of election, it distinguished saints, having been sent from God. It was life, while the sadness of the world was death. In order better to preserve this precious melancholy, Puritans dressed in black. In the same way, Hawthorne's paintings are overlaid with a somber tint. All the passions that stir in his little dramas are inspired by this melancholic vision of human things, as those of true Calvinists are borne out of pious sadness. They had such blind ardor, fierce hate, insatiable anguish, because everywhere they saw only sin. This ardor, this hate, those tortures have vanished, but the constant vision of evil lives on. Hawthorne, no longer a Puritan by faith, is still one in his heart and his imagination. Laws inscribed on tablets of stone are less durable than that those inscribed upon the fleshy tablet of the human heart, where they are written not with ink, but with the essence of the soul.

Our novelists see human nature through different eyes. They see the goodness in man. They can be fatalistic, but only by suppressing, as it were, the evil of human nature, and by displacing it on circumstances, on fate, on society. Thus evil becomes good—our passions are natural things, our vices, virtues. A novelist like Hawthorne is fatalistic in making his characters slaves to Evil. They are born under evil stars, predestinated by their passions, and the author resembles an astrologer who looks for proof in men's lives to justify his horoscopes. Open *The Scarlet Letter* to see what I mean: Hester Prynne, guilty of adultery, recognizes in her child those ardors and follies that were her own, when, at a fatal moment, a spirit descended from on high and sullied her breast with common dirt. The crime of Pearl's birth is a fatal constellation that weighs upon the destiny of this child. Her tastes, her penchants, her destiny will be the logical consequence of adultery. Hawthorne draws everything rigorously from that principle. The Governor and clergymen want to take this child from her mother, as if removing her from Satan's clutches. But the author himself is not far from believing that Pearl is possessed by a demon. She turns on the other children and frightens them with her childish tantrums. A living regret to her mother, she has a mysterious sagacity to guess Hester Prynne's crime. Hester is condemned to wear a red letter on her chest, the first letter of that fatal word that explains her crime. This letter, the color of Hell's fires, tortures and burns her. It is the visible symbol of an ineffaceable evil. And when at last she is able to cast away from her that hideous mark (which has made her suffer like the brand of a burning iron), an invincible compulsion forces her to respect the proof of her condemnation and restore it to her breast.

A third character carries the pain and trace of the same crime: Hester's accomplice, the minister Dimmesdale. He eats away at himself in his vain efforts to erase the evil he has committed. For what purpose are the vigils, the prayers, the scourges, the discipline with which the Calvinist preacher tears apart his chest in secret? How many times, from the pulpit, he is tempted to confess: "I, whom you behold in these black garments of the priesthood,—I, who ascend the sacred desk, and turn my pale face heavenward, taking upon myself to hold communion, in your behalf, with the Most High Omniscience,—I, in whose daily life you discern the sanctity of Enoch,—I, whose footsteps, as you suppose, leave a gleam along my earthly track, whereby the pilgrims that shall come after me may be guided to the regions of the blest,—I, who have laid the hand of baptism upon your children,—I, who have breathed the parting prayer over your dying friends, to whom the Amen sounded faintly from a world which they had quitted,—I, your pastor, whom you so reverence and trust, am utterly a pollution and a lie!" (*SL* 143). A true and dreadful image of crime in Calvinist doctrine—Prometheus' vulture. On one sole day, the adulterous minister is weakened. He throws off the yoke of a ceaseless and inescapable repentance. He sees Hester again and will flee with her. The fight has ended in his heart. What is there to say? Does the drama of adultery begin, the drama of an unyielding passion, that drags us in its wake, across bitter joys, toward a denouement that is terrible for the crime or painful for moral sentiment? No—it is the intimate and curious drama of a soul freed from the power of Evil—even, one might say, from demonic possession. Returning home, after his encounter with Hester, Dimmesdale meets one of his deacons, a good old man whom he has always respected as if he were his superior. Their meeting lasts only two minutes, and he takes great pains to stop himself from expressing who knows what blasphemous thoughts upon the sacrament of communion. He trembles and becomes entirely pale for fear that his mouth will betray his will, and yet he cannot contain his laughter at the idea of the fright that the old man would feel in hearing such impious words. Another incident: an elderly, pious lady finds herself in his path, a poor widow without children, without fortune, whose sole consolation is in her Bible and in some words from her pastor. Would she not blaspheme Heaven if the pastor were not to offer her words that would change her suffering into a source of joy? Dimmesdale no longer knows a word of the Bible. Satan would not be more hard pressed to find a text. Diabolical verses come to him. His mouth murmurs, without his willing it, who knows what pithy, irresistible arguments against the soul's immortality. These funereal words, distilled in the ear of this poor woman, like a subtle poison, might have killed her outright if she had understood them. A third encounter: a newly converted young woman in the minister's chosen flock, a young and candid soul, touched by his recent sermons, resolute in changing the passing pleasures of the world for the everlasting life of Heaven, beautiful and pure like a lily in the garden of Eden. He knows that his own image is enshrined within this stainless heart, that he is there, hidden beneath the white veils of modesty, imparting to religion the warmth of love, and to love, a religious purity. When this young girl approaches, an infernal power whispers something in his ear. If he could only concentrate in one word the venom of Hell, and place in her chaste breast the seed of Evil, to grow there in the dark, to bear one day its sinister fruit! He knows that this is the power he holds over this soul. One look from him could lay waste to the field of innocence, one word plant corruption there. It takes a terrible effort on Dimmesdale's part to pass her in silence, covering up his face with his coat, hurrying his step, pretending not to know her, leaving the poor girl with the scruples of an agitated conscience that betrays her the next day in her swollen eyelids.

I would like to imagine this scene upon the stage: in the theater, we only believe what is human. The supernatural power of Evil is as unbelievable there as that of Good. The conversion of Félix in *Polyeucte* leaves us cold;[8] a demonic possession would leave us laughing. Dimmesdale is nothing else, and yet he strikes us forcefully. The novel is nourished not only by what is, but also by what might be. It has no limits but those of the human soul, and the soul is not content with this world: it still embraces Heaven and Hell.

Death's approach makes the curtain fall, and the soul, little by little letting go of the flesh, knows itself better. Remorse overtakes Dimmesdale: his crime begins burning his heart anew. We see him again, as he has done for many years, painfully holding his hand to his chest. I am afraid to make a profane comparison, but the adulterous minister carries on his heart a stigmata slowly imprinted by the tortures of conscience, comparable to those produced in other times by the enthusiasm of the Catholic faith. This grandson of the Puritans has robbed it from us: a curious petty theft that carries a Calvinist stamp. A marvelous stigma was to the mystical saints of the Middle Ages a celestial favor, a sign of election. Hawthorne makes of it a withering scourge, the burning imprint of Evil. With the death of Dimmesdale, they discover on his left side (where his heart, now icy, once beat) a scarlet letter similar to the one that Hester wears. Was it a piece of fabric that he glued to his side in order to wear, like his accomplice, the pain and the livery of adultery? Was it a real and miraculous stigma? No two witnesses can agree, according to the author.

The great success of *The Scarlet Letter* is proof of the vivacious power of Puritan thought. In this way, the works of the modern imagination have roots in the beliefs of past centuries. In this way, generations past suffered, fought, and struggled to leave ineffaceable traces in the last of their descendants, and we cannot read the works that enthrall men of our times without reminding ourselves of those ancient doctrines that once enthralled their ancestors. We might say that *The Scarlet Letter* is *Indiana,* that it is *Lélia.*[9] Yes, but with the distinction that here (in its French incarnations) we have novels that reject human corruption, and there, one that exaggerates it. Here, vice does not exist; there, it is irreparable. Here, we flatter all that is in man; there, he is damned without mercy.

II. The New Ethos

Now we confront a person who demands his place in this study. He has been described by all travelers who have visited America; he is well known; he is called the Yankee. Therefore, we can sketch his portrait with broad brush-strokes. Imagine the Puritan of two-hundred years ago, covered with a thick layer of the rust of time and money. His life is made up of work, calculation, and frugality. His time is capital, a relationship he understands with marvelous exactitude. His indefatigable labor knows no rest except on Sundays, and two or three holidays imposed upon him as a citizen of a republic. His economy never fails—even in the heart of a virgin forest, he stingily counts the logs of his hearth. His arithmetic weighs men like bags of money. If he comes into wealth, he behaves like an aristocrat who distinguishes nuances of rank slighter than a hair's breadth. If he sinks into bankruptcy and falls to the bottom of the ladder, he picks himself up bruised but resigned, and renews his weary ascent. Do not speak to him of literature or philosophy until his shop is closed. He will gladly converse with you, as long as it costs nothing and doesn't take too much time. On Saturday night, he buys a newspaper and some quack remedy, in order to adorn his mind and purge his body on the one day when his merchandise does not clamor for him. A theological tract for his clergyman and an almanac for him—that is the only literature he finds indispensable! The work of other writers is irrelevant and can scarcely attract his attention. He has heard, now and then, of some successful authors, but these are rare. He waits until books have proven their worth in the marketplace before he bothers with them. Their dollar value increases, but not enough for him to hold them in high esteem. While waiting, he shrugs and says that Americans will never have great poets like the English, or, even more complacently, that America has nothing to envy of England: that after men like Philip Freneau and Brockden Brown, what else could one hope to achieve in poetry or novel-writing? It is not much of a stretch from Puritan to Yankee. One can find a good deal of the first in the second. Dissident sects were founded, maintained, and multiplied by the peddlers that traversed England with their sacks full of merchandise and fanatical sermons. English proselytism was commercial; it still is. The Puritan was a saint-merchant. The Yankee is a merchant who maintains a place for saintliness in his all-important ledger, just so long as it pays.

Against this spirit of materialism and avarice, new ideas are coming to light. We find them in the writings and lives of Emerson, Ripley, Channing, Curtis, Margaret Fuller, and others. For now, we are going to trace the steps of Nathaniel Hawthorne. He is from Young America; he was a Transcendentalist and a Socialist; he is a Democrat. He has passed through all of these doctrines, without spending much time with any of them, but without forgetting them entirely. A germ of utopianism can be found in each of his books, but he is never enslaved by it. He escapes not by virtue of skepticism, weakness, or calculation: rather by virtue of good sense and generosity. In him we find the persistence of the old American ethos. Even his socialism is Puritan. In the old American ethos we discover a new principle: utopianism is by its very nature antipathetic to a young civilization.

On paper, or in our minds, we can invent new social states in Old Europe; however, we have a hard time realizing them. In America, the proof is in the pudding. Would you like to become a Mormon? An Icarian?[10] The path is clear. Imagine a new way of living—big tracts of land are there waiting for their masters. In one of our salons, we can prattle ad nauseam (as they did in the eighteenth century) about Nature's superiority to Civilization. In America the question is moot: the ever-present wilderness swallows it up. Americans have nature at their door. What could be more preposterous than to question it? Hawthorne loves nature: he, too, gives short shrift to social niceties, prejudices, and conventions. He goes back to the Assabet River with his friend Channing, alights in some very rustic spot, kindles his campfire, prepares his meal as a tattooed Indian might have three hundred years ago, and returns in the evening, reconciled with social life. America is a laboratory of the new. Paradoxical republics, impossible societies, combinations, associations—everything is imaginable there, everything ferments there, everything goes into the pot, into the mill. By and by, diversity has been distilled into the common air. Ask, choose—there is something for every taste. Every experience has happened or will happen. There is also no country where projects for the renovation of the human race are more frequent or less durable. Hawthorne was part of a socialist colony at Brook Farm. He is enthusiastic; he hopes for much in the future. But the multitude of dreamers has soured him on utopias. In Concord, the group of empty dreamers who surrounded Emerson, like moths around a flame, alienated Hawthorne from philosophical and humanitarian speculation. We can see that rabble of bizarre men, with their dubious looks, their motley dress, who believe themselves, each and every one, called to regenerate the world—true nightmares to thought and common sense. Such has been the unfortunate influence of that original thinker: those who live too close to him have been besotted by his breath and saturated by false originality. Truth goes to their head like wine. Such is the vulgarity of innovation, the originality of bad taste that would make a man abhor all ideas that predate his own century.

Imagine, in the time of Plato and beyond the gates of Athens, vast lands to be cleared, virgin Nature, a world offering itself to any hands that would take hold of it. It is likely that such a Republic, full of dreams and poetry, would have ignored his Dialogues. In one little corner of the realm,

Antiquity would have seen established a community of chattels, women, and children—lasting for at least one generation (time enough to give rise to little citizens). What would have been the result of this? It is probable that humanity, constrained or misunderstood, would have taken its revenge. Selfish interests, stripped of their appearances, would have fought back one beautiful night; and from this would come divisions, the rupture of society, and the fall of the Republic. Dreaming of riches in the land beyond, every man would have run to claim his share of the Goldrush of drachmas, perhaps even abandoning his wife to the Republic because of the impossibility of reclaiming her as well as his money. That, realistically, is what would have happened with such an experiment. Undoubtedly, Plato's beautiful book would have suffered: the actual Republic would have compromised the imagined Republic. And Antiquity would have found some Nathaniel Hawthorne to recount the greatness and decadence of Platonopolis.

We know that events like this have occurred in the literary and philosophical world of New England. There we find the same situation: the same thoughts of reformation; a democracy attached only to its traditions and to its material needs; men of science and talent who do not have sufficient room for their ambition; a master who is both poet and philosopher and whose name serves as his flag; disciples who have their own ideas, but who come with them to this new Plato, like those who have found precious gems and show them to a jeweler in order to find out their value or to bring out all of their beauty; young, enthusiastic men who leave their professions as poets, journalists, ministers, lawyers to become laborers and workers, spade in hand, for the progress of humanity. Then, likewise, the ruin of this beautiful and generous utopia, this lost illusion: reformers disenchanted with their fellows; the poet, the journalist, the lawyer who return to their half-begun poems, to their indulgent subscribers, to their faithful clients; they all come back to their lecture halls, their picture galleries, their noisy sidewalks, their dinners at the Hotel Albion, the billiard parlor, the concert, the theater. At last, they reclaim their true selves, in which dreams have not obliterated either the moral sense of their Puritan ancestors or the shrewdness and practicality of the Yankee. Then one appears who dares to tell the truth, who first sounds the alarm about utopias, and who tells the story of the communal error.

The Blithedale Romance is such an idealized story. This work is already known in France; we need not waste time describing it. If we wanted to analyze Hawthorne's best novel, we would not choose this one. Still, it is of a piece with the storyteller's other tales. The development of its plot and its characters does not concern us. Instead, let us consider the contest between the modern mercantile spirit and the lingering sense of an older morality: this is what we can draw out from *Blithedale* (and from all of Hawthorne's other works). This is what is important. This is what remains to be said.

The vaguely communistic association that was Brook Farm, attempted sixteen years ago, was a protest against the mercantile spirit that we have already sketched. In other words, its members did what was least Yankee-like in the world: they freely renounced all conveniences in life, all that was comfortable. We make note of this point, because attempts at communism in the Old World have had a different bearing. Those who flirt with communism generally have had nothing to lose, and think that they have everything to gain. The masses are brought to it by poverty and irresistible ambition. Those American communists were of a different order. They left their carpeted offices, well furnished with curtains, where they could have let in the sunlight at will or kept cool in their shadows. They forsook their tables covered with books and periodicals, their offices with their poem or article just begun. They deprived themselves of capacious sideboards, covered with entrées, their entertainments, their teas. And why? To hoe, to reap, to sweat, and to tire themselves out. To serve as chambermaids to a pair of bulls and a dozen cows. To eat a little salted beef earned by the sweat of their brows, to win the honor of fever and consumption by working too hard. A dozen Yankees played at Arcadia, but unlike shepherds at the Opera, they were not dressed in doublets decorated with ribbons, in pants and silk stockings, in court shoes tied with artificial roses:

> In outward show, I humbly conceive, we looked rather like a gang of beggars or banditti, than either a company of honest laboring men, or a conclave of philosophers. Whatever might be our points of difference, we all of us seemed to have come to Blithedale with the one thrifty and laudable idea of wearing out our old clothes. Such garments as had an airing, whenever we strode afield! Coats with high collars and with no collars, broad-skirted or swallow-tailed, and with the waist at every point between the hip and arm-pit; pantaloons of a dozen successive epochs, and greatly defaced at the knees by the humiliations of the wearer before his lady-love;—in short, we were a living epitome of defunct fashions, and the very raggedest presentment of men who had seen better days. It was gentility in tatters. Often retaining a scholar like or clerical air, you might have taken us for the denizens of Grub Street, intent on getting a comfortable livelihood by agricultural labor; or Coleridge's projected Pantisocracy in full experiment; or Candide and his motley associates at work in their cabbage-garden; or anything else that was miserably out at elbows, and

most clumsily patched in the rear. [We might have been sworn comrades to Falstaff's ragged regiment. Little skill as we boasted in other points of husbandry, every mother's son of us would have served admirably to stick up for a scarecrow.] And the worst of the matter was, that the first energetic movement essential to one downright stroke of real labor, was sure to put a finish to these poor habiliments. So we gradually flung them all aside, and took to honest homespun and linsey-woolsey, as preferable, on the whole, to the plan recommended, I think, by Virgil,—'*Ara nudus; sere nudus*'—which as Silas Foster remarked, when I translated the maxim, would be apt to astonish the women-folks.

(BR 63–64)

The moral thinking of the association would not contrast any less than its appearance with the national ethos. It is a not a question of suppressing the spirit of competition that preempts one's neighbor, and wins before him, by force or by ruse, the bread upon which he already has a hand. Competition is the life of modern peoples, but to the American, it is the soul of his life, the blood of his heart, the marrow of his bones. One cannot know the meaning of ruthlessness unless one knows America. That is what was supposedly conquered by the forces of the little community at Brook Farm. A naïve, or even crazy thought, if you will, but a generous one. Those poets wanted to elevate manual labor to the level of their poetry; they tried to spiritualize fatigue and sweat. Labor was supposed to be their prayer and the liturgy of their devotions. Every stroke of the spade was destined to uncover some root of wisdom with its invigorating balm, hidden until now from the light of day. Every time they took a break to wipe the sweat from their brow in the breeze, they were supposed to look heavenward to find some sign of infinite truth. Nature's smile sometimes recognized her elect. But these happy accidents became more and more rare. No matter how much or how often they ploughed, they could not successfully transform such drudgery into sublime thoughts. Instead of absorbing manual labor into the poet's soul, the poet's soul became absorbed by his work, and his thoughts became heavy like the clumps of soil he tilled. In this way, these men of letters, who at first feared themselves not to be workers enough, feared themselves at last to be nothing else.

And that is not all: that mental work, however weighty, was not wholesome. The diverse opinions brewing in their heads made them spin. Blithedale was a sort of Bedlam. After a short stay, they lost the sense of the real. In the middle of the most varied discussions about the new world to be established, they ended up no longer knowing the one in which they were living. Everything became indecisive and irresolute. It seemed as if the earth's crust was no longer solid, and that it could easily shift underfoot. Hawthorne (who hides behind the name of Coverdale) concluded that, were he to live exclusively among these reformers, he would lose his reason. He felt that it was time to return to the world of merchants, professors, men of affairs. He needed to feel the earth under his feet. In the blur of opinions, he was looking for men who had two or three ideas hatched prior to yesterday. The Yankees certainly got their revenge.

Thrown into the middle of this vortex of progress and regeneration, Hawthorne is said to have met women reformers there, too. Brook Farm counted women among its inhabitants, and the storyteller masquerading by the name of Zenobia is the celebrated Margaret Fuller, that imperious muse of Transcendentalism. If the sentiments of the poet Coverdale are indeed those of Hawthorne, one must admit that he came under the powerful charms of that rich nature. Envious of his liberty in a utopia that was, in fact, already partial to residents with whiskers, he nevertheless submitted gladly to the charm of feminine eloquence when she appeared. But this illusion could not last for long. Hawthorne was one of the first to revolt against the pride of that American Aspasia.[11] No one, in that land of Bloomerism,[12] has had a better grasp of petticoat charlatanism and pedantry. Without passion, without bitterness, he saw that women reformers were always women whom destiny or error had diverted from their natural path. At first they stray from it imperceptibly, but necessity pushes them on. They veer off, so to speak, at an inappreciable angle, made as inconspicuous as possible. But, going farther and farther afield, the course they have set for themselves—adjacent to the normal one—opens an abyss between them and society.[13]

How does it happen that these women of the Anglo-Saxon race, a race superstitiously attached to old traditions, should present to us this spectacle of restless ambition and declarations of rights of which our constitutions have never dreamed? Is it because private life is disappearing more and more? In America particularly, public life invades everything: all citizens live under each other's eyes; no one hesitates to call attention to himself or his family. All aspects of private life are broadcast—even domestic matters of the hearth and table. They clamor for public notoriety by every means. A respectable citizen announces in a newspaper that, having a kettle that whistles pleasantly on the stove, he has baptized it after the name of his favorite singer. Every house is open to the public, invited by those who live in them: not even the birth chamber is off limits. Take away from women the domain and the empire of private life that belongs to them, and what do they have left? Let us leave the home. What do we see? Clubs, salons, assemblies where one hears endless chatter but never true conversation. Politics, business, the "institution" (that is to say, slavery), commerce, annexation, compromise, the territories—gracious themes, inexhaustible subjects! From the stuffy talker who holds you by your buttons to the long-winded orator who preaches his gaudy eloquence from the rooftops, you hear nothing else. Take conversation away from the women who are out of the home, and what do you expect them to do? They will become orators, they will make themselves *male* citizens. Their path has already been set out before them. For a very long time, it has been observed, English and American women have been becoming men. By now we can see that the women of that race have had all the virile liberties that decency will tolerate. "We seldom meet with women, now-a-days, and in this country, who impress us as being women at all; their sex fades away and goes for nothing, in ordinary intercourse" (*BR* 17). Eloquence—or, rather, let us say slickness—is the dominant character of the people of the United States. The gift of the nation is the gift of gab. It is an art that is practiced at every hour in every place from one end of North America to another. Is it possible that women would not be jealous of the privilege of masculine loquacity? What? There is only one manner of speaking practiced in this country! And they ask women to abstain?

The American women reformers have only one object: speaking. To fight for the rights of women to be heard, that is the great female reform, the great women's charter. Other rights are only occasions to use this great right. But when one talks, it must be about something.

> "It is my belief [Zenobia says]—yes, and my prophecy, should I die before it happens—that, when my sex shall achieve its rights, there will be ten eloquent women, where there is now one eloquent man. Thus far, no woman in the world has ever once spoken out her whole heart and her whole mind. The mistrust and disapproval of the vast bulk of society throttles us, as with two gigantic hands at our throats! We mumble a few weak words, and leave a thousand better ones unsaid. You let us write a little, it is true, on a limited range of subjects. But the pen is not for woman. Her power is too natural and immediate. It is with the living voice, alone, that she can compel the world to recognize the light of her intellect and the depth of her heart!"
> (*BR* 120)

The woman who silently pursues her life on the straight path made for her by the world's prejudices is the female Yankee. Anything outside of her rut, anything new always shocks and displeases her. She takes cover as soon as her traditions are wounded. That is what most of those pale and somewhat sad women from New England are like, great granddaughters of Puritan matrons, arrived long ago from England, with drab clothing, but with a more vigorous temperament and more blooming complexions. From the breast of this timid generation springs Margaret Fuller, the Madame de Staël of the United States. To what extent is she represented by Zenobia? The author has given her beauty and weaknesses that Fuller did not have, while preserving her ambition, her disdain, her caprice. He has profited from his memory of her eloquence. Perhaps even the tragic ending (in which Zenobia drowns, achieving neither the goals of her ambitions nor the object of her love) is destined to recall Margaret's tragic shipwrecked drama: her arrival from Italy and capsizing in sight of land, lost at sea with her husband, her child, her manuscripts—all of her life—her current love and her ambitions of yesteryear. Despite several attempts to throw off the reader, the public was not mistaken in seeing Fuller's image.

Male and female Yankees—that is what American society is made up of, following in the footsteps of our philosophers and socialists. Everyone thought that there was much to change in intellect, in life, in institutions. Some went all the way; others stopped midway. Some established Brook Farm; others were happy to visit there on a few occasions. Today, enthusiasm has cooled. The school has dispersed. Those who strayed farthest are also those who distance themselves most from their error. Hawthorne is among these. Should we say he loves what he has consigned to the fire? Among all the illusions to which he attached himself, disgusted with vulgar reality, does anything remain but a distrust of his first faith and a regret for having aspired to a better ideal? He gives us the residue of his enthusiasm in the last chapter of *The Blithedale Romance*. These words reveal a sincere soul, a heart without venom, half-impassioned, like so many these days. They are still the words of a democrat, but a democrat who needs some rest. As with so many today, his faith is tepid, almost nonchalant:

> I by no means wish to die. Yet, were there any cause, in this whole chaos of human struggle, worth a sane man's dying for, and which my death would benefit, then—provided, however, the effort did not involve an unreasonable amount of trouble—methinks I might be bold to offer up my life. If Kossuth, for example, would pitch the battle-field of Hungarian rights within an easy ride of my abode, and choose a mild, sunny morning, after breakfast, for the conflict, Miles Coverdale would gladly be his man, for one brave rush upon the leveled bayonets. Farther than that, I should be loth to pledge myself.

(*BR* 246–47)

III. The Author's Manner

It is not contingent upon an author to give one shape or another to his thoughts. The needs and habits of the public predetermine the occasions it will devote to its novelists, even the length of its attention. America's interest in its writers is fleeting. The American public is like Judge Pyncheon, whose busy itinerary fills his whole day. He has no need to carry a watch in his pocket, because his internal chronometer ticks perfectly and never needs winding. He sets aside half an hour for his family, or almost that, leaving margin for the presence of women, whose garrulity demands it: they use a hundred words when fifty would suffice. Next on his date book comes a list of things to do. See a broker who will invest several thousand dollars (spare change, really) in snug securities, paying heavy interest. Half an hour later, attend an auction at such and such a street, at such and such a number—a lot that would fill out his property perfectly. Four-score years ago, the parcel was alienated from the Pyncheons; but ever since he was old enough to reason, the Judge has been waiting for the moment when he could buy it back. Be prompt: you don't want to arrive to the sound of the gavel fatally marking a prior sale. Buy a horse to replace the one no longer worthy of a worthy American, accustomed to breaking his neck in pursuit of money. If all this can be accomplished expeditiously, attend a meeting of a charitable society, whose name he has not written down, a small detail forgotten amid the multitude of things to be done. If there is time, go to the cemetery to have a family tombstone replaced, possibly that of Mrs. Pyncheon, who passed away, a good woman, in spite of her rattled nerves and her unreasonable taste for coffee. She departed without even a prayer—why haggle now over a piece of marble? Even death has its rightful place in his crowded date book. The Judge will find a moment to cry, provided that his tears are dry before his appointment with a political committee. By and by, give orders to expedite the delivery of fruit trees (a rare variety) to your country home. What marvelous peaches you will eat next Fall! Be punctual for the committee meeting where you will endorse one of the party's candidates: the fate of the country is at stake! Pay a visit to the widow of one your old friends (who has a *very* pretty daughter). Attend a dinner where there will be much conversation after the remains of turtle, salmon, English mutton, and roast beef. Go home with ambitious plans and a huge headache, go to sleep while planning out tomorrow. That is the life of an American. How can literature find a place in an itinerary so crowded? Only by making itself modest, by shrinking down to fit in a small volume. That is why short stories and novellas are so popular.

From this we can hazard a generalization: a lot of American novels are only diffuse short stories. Hawthorne has written a multitude of tales, and even his novels are tales. It seems as if the author's imagination, accustomed to this mold, did not want to change, even when celebrity and the assurance of having a readership permitted him broader scope. *The Scarlet Letter* and *Blithedale* present very few incidents; *The House of the Seven Gables* hardly has any more. There are barely two or three situations: just enough to construct a short story, but by superadding philosophy, feeling, and humor, Hawthorne has made a novel out of it. Hawthorne is never diffuse because he is a thinker and an artist. But he is like a poet who conceives a drama in one act and then wants to spread it into three. However, he does not take sufficient trouble to invent incidents, to complicate the action. With what, then, does he fill this enlarged framework? This leads us to speak of a second characteristic of the author.

After busy-ness, one of the most salient traits of the American is curiosity. He lives on the run, but not in a straight line; he loves adventure. Everything that strikes him has a claim to his attention, and he feeds at the breast of a nature that always brings novelties to him. He also has a genius for details and particulars. He is an intrepid observer. What are the formulas we most often encounter in American literature? "A skilled observer would have easily surmised from this person's movements, etc. . . ." "Nothing in this room would have jumped to the observer's eyes, but soon, etc. . . ." The word *spiritual* is always on the lips of spirited people (or spilling from their pens)—they can't help it—in the same way that curious people speak without end of penetrating observers. But there are different kinds of observation: the one of which we speak delights in infinite detail. For example, if there is an old family in decline, as in *The House of the Seven Gables,* the author analyzes this decadence down to the chicken coop, where three or four emaciated descendants of some aristocratic hen reside. The rooster, no larger than a partridge perched on two little stilts, struts with a dignity that recalls his many forefathers. His two wives have grown to the size of a quail. But all interest lies in a tiny chicken who would seem still to be able to make a home for himself in his egg, but whose antiquated, withered, and wizened air make him the worthy founder of this lineage. All the perfections and all the singularities of his race are summed up in this little body. His mother, thus, looks at him as if he were the one chicken of the world, necessary to the existence of the universe. No lesser sense of this runt's importance could explain how she ruffles her feathers (until she is twice her normal size) and flies in your face if you even look at this child of gallinaceous ancestry. What nervous clucking when he is hidden from sight by tall grass! What pleasurable cooing when he is back under her wing! By degrees, the *observer* comes to feel as much interest in this little fowl as its mother. This chicken is no more than a symbol of the noble and funereal Pyncheon household, an enigma covered in feathers, a mystery hatched from an egg.

Hawthorne, the prototypical American, is one of "those storytellers who have never seen anything except with a microscope."[14] He says through Zenobia in *The Blithedale Romance* that he looks at things through opera glasses, like all the other poets of his day.[15] Yet, his glasses do not stop at the exterior surfaces of things. They resemble the pince-nez of Delphine Gay in the novel of the same name: they penetrate through to the soul.[16] But in surveying the recesses of the conscience, they also reveal the train of thought. Hawthorne does not simply disclose the private ruminations of his hero, but (what is more) how he perceives them. His glasses have no magical or inexplicable powers like a talisman. Rather, by directing his magnifying glass at the fleeting expressions of the face, the mysterious relations of our physical attitude and our moral state, the timbre of our voice and the music of our soul, the storyteller comes to grasp the birth and torment of feelings, much as the biologist examines microbes in a drop of water. Hawthorne has all the curiosity of a physiognomist and all the patience of a psychologist. His method is too experimental not to cast a chilling pall over the drama. In order to move the reader, a writer must work sympathy and tears into a novel; if an author wants warm tears to fall on the reader's heart, he must work quickly or they might freeze up. I fear that Hawthorne may have painted himself when he has Holgrave say these words in *The House of the Seven Gables:*

> "Undoubtedly . . . I do feel an interest in this antiquated, poverty-stricken old maiden lady; and this degraded and shattered gentleman—this abortive lover of the Beautiful. A kindly interest too, helpless old children that they are! But you have no conception what a different kind of heart mine is from your own. It is not my impulse—as regards these two individuals—either to help or hinder; but to look on, to analyze, to explain matters to myself, and to comprehend the drama which, for almost two hundred years, has been dragging its slow length over the ground, where you and I now tread. If permitted to witness the close, I doubt not to derive a moral satisfaction from it, go matters how they may."
>
> (*HSG* 216–17)

Hawthorne derives pleasure in evoking touching dramas and looking on with a cold heart. The reason for this is that he yields to commiseration less than to curiosity. He is American to the core. Zenobia expresses this, when she says to the poet Coverdale:

> "[I]t has gratified me to see the interest which you continue to take in my affairs! I have long recognized you as a sort of transcendental Yankee, with all the native propensity of your countrymen to investigate matters that come within their range, but rendered almost poetical, in your case, by the refined methods which you adopt for its gratification."
>
> (*BR* 162)

Zenobia says it all: Hawthorne's optic is the magnifying glass of Transcendentalism.

This method has its advantages. It gives something of the Ideal to the novelist's conceptions. Especially in America, the Ideal is something precious and rare—no less in demand for its scarcity!—because America was just born yesterday. Some look for it in the novel of the sea or the novel of the frontier. Strangely for us, others see the Ideal in Europe (which we would not have guessed so poetic). Hawthorne has found his own Ideal in a philosophical view of objects. This method also has some disadvantages: the pace of the narrative slows to a crawl; every topic invites digression; the illusion of reality is suspended at every moment. Standing at the counter where she has replaced her elderly cousin, Phoebe sees a relative enter whom she does not know—Judge Pyncheon. "'Is it possible that you are Phoebe Pyncheon,'" he inquires, "'only child of my dear cousin and classmate . . . ? Yes; yes; we must be better acquainted! I am your kinsman, my dear'" (*HSG* 117–18). In response to these words, Phoebe curtsies. The judge leans forward across the counter to place a paternal kiss on Phoebe's cheek. Unfortunately, Phoebe backs away at this moment, and leaves her respectable relative, with his body sprawled on the counter, lips pursed outward, to experience the pleasure that Ixion must have felt kissing the void.[17] The author takes this critical moment to create a study of Judge Pyncheon's face and Phoebe's involuntary repugnance. All sorts of expressions succeed one another in the physiognomy of this giver of kisses. First, his face displays a satisfaction as wide and as massive, as it were, as the person of the Judge himself. Then, as quickly as a country landscape darkens when a thundercloud advances, his face becomes cold, hard, implacable. Next, his demeanor abruptly reveals an unexpected resemblance to a portrait that hangs in a lower chamber of the House of the Seven Gables (and at which Phoebe cannot look without trembling): the portrait of an ancestor that prophesies all the grim inflexibility in the face of this descendant. Herein are reflected all the weaknesses, the bad passions, the vile tendencies, the moral maladies that lead to crime: all of them perpetuated from generation to generation (with corresponding facial traits) by an inheritance inscribed on the book of destiny. At last, the nimbus cloud breaks up, the fatal resemblance fades away. Then comes a smile that operates on poor, trembling Phoebe like a warm ray of sunshine on a flower or the entrancing gaze of a snake upon a defenseless bird: "'I like it much, my little cousin! You are a good child, and know how to take care of yourself. A young girl—especially if she be a very pretty one—can never be too chary of her lips'" (*HSG* 119–20). The scene is over, but two pages of psychology, during which a character is left in such a difficult and inconvenient position, is a stretch. We prefer the long speeches that Homer's heroes give when they already have their arms raised in combat.

The most remarkable use of this psychological method is the long and interesting study of an intelligence happily gifted in principle, but ruined by the outrages of unhappiness and injustice, and waking up from its lethargy through the feeling of the beautiful, by an unexpected communion with life and youth. We mean to speak of Clifford and Phoebe in *The House of the Seven Gables,* the book to which we return often because it is Hawthorne's best, and about which we have the privilege of speaking more or less first.[18] Even the title is a Puritan idea: anyone can see that the seven gables of the doomed mansion are meant to signify the seven deadly sins. Founded on avarice and transgression, the house has been haunted periodically by avarice and transgression. At the present moment, an elderly Clifford lives in it with his elderly sister, Hepzibah. Superstitious terrors, ghosts, and memories of old crimes reside there with them. But they dare not leave. Submitting to their destiny, they become their own jailers. On circumstantial evidence, Clifford had been accused of killing his uncle; he would have been condemned if it were not for the influence of his cousin, Judge Pyncheon. But the truth is that the Judge placed the blame of that frightful accusation on an innocent person, seeking to destroy his cousin's reputation while enhancing his own. That uncle, however, died of an apoplectic attack, a genetic condition in the family passed down ever since the original patriarch of the Pyncheon line first atoned for his crime by that horrible death. Clifford's reason is wrecked by this unhappiness. With a past that was painful (and, in others' eyes, criminal and bloody), with a future that is nothing more than a great and terrifying void, for him the present can only be peopled by terrors, sorrows, and ghosts. He lives in a house that weighs upon him like one of those capes of lead that Dante placed upon the shoulders of certain of the damned.[19] How can poor Hepzibah, his sister, with her incurable nostalgia and her equally incurable scowl (both fatal and hereditary) hope to restore his mental balance and the health of his soul? How can Clifford not be crazy?

Have you not met the man we have been describing?—do you not see all around you, dear reader (even, perhaps, in your own person) people who find only unhappiness and suffering in what, for others, would be a source of happiness and peace? They are forever fighting against the current: in whatever broad social channel fate has thrown them, inevitably they cannot go with the flow and the torrent passes over their body. Gladly they destroy all the promise of their intelligence, the flower of their youth. They starve themselves of the very food essential to their elite nature; they are the instruments of their own torture, and prepare with their own hands the poison with which they will nourish themselves at the very start of life's grand banquet. It is easy for them to arrange a passable existence: they accustom themselves to alienation, solitude, torture. Let us not mock these poor souls, and let us not say, with superior wisdom, that there is an art to being unhappy. Let us be sympathetic to them. These are the souls whose bitter chalice is never empty, because they have a cruel need bring it to their lips. Its bitterness never goes away for them. They brood over it slowly, perpetually, so well that they eventually succumb to it. Others drown their reason in the cup of pleasure: they die, distilling until the end life's absinthe.

Such a man is Clifford. His whole life is a relentless study of the secret of suffering, and the fruit of this long effort is a sort of lunacy. To speak in Transcendentalist terms, he is the Representative Man of all souls devoted to unhappiness. The term comes from Hawthorne himself. He has not shrunk from applying to a character in his novel the philosophical term applied by Emerson to the greatest men of history. Clifford, creature of his fantasy, seems to him worthy of analysis, as it were, in the same way that Plato, Swedenborg, Montaigne, Shakespeare, Napoleon, and Gœthe appealed to Emerson.[20] Is there any other trait that can better establish the importance that the storyteller attaches to his fiction? Those of us who are critics are sometimes touched by a scruple in the presence of these English or American works of the imagination: "Let us not take these novels too seriously," we are tempted to say to ourselves; "are they anything more than games of fancy played for the amusement of others? Can we really hope to find in them the expression of a society, the faithful mirror of a country, an epoch, and a people?" Well, yes! There are some pages that reassure us, that require us to treat these works without disdain or levity. Here is a very distinguished writer, a *philosophe*, who makes with his own hands an imaginary being, and sets out to study him as if he were an historical figure. He employs the same zeal and curiosity to explain Clifford that one would expect from any other case history of dementia (the poet Cowper, say, or King George III). Here, he begs the reader's indulgence: "The author needs great faith in his reader's sympathy; else he must hesitate to give details so minute, and incidents apparently so trifling . . ." (*HSG* 150). Elsewhere, when Phoebe's presence restores to the old man a smile and a glimmer of reason, the author says, "But we strive in vain to put the idea into words. No adequate expression of the beauty and profound pathos with which it impresses us, is attainable" (*HSG* 142).

The arrival of little cousin Phoebe in the doomed house produces an effect just like that of a drop of rose oil sprinkled in a large chest crammed with all kinds of things—even mourning clothes. An unexpected balm permeates the darkness, lends its fragrance to all those souvenirs, dispels the air of melancholy. Phoebe's beauty, her voice, her youth remind her old cousin Clifford of the notes of some forgotten melody, a tune familiar in his youth. In Phoebe's presence he becomes a child again, he begins life anew. Hawthorne's delicate analysis of Clifford's regeneration is charming, as little by little his mind loses its somber cast through the simple incidents of the drama. His cousin the Judge, inheritor of the Puritan physiognomy and of the Pyncheons' hypocritical avarice, receives his punishment just at the moment when he is about to complete his crime. Persuaded that Clifford knows the secret of a treasure passed down by a common ancestor, the Judge threatens these vulnerable inhabitants of the House of the Seven Gables if they do not agree to reveal its whereabouts to him. At this moment the blood of the Pyncheon family rises to the throat of their worthy descendant and strangles him. This death lifts thirty years of anguish, degradation, and insanity from the breast of the poor lunatic. He then finds the courage to flee the voluntary prison with his sister. Poor frightened owls, they escape from their darkness to the streets, where the townspeople are stunned to see them. As if by instinct, they run to the train station, jump into a car, and depart without knowing where—so long as it is far from their tyrannical hypocrite, far from that fatal house, far from damnation, from pain and madness. Clifford's flight affords Hawthorne one of his most charming chapters; delightfully, we see him regain his senses and rediscover the happiness of breathing, of living, of letting his imagination run free.

Next to the Pyncheons (the sly persecutor, and the fallen persecuted), next to the vivacious Phoebe (a young, positive, and steady girl—descended from Puritan stock but brightened by a golden thread of gayety), the author places Holgrave, the daguerreotype artist. He is the image and the model of an adventurer in a country where everyone is invited to do the same. He is Gil Blas in a Puritan and democratic country.[21] He has held every job that an honest man can have, and, thus, he has also been a man of letters.

He is only twenty-two years old. He was first a country schoolmaster, then a salesman in a general store. From there, or perhaps at the same time, he was the publisher of a political newspaper. Before long, he was a peddler of cologne and other essences for a Connecticut manufactory; then, by and by, he practiced dentistry—just another episode in the drama of his life. As a supernumerary officer on an ocean liner, he visited Europe and found a way, before coming back, to see Italy, a part of France, and Germany. In a more recent period, we find him in a Fourierist association, and, lastly, lecturing on animal magnetism. Today, he works with daguerreotypes, but is no more interested in this than in his other professions. There is one thing, however, that he holds dear: he has retained his conscience, and we are grateful to him for it, because after so many various adventures, it would be difficult to keep.

Holgrave is from the generation that believes that the world is not made of granite, and that it is easy for him to change its form. The human race—an old and evil subject, with grey hair and a wrinkled complexion, more decrepit than respectable—appears to him in the shape of a beautiful adolescent, capable of infinite progress and every virtue. He has reason to believe that we are not condemned to mope around an old and unhappy rut. It would be better for the young man never to have been born, and for the aged man to die, than to believe in such a pitiful doctrine. But his mistake is to think that the time in which he is living is destined, by a flattering privilege, to strip off Antiquity's rags and to furnish itself in a brand new outfit, instead of replacing its garments (as our fathers did, bit by bit) by means of mending. He believes himself to be a thinker. His intellect is shallow; he has barely been educated; but his nature is forceful. His culture is incomplete, but sturdy; his philosophy is rude, coarse and vague; but these traits are accompanied by a practical mind, a discreet ambition, an ardor for human progress, a distrust of old institutions; in him are faith and infidelity. With what he has—and what he lacks—Holgrave is the modern American type, the Representative Man of generations who will call themselves tomorrow the Republic of the United States. Let us hear some of the words of this American Gil Blas:

> "Shall we never, never get rid of this Past<?>[!" *cried he, keeping up the earnest tone of his preceding conversation.*] It lies upon the Present like a giant's dead body! In fact, the case is just as if a young giant were compelled to waste all his strength in carrying about the corpse of the old giant, his grandfather, who died a long while ago, and only needs to be decently buried. Just think a moment; and it will startle you to see what slaves we are to by-gone times—to Death, if we give the matter the right word!
>
> [*"But I do not see it,"* observed Phoebe.

"For example, then," continued Holgrave,] [A] Dead Man, if he happens to have made a will, disposes of wealth no longer his own; or, if he die intestate, it is distributed in accordance with the notions of men much longer dead than he. A Dead Man sits on all our judgment-seats; and living judges do but search out and repeat his decisions. We read in Dead Men's books! We laugh at Dead Men's jokes, and cry at Dead Men's pathos! We are sick of Dead Men's diseases, physical and moral, and die of the same remedies with which dead doctors killed their patients! We worship the living Deity according to Dead Men's forms and creeds. Whatever we seek to do, of our own free motion, a Dead Man's icy hand obstructs us! Turn our eyes to what point we may, a Dead Man's white, immitigable face encounters them, and freezes our very heart! And we must be dead ourselves before we can begin to have our proper influence on our own world, which will then be no longer our world, but the world of another generation, with which we shall have no shadow of a right to interfere. I ought to have said, too, that we live in Dead Men's houses; as, for instance, in this of the Seven Gables!"

"And why not," said Phoebe, "so long as we can be comfortable in them?"

"But we shall live to see the day, I trust," went on the artist, "when no man shall build his house for posterity. Why should he? He might just as reasonably order a durable suit of clothes—leather, or gutta percha, or whatever else lasts longest—so that his great-grandchildren should have the benefit of them, and cut precisely the same figure in the world that he himself does. If each generation were allowed and expected to build its own houses, that single change, comparatively unimportant in itself, would imply almost every reform which society is now suffering for. I doubt whether even our public edifices—our capitols, state-houses, court-houses, city-hall, and churches—ought to be built of such permanent materials as stone or brick. It were better that they should crumble to ruin once in twenty years, or thereabouts, as a hint to the people to examine into and reform the institutions which they symbolize.

[*"How you hate everything old!"* said Phoebe in dismay.—*"It makes me dizzy to think of such a shifting world!*

"I certainly love nothing mouldy," answered Holgrave. *"Now this old Pyncheon-house! Is it a wholesome place to live in, with its black shingles, and the green moss that shows how damp they are?—its dark, low-studded rooms?—its grime and sordidness, which are the crystallization on its walls of the human breath, that has been drawn and exhaled here, in discontent and anguish? The house ought to be purified with fire—purified till only its ashes remain!"*

"Then why do you live in it?" asked Phoebe, a little piqued.

> "Oh, I am pursuing my studies here; not in books, however!" replied Holgrave.] The house, in my view, is expressive of that odious and abominable Past, with all its bad influences[, *against which I have just been declaiming. I dwell in it for awhile, that I may know the better how to hate it.* By-the-by, did you ever hear the story of Maule, the wizard, and what happened between him and your immeasurably great-grandfather?"
>
> "Yes indeed!" said Phoebe. "I heard it long ago from my father, and two or three times from my Cousin Hepzibah, in the month that that I have been here. She seems to think that all the calamities of the Pyncheons began from that quarrel with the wizard, as you call him. And you, Mr. Holgrave, look as if you thought so too! How singular, that you should believe what is so very absurd, when you reject many things that are a great deal worthier of credit!"
>
> "I do believe it," said the artist seriously—"not as a superstition, however—but as proved by unquestionable facts, and as exemplifying a theory.] Now, see! Under those seven gables, at which we now look up—and which old Colonel Pyncheon meant to be the house of his descendants, in prosperity and happiness, down to an epoch far beyond the present—under that roof, through a portion of three centuries, there has been perpetual remorse of conscience, a constantly defeated hope, strife amongst kindred, various misery, a strange form of death[, *dark suspicion, unspeakable disgrace,*]—all, or most of which calamity, I have the means of tracing to the old Puritan's inordinate desire to plant and endow a family. To plant a family! This idea is at the bottom of most of the wrong and mischief which men do. The truth is, that, once in every half-century, at longest, a family should be merged into the great, obscure mass of humanity, and forget all about its ancestors. Human blood, in order to keep its freshness, should run in hidden streams, as the water of an aqueduct is conveyed in subterranean pipes.
>
> (HSG 183–85)

We should say that, once married to Phoebe, Holgrave regrets inheriting a country house that is not made of stone. The rich democrat becomes conservative.

For those who would like to get to know the principal gifts of this author in a single book, we confidently recommend *The House of the Seven Gables*. Here are brought together all the traces of the old Puritan ethos, the new ethos (in its successive forms), and the most striking example of the psychological manner of the storyteller: in this one book, as we see it, we find Hawthorne complete. Once a Transcendentalist in his theories and his political opinions, artistically he is still one in the conception of his characters. After having influenced his convictions and his life, these doctrines only leave traces in his novels, but they give them their particular originality.

Earlier we imagined America as a hypothetical form of Plato's Republic. What would have become of this platonic Union if, in one of those unanticipated movements that such tentative loyalties might have provoked in Athens, the slaves awoke and cried out for liberty? Would it have declared itself to be for or against the slaves? Would it open its eyes to this new light, or, like Aristotle several years later, would it declare slavery to be an inevitable fact of human societies? There is evidence that this colony of Platonists would have divided, some pushing to extremes the logic of their ideas and the boldness of their temperament, others faithful to the interest of the State and to traditional ideas. That is what has happened to the American philosophical school. The question of slavery, the Sphinx of American society, has placed itself at the center of the Republic at a crossroads where all paths end. No one can avoid it and everyone must have an opinion about it. Each one of them has responded in his own manner. Some, and among them the head himself, have become abolitionists or "free soilers." Others, having made so many other concessions to the Yankees, have remained loyal to their party and acknowledge rightful ownership of slaves. The former are in the opposition, the others have the confidence and favor of the government. Uncle Sam (the popular name of the latter) reserves its spoils for them, including Hawthorne. An elegant and quick biography of Franklin Pierce (an honorable service rendered to a friend, and a consecration given by a popular pen to the politics of the Compromise) earned the novelist the lucrative position of consul at Liverpool, which he has held for four years. Never has a literary prize been so handsomely awarded. All the same, we can hope that slavery will not be for the United States what the hereditary curse is in *The House of the Seven Gables,* an incurable evil to which the Puritan ethos resigns itself perhaps too easily. "Slavery," says Hawthorne in his biography of Pierce, "is an evil beyond human remedy. Only Providence can efface it."[22] All in good time, Hawthorne urges; but would it not be wise and human to clear the path? Do not the partisans of the Compromise and all the other laws protecting slavery make the work of Providence that much more difficult?

Revue contemporaine (30 May 1857)

Notes

1. Étienne alludes to Charles Baudelaire's *Flowers of Evil* (*Les fleurs du mal*), first published in the *Revue des Deux Mondes* and then assembled later for publication as a collection by Auguste Poulet-Malassis in June 1857.
2. Roman gods of the household.
3. First published in *The Snow-Image, and Other Twice-told Tales* (1851).
4. First published in *Mosses from an Old Manse* (1846).
5. Published in 1563, this work is an account written by English Protestant John Foxe as a chronicle of those precursors to the Protestant Reformation.
6. Étienne refers to François-René de Chateaubriand's (1768–1848) *René* (1802), whose main character epitomized the ideal young Romantic hero.
7. Lord Byron's *Childe Harold's Pilgrimage*, published between 1812 and 1818, chronicles a young man's life and frustrations at the onset of the nineteenth century.
8. Pierre Corneille's (1606–84) classical drama about Christian persecution in Armenia was first performed in 1643.
9. *Indiana* (1831) and *Lélia* (1833; 1839) were both novels of passion written by George Sand.
10. Followers of Frenchman Étienne Cabet's (1788–1856) utopian socialist philosophies. They set up a community in Nauvoo, Illinois, during the middle of the nineteenth century. The movement disbanded at the end of the nineteenth century.
11. Aspasia (470 B.C.–400 B.C.), a woman involved in the political sphere in Athens.
12. This remark refers to Amelia Jenks Bloomer (1818–94), an American advocate for women's rights and temperance, best remembered for her campaign to remedy the deleterious effects of restrictive feminine fashion, preferring loose-fitting trousers ("bloomers") to corseted dresses and skirts.
13. Étienne's gloss bears remarkable resemblance to a suppressed passage in Hawthorne's *French and Italian Notebooks*, notoriously published by Julian Hawthorne in his 1885 memoir, *Nathaniel Hawthorne and His Wife*. Hawthorne's reflections on Margaret Fuller provoked a firestorm of criticism from her defenders, but their sting has left a mark on much later criticism of both writers. Trying to understand and explain Fuller's possibly dubious relationship with Giovanni Ossoli, an Italian revolutionary (whom Hawthorne considered a "boor," a "hymen without the intellectual spark"), the novelist was led to conclude:

> As from her towards him, I do not understand what feeling there could have been, except it were purely sensual; as from him towards her, there could hardly have been even this, for she had not the charm of womanhood. But she was a woman anxious to try all things, and fill up her experience in all directions; she had a strong and coarse nature, too, which she had done her utmost to refine, with infinite pains, but which of course could only be superficially changed. The solution of the riddle lies in this direction; nor does one's conscience revolt at the idea of thus solving it; for—at least, this is my own experience—Margaret has not left, in the hearts and minds of those who knew her, any deep witness for her integrity and purity. She was a great humbug; of course with much talent, and much moral reality, or else she could not have been so great a humbug.

But she had stuck herself full of borrowed qualities, which she chose to provide herself with, but which had no root in her.
(Centenary Edition, vol. XIV, *The French and Italian Notebooks,* 155–56)

14. A quote from *Le dépositaire infidèle* or *The Faithless Depositary* (Book IX, Fable I) in *Les fables* (1668), the renowned work of Jean de la Fontaine (1621–85).

15. In chapter 20 of *The Blithedale Romance,* Zenobia says to Miles Coverdale, "'You are a poet—at least, as poets go now-a-days—and must be allowed to make an opera-glass of your imagination, when you look at women'" (Centenary Edition, vol. III, 170).

16. Étienne refers here to "*Le lorgnon,*" by Madame de Girardin (Bruxelles: Hauman, Cattoir et Cie, 1837). Delphine de Girardin née Gay (1804–55) was a French author of contemporary sketches who wrote under the pen name "Vicomte Delaunay."

17. Ixion, from Greek mythology, who slept with a cloud resembling Zeus' wife Hera while visiting Olympus.

18. In "Poètes et romanciers américains: Nathaniel Hawthorne" (1852), E.-D. Forgues makes brief mention of *The House of the Seven Gables.*

19. Dante envisions this curse for Hypocrites in Canto XXIII of the *Inferno.*

20. Emerson devotes a chapter to each of these figures in *Representative Men* (1850).

21. Gil Blas, the main character of the picaresque *Histoire de Gil Blas de Santillane* (1715–35), written by Alain-René Lesage (1668–1747).

22. Étienne paraphrases the most notorious passage from Hawthorne's campaign biography. Slavery, Hawthorne writes, is

> one of those evils which divine Providence does not leave to be remedied by human contrivances, but which, in its own good time, by some means impossible to be anticipated, but of the simplest and easiest operation, when all its uses shall have been fulfilled, it causes to vanish like a dream. There is no instance, in all history, of the human will and intellect having perfected any great moral reform by methods which it adapted to that end; but the Progress of the world, at every step, leaves some evil or wrong on the path behind it, which the wisest of mankind, of their own set purpose, could never have found the way to rectify. Whatever contributes to the great cause of good, contributes to all its subdivisions and varieties; and, on this score, the lover of his race, the enthusiast, the philanthropist of whatever theory, might lend his aid to put a man, like the one before us, in the leadership of the world's affairs.
> (Centenary Edition, vol. XXIII, *The Life of Franklin Pierce,* in *Miscellaneous Prose and Verse,* 352)

IX

Émile Montégut

"A Pessimistic Novelist in America" (1860)

The solemn feast days of literary criticism are becoming rare, and it seems Providence has decreed that, in the future, they will become rarer still. The critic's work and his research will not be altogether without reward, but typically he will have to make do with small joys and modest pleasures—those that come from perusing ingenious essays, amiable stories, and meritorious poems. Only after long intervals can he savor a greater and more congenial pleasure—the best satisfaction for a mind dedicated to study—namely, to recommend a beautiful unknown work to the public, an original talent that seeks new byways, a man of genius who has discovered and explored some new region of the soul and heart. Welcome, then, is such an explorer (from wherever he comes), as is the report from the territory he has discovered and visited (even if it be a cavern or an abandoned cemetery!). Welcome is the true talent in whatever form he appears and with whatever subject he takes up! If talent has always been the rarest gift bestowed upon Adam's descendants, never has nature shown herself to be more greedy than at the present hour. "Why should this gift not be rare, and why should nature not be stingy?" we ask. Nature weakens herself every time she makes this concession to mankind: it is a part of herself she abandons, a part of her life cut off, a force from which she retreats. A man of real talent is, as the saying goes, a son of life in whose veins runs that music of the blood (as a great Spanish playwright has said) that rings out across all the generations of the same race.[1] He can be identified by the ties of his soul and heart to all those invisible relatives whose mysterious voices he hears singing inside of him—so well identified that when he thinks he is explaining only his feelings, in reality he uncovers life's secrets, and when he believes he is disclosing his individual thoughts, he uncovers nature's mysteries. The critic who knows of what real talent is made and from what illustrious origin it comes is not then surprised that this gift is so rare. Moreover, when he perceives the marvelous glimmer of light that announces talent or genius, the critic hastens to run toward it because he knows that to penetrate the soul of a man of talent is to uncover the secrets of nature herself. He gladly abandons his ferule and his aesthetic scales, he throws off his professor's gown, and agrees for a time to become once again an ignorant schoolboy, a naïve child. Attending to a real man of genius is like attending a new academy: the critic makes his way there, not with the idea that he will complete a task, but rather with the conviction that his experience will be pleasant and that he will receive an important lesson. Before embarking on this new voyage, he says to himself, "What shall I learn that is new?"—not "what conventional warrant shall I promulgate?" or "what laurels shall I bestow?" He knows that to hold men who are truly gifted accountable to the dictates of ordinary justice is to do them profound injustice. The only honor that is worthy of their merit is, at the utmost, understanding—or even, possibly, love.

It is to one of those rare fetes of literary criticism to which Nathaniel Hawthorne invites us yet again. With him we are in the presence of a man who does not worry about being judged, one who, I believe, does not worry much more about being loved, but who demands above all to be understood and interpreted. Without a doubt he cares very little about our sympathy or even our admiration: rather, he implores us to understand all the pains he has taken, to do justice to all his little labors of love in his works. If you were to express your admiration to him, your praise would leave him cold—possibly would not even provoke a response (unless, that is, he preferred to advise you to keep your admiration for those things that are truly admirable—in short, things that are healthy, simple, and robust). If you were to tell him that you loved him, he would probably ask you by what misfortune, or which infirmity, and through what perversity of heart you bring your affection to works that only recount abnormalities of human feeling, the stoicism of disenchanted and vanquished souls, works that seem made to inspire a desire to love nothing, to take no delight in anything. Keep your admiration and your love, then, but understand this if you can: the man and his work are worth your trouble. For the first time, eight years ago, I made the acquaintance of Hawthorne's works through that strange novel, *The Blithedale Romance,* in which he recounts the disappointments and the misadventures of his life as a utopian and reformer. Since then, he has not given any more news to the lettered public of Europe. On that occasion I examined with a fearful, antipathetic, yet real curiosity those funereal flowers with which he loves to compose his literary bouquets. I also noted the impression (much like a nervous shudder or even more so a moral shudder, a presentiment) I felt in contemplating them and inhaling their strange aroma.[2] A new occasion, offered by the author himself, has given me the pretext to verify and test my former impressions, and I have not found them to be wrong. I felt the same curiosity of mind, the same antipathy of heart, the same shudders of the soul, in front of these bizarre flowers, not one of which does not contain a hungry worm or a poisoned perfume. It is only that in smelling these flowers a second time I find them more pungent, more acrid, more penetrating. Far from diminishing after a second go-round, my esteem for Hawthorne has grown and gotten stronger. Thanks to the interval that has passed between reading these two books, the experience has permitted me to recognize as true what up to now I only had felt, confirming exactly what I had all along suspected. I had not said too much and I must admit to the contrary that I had not said enough. Hawthorne is certainly the least lovable man of genius; however, in many ways he merits this illustrious title, and we shall give it to him without his asking.

He is, as I said, the least loveable man of genius, and yet he forces the recalcitrant mind to acknowledge him and to pay him due respect. It is not rare in life to meet disagreeable characters to whom we cannot refuse our esteem or admiration. We tolerate them and even, sometimes, love them out of sympathy for the virtues and the rays of intelligence that it pleased the Almighty to add to the intolerable or indecipherable mélange that makes up their nature. Even while hating them, we cannot prevent ourselves from recognizing those marks of a high moral life that (even in detestable beings) demand our respect. But this phenomenon is much more rare in the pure regions of intelligence and art. There we are no longer obliged, as in everyday life, painstakingly to pursue traces of truth and beauty through a labyrinth of skin and blood. We can be partial without scruple and even unjust without iniquity. We go straight to works that have an affinity with our soul, to the light that has an affinity with the gleam that shines in us. There love, hate, and indifference are determined exclusively by intellectual and moral motives (devoid of passion), and are only more absolute and less subject to hesitations of judgment. What we do not love in the regions of art is what we do not understand. What leaves us indifferent has no affinity with our nature. We refuse to give great artists and poets the benefit we give to the most vulgar of men. To say to a man that we do not love him, but that we respect him is to say something. To say to an artist that he is repugnant to us, but that we recognize in him a certain merit is to say nothing at all because it is reserving our judgment. In literature and art, the thing that seems worthy of our love is at the same time the thing that seems beautiful and true. Literary justice, you see, is more difficult than social justice. Generally speaking, we can affirm that only minds and hearts of the same order are able to do justice to each other. Consequently, we can never do justice—however impartial we might be—to works and men that do not establish an intimate rapport with our own nature.[3]

It is not so with Hawthorne. He forces recalcitrant attention to listen to him. He imposes himself on the imagination that would like to turn away from the spectacles he presents, and he seems to defy it to repudiate his lugubrious fantasies or his revelations of sinister secrets. He does not insinuate himself by flattering or caressing the reader's mind. He positively violates him. He forces open the doors of the soul that close before him. Never has an entertainer, never has a poetic fiddler presented such an inhospitable face to the public, displaying instead the features of a killjoy. He introduces himself to the reader almost as old Knox did to the attendants of Mary Stuart: to uncover the head of a corpse hidden behind a flowery visage and to propose a knowing and instructive anatomy lesson on the human skeleton.[4] You grimace and listen to him with antipathy, then with interest, and at the end of the recital you beg him to come back another night. He does not imitate those artists and poets who traitorously present you with their lethal potions in your preferred cup; the underhanded homicides of the typical poetic poisoner are not for him. He comes from too good a family to practice the art of literary treason. He follows the rules, engages in fair play with his readers. A wise toxicologist, he presents you with his drugs in small, carefully labeled vials which reveal the murderous liquid, and then asks you candidly if you would like to inhale the aroma, to savor the taste, and to suffer the particular devastation each one of them can inflict upon the mind and nervous system. First, we have the poison of remorse that has the property of staining everything black to the eyes of the soul and enveloping the universe in mourning crepe. Next, the poison of egoism that gives you the faculty to penetrate the most subtle thoughts of those who surround you and that bites your heart like the fangs of a reptile. Then, the poison of poverty that induces in the soul all sorts of little nervous tremors, little bizarre apprehensions, little beneficent timidities that (by paralyzing the forces in you that make you desire happiness) stop you from feeling the heavy burden of your misfortune. Last, the poison of pride that makes you believe that there exists a wall of ice between you and other men.

You resist and respond that if the wise chemist had put his drugs in your potage or coffee without your knowledge, you might have been happy to have had the experience. Nevertheless, you consent to the experiment in spite of it all; you thank him for it even though he has made you somber for an entire day. Hawthorne presents the fairly curious and extremely rare spectacle of a man who knows how to make himself heard through no strength of persuasion, no gift of poetic flattery, but simply through the singular power of real talent, stripped of artifice. He does not inspire tenderness in his readers (unless they be misanthropes or pariahs of sentiment), but no one can become acquainted with his works—and do justice to them—without taking away the conviction that one has encountered a singular and rare man.

The great power that he wields over the contemporary reader's imagination, he will wield still more after his death, I believe, on posterity's judgment. Hawthorne will not be more popular with generations that follow us than he is now, because hearts do not yield to those who do not possess tenderness; still, his name will not be forgotten. When our generation has disappeared, much time will pass again before some of his works fall into the abyss of oblivion that ends up swallowing everything. Not one of his works is marked by a sign of absolute immortality, but several of them will last for centuries. In each generation, there will be about half-a-hundred or so of those true connoisseurs of literature who know that the oblivion into which certain works disappear is not tantamount to condemnation, because (sooner or later) oblivion comes inevitably to all works that are neither the expression of sentiments readily familiar to the vast majority of men nor impersonal enough to be easily understood by all. Kindred intellects of those today who are happy to read *The Anatomy of Melancholy,* the dramas of old Webster, or *The Baron of Foeneste,*[5] those intelligences that can penetrate the banal and deceitful surface of human sentiments (where most readers stop for their pleasure), and those as well who, in reading old books, love to find the proof that there was once an original man—exceptionally gifted with a piercing vision that could not be tricked by the world's illusions—will look for and will read with curiosity *Mosses from an Old Manse* and *The Blithedale Romance.* From time to time, an ingenious and knowledgeable critic will cite his name in the *revues* of the future or will bring to light some passage of his writings that will make the reader quiver with surprise or even admiration. Maybe even, twice a century, they will exhume him and make him endure the honors of a resurrection, the kind of literary revival so fashionable today.

Thus, brought to light again, he will be reprinted in Elzevirian[6] collections of rare and curious authors for connoisseurs and blasé minds for whom the classic literatures have lost some flavor. It will remain this way a certain number of centuries, after which the lugubrious Hawthorne will be more forgotten than the doctrine of ages past and he will return forever to that abyss of nothingness from which he had escaped to conquer the celebrity of the moment, to say some unpleasant truths to a distracted and busy humanity, to give voluptuous literati a few minutes of morbid pleasure and—to delicate consciences—some minutes of bitter contemplation. Among all the lessons he has given on human vanity and pride, Hawthorne has forgotten this one. It is not, however, the least striking or the least instructive of all.

Perhaps you are stunned to see an epithet of antipathy awarded to this author for whom, nevertheless, I have the greatest respect? His bitterness and misanthropy, you might say to me, cannot offer sufficient reason for repugnance. Literary history abounds with examples of morose, melancholic, desperate, violent, and even hateful poets and writers who invincibly hold the reader's sympathy, even more so, who warm, lift his heart, and fill his soul with enthusiasm—a Byron, a Shelley, a Rousseau. They have only words of sadness or rancor, yet our ears drink their words avidly; and, a strange phenomenon, sometimes after having heard them, far from feeling somber and sick, we feel capable of the most noble actions and most generous aspirations. From their desperation we draw out the force of courage, and in their hate, the force of love. Do you know why? Their despair and bitterness are passionate, and nothing is without remedy as long as passion exists and strengthens the soul. We feel that their arguments with humanity are only lovers' quarrels, and no matter how sharp the reproaches, they are neither the prelude to nor the sign of a rupture. Great moralists and great saints are pleased in turn to humiliate human nature, to spread out under our eyes the skeleton that we will become someday, to declare to us that we are only rot and ash, yet their words do not leave us weaker, and we welcome them as promises of resurrection and spiritual life. With Hawthorne, we have none of these compensations: there is nothing that makes the heart grow, that inspires enthusiasm and hope. He afflicts us and does not know how to console us; he alarms us and dares not reassure us. He is coldly cruel without knowing it, like the doctor who gives up hope on a patient and declares to his face that he has no chance of getting better. Our miseries appear irrevocable, our souls a realm of sin. The only remedy is death—with neither the dream nor the hope of an afterlife. Other moralists doubtlessly believed they were truly galling by comparing our vices to scorpions and vipers. But what is their eloquent and *enraged* bitterness compared to the bitterness of a pacific Hawthorne, who, with a tranquil air and an icy smile on his lips, comes to say to us that our virtues are gentle snakes that should not be thought harmless, because, in their long consanguinity with the other reptiles that dwell in the heart's cavern, assuredly they have assimilated too much venom for it not to be dangerous to touch them without precaution. Thus, in vain do we believe in the power of good: the struggle against evil is chimerical, senseless, and useless. It is a quixotic act, a pastime that might tempt children, but in the face of which a sage will only smile and walk on. In one of his short stories, "Earth's Holocaust,"[7] he mocks the powerlessness of good in this world and condemns the desire for perfectibility that can trouble man's heart and inspire him to accomplish so many wonders. The human race, in a moment of enthusiasm, decides to purify itself on the night of August 4th.[8] On the great plains of the New World, humanity finds a site for a conflagration that will devour all prejudices and all vices. There, successively thrown into the fire are all engines of vanity, hate, and pride that sustain the domination of evil in this world, all the emblems of fanaticism and superstition, all the instruments of tyranny and destruction: scepters and crowns, noble titles, genealogical pedigrees, crosses and miters, sacerdotal vestments, jewels and *objets d'art,* toilette mirrors, baubles, instruments of pleasure, books and newspapers. Nothing is forgotten that perpetuates vice among men, and the disciples of temperance have the joy of watching flame up—to the last drop—the stocks of brews and spirits that the human race preciously has conserved in basements and cellars for the sole purpose of disturbing reason and perverting instinct. The holocaust consumes it all; men have returned to a state of nature. What, then, prevents them from being good? "You still have one last sacrifice to carry out," one ironical fellow cries out to those at the edge of the inferno, someone you might take, if you please, for Satan himself, but whom we would prefer to take for some disenchanted philosopher who had nothing else besides the vanity of others to throw in the flames. What they have forgotten is the human heart itself. Nothing will be done as long as they have not destroyed that arsenal of all the vices and sins. From the ashes of this universal holocaust, evil will be reborn like the phoenix—younger and more charming—with a new set of feathers and a warble that would make the devil's courtiers faint with admiration. These men believed that they were obeying divine inspiration, the poor fools! Did they not see that they were playthings of the devil, who felt the need to renew his engines of damnation? The old machines of moral destruction were out of service—they clanked and were rusted—and what better occasion to renew the materiel of hell? All the equipment could now be replaced with the latest models, and, undoubtedly, all would go better.

"Amen!" Hawthorne calmly replies in a tone that seems to say, "Just what I expected." You understand now the sort of dread—verging on terror—that Hawthorne's writings inspire, a dread all the more remarkable because the reader feels it without being able to do anything about it; it acts on him with a sort of displeasing fascination. The spirit of Hawthorne seems gifted with the power that the popular imagination credits to the look of the fabulous basilisk: he who meets the dragon's eye cannot take a step, or make a sound; his feet are nailed to the earth, his blood is frozen, his tongue is paralyzed.

This impression of cold and sadness is even more powerful when Hawthorne's bitterness is undiluted; then his bad opinion of mankind affords no compensation. Hawthorne is a determined and convinced pessimist. The modern Hegelians will teach you, if you hold to their beliefs, that evil is only an inferior form of good. Hawthorne, however, goes much further and would return the proposition this way: the good that men accomplish is only a superior form of evil. Great optimistic sentiments—faith, hope, and charity—do not exist for him; or, even worse, they exist only as phantoms. Unsparing analysis has killed the sympathetic fiber in him. When he leaves the somber cavern of the human heart, he passes into a sort of vague and abstract region, illuminated by a frigid sun, in which light we see good instincts and noble sentiments crawling, shivering—haggard and crazy—like sick or old people who avidly yearn for the pale sunshine of November. How little this light warms! How decrepit these impulses appear! Doubtless their days are numbered and they will die. We step aside when we see them pass by, less out of respect than from an upwelling of involuntary sadness. What! These are the great sentiments, the proper pride of mankind, toward which we turn, in our moments of distress, in order to find support and consolation! They are the ones who really ought to be supported and consoled. If you are going to ask this consolation of Religion, perhaps you will come away weighed down with despair. She is not precisely the good buxom nanny you imagine: she is an old girl—dry, cantankerous, without love—who will find a way to wound you cruelly. Don't you hear her say in a voice that is bitter and sweet, "Here you are, perverted child, a being born of sin. Go—go—be without worry and find respite in the justice of God. When we have left this valley of tears, we shall all be damned." What a cordial welcome! You would do well, if you were wise, not to trust to Hope. She is a crazy woman (lovable enough in appearance, but dangerous in reality) who will drag you with her, not chasing butterflies in the meadow, but pursuing a will-o'-the-wisp in some six-foot trench, excavated in advance by a tireless gravedigger (with foresight) who does not like to be caught off guard. Do not come near Friendship. She is a lunatic and has the deplorable habit of biting: generally speaking, her bites are harmless, yet some have been seen that have caused cases of hydrophobia. Here is Clemency. Lord! She is weak! She is on her last breath, and will have expired before having the time to pronounce the words of pardon that were familiar to her lips in other times. Resignation is sitting in the corner. She is indeed resigned. She thinks no more. Nothing can move her. She has lost the memory of past good and evil and the consciousness of present good and evil. These are the decrepit images of great sentiments that present themselves in Hawthorne's work. As for the light under which they stir, it is a cold and deceitful radiance that reveals objects without warming them, that outlines forms but washes out colors—light that does not spread like that of the moon (which, some say, is a dead star), under whose clear reflection the phantoms of intelligence and imagination are happy. We all know this light: call it by any name you like—philanthropy without charity, idealism without conviction, utopia without confidence, mysticism without love—flattering sayings ingeniously invented to uncover the emptiness of the soul, beautiful epitaphs that we love to chisel onto the tomb of faith to lessen the horror of the catastrophe that has befallen us.

That vague idealism, that uncertain mysticism, that democratic philanthropy—all are powerless to replace love in Hawthorne's writings. Never will his aspirations for human betterment take flight—they are missing warmth and wings. The being of beings, by whichever name we call Him, will never hear them because these wishes have neither the ardor of a prayer nor the passion of a curse. Hawthorne's hopes for human progress betray an almost decorous politeness toward mankind. Stripped of love, his writings are also stripped of hate. Hawthorne's misanthropy is in no way aggressive or bellicose. One feels that it is not a motivating force in him, but rather a habitual moral state—an acquired taste of the soul—savored in the same way that pious Buddhists grow to like nirvana. He does not explode, he does not get angry or carried away; however, one honestly might prefer the most violent insults to those words of peaceful civility that he whispers privately in your ear. He assumes a mysterious air to tell you what other men say out loud and with indifference. In truth, you thank him for his reserve because no one would be comfortable hearing the compliments that he quietly makes to you. His expressions of cordiality are so original (and he has an exceptional way of asking after your health, your work, and those who are dear to you) that you know it pleases him to be discreet. For example, he will ask you, "How is the serpent that you have in your heart? Is it fattening up or having little ones?" He will push the limits of charity until he says to you that you should count yourself lucky because there are serpents bigger (and even more prolific) than your own. Your studies of philosophy are paying off, we can see. Your last work was excellent. We can measure your progress in the desiccation of your soul, a credit to your labors. You are truly a new Hercules. How you have worked to drain the swamps of faith in you, so fecund with hydras and dragons! Now they seem like the Russian steppes. One may walk there without fear of bogs or quagmires. With a few more swings of the ax, the last overgrowth fallen, you will have the pleasure of receiving directly on your head, without losing the slightest ray, the full light of day! Don't you find that Hawthorne is right to speak quietly when he whispers these strange compliments in your ear? Note once again that he hasn't the slightest wish to offend you. Never do we find in him the aggressive intentions that we find in a Swift or a Voltaire. This absence of malice, for those who know, is perhaps even more cutting than the absence of love.

I have said that the bitterness of Hawthorne is not diluted, not mitigated in any way. Other misanthropes, for example, know laughter. Hawthorne absolutely ignores it. Never does he have a ray of that redeeming light that extends even to the most somber works an air of health, and that gives an air of celebration to the dungeon where the soul is locked up. I do not know who could so blindly confuse the qualities of human genius and so completely lose the appreciation of nuance to say that Hawthorne is a humorist. Hawthorne has wit and imagination; but to no degree does he possess that joyous opening up of the heart, that intellectual cordiality, that unexpected expansion of sympathy, the amicable jokes or complex fusion of high spirits and choler to which the English have awarded the name *humor*. The spirit of a humorist is similar to weather that the thermometer qualifies as variable, and during which, according to the popular proverb, the devil beats his wife. Hawthorne's spirit is stubbornly misanthropic. Never has tranquil disdain been the stuff of *humor*. Humorists may have lovers' quarrels with humanity, but love, and fervid love, unchangeable in men, underlies their comedy. But Hawthorne does not laugh. Sometimes he tries to smile, but his smile is so sad that it afflicts you even more profoundly than his bitterness. You perceive that the smile has cost him too much effort. A propensity for sad feelings appears to make him powerless to express the happier sentiments of the heart and the joys of nature. In all of his works, I have seen only one true Spring sunbeam, the little story called "David Swan."[9] Never does that sweet joy, never does that amiable abandon come for a minute to brighten the taciturn physiognomy that we see in his portraits or to open lips that, it seems, prefer to remain quiet even in the intimacy and company of his dearest friends. We have no trouble believing that Hawthorne deserves the compliment that Emerson paid him at the end of an evening when, gathered with others in the Transcendentalist circle, he had kept company with his lugubrious chimeras and had not taken part in his friends' conversations: "Hawthorne rides well his horse of [the] night."[10]

Hawthorne's talent at first presents an indecipherable enigma, but on closer inspection, it can be solved rather easily. All the characteristics of this talent are found whenever culture reaches its apogee. He has the morbid love of abnormalities that distinguishes blasé minds, the intelligent taste for rarities that distinguishes connoisseurs of human nature. He has the same fancies and caprice that we find in societies consumed with boredom and eager to experience new sensations. He is a casuist, a collector of curiosities, a horticulturalist of exotic plants. He translates only the feelings of souls in ruin, the scruples of consciences that have been refined beyond the point of civilization. In him we find nothing of the vigorous, popular—or, I gladly say—plebeian. "What!" you ask with astonishment, "Why should young and democratic America send us these strange flowers—the kind we thought peculiar to ancient civilizations, where ruins lie in heaps?" Astonishment ceases, however, when we remember to what lineage and society Hawthorne belongs. Hawthorne belongs to the old America, and not to the new, to the America of the Puritans and of the founders of the Republic. Democrat though he is and (would-be) socialist that he was, Hawthorne has an aristocratic genealogy; he has ancestors and a pedigree. He is one of the last descendants of those austere and hearty Pharisees, great burners of witches, great whippers of Quakers, great hunters of heretics and libertines, who "laid the foundation of New England." In the preface to one of his novels, Hawthorne recounts their history and fancifully engages them in dialogue across the gulf of time. He represents these ancestors as looking with contempt at the last-born of their strong race and saying, "Who is this fiddler, this violin player, this vagabond artist? Is this any way to praise God and serve Him in this world?" "Yet," adds Hawthorne, "let them scorn me as they will, strong traits of their nature have intertwined themselves with mine" (*SL* 10). Nothing is more correct. That morbid love of cases of conscience, that turn of taciturn and disdainful wit, that habit of seeing sin everywhere and the yawning gates of hell, that somber look surveying a damned world and a nature draped in mourning, those lonely conversations of the imagination with the conscience, that pitiless analysis resulting from perpetual examination of self and the tortures of a heart closed to men, but always open to God—all those traits of the Puritan character have been passed on to Hawthorne, or, better yet, have *filtered down* to him across a long line of generations. If we do not recognize them all at once, we should not be surprised; the soul of the Hawthorne family necessarily was modified in each *avatar* that it sent forth, but the substance has remained the same. With each generation, something has been lost: first, religious ardor; next, political readiness; and, then again, the fervor of hate. Everything owing to spiritual conviction has disappeared, all that was from nature has stayed. The visions that haunt Hawthorne's mind are the same that his ancestors knew; but these phantoms have kept up with the fashion of the times and have renewed their sinister costumes. Long ago, they wore a Christian shroud, now they don philosophical togas. Hawthorne's ancestors knew where these visions were coming from because they knew that they had been besieged by two enemy powers, Satan and Christ, who battled for their hearts like a fortress. They were skilled in distinguishing the visions that came from heaven and those that came from hell. Hawthorne's vision comes neither from heaven nor hell; these two words have lost all meaning for him. Heaven is replaced by the black room of the imagination, and hell by the cavern of the heart. His books are thus the final product of an old civilization, or, if you prefer, the chemical residue of substances once pure and salubrious, but long since contaminated by the deleterious admixture—too frequent and imprudent—of certain elements that were hostile to them. In these little literary urns are contained the ashes and the earth of Puritanism. The divine life that animated Puritanism has disappeared: all that we feel now is its dissolving earthly substance.

The heavenly spark having been extinguished, it is, so to speak, during the night, by feeling and only by a sense of touch, that we are permitted to find in Hawthorne the traits of a Puritan physiognomy. But whoever has seen the Puritan genius working in literature and history will recognize quickly his habits of mind and his methods of action: for example, that honesty that is at once brutal and loyal, that makes not one effort to conceal interior feelings, to smooth the wrinkles of a too-worried forehead or to recover with a smile the folds that disdain has printed on the lips. Hawthorne presents himself to his readers as the old Puritans stood before their enemies and explains to them what he is from the very first page. But the most conspicuous trait of Puritan nature that he has in him is perhaps the ease with which he manipulates the old literary form called the allegory. Allegory is the preferred form of his genius, and it was, if we look closely, the favorite form of the Puritan imagination. This preference, which seems singular at first glance, resulted naturally from the moral habits of the old Puritans, from the perpetual conversations that they had with themselves. Such incessant examinations of conscience subjected them to psychological hallucinations, owing largely to a vigorous—an obstinate—force of resolve that the world had never known before them, that it has not known since, and that brought back all their thoughts to a fixed and unwavering preoccupation. These exclusive and haughty souls, all aquiver with retribution and hate, rejected outside of themselves the obsessions to which they were prey with a vigor equal to the torment they felt. We should not be surprised that these abstract obsessions became living characters. They were nourished with the heart's flesh and blood, they were watered with tears that they made flow, they were warmed by the fire of fevers they had lit. For all his apparent moral solitude, the Puritan, in fact, was surrounded by the most peculiar company imaginable. Sin, Death, Justice, Faith, Despair were not the abstract characters that their names present to our understanding, but loveable or perverted gentlemen, powerful princes, coquettish ladies, or those devoted to the good. This is the reason for the preference given by the Puritans to allegory, or, to say it better, of the imperious—almost fatal—necessity that constrained them to use it, and, at the same time, the reason for the vigor and the life that they knew how to imprint on this old literary form. For a long time, allegory has been labeled and classed in books on rhetoric as suiting the needs of the lazy and pedantic. But the Puritans found it where we find all the great things, in nature or in the contemplation of the world, and recreated it for the needs of their hearts.

Their sickly and melancholic descendant has inherited the same gift. He knows, as they did, how to give life to abstraction and how to creep up on the most hidden secrets of interior life. Any psychologist is necessarily an egoist. But we can say in all truth that the egoism of Hawthorne is heroic and disinterested. Not one of the movements of the self eludes him, even in such moments when, the opposite of Galatea,[11] it has wanted to escape and not be observed. This method of extreme egoism, this procedure of excessive *personality*, detracts nothing, however, from the *impersonality* of the characters he draws and the protagonists that he puts into his work. By expressing his individuality, Hawthorne expresses general human nature. His short stories above all have the air of confessions that your soul makes to itself. They are so many small slaps that the author applies to your face. You would swear that they apply personally to you, so much so that you want to say to the author, "How do you know that and who told you so?" Since he is himself, Hawthorne succeeds in being us. His observation of himself is sincere and serious; his egoism becomes humble because of its veracity; and he directs this merciless force against himself with the relentlessness that, typically, we direct against others. He accuses us while accusing himself. Give to that egoism a speck of frivolity, or vanity, or hypocrisy, and instantly it will seem untenable to us, and we will rise up with good reason against such an audacious personality. But since Hawthorne presents himself to us disarmed against himself, he makes us tremble. This is the force that truth possesses, even when it is unpleasant.

Here is a question that has tormented certain English critics and that not a single one of them has been able to resolve in a satisfying manner: Are Hawthorne's writings immoral?[12] I see why they ask this question and yet hesitate to respond to it. In Hawthorne's work, not the smallest word is spoken against morality or virtue, not even against what we might call *official* virtue, which certainly has its price and holds a place in the government of societies (which is even necessary for the education of the soul just as the academies and masters are necessary for the study of drawing), but is much less respectable in total than true virtue, and which has had the honor—more than once—of capturing the attention of the greatest writers. Never does he allow himself a jest: no silly French licentiousness, or withering English cynicism. All of his pages are scrupulously decent; we would search in vain for sensual tidbits or paradoxical lapses of forgetfulness. Nevertheless, when we read him, we feel prey to a disturbing impression that we cannot get rid of. The truth is that Hawthorne transports the reader's soul to an atmosphere other than the one that it customarily breathes. He makes it descend to the depths, to the caves of the underworld, and makes it inhale the stale air and gas that are contained within. The soul is, so to speak, akin to those rudimentary animals that open their shells, or, better yet, to those plants that have no need for roots. It breathes and can only breathe on its own footing. If the soul wants to live freely and happily, it must consent not to ask too many questions or in a manner too pressing. It will ignore the subterranean alchemy by which the elixir that nourishes it is prepared; it will not attend to the laborious work by which nature keeps and maintains it; but it will enjoy everything naïvely and with confidence. It will not know it, but it will live, and it will live precisely because of what it does not know. If it wants to know itself and to ferret out the truth, then it will change. This malevolent analysis will teach it that poisons transformed by a subtle and knowledgeable art have entered into the composition of the source of its nourishment and will strip it of all joy and all happiness. Do you want to live happily? Don't follow the counsels of somber Hawthorne— live life on the surface. If you do, from your thoughts you will have only light, from your feelings you will have only perfume: you will not know sadness because you will never have explored the underground galleries of the soul; you will only have known the superficies of moral life, where, as with visible nature, all is grace and smiles. All the elements will work for you, and you will be like the plant described by the poet: *Qu[e]m mulcent aurae, firmat sol, educat imber.*[13] But if you want to penetrate your own depths, the soul will no longer find itself in its accustomed atmosphere: it will miss the air, and with it, health, joy, and love. Repeat, then, if you are wise, the desperate wish of that Faust who lived in science as in a prison, and say with him: "Ah! If only I could live, spontaneously, like the plants and the trees!" Leave nature to its alchemy: the secrets of life are not life itself, and knowing the elements that enter into the composition of life is not the same thing as living. The goal of man is to live, as the goal of nature is to foster and shape life.

There is in the abuse of this power of analysis a veritable immorality, immorality in two senses. On the one hand, Hawthorne's writing represents an illicit usurpation of powers that were not given to man, an illegitimate curiosity for secrets that have been hidden from him, a yearning that forces the soul to breathe an atmosphere (in some ways *above* itself) for which it is not made. That is the immorality of which we are vaguely aware when we read Hawthorne's writing. On the other hand, there is an immorality of a different type that has nothing to do with individual life, but rather with social life. Everything that Hawthorne tells and teaches us is true, but in the end we ask ourselves if it wouldn't be better to ignore him. What would happen if all men possessed the talent for delving into others, or if this fatal gift were the common inheritance of mankind? Secure and confiding relationships would be unimaginable, and society—which is only established on the vows of the human heart—would become, if not impossible, at least very difficult. It would be a grave error to believe that society rests on very deep moral secrets and very esoteric metaphysical notions. Laws, civic institutions, political government: all of these rest on very elementary moral principles—neither complex nor profound—and whenever someone meddles with them too aggressively, they become false, infallibly perverted, and sometimes even completely dissolved. Society cannot be based upon the secret depths of the soul, but rather upon the soul's explicit confessions. Hawthorne does not attack these confessions, and does not see them as a necessary hypocrisy, as so many great misanthropic minds have made him out to do. He is too subtle not to know that these confessions are sincere and, for that matter, perfectly legitimate, because the soul never makes shameless admissions without detriment to its morality and its happiness. He never attacks those forms of consent that have become the facts that we call institutions; but he looks at them indifferently and moves on. Then, all of society, with its outward customs and manners, disappears, and we watch a curious, yet desperate spectacle—souls that act only in accord with the incentives of their own egotistical nature, no longer prompted by motives of action endorsed by social morals.

This, if I am not wrong, is where the immorality of Hawthorne's work lies. There is nothing in it that resembles what men generally call immorality. Hawthorne is too deep to be immoral in the usual sense of the word. Profundity necessarily excludes immorality in its three most common forms: exhibiting lightness and frivolity in mind and heart; audaciously attacking the most sacred sentiments; or deliberately preferring voluntary vice instead of virtue. With these, a truly profound mind has nothing to do. Thus, when we are speaking about the immorality of Hawthorne's works, the very particular and unusual definition we have given to it must be understood. Once these qualifications have been made, Hawthorne's pessimistic psychology can be seen, above all, as a testament to human nature. In this psychology, the conception of the soul is not grand or noble, but neither is it ignoble and paltry. When we finish reading Hawthorne, we feel a particular esteem for the soul (a rare opinion) much like that marked deference that we experience toward certain people whom we distinguish without affection, but whom our mind picks out as kindred spirits. They appear to us as unhealthy, subject to all sorts of moral rheumatisms and spiritual neuralgias, but interesting because of that. Hawthorne has made a very important psychological discovery: sensibility is the dominant function of the soul, the one that commands all the other functions and dominates the moral organs. Nervous agitation is the permanent state of the soul: its sensitivity defies all comparisons. The smallest things wound and trouble it; the lightest apprehension destroys its calm and all its happiness; an indifferent reproach fills it with sadness; the shadow of a guilty thought tarnishes its candor; the phantasmagoria of a bad dream torture it as if the event were real. The unappreciable variations of the moral atmosphere that surrounds it make it shiver like the needle of a compass. By contemplating this excessive sensibility, we appreciate the advantage of having a body, and we no longer have any desire to treat it merely as the soul's trumpery or inconvenient costume. That body is no longer an embarrassment; it is a protection and rampart for the soul. We feel happy and reassured by thinking that our feelings, our ideas, and our impressions will have to cross the thickness of our flesh, and will only arrive at the soul dulled in some way, having lost during the journey some of their original intensity. At the same time, we absolve the body of all the faults and vices of which we too hastily accused it. How does this fine substance, delicate and susceptible, resist sickness and disorder? No need for heavy sins to flatten and kill it: a modest injection will suffice, a small infiltration, a speck of dust, and all is finished. When we say, then, that the soul is sick, let us stop ourselves from believing that it is prey to some hideous infirmity, to some crushing remorse, to some criminal and sinful habit. If Hawthorne had not shown us the well-known monsters of sin and recrimination, he would not have made a discovery, and simply would have repeated in a more or less pleasing form what the psychologists have attested since man began to think. His discovery is this: there are no little things for the soul, because it does not judge things based on their material proportions or their volume; the soul conceives them much less from their exterior form, but instead from their pure essence. Thus, it does not judge a crime based on the exterior act it manifests, but rather on the idea of which the act is merely a representation: as far as the soul is concerned, the thought of the crime equals the crime itself. He therefore traces light shadows over the soul, and those shadows cover it like real darkness. He assaults it with imagined dread, and that dread assumes the equivalent reality and peril of present danger.

We must not occupy ourselves with the details of each of Hawthorne's writings. We have already performed that service for readers of the *Revue*,[14] and were preceded in that task by an inspired critic.[15] The goal we propose today in taking up Hawthorne's writings for the second time is not to make them known, but to make them understood and felt. We have not wanted to analyze or to dissect them either, but rather, as it were, to distill them: to extract the essence and aroma; to inquire, that is to say, into their principle and soul. If we succeed in suffusing our reader's mind with this unnerving perfume and make him appreciate the flavor of this bitter liquor—if, in a word, we provide him with the exact sensation of this original talent—our goal will be met.

In spite of our respect and even our admiration for Hawthorne's talent, his works are less than masterpieces and we cannot expect all of them to have equal value. Hawthorne's talent is very uneven, and this inequality has a character worthy of remark. The talent is not unequal in its carriage, because it proceeds at a regular pace, a slow trot, with a sort of cold vivacity and self-assuredness. What is unequal in him is his physiognomy, which is mutable like the beauty of faces that have seen better days (as they say, vulgarly). There are thus entire pages where that physiognomy is intolerable and even tedious to look at, and where the charm of sadness that animates it has disappeared.

We don't really love Hawthorne, for example, in the writings in which the allegory is intellectual or aesthetic instead of moral, when it is an allegory of thought rather than an allegory of the heart. In these he is not only cold, but affected, exhibiting a dry and slightly artificial refinement. We like him less when he tries to express relatively happy feelings. I say relatively because happiness for him is only a faded blending of two dolorous shades, instead of being what it is for the rest of the world, an absolutely bright color, clearly demarcated from its absolutely somber opposite. Thus, without regret, we can dismiss one of his novels, *The House of the Seven Gables*. Of this novel, we like only the first part, where he sounds every note in his familiar key, that of unhappiness and destitution. As he deftly describes the trembling soul of old Miss Hepzibah Pyncheon, a noble daughter of America as much as a daughter of America can be, who, in her last days, is obliged to open a cent shop in order to survive! Hawthorne admirably succeeds in making us understand the deep feeling of loss that fills the soul of this descendant of the Puritans, this gentlewoman from the land of the Yankees. Never in aristocratic countries has a monarch been stripped of his kingdom, or a ruined nobleman been so cruelly tormented by the bitter sentiment that would seem to be only a morbid illusion in a democratic country, but which, instead of being lessened there, to the contrary is multiplied by the equality of social conditions. As Hawthorne finely remarks, in democratic countries rank has no *spiritual existence* that survives independently of money. Stripped of her fortune, Miss Hepzibah Pyncheon is no longer a lady, but a poor woman, the equal—perhaps the social inferior—of the middling gossips who come to frequent her counter, their equal or their inferior according to the gossips' more-or-less shabby raiment cut from more-or-less shabby material: such miniscule distinctions in the quality of one's clothes determine equality or inequality. Oh! The vanity of the world! Such has been the painful descent of Colonel Pyncheon, that solid Pharisee with a predatory and cruel heart, who had Matthew Maule burned as a witch, in order to acquire the commoner's possessions![16] The malediction that the victim cast from his pyre was heard, it seems, and recorded in Heaven. How Hawthorne's mind is at ease, at home, in the company of these painful sentiments! Imagination, a faculty without pity, derives its enjoyment from the greatest pains as well as the greatest pleasures, follows with a voluptuous and cruel curiosity the movements of this poor creature crushed under the burden of her misfortune. But, as soon as Phoebe's arrival brings a glimmer of youth and Spring into the old house, interest starts to wane, and the disappointed imagination of the reader would gladly say to the writer: "Snuff out this sunbeam, chase away the Spring, give us solitude, and speak to us again of the tremors and terrors that grip the souls of the destitute!"

In truth, in spite of the admiration that the story entitled *The Scarlet Letter* merits, I do not think that Hawthorne was born for the long novel. The feelings of which he is fond, that he prefers to describe and that he truly knows—solitude, destitution, meditative ennui—necessarily exclude movement, noise, life. Thus a novel must be a small world in miniature as soon as it transcends the limits of a simple short story or a so-called psychological study. Left to themselves and sequestered from humanity, his characters do nothing more than lugubriously dream, brood, and nourish themselves with their sadness. Protected by that barrier that sadness erects between those it has touched and the rest of men, they see their peers move away from them on an impulse of respectful fear. The drama is entirely interior and remains, as it were, invisible. It cannot be translated by exterior acts, by passionate deeds, by adventures. It plays out among three or four characters—equally sad, wounded, and deaf—who look at each other dolorously while nodding their heads, who let out sighs that contain an entire world of sorrows, and drift apart, taking with them the secret that gnaws inside of them. The result of this is that Hawthorne's novels never give an idea of life: they only provoke an idea of death and destruction. That singular spectacle is in particular what the novel entitled *The Scarlet Letter* presents, a book that is completely black, without precedent even in the somber literature of England.

When the novel begins, the passionate drama has already ended, stormy and overwhelming sentiments have done their work and retreated, making way for other feelings (just as intense) that thrive on solitude and silence. We attend to the slow destruction of three hearts, all differently, but all equally wounded. Each one of these hearts is prey to a sole sentiment that absorbs all others: for Hester[17] (the adulterous woman, condemned by the Puritan tribunal eternally to wear the infamous red letter which assigns her shame) it is remembrance of the sin committed; for the young minister (her accomplice) it is remorse; for the outraged husband, it is the feeling of indignation and an irresistible desire to know the offender. The novel is composed around the description of this triple agony, and the spectacle is frightening in its truth and horror. We follow line by line—all of them marking the minutes, the steps of time toward a fatal and inevitable conclusion—the slow, continuous devastation of these three hearts under the incessant labor of Death, whose spade we seem to hear. A chorus of sobs and lamentations accompanies and encourages the work of Death, who appears in the novel with a peculiar physiognomy worthy of remark. Here, Death displays nothing ironic or macabre; it has no stupid follies and would not tolerate the smallest lugubrious pleasantry. No, it is a solemn Puritan matron—serious, dedicated, laborious—a Death that is completely earnest, hard at work, always conscientious. It knows the price of time: time is decay. It does not allow itself a minute's rest, and does not allow the hearts it destroys truce or pity. Life is still represented in this book, but in a form that is in perfect harmony with the author's thinking. It is represented by Pearl, the child born of the adultery, a little creature living like the forbidden desire that gave birth to it, charming like shared pleasure, irresistible like temptation.

Small doubting flame, we would not know to say exactly where she caught fire, if she clings more to God or the devil, if she is a will-o'-the-wisp in the cemetery or a celestial meteorite. Whatever she may be, she is the only one to brighten the story, and reconciles the imagination with the world. Read this book, if the experience of life has left you qualified to understand it. It is worth the while and, in the event that this disturbing reading frightens you, be reassured by the thought that there is no second *Scarlet Letter* in all of literature, and that you do not run the risk of encountering again such a distillation of misery. It is a good impression to have once—to know just how far art can push the expression of moral sadness. *The Scarlet Letter* is such a tour de force: good to read through once, but not to be revisited. The book is exceptional, but it is beautiful, and anyone who has read it will never forget the dreadful scene where the minister, gasping with remorse, is found at night on the scaffold where Hester's shame was laid bare, or the revealing *thee*ing and *thou*ing with which the author insinuates the secret in the mind of the reader when Hester pleads before the Puritan council not to have her child taken away from her, her incarnate punishment and the living hope for her reconciliation with God.

While I hesitate to recommend *The Blithedale Romance,* this—of all of the author's novels—is the one I prefer. In this book, Hawthorne summarizes all the experiences of his life as a dreamer and utopian, and recounts his memories of his stay at the Fourierist commune Brook Farm, which he helped to establish and probably as well to dissolve. The names of the novel's characters are pseudonyms that mask well-known personalities: Doctor George Ripley and his wife, Henry Channing, Margaret Fuller, Hawthorne himself. This novel is one of the most remarkable books that has appeared in the last ten years. Here, Hawthorne has painted a particular subset of the human race, the race of utopians and dreamers of social reform, an equivocal race, not well known and generally underappreciated, a race apart, neither large nor small, and for which seems to have been found the qualification, "eccentric." Eccentric, indeed, are all these characters whose hearts are hardened against experience and whose ebullient heads boil like a kettle. Unfortunately, this novel, which, like all masterpieces has a distinctive merit (it introduces readers to a particular corner of human life, a race of unknown men: in a word, it has something new and important to say), necessarily is condemned to near oblivion. The book is too particular to our time and will no longer be understood by anyone when those contemporary follies will have gone to rejoin the nothingness, the nonsense of days gone by. The society of men and women that Hawthorne describes is too exceptional, too removed from the way of life and thinking of the human collective, actively to interest a really large number of readers. In the society of Blithedale, we enter into a sort of middling region among whose inhabitants we find neither the most exalted nor the meanest forms of humanity. The characters' methods of thinking, their passions, their motives of action differ entirely from those of other men. Moreover, the residents of the community never excite sympathy, and the reader hesitates to recognize them as his brothers. They awaken curiosity, but a disturbing curiosity, and, even further, will stimulate only those who are eager for instruction and fearless of nothing. Thus, the heart repels them, and only with effort can the head understand them. The audience for such a book necessarily must be limited. *The Blithedale Romance* is made to be understood and felt only by a hundred or so people among the generation currently alive. It is a diamond, but a diamond whose value even lapidaries and connoisseurs of precious gems themselves cannot completely comprehend, and that is destined to be hidden again under a thick layer of oblivion in about twenty or so years. But those who have learned sorry lessons from close encounters with utopians, lovers of chimeras, and what we might call in a word *alexandrine* souls, will recognize the hand of a master in the portraits of Hollingsworth, Zenobia, and Miles Coverdale. There they are—just as you have met them—dreamers without poetry, philanthropists without love, politicians without a mind for innovation: all agitated, yet passionless hearts and cowering intellects. They have been captured and described with the artful finesse and suppleness of a truly admirable talent. And yet, the moral that comes from this work is ambiguous and uncertain. For those who have met such people, reading the novel is taxing; it registers like a painful memory we would prefer to forget, and we are not in the least grateful to the author for having awakened it. And for those who have not known those people, reading the book will be of no benefit; it will not protect them against any danger because they will not understand the risk.

In my opinion, all of Hawthorne's talent effloresces wherever he is truly himself—in his short stories, in rapid sketches, in tidy and concise moral allegories. That is the genre in which he triumphs and which best conveys the nature of his talent. The secrets he is contented to keep for us are too painful—too unhealthy—to be pursued through five or six hundred pages. No one, I imagine, wants to drink tears from a cup filled to the brim. It would be a veritable debauch to take sadness in such large doses. Readers of one of Hawthorne's novels can be accused of this type of orgy. At the same time, no one who is curious about or erudite in moral chemistry, no spiritual toxicologist taken with his art, would refuse to drink a few drops of this essence of tears if they were given to him. That is the particular merit of Hawthorne's short stories. What he wants to teach us is quickly said, and the mind does not have to fear losing its sanity and joy in hearing his disillusioned words for too long. Instead, we swallow the bitter lesson like a tonic, and if the heart asks for no more, we put down the book and do not pick it up again except at our leisure. Yet, whatever the value of Hawthorne's short stories, I do not recommend them all equally; one needs to be selective. Only half of *Twice-told Tales* and those in the volume entitled *The Snow-Image* are worth keeping, because in these short stories his talent has not yet arrived at maturity. He tries out and fumbles. The series of short stories entitled *Mosses from an Old Manse,* however, should be read from cover to cover. A light of true genius has touched some of these allegories: "Rappaccini's Daughter," "The Birth-mark," "Young Goodman Brown," "Egotism; or the Bosom-Serpent," "The Christmas Banquet," "The Artist of the Beautiful," etc.

Hawthorne's last novel, *Transformation, or the Romance of Monte Beni,*[18] is—as always—an allegory of the heart, a psychological drama determined by exterior circumstances that, in the book, play only a secondary role. The story takes place in Italy, but the choice of setting is completely arbitrary, and the drama just as well could have been set in another region because it is timeless and universal. I see no other determining factor behind this choice other than the author's resolution to use the notes from his travels, the desire to communicate to his compatriots the aesthetic impressions that he felt in that classic land of the arts. Hawthorne wanted to frame one of those somber histories familiar to him with a border of Italian flowers and to populate the landscapes that he had admired with a society of his choosing. The unity of the work and the interest it should have inspired necessarily have suffered from this combination. The novel is really two, as it were: it contains both an aesthetic novel and a psychological novel that are at war with one another, and that, like two rivals, compete for the reader's attention. It belongs to that class of hybrid books with contrary claims (of which *Corinne* is the prototype),[19] and in which—for the sake of fusing two opposites—the author squanders a sum of talent that would have been more than sufficient to write two beautiful books belonging, respectively, to each of the genres artificially brought together. Literary criticism frequently has shown this falseness in the historical novel. But what is that falseness next to the one that distinguishes the aesthetic novel? "I read *Corinne* two times," an intelligent woman said to us one day, "and yet I can say that I've only read it once. When I wanted to read the novel, I skipped over all of the author's descriptions and reflections. Later, I read those descriptions, and left the novel aside." These words indicate the veritable pitfall of this kind of book, and it is not surprising that Hawthorne, having encountered the same obstacles as Madame de Staël, was no better able to avoid them.

As a general rule, this genre is only tolerable when aesthetic sensation is the real subject of the story, as in Hoffmann's *Don Juan*.[20] The work of art that produces this sensation is not simply a model of beauty left to passive admiration—it is transformed into a fantastic avatar and somehow becomes a living character that asks for our tenderness or our pity. The soul of the work speaks distinctly to the ear of the spectator; the spectator answers it, and that double dialogue engenders the poetic hallucination, the illusion of reality. In this particular case, the sensation produced by the work of art must have lost, absolutely lost, what generally characterizes these sorts of sensations: it cannot invite criticism. Intelligent admiration is not enough—there must be passion, that is to say, the abandonment and oblivion of self. In other words, the sensation must be strong enough to go beyond the ordinary limits where emotions (even the most extreme that art can evoke) stop, to join up with the most exceptional, the most poignant, the most ardent feelings of life. The work must weaken your entire being, fill you full of love like a woman, of hate like an enemy, of terror like a persecuting fatality. If the impressions felt are not capable of accomplishing such miracles, what are they doing in the novel? I know no crueler disappointments than those that are reserved for us by stories with aesthetic pretensions. We go out to accompany two lovers during their walk, surely counting that they will chat about their love and that they will acquaint us with their rapture. Not at all. Instead, they lead us in front of an arch of triumph and begin to take notes like British tourists. We follow a woman who goes to confession; respectfully, the author stops you at the door and asks us to read an historical account about the church she entered, while waiting for the return of the beautiful penitent. All in all, the reader has the air of an indiscreet being whom we suspect of wanting to be involved in things that do not concern him, and whose curiosity we evade by the most general conversation available. The reader truly feels this indirect reproach, admits his fault mentally, and promises never to return. He will put down the book and never come back to it if he is intelligent and devoid of pedantry; if he has a trace of pedantry, he will come back to it indefatigably, without being shocked for a moment to meet professors of archeology and eloquence instead of the friends he was hoping to find. Thus, all tastes are satisfied, and all is for the best in the falsest of all literary genres. This is my humble opinion about the aesthetic novel. I offer it without the impertinent pretension—God forbid!—of wanting to impose it on anyone. If, then, you like aesthetic novels, you may continue at your leisure to indulge that pleasure, something I shall never hope to disturb, and I beg you not to be angry with me.

Nonetheless, an eminent thinker's impressions of art, nature, and religion will always have great interest and the opinion that we expressed, having to do exclusively with the genre in which these impressions are presented, takes away nothing from their merit. Hawthorne's observations and thoughts on Italy, Italian arts, art in general, are such as we would expect from his sharp and subtle mind. He penetrates beneath the surface and goes to look for the hidden soul of things, but somewhat at random and with a degree of hesitation that indicates that the author is not absolutely sure of himself. He speaks self-consciously, proposes his opinions without conviction, in a muffled voice, and suddenly interrupts himself as if he were afraid that he had gone too far and dreaded the judgment of those whom he is addressing. We sense in his opinions, as in those of all of his compatriots in the arts, a certain intrinsic weakness that results from a fundamental deficiency in education, a deficiency that the historical circumstances of America have created, and that her best endowed minds will need much time to overcome.[21] Hawthorne lacks neither the depth nor the subtlety of mind to understand exactly certain great things; what he needs is practice. Neither mind nor even genius can take the place of educational familiarity in understanding the value of great works of art. Nothing can substitute for this primary schooling, not even the most exquisite sensitivity. Any European of ordinary judgment, even with a soul lacking elevation and of only moderate sensibility, will surpass Hawthorne in this arena. I do not want to say that he will better comprehend than Hawthorne the essence and the aim of art; he might not comprehend them at all; but he will be less deceived as to the productions of art, and will not fall into the same errors of detail. After having listened with curiosity, with admiration, perhaps, to the aesthetic opinions of Hawthorne about art in general, he will regain all his advantage as soon as they move on to particular applications and practical appreciation of various works of art. He will be surprised that the names of painters cited by Hawthorne belong only to the third and fourth rank, like that of Guido for example.[22] "You have been taken in," he would say to him, "by processes and artistic contrivances; you are the victim of your own sensibility. You admire Guido. Do you want to know why? It is because he presents to your sensibility emotions that do not unsettle you and that flatter without greatly disturbing you, emotions that are not too far removed from those already familiar to you. You admire him because he engages you through his insinuating, coaxing air, typical of a flatterer or a courtier. All his heads incline toward you with the most encouraging smiles and appeal to your sympathy and pity. You award both to them, and that is all very well. But ask yourself why, and you will see that it is not because they appear to you great, but because they appear *lovable*. Guido does not express beauty, but a graceful prettiness, and that is what produces an immediate impression on your sensibility. On entering this new world of art, your heart and thoughts, in spite of yourself, attach themselves to works recalling emotions that are familiar to them. Fully to comprehend the arts, your mind and heart require new experiences. Like yourself, I fancied Guido or some other painter of the same class because his works insensibly revived emotions that I had had before I ever entered a gallery of paintings, and that I was sure to encounter again upon leaving it. I was charmed by the graceful sadness of a Virgin because it was not far removed from the sadness I contemplated in my mother's face; I was captivated by the smile of this or that saint because it reminded me of the smile of a sister or of some object of my youthful dreams. The charm passed quickly because I was not long in discovering that the amiability of a painting bears no comparison to the amiability of real life, and I went on to contemplate works that would excite exceptional and ideal emotions. All the same, Guido and his kind have their merits, even in their defects and their want of elevation. They are the initiators; they open the doors of Art to you and lead you, step by step, into the splendors of its palace. By the ordinary emotions they provoke in you, they prepare you to feel more exalted ones." Our European continues, "Your opinion on the cerebral debility and the mental vacuum that a prolonged stroll in a picture gallery leaves behind is also equally superficial. You almost come to the conclusion that painting is an artificial thing with nothing human about it. But I have also noticed that this cerebral fatigue, which is real, can be traced to two principal causes: first, the diversity of subjects and styles that clash together in a gallery; and, second, the hasty and commonplace—I would almost say impudent—curiosity, of the stroller whose principal ambition is to see the greatest number of paintings in the shortest possible space of time. One beautiful painting is of itself sufficient to occupy the mind and to exhaust whatever provision of admiration you may have the moment you contemplate it. What would you think of a man who, in the space of an hour, should amuse himself with a scene from Shakespeare, a poem by Byron, a pamphlet by Swift, two or three of Wordsworth's sonnets, and several pages in one of Bishop Taylor's sermons, and then finally declare that literature is a *capharnaum*[23] that deranges and disorders his mental faculties?" This is how our European would speak, without needing the genius or mental grasp of Hawthorne. Yes, without a doubt, from childhood he has been raised with a familiarity with the arts. He has spent his youth in museums, in the shadow of palaces; at every moment, he has seen, felt, and been moved by the most beautiful works of art in every possible form. Would that Hawthorne not feel wounded by our observations because the customs that encourage conviction in matters of taste do not necessarily imply a great understanding of art any more than an ease in manipulating the instruments of modern science implies a deep understanding of science. If Roger Bacon or Albert the Great came back to the world, they would fumble around in any modern laboratory: even beginning chemistry students would laugh at their clumsiness. Hawthorne's sojourn in Europe was not long enough to insure him the security of taste that only familiarity creates, that is all.

The aesthetic discourses of the American romancer have less to do with painting than with sculpture, and his remarks on this latter art are generally acute and profound. It would be very difficult for us to say why he has understood sculpture better than painting because the nature of his own talent would seem—on the contrary—to foreordain for him a stronger appreciation for the art of color instead of form. This is one of those strange things one encounters so frequently in the realm of intelligence, and which seems to be the work of a mischievous sprite who takes pleasure in subverting common sense and logic. Whatever it may be, he has clearly comprehended the principles upon which the art of sculpture rests and has shown very well the reasons why, henceforth, sculpture is an art powerless and condemned. Let us translate the thoughts he has developed and put into action in the course of his story. Sculpture, which at first glance seems to be the most masterful of all the arts, is actually the simplest and most primitive. Far from supposing a brilliant and advanced civilization, it supposes a society in which men lead a simple life, the elementary kind led by pastoral innocents. The idea of sculpture implies the idea of an approximate state of paradise, of a pagan Eden like that shown to us by poets of Antiquity, peopled with nymphs and fauns, which is to say beings whose conscience is inseparable from their instincts, whose soul is allied to their senses, and who stand in almost immediate relation to the elementary forces of nature. Sculpture needs models that are docile and obedient to nature's laws, ignorant of evil and never troubled by thoughts of sin. Only in models like these will the sculptor find that perfect harmony and repose of the body that are the essential conditions of his art. Now the living model has no repose except on condition of not being goaded by the soul and ignoring his duality—ignoring that he is made up of flesh and spirit. Sculpture does not absolutely exclude the idea of moral life, but it only admits it unconsciously or rudimentarily; it forcibly excludes the idea of moral life founded upon the redemption of the soul through suffering, that is to say, through the knowledge of evil. Sculpture is thus impossible as soon as man has acquired the knowledge of thoughtful beauty.

Hawthorne has developed and put in action this aesthetic truth in an ingenious fable that links all his different dissertations on art. The studio of Kenyon, an American sculptor established in Rome, is constantly frequented by a youth just entering manhood named Donatello, the Count of Monte Beni. No one is more lovable than this young Italian, who, nevertheless, has neither great beauty nor great gifts of intelligence, and whose education seems in certain respects to have been deplorably neglected. As soon as he appears, the studio comes alive, all hearts expand, and the beautiful Miriam, a young English girl with whom he is in love, tries to entice him with the most amusing pleasantries. His charm is due to his perfect candor and to the profound moral security that his ignorance of evil makes possible. Nothing occurs to destroy the equilibrium of his nature. Ignorant of shame, he ignores human respect and gives himself up, in the midst of Roman society, to impulses of inoffensive gaiety with no more concern than a bunny rabbit in the lanes of a park or a young deer in the shade of his native forest. He is, in every sense of the expression, a child of nature, a young faun or satyr from Antiquity, so much so that when looking at him, his friends at the studio conclude that he bears a certain resemblance to the *Faun* of Praxiteles. "Come forward, young companion of the god Pan," Miriam says to him one day, "so that we may see if you have the velvety ears of your brothers and your cousins of the forest." Now, strange to say, Donatello does have pointed and slightly furry ears. The sculptor Kenyon has repeatedly expressed the desire to model his bust, but before he is able to accomplish this, the opportunity has fled. The existence of fauns is short these days, even in Italy, their preferred country, and they soon lose, in our complicated societies, their good nature and naïve simplicity. Only a few days after Miriam verifies the traits of consanguinity that Donatello shares with pastoral divinities, out of love for her he commits a crime. A personage of dubious character, whom the author has left partly a mystery and whose secret motives he does not bother to explain, pursues Miriam with an assiduity as importunate and menacing as if prompted by remorse and vengeance. With one look from Miriam, Donatello punishes him as if he were a traitor to ancient Rome, by casting him down from atop the Tarpeian Rock. As soon as the act is done, the faun's nature begins to disappear. The seed of a new man is sewn in him by the crime and gradually develops. Gone forever is the joyous creature in whom were revived the lost innocence and simplicity of ages past. When Kenyon models his bust, the sculptor is terrified by the image he has reproduced so accurately. With moral anguish, the face has lost its repose, and in place of the insouciant physiognomy of a young, happy boy, his fingers set in stone the agitated countenance of a corrupted man.

The whole novel is contained in that title, *Transformation*. As we have just seen, Hawthorne wants to show how the faun transforms himself into a man, and the price he has to pay for a moral life. Alas! It is a sad story because sin plays the principal role. In order for man to be elevated into moral awareness, he must lose his innocence and his happiness. The supreme crown of the soul is sadness; it is not until it receives this diadem that it is conscious of its royalty and nobility. The history of Donatello is emblematic of this moral fact. Hawthorne's narrative is thus an allegory that touches reality only through the truth of its psychological insights. The exterior circumstances are fabulous; the dramatic incidents are, in a way, symbolic. With more audacity than felicity, the author has based a contemporary drama on eternal myths. Hawthorne does not confine himself to a vague resemblance between Donatello and the *Faun* of Praxiteles: he traces his descent directly from a race of fauns that were born in mythological times through the union of a god of the woods and a mortal woman. This happy couple lived near a spring that flowed in the domain that would later belong to the Counts of Monte-Beni. Several times a naiad had appeared to the ancestors of Donatello and had informed them that her race was related to theirs. One time even, her lips touched those of a knight of that house as he bent to drink its waters. But one day, when he returned to her with a bloodstain on his hands, she dove into the spring, and he never saw her again. Donatello has never seen her, even though this has been his preferred resting spot throughout his childhood. Maybe the marvelous nymph knew in advance that his hands would be covered in blood one day? No one has doubted the illustrious origins of the Monte-Beni family because over all the course of its long existence its members have always shown moral or physical peculiarities that could be traced to the blood of the antique fauns that flowed in their veins. Sometimes it might be furry ears such as Donatello's; in others, it was a character whose joyful temperament contrasted with the somber society of the Middle Ages, or a charming innocence that defied the corrupt refinement of the Renaissance. Regarding Donatello, his childhood was marvelous, and the peasants recount that just his presence sufficed to illuminate their stables and hovels. He reveled in his truly extraordinary personal gifts—the ability to speak a primitive language, for example. He would sit by the edge of the fountain, his family's cradle, and sing a sort of familiar tune—caressing, pathetic—which no one had ever taught him, and which he had found in the instincts of his innermost self, when he wanted to express his love for his mother, Nature, and the chaste voluptuousness that he felt in the beauty of Her sun and the freshness of Her woods. When his voice filled the air, the beasts of the forest would come out of their dens, the birds would forsake their nests, even venomous reptiles would abandon their holes, all coming to make a circle around him. It is a sad day for Donatello when, at the request of the sculptor Kenyon, he tries once more to exercise the power of this ancient enchantment. Kenyon, who has gone away and hidden behind a tree (so as to not frighten the native denizens of the forest by his presence), feels his heart beat in sympathy and his eyes fill with tears upon hearing this melody invented by the genius of instinct. But the inhabitants of the forest do not respond in like manner. Kenyon hears the shuffling of dry leaves, he sees the fronds of the trees moving, but not one of the creatures whose presence has been revealed by these signs dares to approach. "They, too, have abandoned me!" moans Donatello, crying hot tears. "They know they are no longer my brothers, and perchance, if I continue, I will see them turn against me!"

The allegory is beautiful and profound. It is unfortunate, in our opinion, that Hawthorne believed he had to extend it to fill three volumes. This poetic theme is parceled out from one chapter to another, taken up, abandoned, taken up again, and forgotten anew. Condensed in just a few pages, it would have held a dignified place next to "Rappaccini's Daughter" and "Egotism; or, the Bosom Serpent." Hawthorne could have given us one of his admirable psychological tales—to which he possesses the secret—but instead he offers us an inferior romance that will add little to his fame. Rather carelessly, he symbolizes the unfortunate destiny of this beautiful idea in the chapter of his novel titled "Sunshine." This is also the name of a wine, the proprietary rights to which belong exclusively to the Counts of Monte-Beni: the first glass inundates the heart with light but, once uncorked, the vintage rapidly loses its freshness; and so it is with Hawthorne's subject, which evaporates in the long pages of his narrative. The adventure of Donatello is almost that of Hawthorne. The genius that is his own, but unrecognized by him and betrayed by his description of museums and cathedrals, abandons him like the animals in Donatello's forest. Hearing the call, he behaves as they did, seeming to come forth; we hear him rustle the dry leaves of his aesthetic dissertations, but he does not want to show his face.

The book has another capital fault: it is obscure, and *willfully* obscure. One cannot figure it out for this reason. From beginning to end, the fates of the characters are crossed by a secret that it is impossible for us to explain to the reader, because the author has not explained it to himself, and he is careful to warn us that even he does not know of what it consists. We know very well that such things can happen in real life, but we expect a novel to be more explicit than real life, and we have some trouble being satisfied by the excuses Hawthorne presents to the reader at the end of the book. "The gentle reader," he writes,

> would not thank us for one of those minute elucidations, which are so tedious, and, after all, so unsatisfactory, in clearing up the romantic myster-

ies of a story. He is too wise to insist upon looking closely at the wrong side of the tapestry, after the right one has been sufficiently displayed to him, woven with the best of the artist's skill, and cunningly arranged with a view to the harmonious exhibition of its colors. If any brilliant, or beautiful, or even tolerable effect have been produced, this pattern of kindly Readers will accept it at its worth, without tearing its web apart, with the idle purpose of discovering how the threads have been knit together; for the sagacity by which he is distinguished will long ago have taught him that any narrative of human action and adventure whether we call it history or romance—is certain to be a fragile handiwork, more easily rent than mended. The actual experience of even the most ordinary life is full of events that never explain themselves, either as regards their origin or their tendency.

(*MF* 455)

Truthfully, the obscurity that prevails in the novel makes one pause. In general, mysteries exist only for the reader; but here they exist for the author himself. The romancer does not hold the strings that move the characters whose destinies he recounts. Better yet, the actors of the drama themselves seem oblivious to the secret of the perils that pursue them and the adventures that are completely their own. Miriam herself declares not to know exactly the motive for the hate with which she was pursued by that strange character whom Donatello hurled into eternity upon a meaningful look from her beautiful eyes; indeed, if one were to judge based on what she has told us about him, it is probable that he does not know any more than she. The pleasure of doing harm is felt greatly in certain natures, and often there is no need to look for any motive more secret or profound than that one—already hidden by shame—as all moralists (and Hawthorne, in particular) know. Another mystery. The only witness to Donatello's crime is the young American by the name of Hilda. Charged by Miriam to carry a packet of letters to the old palace of the Cencis, she disappears in the course of this errand, without anyone being able to know what has become of her; later, when she is reunited with her friends, she refuses to reveal what has happened to her. This novel is a true masquerade, similar to that on the Corso, where all the characters meet each other for the last time and talk to each other from behind their masks. We cannot know even if Miriam and Donatello are united or separated, and the author does not leave to the imagination of the reader the pleasure at the end of a novel that is especially sweet to him—namely, to anticipate the future lives of the characters.[24]

Hawthorne understood Italy and speaks of it fondly, in spite of the inevitable prejudices of his race and religion. Descendant of Puritans that he is, nevertheless he feels the profound charm of Rome, that city of which every visitor likes to speak ill, but from which, as it were, they cannot tear themselves away once they have spent a fortnight under its spell. "When we have left Rome in a bad humor, inflamed because the ravenous population native to her sleeping quarters has feasted on our flesh, disgusted with the bad cookery, weary from treading the poorly paved streets, desperate for a ray of sunshine," Hawthorne tells us, "we are astonished by the discovery, by and by, that our heart-strings have mysteriously attached themselves to the Eternal City, and are drawing us thitherward again, as if it were more familiar, more intimately our home, than even the spot where we were born."[25] In effect, Rome is a transcendent country, a place where our souls are born, no matter where on earth our bodies are conceived. Just as a child has no memory of its birth, the soul has no memory of the place where it quickens. But when the serendipity of life puts it in the presence of this matriarch of European cities, an innate instinct makes the soul recognize its homeland. This city is its mother—of this there can be no doubt. In Rome's familiar grandeur and smiling austerity the soul recognizes traits that only a mother's face can possess, and which, as all travelers attest, make up the sovereign charm, the ineluctable allure of the eternal city. Hawthorne tells us this: we feel at home in this maternal abode. We have no trouble understanding it as such. Everywhere else, man is the enemy or the rival of man. Only here does he feel his consanguinity with the greater human family; only here does he find himself a citizen of the world. A distinctive trait of Hawthorne's book is his respect for Catholicism and his obvious relish for the practice of confession. It is not difficult to explain how this descendant of the Puritans arrived at admiring the one principle of dogma that would have been most antipathetic to his ancestors. It is one of those unanticipated reversals of abstract logic that subvert human reason: those who lay down the most rigid doctrines are often confronted with outcomes completely opposite from what they would have expected. Hawthorne is no longer animated by the hatred of Rome that his ancestors held; and, deprived of this moral buttress, his mind (which has retained all their propensity for merciless analysis) inevitably must feel the religious reason for and the philosophical value of the sacrament of penitence. He has attended too many examinations of conscience, he knows too many of the mind's inner secrets, he has described too well those moments of extreme anguish when the soul, pursued by invisible enemies, feels the irresistible desire to proclaim aloud in front of assembled crowds its guilt or its innocence, when the terrified imagination sees no recourse against the monsters of Hell other than God's protection, not to understand the soothing properties of the religious remedy. Thus, the

Puritans' science of analysis turns against itself, and the excessive susceptibility of conscience that was their great virtue ends up justifying the enemy church. Hawthorne does not accept confession as a regular practice, but he sees it as the only resource for the soul in certain desperate cases. Here is an example of one of these exceptional cases. Hilda is a young American, a fervent Protestant, but with mystic tendencies that promote the sweetness of her character and her absolute candor. As with all innocent persons who are ignorant of life, she experiences religion more as spiritual rapture than a sovereign remedy. Piety, that charming virtue that Catholicism prizes more than any other religion, spontaneously flowers in this Puritan girl's soul. Though Protestant, she has no degree of aversion to Rome, and she does not worry herself in the least about trimming the lamp that burns in front of the Madonna at the foot of the tower in which she lives. Such a soul has no need for the rescue of confession, because purity is its life. Yes, but the day when that ermine whiteness is stained, what will happen? Hilda has seen the crime committed by Donatello, and from this moment on, her conscience gives her no rest. All the fears that innocent souls have known assail her. Because she has been a witness to the act, it seems to her that she has taken part in it. Because she has seen the crime, it seems to her that she is an accomplice. This secret, kept for too long, soon fills her with remorse. Finally one day, at the end of her strength, she wanders into that church, Saint Peter's, where confessionals are planted here and there for every language of the globe, where men of all nations may come to seek absolution for their sins. She enters one that has the following inscription, *Pro anglicá linguá,* and leaves with her soul at rest, cleansed of the apprehensions that have tortured her. Like the most fervent Catholic, she devoutly receives the benediction of the old father who has heard her avowals. But when he presses her to complete the action she has just taken by converting, Hilda refuses to betray the faith of her fathers. The good priest does not insist further, doubtless understanding that Hilda's deed is a poetic and charming act, inspired at once by nature and by grace, making any awkward appeals to her conscience unnecessary.

Before sealing this long *salaam* and sending it across the ocean to the sagacious Hawthorne, we will add a short postscript for the reader. I feel that I have to apologize to him in some ways for having discussed at such length the writings of a man who only likes to play the most plaintive chords, all deliberately orchestrated as the bass note of the human heart. For me, reading Hawthorne's books has been a pleasure, but what pleasure will they give you? My answer—and justification—is twofold. First, the human heart is not an exclusive repository for healthy, moral, and robust sentiments: it also harbors feelings that are diseased, ambiguous, and malicious. The expression of these sentiments—as long as it is frank, sincere, and vibrant—entitles a man to claims of genius because, by complementing the expression of the most saintly and irreproachable sentiments, he has added a page to the great history of the human heart, a chronicle that poets and writers have told and retold for centuries. Do you desire an infallible criterion that will permit you to put an author in his true place when you are having trouble classifying him? Do not let yourself be fooled by the titles of books or by the hierarchy of genres. Do not even ask yourself if the nature of his thought and feeling pleases or displeases you. Instead, resolutely ask yourself this question: Does the author merely repeat what his predecessors have said, without correction, without amendment, or, does he have something new to say that has not been said before? In a word, has he contributed a new page to the moral annals of mankind? Happy is he who adds something in whatever form to this great history, even if it were a footnote to the work of one of our predecessors! (Provided that the note is essential and that it has been omitted from previous editions.) It matters little, I assure you, whether the added chapter be happy or sad, pleasant or morose. What is important is that it be written at all, since the adventures he recounts and the secrets he unveils are true and real. This is the claim with which Hawthorne presents himself to us: he has written a chapter in this moral history. Doubtless, this chapter does not do the soul or the human heart the greatest honor. All the same, the chapter is true and thus merits comment and explanation because critics and philosophers are no more allowed to avoid a truth by virtue of the fact that it is unpleasant than an honest man, in ordinary life, can pretend not to see an obvious fact under the pretext that it is bothersome.

Second, can we not draw a moral even more elevated and pure from the contemplation of the most austere virtues? Is it not true that the minute understanding of evil may be a more active agent for good than that overly superficial and delicate repugnance that turns away from evil less in virtuous horror than in elegant distaste? Hawthorne's works, wisely read by a meditative mind that dilettantism has not perverted, and by a heart that experience has instructed without hurting or sullying, will thus be truer and nobler agents of moral elevation than many other works, outwardly more severe and irreproachable. We can apply to Hawthorne's works the words that the sculptor Kenyon applies to Donatello at the end of his book. Thus, let us permit the author himself to explain the morality of his writings: "Here comes my perplexity," Kenyon says,

> "Sin has educated Donatello, and elevated him. Is sin, then—which we deem such a dreadful blackness in the universe—is it, like sorrow, merely

an element of human education, through which we struggle to a higher and purer state than we could otherwise have attained? Did Adam fall, that we might ultimately rise to a far loftier paradise than his?"[26]

(*MF* 460)

Revue des Deux Mondes (1 Aug. 1860)

Notes

1. For the correct attribution of this phrase, see chapter IV, note 6.

2. Montégut's note: "See 'Un roman socialiste en Amérique,' *Revue des Deux Mondes*, Dec. 1, 1852."

3. Montégut's note: "This remark applies only to works that are undeniably superior and to men who are genuinely exceptional. Our antipathy toward certain works and certain men arises in direct proportion to their greatness, to the ability of these men to express more powerfully those forms of mind that are different from ours. The case must possess real grandeur in order to legitimate such intellectual injustice. A Gœthe shocks a Christian as a declared enemy, a Rubens shocks an idealist as a mockery incarnate of his purest thoughts. However, nothing is easier than to render justice to lesser men who are not of our party and to lesser works that have been conceived outside of the sphere in which we breathe."

4. After her execution, the Protestant theologian John Knox (ca. 1513–72) confronted those still loyal to the deposed monarch Mary Stuart (1542–87) with her severed head.

5. Montégut alludes to Robert Burton (ca. 1577– ca. 1640), who published *The Anatomy of Melancholy* in 1621; to John Webster (ca. 1578– ca. 1632), Renaissance playwright and dramatic collaborator, best known for *The Duchess of Malfi* (1623); and to *Les aventures du Baron de Faeneste* (1617, 1619, 1630), by Théodore Agrippa d'Aubigné (ca. 1552–1630), French poet and Huguenot soldier known for *Les tragiques* (1616).

6. The name (properly Elzevier) of a family of Dutch printers, famous chiefly for their special editions of the classics, much valued by collectors.

7. First published in *Mosses from an Old Manse* (1846).

8. August 4, 1789, was the date on which the Constituent Assembly, the legislative body that was formed in revolt against the meeting of the Estates General in Paris in May 1789, declared an end to long-held class privileges as a response to mob violence that had spread from Paris to the countryside in July of that same year. This was soon followed by the establishment of the Declaration of the Rights of Man and Citizen on August 26, as France moved toward the (temporary) end of autocracy. In Hawthorne's story, no calendar date is specified, but the analogy that Montégut suggests is certainly apropos.

9. First published in *Twice-told Tales* (1837).

10. Emerson's remark was recorded by George W. Curtis (1824–92) in the sketch of Hawthorne that he included in *Homes of American Authors*, a miscellany compiled by various hands (300). Montégut wrote a brief notice of this volume for the *Revue des Deux Mondes* (1 Aug. 1853): 632.

11. A sea nymph, unashamed of displaying her charms.

12. Not surprisingly, Hawthorne's works provoked considerable censure in the religious press. Writing in the *Church Review* (Jan. 1851), Arthur Cleveland Coxe, an Episcopal bishop, alleged that *The Scarlet Letter* had "already done not a little to degrade our literature, and to encourage social licentiousness." Coxe worried openly whether Hawthorne was "making fun of all religion, or only giving a fair hint of the essential sensualism of enthusiasm." His and other contemporary reviews are collected in *Hawthorne: The Critical Heritage*, edited by J. Donald Crowley (New York: Barnes & Noble, 1970); quotation 182.

13. From Cattalus (ca. 82 B.C.– ca. 54 A.D.), Ode 62: "Which the winds caress, the sun strengthens, the shower draws forth."

14. Montégut here cites his earlier essay on Hawthorne, "Un roman socialiste en Amérique," translated in chapter VII.

15. E.-D. Forgues, "Poètes et romanciers américains: Nathaniel Hawthorne," translated in chapter VI.

16. In Hawthorne's novel, Maule is hanged from the scaffold, not burned on a pyre.

17. In Montégut's original text, he uses "Esther" instead of "Hester," perhaps to facilitate a French pronunciation of the name.

18. The London firm of Smith, Elder & Co. published Hawthorne's 1860 novel under this title; in America, Ticknor & Fields issued it as *The Marble Faun; or, The Romance of Monte Beni*, which the author much preferred.

19. Madame de Staël's *Corinne, ou l'Italie* (1807) is an early example of French Romantic writing, set in France, England, and Italy.

20. *Don Juan* (1813) was one of many Romantic tales authored by the German writer and composer Ernest Theodor Amadeus Hoffmann (1776–1822), whose work inspired many later musicians, most notably Jacques Offenbach (1819–80) and Pyotr Ilyich Tchaikovsky (1840–93).

21. The next several paragraphs of Montégut's essay were translated (anonymously) as "Hawthorne in Relation to Art" in the American art periodical *The Crayon* (7 Oct. 1860): 298–301.

22. The portrait of Beatrice Cenci, until recently attributed to Guido Reni (1575–1642), figures largely in Hawthorne's novel. Guido's predilection for Classical restraint, delicate coloring, and the representation of tender emotion earned him the scorn of Ruskin and other art critics of the late nineteenth century, although Hawthorne seems to prize these same qualities.

23. An ancient city in Palestine at the crossroads of many important trading routes; hence, a place of confusing spectacle.

24. Montégut may have been even more exasperated had he seen the second edition of *The Marble Faun*, issued just several weeks after its first printing. To it Hawthorne added a factitious "Postscript," which presumably was written to satisfy "a demand for further elucidations respecting the mysteries of the story" but which did little or nothing to resolve them (*MF* 463).

25. Montégut paraphrases liberally from the opening paragraph of chapter 36 of *The Marble Faun*:

> When we have once known Rome, and left her where she lies, like a long decaying corpse, retaining a trace of the noble shape it was, but with accumulated dust and a fungus growth overspreading all its more admirable features, left her in utter weariness, no doubt, of her narrow, crooked, intricate streets, so uncom-

fortably paved with little squares of lava that to tread over them is a penitential pilgrimage, so indescribably ugly, moreover, so cold, so alley-like, into which the sun never falls, and where a chill wind forces its deadly breath into our lungs,—left her, tired of the sight of those immense seven-storied, yellow-washed hovels, or call them palaces, where all that is dreary in domestic life seems magnified and multiplied, and weary of climbing those staircases, which ascend from a ground-floor of cook shops, cobblers' stalls, stables, and regiments of cavalry, to a middle region of princes, cardinals, and ambassadors, and an upper tier of artists, just beneath the unattainable sky,—left her, worn out with shivering at the cheerless and smoky fireside by day, and feasting with our own substance the ravenous little populace of a Roman bed at night,—left her, sick at heart of Italian trickery, which has uprooted whatever faith in man's integrity had endured till now, and sick at stomach of sour bread, sour wine, rancid butter, and bad cookery, needlessly bestowed on evil meats,—left her, disgusted with the pretence of holiness and the reality of nastiness, each equally omnipresent,—left her, half lifeless from the languid atmosphere, the vital principle of which has been used up long ago, or corrupted by myriads of slaughters,—left her, crushed down in spirit with the desolation of her ruin, and the hopelessness of her future,—left her, in short, hating her with all our might, and adding our individual curse to the infinite anathema which her old crimes have unmistakably brought down,—when we have left Rome in such mood as this, we are astonished by the discovery, by and by, that our heart-strings have mysteriously attached themselves to the Eternal City, and are drawing us thitherward again, as if it were more familiar, more intimately our home, than even the spot where we were born.

(Centenary Edition, vol. IV, 325–26)

26. Significantly, the sculptor's fiancée, Hilda, immediately repudiates this assertion, and Kenyon himself withdraws from it, affirming his desire to confine himself to the horizons of her orthodox moral vision. In his 1864 essay, Montégut revised his estimate of *The Marble Faun,* claiming that he owed "a reparation to the author's memory." While still not discounting the novel's faults, he now felt that he could not "say too much in praise" of it; "it is worthy of all the meditations of a philosopher." (See chapter XI, "Nathaniel Hawthorne.")

X

Louis Étienne

"The Transcendentalist Novel in America" (1860)

Is mythology back in favor? Pans, satyrs, and fauns are returning by leaps and bounds. There is a satyr in the new novel by this American storyteller. Along with *La légende des siècles*,[1] that makes two of them over the course of several months:

> On connaissait Stulcas, faune de Pallantyre,
> Gès, qui, le soir, riait sur le Ménale assis,
> Bos, l'ægipan de Crète; on entendait Chrysis,
> Sylvain du Ptyx que l'homme appelle Janicule,
> Qui jouait de la flûte au fond du crépuscule;
> Anthrops, faune de Pinde, était cité partout;
> Celui-ci, nulle part.

> [We knew Stulcas, the faun of Pallantyre,
> Gès, who, at night, laughed while sitting on the Menalo,
> Bos, Crete's aegipan; we heard Chrysis,
> Sylvain of the Ptyx, whom man called Janiculum,
> Who played the flute as the sun began to set;
> Anthrops, Pindar's faun, was cited everywhere;
> This one, nowhere.]

More or less twins in time, these creatures nevertheless are very different. The poet's faun has morals worthy of the parents whose lower body he resembles. In the past, French verse behaved like a great lady, with great decorum (like tragedy in Horace), and never would have danced the saraband, blushing with shame, with an illiterate satyr: *Intererit Satyris paulum pudibunds protervis*.[2]

The novelist's is neither Pan nor Aegipan. He is just as much a faun as they, but he is also the heir of all the ages, the most charming model of a young man, except that he sports a pair of slightly pointed ears crowned with small tufts of fur. Don't let the keenness of these auditory organs alarm you. They are not the symbol of any brute instinct; they are simply signs of a sylvan nature, alert to the slightest noises of the forest. Hawthorne's satyr is the *Faun* of Praxiteles, whose innocent peace is troubled not even by a cloud. He is eternal adolescence and unfailing and pure joy.

That is not all: the poet's satyr is a veritable allegory, a more or less poetic form embodying pantheism. As long as the allegory is graceful, it hardly matters that it lacks the feeling of loss conveyed by Gœthe's "Ganymede"—so short, so sober, and so impassioned.[3] The novelist's is a real character, an Italian, Donatello, Count of Monte Beni: he lives there, walks there, talks there without being aware of anything in the world called pantheism.

These two beings are separated by a distance, a distance equivalent to that which separates America from Europe, the sites of their respective nativities. And yet it is impossible that they are not related. It is not by caprice that we compare them; it is it not by chance that they were born at the same moment in the Old World and the New. The same philosophical inspiration that seems to be in the air has given birth to them. This doctrine has a name, but it serves to designate two very different systems. Today I want to shed light on the particular system to which Hawthorne is attached by examining his very curious novel, *Transformation*.[4] Never has he been more metaphysical; no other work reveals the extent to which he has been schooled by his philosophical master. Up until now, he seemed most conspicuously to be the great nephew of the old Puritan founders of New England, and we studied him from this point of view ourselves.[5] We knew very well that this son of the Puritans was, at heart, a Transcendentalist. But we deferred considering the latter for a more favorable opportunity, and that opportunity has arrived. Though it might seem illogical to combine philosophical and literary analysis (two things that address two different orders of readers), in this case it is not impossible to answer the expectations of both.

As a disciple of Emerson—that rarest of intellects, no less distinguished as a poet than as a philosopher—Hawthorne took from Transcendentalism its poetic element. He does not write novels to spread a philosophy, but he quarries philosophical ideas that give life and inspiration to his novels. This is the important thing: the principal concern of a novel is the story itself; but it also needs an ideal, and that it seeks from philosophy. To whom does the novelist owe the idea of his modern faun, the most important conception in his book?

To our surprise, he came looking for his ideal in this old Europe, the mother of genius, the old wet nurse to so many. She told them so many beautiful tales in their childhood that even those who crossed the ocean remember them and never grow weary of coming back to ask for them again. America is too young a mother to know many of the old stories. Everything there is new, well organized, well constructed. There are no edifices in ruins. Legends find no old walls to which they can attach themselves. The Ideal is like parietaria[6]—it cannot grow on newly quarried stones. Thus, it was to Rome, the metropolis of the Ancient World, that the storyteller came to seek his inspiration. No doubt, one day, when he was strolling through those Vatican galleries (with his Poet's admiration and his American skepticism abreast and side to side), suddenly he stopped himself in front of that *Faun* of Praxiteles—so alive, so young, so handsome. He, the Puritan, the Transcendentalist, the citizen of a sad, mirthless nation, arrived in front of this beauty, this youth, this freshness, this childish laughter, and cried to himself, "I've found it!"

But can we be sure that this conception was new to him? Before having met it in all of its plastic beauty, realized for the eyes but imprisoned in marble, did he not see it floating in the ethereal regions of the imagination—less striking, true, but free and pure like an idea? Could he not remember having perceived on a certain day, at a certain moment of his life, a being that was neither man nor animal, but a beautiful intermediary between the two: an attempt by Nature to outdo the Creation, a supreme and final retouching of a being stripped of reason? Another touch of the Divine finger, another brushstroke of the eternal Painter, another beam from the source of Light, and a new man is created. Perhaps he resembles other men, but he has not yet been altered and made sophisticated by civilization, retaining all the innocent characteristics of creatures who live in the forests and the fields. Woods, verdure, flowers, streams running under the overhanging branches, flocks in the field, wild beasts in the woods: all of this was melted down and condensed in the graceful creation of the faun. I repeat, was the marble of the Greek artist a new discovery for the storyteller? If I am not mistaken, he could have said the same words to this marble statue that his master addressed in a similar circumstance: I know you; the beauty of your lines is surprising me for the first time, but you are "the old, eternal fact I had met already in so many forms,—with which I lived, and which I left at home in so many conversations." Nothing has changed around me except the place, "and I said to myself: O! 'Thou foolish child, hast thou come out hither, over four thousand miles of salt water, to find that which was perfect to thee there at home?'" That done, "It traveled by my side; I imagined that I had left it in Boston, and I found it in the Vatican. . . ."[7]

One might ask in which area of America the storyteller found his faun: if it were in some virgin forest or among some remnants of the Chippewa or the Huron tribes. I would answer that mythology is not the exclusive domain of the arts or poetry, and that at the source of all myths will be found latent distillations of philosophy. It was no doubt some great, yet unknown philosopher who invented the first hybrid beings, the satyrs, to provide the missing link between the animals and man. One day when he was "God-intoxicated" (as Novalis said of Spinoza),[8] this unknown philosopher (who nevertheless existed) gave birth to this poetic monstrosity. That very day, the god Nature "who stirs silently in the waters and winds, who sleeps in the plants, who gives life to the animal, and who gives reason to man,"[9] created a new being, a consciousness midway between simple waking and reason, between animal and man. That was the day that pantheism was born.

Thus we can believe that Hawthorne's faun was sired neither by the wilderness nor by solitude (like the satyrs of Plutarch or certain Fathers of the Church), but simply by philosophy, much like the *homunculus* of Doctor Faust.[10] We would not even be surprised to catch a glimpse of the nest where he was hatched in one of the most abstruse and shadowy corners of Emerson's *Essays*. "The universe is represented in every one of its particles. Every thing in nature contains all the powers of nature. Every thing is made of one hidden stuff; as the naturalist sees one type under every metamorphosis, and regards a horse as a running man, a fish as a swimming man, a bird as a flying man, a tree as a rooted man."[11] Without insisting on Emerson's pantheism, which is hardly in doubt, it will suffice to take my readers for a walk in the groves of Transcendentalism, and to find there some traces of the romancer. That same hidden stuff, those metamorphoses, are purely identical, and, if we look carefully, we will find the very same expression. But let us quickly escape these big metaphysical words, and say simply that Hawthorne's faun is much more a literary experience than a philosophical study. Another time, perhaps, we shall get the metamorphosis of a plant into an animal. But for now, let us be content with this very modest and very ideal metamorphosis of the most charming of animals into an individual of the human species.

How will this metamorphosis happen? The very title of the book, *Transformation,* proves that this is the central subject of the novel. It would take all the art of a philosopher—together with that of a poet—to make today's readers accept this utterly fantastic idea. For his faun, he provides an Arcadia, Rome and its ruins, even a Rome seen from atop Saint Peter's, from the Capitol to the Tarpeian Rock, from summits that the noises of real life never reach.

Donatello, the Count of Monte Beni, noble descendant of one of the oldest families of Tuscany, has followed to Rome a foreign woman of rare beauty, Miriam, whose family lineage is obscure, but which reputedly is allied with one of the most powerful houses in the city of the Popes. The love of the Count and the signora is not one of those Italian loves that expresses itself in sighs, in gallant gifts, in amorous sonnets, reminiscent of Metastasio or Petrarch.[12] An ordinary and common flame cannot exist between two beings who so little resemble their surroundings; doubtless, only a man as handsome as Donatello, Praxiteles' marble faun come to life, could suit Miriam, a beautiful living image of some Amazon from Antiquity. Is Miriam Italian? Her independent existence, without parents to live with her, without a husband or lover, does not permit us to think so. With her freedom of expression and judgment, we would be tempted to take her for an Englishwoman, but a closer look at her eyes and her skin tone (darkened by the desert sun of the Orient) prevents us from accepting that conclusion. Whether she be Roman, English, or Jewish, Miriam has something in her very being that intimates a premonition of unhappiness. Is it sadness, a painful memory, an inexplicable anxiety? Mystery surrounds her soul as well as her person. Only a vulgar fool would be baited by this mystery, and he would soon see himself punished for it. Any man who dreams seriously of joining his destiny to Miriam's would be truly imprudent. Besides, the beautiful signora defends herself with scornful and ironic pride. She has a strong arm against all weakness and a secret that is impossible to share and upon which her life and honor seem to depend.

To complete the picture, beautiful and rich foreigner that she is, Miriam has the habits and even the talent of an artist. She occupies a Roman palace, since that is what they call those dilapidated aristocratic residences. The main salon of her palace is an artist's studio. There, if it is true that the paintbrush has something to say about the painter's soul, perhaps we can discover some clues about Miriam's secret. Her favorite paintings (and, what is more, the only canvasses she has done for some time) tell only of retribution and murderous passions. The artist's brush is almost drunk with blood. Here, a triumphant Judith, who holds the head of her enemy, and who looks with an implacable eye at the blood that flows in streams.[13] Only unquenchable vengeance can reach such heights of energy. Elsewhere, with invincible horror, Herodias contemplates the severed head of John the Baptist, murdered by her command.[14] One might say that the hand that satisfied itself in drafting these images of cruelty also expressed, in spite of itself, an anticipated remorse. What if all of those canvases, whose bloody fantasies are admired but laughingly dismissed by Miriam's friends, are confessions written with a paintbrush? Yet this studio, solitary domain of a woman's soul, is haunted not only by murderous thoughts: the palette held by that white hand has known more joyous colors than that of blood. Here and there, we see clearly images of happiness smiling, sketches of the joys given to man. But even here, worry is not absent, an ever-present witness to the happiest moments in life. Sometimes we see depicted a naïve love barely aware of itself, of the hour that is passing, and the austere future that is approaching. Sometimes it is a strong and calm love, the saintly love of husband and wife, between the hearth and the cradle. Sometimes it might be a fresh pastoral replete with dancing, music, and flowers. But in the background of all these paintings, otherwise relaxed and rejoicing, there is always a somber figure who attends all these joys with envy, and this figure has a certain vague resemblance to Miriam.

Why does Miriam show, if not love, at least a marked fondness for the Count of Monte Beni? How is she able to let that truly primitive and innocent soul attach itself to her? For that very reason, we might take her for a novice—even a virgin. This young man is beneath the love of a woman such as Miriam; but the origin of his inferiority also renders him more worthy of attachment and interest. One loves a child, not with ardor, but with tenderness. Donatello is something more—and less—than a man.

Donatello is, as it were, the ravishing figure that appeared to Praxiteles the day he conceived his *Faun*. He is the Faun himself. Only instead of being born in the artist's workshop, he was newly delivered from the hands of Nature and carries her recent imprint. His joyous and unselfconscious soul resembles . . . the gentle type that Virgil, Nature's poet, ascribes to young animals. He has no idea of evil—not even a taste for it, or an aversion. His innocence is natural—perhaps a trifle pagan, but gracious: the only innocence that the Ancients knew. It is the innocence of fauns who bound through the forest and the bird who pushes itself out of the nest while trilling its song for the first time. The air and the forest alike are home to his brothers. Donatello knows them, calls to them, and they respond to his voice.

A modern poet has anticipated and sketched out the poetic figure of Donatello, and we shall avail ourselves of his work to characterize the young

Count of Monte Beni. Let us remember only that the latter has no idea of his gifts and even less of his deficiencies.

> And such I knew, a forest seer,
> A minstrel of the natural year,
> Foreteller of the vernal ides,
> . . .
> It seemed that nature could not raise
> A plant in any secret place,
> In quaking bog, on snowy hill,
> Beneath the grass that shades the rill,
> Under the snow, between the rocks,
> In damp fields known to bird and fox,
> But he would come in the very hour
> It opened in its virgin bower,
> As if a sunbeam showed the place,
> And tell its long-descended race.
> It seemed as if the breezes brought him,
> It seemed as if the sparrows taught him,
> As if by secret sight he knew
> Where in far fields the orchis grew.
> There are many events in the field
> Which are not shown to common eyes,
> But all her shows did nature yield
> To please and win this pilgrim wise.
> He saw the partridge drum in the woods,
> He heard the woodcock's evening hymn,
> He found the tawny thrush's broods,
> And the shy hawk did wait for him.
> What others did at distance hear,
> And guessed within the thicket's gloom,
> Was showed to this philosopher,
> And at his bidding seemed to come.[15]

Take away from this portrait of the lover of nature everything that reminds us of the sage and the philosopher. In place of reflection put instinct, and you have Donatello.

For most men, the beauties of nature speak a language that explains itself little by little and penetrates the soul. Donatello senses them with the impetuosity of passion. When his organization (a rustic one, we might say) tires of the artificial atmosphere of the city and shivers at the cold and severe aspect of statues, churches, and ruins, he runs to the Borghese gardens, where Art does not impose itself however far and wide one rambles. There the breath of an almost wild nature intoxicates him, as if it were a full-bodied wine. All alone he runs down the paths, he leaps to catch a branch of a tree and swings himself through the air. He is exultant, divinely mad. He has raptures in which he embraces the trunk of a sturdy tree—as if he heard a heart beating under the bark that responds to his hug—strikingly like the faun of Antiquity who tried to clasp the body of a Nymph who lived within the tree's rough outer shell, ready perhaps to wake in his arms. At other times, he stretches himself out on the ground, so as to hold the maternal breast of the earth closer to him, and he presses his lips to violets and daisies that seem, in spite of their natural modesty, to kiss him back.

While he is lying motionless on the turf, it is pleasant to see how green and blue lizards leave their rock in the sun to span the length of Donatello's person with their little feet, or how birds leap and sing their chorus about him. Perhaps they recognize him as one of theirs. Perhaps they think he is rooted there, and that he grows like any other tree. What is certain is that they do not see him as an enemy (like other men), and that they are no more fearful of him than they would be of a hillock of grass and flowers.

We could go on forever if we only wanted to recall all the strange things to be said about this young Count. About one thing, however, we cannot be silent: the origin of his family. His genealogy is pure mythology, but it lends romantic interest to his lineage. According to tradition, the Monte Beni go back to that Pelasgian era when the beings and gods of the forests took little care to hide themselves in the shrubbery. The father of the first Monte Beni was one of these savage gods, who had loved a mortal maiden, having won her charms either through unexpected courtesy and delicacy or, perhaps, by means more in keeping with his brutal nature. Either genealogists have sought to give this family a very flattering link to Antiquity, or, more likely, the pointed ears that have renewed themselves from time to time in the house steered their imagination in their prehistoric research. Donatello passes for the veritable son of fauns (like Aeneas, the offspring of the goddess Venus, and Romulus of Mars).[16] As to the rest, a little of the fantastic is not unusual in the towns of Etruria,[17] and, if my memory serves me right, Boccaccio, in his poem *Ameto,* has the first forefather of the Florentine people born of a satyr and a human woman.[18]

Does the Monte Beni family derive its glory from their pointed ears, as certain houses do of physical deformities to which they are privileged (like the protuberant lower lip of an illustrious reigning house)?[19]

Are they proud or ashamed of these bizarre traditions? Of this we cannot be sure. It often happens that they cover their ears (as did the imposter Smerdis—from whom they were cut);[20] thus it is difficult to make any statement about the presumptive acuity of that auditory organ. But doubtless other signs of that lineage (intellectual and, especially, moral) are visible from time to time in this member of the family: beauty, strength, bravura, generosity, sincerity, and simple tastes—a love for ordinary country pleasures, a certain secret gift for befriending wild beasts and birds, a certain sympathy for trees among which he takes pleasure above all. For all these gifts, he also possesses singular deficiencies in intelligence and heart (the higher human faculties); these become more conspicuous as the years pass while the primitive gifts have had time to become corrupted and altered.

Such is the young Count of Monte Beni who renounces his happy Tuscan solitudes to follow the mysterious Miriam: he is sad, but trusting, when he sees a cloud on her pensive brow; happy when he sees her smile. And he asks for no other happiness than to follow her steps like a handsome spaniel, wanting only a caress from time to time, and permission to sleep at its mistress's feet.

These youthful joys could have lasted for a long time if a strange incident had not awakened in Miriam a memory of an inexorable past and, in Donatello, feelings of hate that he had never known before. One day, accompanied by Donatello and two American friends (like her, sculptors and painters), Miriam is exploring the catacombs. All of a sudden, they notice that the beautiful artist of bloody canvases is missing. To describe Donatello's anguish while he searches for Miriam in those funereal subterranean depths would be difficult. Like a faithful dog who has lost track of his master, he is the first to find her. But discovered with her is someone with a strange demeanor, from whom Donatello instinctively is repelled: more sagacious than human reason, his nature tells him, "This is the enemy." Miriam's pallor, the agitation and horror that betray themselves in her whole person, confirm for Donatello the voice of instinct. From that day forward, he ceases to be the joyous child of the forests because he no longer sees Miriam's smile. An unknown figure shadowing the woman he loves, incessantly renewing his terrors yet exercising over her an inexplicable dominion, would have thrown any other man into a frenzy of dismay, wavering between disgust and defiance, disdain and jealousy. For Donatello, the unfortunate presence of this stranger casts a first pall of gloom over his life. It provokes his anger without diminishing his confidence in Miriam, and changes the impassioned instincts of his lively nature into savage impulses for vengeance. Gentle and harmless like the most innocent of animals, he is drawn without hesitation to the idea of murder.

For her part, Miriam fears this character no less than she hates him. Is he linked to the secret that makes her tremble? Does he have the power to destroy her honor—or some far worse terror yet? Is Miriam innocent? Or are the visions of murder that occupy her artistic imagination images—only too exact—of real blood that has stained her small feminine hand? Then again, as happens to so many innocent people, perhaps she holds the fatal responsibility for a crime that others have committed? After the encounter in the catacombs, where he seemed to be hidden until then, nothing can quell the stranger's obstinacy. At night, he sleeps at Miriam's door, like one of the thousands of beggars who take refuge in the porticos of Italian palaces. During the day, we can be certain that he will emerge from behind a ruin or suddenly appear in the midst of a piazza like Hamlet's ghost. Miriam's imagination is no less besieged than her palazzo and her person. The figure of the stranger always slides through the bristles of her paintbrush to occupy a corner in her canvases. At last he is called Miriam's *model*.

The heavy chains that bind together two beings who hate one another most often are forged in a furnace of evil passions and misdeeds. Only death can break them. Miriam foresees that death will be her only deliverance. But she seems to believe in her innocence, and this makes her cling to life. When her eyes fell on Donatello—perhaps happiness might still be hers? Amid these fluctuations of thought, time passes and the hour approaches when the stranger will fulfill the threat of his vengeance or his jealousy. More than once Miriam has contemplated a poison that could put her torment to an end, or the Tiber into which she might disappear. More than once, she realizes that Donatello (that overgrown child, tender and mirthful) has only been waiting for a sign to become a man of blood. Only her most desperate prayers have saved the life of her tormentor.

One evening, during a promenade on the Capitol, Miriam and Donatello stay behind their friends on a little platform surrounded by a parapet, from which they overlook the houses of Rome in all their infinite multitude. Left by themselves, their conversation turns to memories of the Tarpeian Rock, where they have found themselves. Silence and solitude seem to surround Donatello and Miriam: their talk continues; Donatello questions Miriam about the rock from which traitors in ancient times were thrown. While listening, the former seems distracted by something strange, like a hunting dog that is striving to obey his master, but whose attention nervously is focused on something further off. They are not alone: a shadow emerges from the depths of a niche once occupied by a statue. It approaches Miriam; it is the *model* who now stands between Miriam and Donatello, between his victim and his enemy, at the edge of a precipice. At that moment, a violent scene transpires between these three beings who are fatally chained together, all of whom know that a supreme crisis has arrived, at that height and that distance, in the silence of the night, far removed from the tranquility and peace in which the rest of humanity are immersed. There is a struggle, but not a long one. And when a friend of Miriam's, who has noticed her absence, retraces her footsteps, she sees Donatello holding a man suspended above the precipice, possibly questioning Miriam with his eyes.

Before letting the stranger fall into this empty space (in which we see numberless gables and steep-pitched roofs), or saving his life and rescuing him from this sorry end, let us be permitted to make several reflections on this book and its author. In allowing ourselves this digression (which will not be long), we follow the practice of Homer, who did not hesitate to introduce his most important discourses at the moment when his heroes were holding up their arms to strike the decisive blow. Or, better still, we are following Hawthorne's example, who, like a good philosopher, grasps the fleeting yet somber moment—when the poisoned chalice rises to the lips, or the pike hovers above the wound—to state his moral.

A stranger who possesses a secret he exploits, a young man who blindly loves a woman who is vastly superior to him, a night-time scene of violence at the edge of a precipice—in and of themselves there is nothing new here. Reduced to its bare bones, this story would be the most common of melodramas. But we are not practicing literary osteology; it is more important to grasp the very principle of life which animates a work of art. For better or worse, Hawthorne's novels are always governed by an Idea. In some instances, the Idea is Puritan (as in *The Scarlet Letter*, his most brilliant work, or, in *The House of the Seven Gables*, his most dramatic). In others, it is completely Transcendental (or, to put it differently, informed by Kant, Schelling, and Hegel himself). In these latter works, we can sum things up even better by identifying the influence of a man who has harvested that bumper crop of German philosophy—namely, Ralph Waldo Emerson.

Donatello is happy as long as he is not transformed: in becoming a man through transgression (which is to say out of remorse, out of a knowledge of good and evil), he climbs a step on the ladder of creation. But, at the same time, he falls into the miseries of human life. The chapter in the midst of which we have paused is entitled "The Faun's Transformation," which is the very name of the book. It is also its signature. A long ladder along which elements climb ceaselessly, or rather, one element—at once material, intellectual, and moral: this is the image of Transcendentalism. Hawthorne's faun could be taken for the type of this philosophy, just as another school had Condillac's statue or the first man of Buffon.[21] The word *happiness* is

Donatello's alpha and omega. Having from man only physical beauty, the faun still possesses the quietude of plants and the unselfconscious simplicity of animals. Benefiting from a blind but divine happiness, he breathes the infinite without knowing. This first state is like a golden age for Donatello, scarcely bothered by the dim shadow that occasionally casts on his life the approaching change of his destiny.

Never has Hawthorne written more beautifully than in three chapters meant to discuss the relationship between Art and happiness: "The Suburban Villa," "The Faun and Nymph," and "The Sylvan Dance." There, Donatello surrenders to his rustic merriment and drags Miriam into the middle of a country dance to the sound of the *zampogna*.[22] The illusion is complete: Miriam and Donatello are a nymph of Antiquity dancing with a merry companion of Bacchus. The fearless Romagnols, wearing goatskins or half-naked, are satyrs and sylvans who respond to the sound of the tambourine and join in unison with the crazy joy of Donatello. One might say that the scene resembles a bas-relief from Antiquity depicting the Dionysiacs, detached from the marble vase it had encircled. First of all, these pages are remarkable, coming from the pen of a descendant of the Puritans. They do not seem to comport with the lugubrious tone of so many other of Hawthorne's tales. But only when this merriment vanishes can one appreciate its value. The habit of seeing nature and mankind in mourning renders joy as necessary as sunlight.

Our joyous faun touches again on this side of Emerson's philosophy. Open *The Blithedale Romance* to the chapter about the legend of Zenobia and you will find the definition of this philosophy: Transcendentalists are honest people who quest for a happier life, a better life.[23] Look for happiness, show man happiness in this life: that is the doctrine in its entirety— Transcendental in principle, befitting the school from which it came from Germany, but practical in its results, essential to the Anglo-Saxons. This avowed goal of happiness is the opposite of Puritanism; if we look closely, we can see that, taken seriously, this philosophy would corrupt Christian ideas. Spinoza said it a long time ago: "If science consists in knowing nature, and wisdom in enjoying it, let us repudiate the precepts of abstinence, let us distance ourselves from sadness; wisdom is a meditation not of death, but of life."[24]

The faun enjoys nature without true knowledge. He is unselfconscious, yet lives at the heart of the infinite. Man, aware of himself, is finished. He cannot achieve happiness except by means of knowledge, and by losing himself in the heart of infinity. When Donatello throws himself on the ground to embrace the earth in the Villa Borghese he reminds us of Werther, seated on the grass in his German village, intoxicating himself with the palpitations of the earth whose heart responds to his.[25] Both are Spinozists, but the first is one without knowing it, and the second is not enough of one. If he were more of one, if he knew the dogma of compensation, the philosophy of circles and Transcendentalism better, he would understand why it might be a happiness to be deprived of Lolotte.[26] He would enjoy nature; he would meld his soul into the Oversoul without the necessity of firing a pistol to make that fusion happen.

I have already cited a piece of Emerson's on the philosophy of solitude. Nothing proves better how much the character of Donatello is simply an Emersonian conception. That seer, that lover of nature who is barely still a man is the double for this faun who is not yet a man. Here is a page from Hawthorne. To please his friend, the American sculptor Kenyon, whom he has received in his domain, Donatello consents to demonstrate his knowledge of the language by which (in years past) he could summon the inhabitants of the forests. Even though at this moment he is no longer the joyous *Faun* of Praxiteles, he truly wants to reclaim his secret affinity with the animals.

> "From my earliest childhood, I was familiar with whatever creatures haunt the woods. You would have laughed to see the friends I had among them; yes, among the wild, nimble things, that reckon man their deadliest enemy! How it was first taught me, I cannot tell; but there was a charm—a voice, a murmur, a kind of chant—by which I called the woodland inhabitants, the furry people, and the feathered people, in a language that they seemed to understand."
>
> "I have heard of such a gift," responded the sculptor gravely, "but never before met with a person endowed with it. Pray try the charm; and lest I should frighten your friends away, I will withdraw into this thicket, and merely peep at them."
>
> "I doubt," said Donatello, "whether they will remember my voice now. [*It changes, you know, as the boy grows towards manhood.*]"
>
> Nevertheless, as the young Count's good-nature and easy persuadability were among his best characteristics, he set about complying with Kenyon's request. The latter, in his concealment among the shrubberies, heard him send forth a sort of modulated breath, wild, rude, yet harmonious. It struck the auditor as at once the strangest and the most natural utterance that had ever reached his ears. Any idle boy, it should seem, singing to himself and setting his wordless song to no other or more definite tune than the play of his own pulses, might produce a sound almost identical with this; and yet, it was as individual as a murmur of the breeze. Donatello tried it, over and

over again, with many breaks, at first, and pauses of uncertainty; then with more confidence, and a fuller swell, like a wayfarer groping out of obscurity into the light, and moving with freer footsteps as it brightens around him.

Anon, his voice appeared to fill the air, yet not with an obtrusive clangor. The sound was of a murmurous character, soft, attractive, persuasive, friendly. The sculptor fancied that such might have been the original voice and utterance of the natural man, before the sophistication of the human intellect formed what we now call language. In this broad dialect—broad as the sympathies of nature—the human brother might have spoken to his inarticulate brotherhood that prowl the woods, or soar upon the wing, and have been intelligible to such extent as to win their confidence.

The sound had its pathos too. At some of its simple cadences, the tears came quietly into Kenyon's eyes. They welled up slowly from his heart, which was thrilling with an emotion more delightful than he had often felt before[, *but which he forbore to analyze, lest, if he seized it, it should at once perish in his grasp*].

Donatello paused two or three times, and seemed to listen,—then, recommencing, he poured his spirit and life more earnestly into the strain. And finally,—or else the sculptor's hope and imagination deceived him,—soft treads were audible upon the fallen leaves. There was a rustling among the shrubbery; a whir of wings, moreover, that hovered in the air. It may have been all an illusion; but Kenyon fancied that he could distinguish the stealthy, cat-like movement of some small forest citizen, and that he could even see its doubtful shadow, if not really its substance. But, all at once, whatever might be the reason, there ensued a hurried rush and scamper of little feet; and then the sculptor heard a wild, sorrowful cry, and through the crevices of the thicket beheld Donatello fling himself on the ground.

Emerging from his hiding-place, he saw no living thing, save a brown lizard (it was of the tarantula species) rustling away through the sunshine. To all present appearance, this venomous reptile was the only creature that had responded to the young Count's efforts to renew his intercourse with the lower orders of nature.

"What has happened to you?" exclaimed Kenyon, stooping down over his friend, and wondering at the anguish which he betrayed.

"<Murder, murder!> [Death, death!]" sobbed Donatello. "They know it!"

(*MF* 247–49)

Donatello's anguish adds to the force of the scene. Since he feels guilty, the flight of his animal friends, his brothers in innocence, is a cruel punishment for him. Since evil is no longer unknown to him, the ties that bound him to all living nature are broken. This reflection brings us back to the chapter of the transformation of the faun and to the precipice of the Tarpeian Rock. Excuse this little dalliance in philosophy. For too long now Donatello has been holding the stranger suspended over the abyss. We return to the novel.

Having read in Miriam's eyes the condemnation of her tormentor, the Count of Monte Beni throws him to the bottom of the precipice. The murder is consummated; irremediable evil has been done. After the first feverish exaltation that provokes and follows the crime, after this apparent victory of defiant will over moral law, remorse overtakes the perpetrator with a force he did not foresee and he begins to understand the enormity of his error. He thought himself triumphant, but it was evil that triumphed over good in him, and the guilty one understands that he is his vanquished's prey. He has found an implacable master. At first Donatello and Miriam, freed by murder, breathe a little more easily. However, as soon as the fever has subsided, the crime changes its air. Their victim's face haunts them still, expressing (instead of hate) severity and malediction—the very look they saw (no! not for the last time) at the edge of the precipice. Walking together and leaning on each other, they move toward those from whom henceforth they will feel separated by their crime, much like Adam and Eve banished from Paradise and walking in the immense solitude of the world. But there is blood between them, and a life together that would resemble happiness is not permitted them. They must leave one another, and this separation, in accord with moral sense, is full of truth.

Like many other of Hawthorne's women (witness Zenobia of *The Blithedale Romance*), Miriam—the stronger of the two, not only more energetic, but hardened and in some ways flush with painful experience—braves regret and throws up a challenge to her enemy, who seems to rise from the dead to intimidate her. She is like a rebel angel when she cries to herself, "Evil, be my good!" But Donatello, who gave death blindly, who was Miriam's arm, is absolutely helpless confronting the great fact of conscience that is waking in him. Vainly, Miriam wants to help him bear the burden of moral misery: conscience has an impregnable logic. Donatello, whom Nature made inaccessible to sorrow; Donatello, who seemed a being from the Golden Age, brought to earth to teach men that life used to be joy and sunshine; Donatello must be plunged into the shadows of worry and regret. Because Miriam dragged Donatello into the crime, that very crime separates them.

The young man lifted his hand to his breast, and, unintentionally, as

Miriam's hand was within his, he lifted that along with it. "I have a great weight here!" said he. The fancy struck Miriam (but she drove it resolutely down) that Donatello almost imperceptibly shuddered, while, in pressing his own hand against his heart, he pressed hers there too.

"Rest your heart on me, dearest one!" she resumed. "Let me bear all its weight; I am well able to bear it; for I am a woman, and I love you! I love you, Donatello! Is there no comfort for you in this avowal? Look at me! Heretofore you have found me pleasant to your sight. Gaze into my eyes! Gaze into my soul! Search as deeply as you may, you can never see half the tenderness and devotion that I henceforth cherish for you. All that I ask is your acceptance of the utter self-sacrifice (but it shall be no sacrifice, to my great love) with which I seek to remedy the evil you have incurred for my sake!"

All this fervor on Miriam's part; on Donatello's, a heavy silence.

"O, speak to me!" she exclaimed. "Only promise me to be, by and by, a little happy!"

"Happy?" murmured Donatello. "Ah, never again! never again!"

"Never? Ah, that is a terrible word to say to me!" answered Miriam. "A terrible word to let fall upon a woman's heart, when she loves you, and is conscious of having caused your misery! If you love me, Donatello, speak it not again. And surely you did love me?"

"I did," replied Donatello gloomily and absently.

Miriam released the young man's hand, but suffered one of her own to lie close to his, and waited a moment to see whether he would make any effort to retain it. There was much depending upon that simple experiment.

With a deep sigh—as when, sometimes, a slumberer turns over in a troubled dream—Donatello changed his position, and clasped both his hands over his forehead. The genial warmth of a Roman April kindling into May was in the atmosphere around them; but when Miriam saw that involuntary movement and heard that sigh of relief (for so she interpreted it), a shiver ran through her frame, as if the iciest wind of the Apennines were blowing over her.

["He has done himself a greater wrong than I dreamed of," thought she, with unutterable compassion. "Alas! it was a sad mistake! He might have had a kind of bliss in the consequences of this deed, had he been impelled to it by a love vital enough to survive the frenzy of that terrible moment, mighty enough to make its own law, and justify itself against the natural remorse. But to have perpetrated a dreadful murder (and such was his crime, unless love, annihilating moral distinctions, made it otherwise) on no better warrant than a boy's idle fantasy! I pity him from the very depths of my soul! As for myself, I am past my own or other's pity."]

She arose from the young man's side, and stood before him with a sad, commiserating aspect; [it was the look of a ruined soul, bewailing, in him, a grief less than what her profounder sympathies imposed upon herself.]

"Donatello, we must part." [she said, with melancholy firmness. "]Yes; leave me! Go back to your old tower, which overlooks the green valley you have told me of among the Apennines. Then, all that has passed will be recognized as but an ugly dream. For in dreams the conscience sleeps, and we often stain ourselves with guilt of which we should be incapable in our waking moments. The deed you seemed to do, last night, was no more than such a dream; there was as little substance in what you fancied yourself doing. Go; and forget it all!"

"Ah, that terrible face!" said Donatello, pressing his hands over his eyes. "Do you call that unreal?"

"Yes; for you beheld it with dreaming eyes," replied Miriam. "It was unreal; and, that you may feel it so, it is requisite that you see this face of mine no more. Once, you may have thought it beautiful; now, it has lost its charm. Yet it would still retain a miserable potency to bring back the past illusion, and, in its train, the remorse and anguish [that would darken all your life]. Leave me, [therefore, and forget me."

"Forget you, Miriam!" said Donatello, roused somewhat from his apathy of despair.

"If I could remember you, and behold you, apart from that frightful visage which stares at me over your shoulder, that were a consolation, at least, if not a joy."

"But since that visage haunts you along with mine," rejoined Miriam, glancing behind her, "we needs must part.] Farewell, then! [But if ever—in distress, peril, shame, poverty, or whatever anguish is most poignant, whatever burden heaviest—you should require a life to be given wholly, only to make your own a little easier, then summon me! As the case now stands between us,] you have bought me dear, and find me of little worth. Fling me away, therefore! May you never need me more! But, if otherwise, a wish—almost an unuttered wish will bring me to you!"

She stood a moment, expecting a reply. But Donatello's eyes had again fallen on the ground, and he had not, in his bewildered mind and overburdened heart, a word to respond.

"That hour I speak of may never come," said Miriam. "So farewell—farewell forever."

"Farewell," said Donatello.

(*MF* 198–200)

This scene has been chosen not only because of its novelty but because it illustrates the most salient characteristic of the English and American novel. In it we find the conception of a moralist—in other words, it asks one of those questions that force one to penetrate to the very core of the human heart. Different answers to that question might be found in Paris and Boston: how can we not be interested in comparing them?

If Donatello had continued to obey instinct, to be the *Faun* of Praxiteles, his love would have erased any moral notion: he would have known no other law except his love. But, in gazing over the precipice from which he has hurled his enemy, he has also plunged into the abyss of consciousness. Through this initiation, he has become a man through the knowledge of evil.

This is the fundamental idea of the book. Surround a crime with motives that excuse it, circumstances that explain it, passions that render it inevitable; put in one of its authors a devotion that resembles what the world calls heroism; once the crime has been committed, purge it through remorse and show a means of progress in the evil, a source of education that transforms the primitive and blind man into a complete man, personal and free; touch (in passing) all sorts of delicate and perilous questions, like the union between good and evil, without burning one's fingers; in a word, remake an ingeniously philosophical story of the Fall of Man—that is the book *Transformation*. All that precedes the scene at the precipice is only a preparation and a first stage in a novel that has only two. The rest is a meticulous analysis of the progress of Donatello's soul through the moral regions it has entered through the portal of crime.

At first glance, we see that we might easily be deceived about this: the work might seem to be a new study of remorse in the human soul, a supplement to the powerful pages of *The Scarlet Letter* and *The House of the Seven Gables*. When it comes to the power of evil, these novelists fed on Bunyan and Calvin are prodigious: the American imagination seldom believes in the triumph of good. The victory of the Archangel Michael over Satan would seem to be an improbable subject for an American artist; but, if he did choose it, he would never (like Guido) make of Satan's vanquisher a handsome adolescent, with glistening arms, an undamaged sword, a sky-blue tunic, barely touching his celestial sandal to his down-trodden enemy. No! No! To *his* Methodist eyes, virtue's triumph would be nip-and-tuck; the struggle against a rude adversary would leave his hero more disheveled, more breathless and bruised. In *his* painting, the real Archangel Michael would have lost a good third of his plumage in the fight, and the rest would be as ruffled as the very feathers of Satan's wing. His sword would be dripping with blood and perhaps even broken. His armor would be sullied, his clothing torn, his chest bloody. That is how the American imagination sees the triumph of good over evil.[27]

In *Transformation,* the depiction of evil's effects is robust. But let us not be mistaken, that good might issue from the crime, that evil might be a means of progress: these explanations of the Fall of Man are novel. If the old Puritans were brought back to life, they would find them a trifle unorthodox.

Is it necessary to say where these philosophical innovations come from? Who is the philosopher who only sees oneness in the moral world? Who tells us: "I own I am gladdened by seeing the predominance of the saccharine principle throughout vegetable nature, and not less by beholding in morals that unrestrained inundation of the principle of good into every chink and hole that selfishness has left open, yea, into selfishness and sin itself; so that no evil is pure, nor hell itself without its extreme satisfactions."[28] What a notion! This unfrocked Unitarian minister has almost affirmed that our crimes themselves might be the living stones that will serve to construct the temples of the true God! Who is the head of the school that makes of its philosophy what its disciple makes of his novels: a curious research, a continuous experiment that arrives at no conclusion but tries everything, that plays fast and loose with the facts, never holding one as sacred or profane? What is the doctrine known to its followers as the philosophy of circles? Does not Miriam practice Transcendentalism when she says, in one of the last chapters, while speaking of Donatello: "'So changed, yet still, in a deeper sense, so much the same! He has travelled in a circle, as all things heavenly and earthly do, and now comes back to his original self, with an inestimable treasure of improvement won from an experience of pain'" (*MF* 434).

We have already observed that Hawthorne's new book, unlike most of its predecessors, stamped with the hallmark of Puritanism, is a novel penetrated completely by philosophy. We need only look at the story's conclusion to see this. The separation of Miriam from Donatello is not irrevocable, and the barrier of evil that is erected between them begins to weaken as Donatello's torment subsides, and it falls altogether when he feels reconciled to the moral law. After having lived sad and alone in his tower in the Appenines (at the foot of which there is a precipice that serves as a constant reminder of his crime), after spending time finding ways to ease his pain by becoming more cognizant of moral distinctions, he encounters Miriam in Perugia, at the foot of a statue of Pope Julius II.[29] The warrior pontiff, extending his hand in a venerable gesture, awakens only feelings of peace and rest in the viewer's soul. He is a bronze pontiff, but one who blesses. With a lively and passionate imagination, Miriam has chosen this meeting spot deliberately: she believes that a benign relief to her suffering will fall from his paternal hand. To the same spot, Kenyon brings Donatello (an Italian, raised in the Catholic faith), who kneels at the foot of this bronze confessor. When he raises his eyes, he notices Miriam on her knees like him. Like him, she has come to seek justification, and the hand that extends upon them seems to oblige in according it to them. The barrier has fallen: Donatello and Miriam are reunited in absolution.

To be sure, there is nothing Puritan in this. One might say that their confessional is theatrical decoration, and the priest a simple statue. But there is another confession in the novel, and that one takes place in one of the stalls in Saint Peter's. A good father, in surplice, is seated behind his screen, and a young woman on her knees speaks into his ear. It is a young American Protestant, Hilda, Miriam's friend, who was the involuntary and unforeseen witness to the crime. The crime that she has witnessed, though she has taken no part in it, has weighed upon her; and the remorse of innocence, the burden of truth (described in some of the novel's best pages) can only be relieved for her by cleansing in the waters of penitence. Is the author of *Transformation* favorable to Catholicism?

We do not believe so. In a previous study of the anonymous author of *Scenes of Clerical Life* and *Adam Bede,* we have seen that confession occupies an important place in these books, and yet we find no trace there of any Catholic leanings.[30] For this there were reasons: not only was the writer a woman, as we surmised,[31] but she is also a person whose friends (the editors of *The Westminster Review*) appear to be more attached to certain philosophical doctrines than to a particular church.[32] Hawthorne, in his own right, has produced some remarkable effects with this idea of confession. He has come to it by way of philosophy, and, more specifically, by that philosophy named for the Doctrine of Circles. By following his own path, Donatello has found along the way the redemptive power of evil. "*Be true*"—these two words encompass all the practical morality of Emerson and his disciples. *Be true*—do not hide the wound at your core if you want to heal. *Be true*—these are also the last words of *The Scarlet Letter,* and Dimmesdale, the adulterous minister, ends his life with a public confession.[33]

When Donatello discovers the easing of conscience, the book ends abruptly. It does not matter to the author if his hero surrenders to the penalty of civil law. He does not pain himself to fix the destiny of his characters. What good is it to fret about the social reality of this story? Since it involves the metamorphosis of a faun into a man, the question of his marriage or of his dying heirless is really secondary, and we do not really feel a strong need to learn if the mysterious Miriam becomes the Countess of Monte Beni. The true denouement is in this double philosophical morality:

Either Donatello, made for happiness, comes to understand that human life is something sad and serious, and that men like him must change or perish like antediluvian beings whose existence required a more tropical climate than our own;

Or Donatello, an instinctive and unreflective nature, commits a crime, after which remorse, with its sharp fangs, awakens his slumbering soul, and, with it, a thousand faculties he himself has never imagined. Evil instructs him, raises him. Evil, that blackness spread out across the world, and which horrifies us—could it be, like pain, a simple element of education, through which we rise to a higher and purer state?

Choose between the two explanations, or even take both of them. They both come back to the same doctrine, whose name we have known since Spinoza. This doctrine, watchfully repressed by philosophy, apparently has taken recourse in all forms of literature. Poets, novelists and critics are becoming great philosophers. Literary pantheism is in fashion. If it means replacing Apollo by a God of Nature, and the secret influence of the classic school by immanence, where is the harm? Since it is necessary to admit that contemporary literature does not recommend itself through its treasures of the imagination or its excesses of refinement, we are grateful for anything that seems a new ideal, anything that makes an idea stir under rude and material facts, anything that relieves us from the brutal art of Realism by giving us brushstrokes that make us dream. With the benefit of these reservations, even though human realities please us more, we believe the book *Transformation* worthy of the talent of its author, and we recognize it as one of the most curious signs of the time.

Revue européenne (Nov. 1860)

Notes

1. From the poem "Le satyre" in Victor Hugo's *La légende des siècles* (Brussels: Hetzel, 1851).

2. In the *Ars Poetica*, Horace insisted that scenes of graphic violence be kept offstage in order to maintain the noble decorum appropriate to classical tragedy. His broader aesthetic principle was that different styles and genres should be kept discrete. Here Étienne quotes the last of four lines in which Horace admonishes:

> For as a matron, on our festal days
> Obliged to dance, with modest grace obeys,
> So should the Muse her dignity maintain
> Amidst the satyrs, and their wanton train.

3. Gœthe's poem celebrates the return of spring and the promise of love it portends, but also worries about its ephemeral nature:

> I come! I come!
> To where? Oh, to where?
> Upwards, upwards the urge,
> The clouds are floating
> Downwards, the clouds
> Lower themselves towards yearning love,
> To me, me!
> In your lap
> Upwards,
> Embracing embraced!
> Upwards
> Upon your breast,
> All-loving Father.

Gœthe, *Selected Poems*, translated by John Whaley (Evanston, IL: Northwestern University Press, 1998), 15–17.

4. That is, *The Marble Faun*; as noted in chapter IX, the London firm of Smith, Elder & Co. published Hawthorne's 1860 novel under this title; in America, Ticknor & Fields issued it as *The Marble Faun; or, The Romance of Monte Beni*, which the author much preferred.

5. See Étienne's earlier essay, "Les conteurs américains: Nathaniel Hawthorne," *Revue contemporaine* 31 (30 May 1857): 633–63, translated in chapter VIII.

6. *Parietaria officinalis*, Pellitory-of-the-Wall or Lichwort, a plant that commonly grows between cracks in rocks and stone edifices.

7. Étienne's note: "From Émile Montégut's translation, *Essais de philosophie américaine*, by Ralph Waldo Emerson (Paris: Charpentier, 1851) [47]." The full text from Emerson's essay "Art" reads:

> When I came at last to Rome, and saw with eyes the pictures, I found that genius left to novices the gay and fantastic and ostentatious, and itself pierced directly to the simple and true; that it was familiar and sincere; that it was the old, eternal fact I had met already in so many forms, unto which I lived; that it was the plain *you and me* I knew so well, had left at home in so many conversations. I had the same experience already in a church at Naples. There I saw that nothing was changed with me but the place, and said to myself, "Thou foolish child, hast thou come out hither, over four thousand miles of salt water, to find that which was perfect to thee there at home?" that fact I saw again in the Academmia at Naples, in the chambers of sculpture, and yet again when I came to Rome, and to the paintings of Raphael, Angelo, Sacchi, Titian, and Leonardo da Vinci. "What, old mole! workest thou in the earth so fast?" It had travelled by my side: that which I fancied I had left in Boston was here in the Vatican, and again at Milan, and at Paris, and made all travelling ridiculous as a treadmill.
>
> (*Collected Works of Ralph Waldo Emerson* 2: 214–15)

8. Novalis, or Georg Philipp Friedrich Freiherr von Hardenberg (1772–1801), a phi-

losopher of German Romanticism, spoke these words about Dutch philosopher Spinoza (1632–77).

9. Étienne paraphrases traditional Catholic doctrine. Cf. Édouard Thamiry, "Immanence," *The Catholic Encyclopedia*, 15 vols. (New York: Robert Appleton Company, 1907–12), vol. 7, 686.

10. In Gœthe's *Faust* (Part II), the sorcerer's former student, Wagner, creates a homunculus, who then converses extensively with Mephistopheles.

11. Emerson, "Compensation," in *The Collected Works*, 7 vols. to date (Cambridge: Belknap, 1971), vol. 2, 59.

12. Pietro Metastasio (1698–1782) and Petrarch (1304–72), famous Italian poets known for verses about love.

13. Judith is a biblical figure who beheaded the Assyrian general Holofernes (Judith 13).

14. A reference to the beheading of John the Baptist at the request of Herodias, a Jewish princess (Matthew 14:6–11).

15. Étienne cites the second stanza of Emerson's "Woodnotes I" from Émile Montégut's Introduction to his 1851 translation of Emerson's *Essays*. Montégut translates the lines in the form of a prose paragraph. See *Essais de philosophie américaine, de R. W. Emerson, traduits de l'anglais par E. Montégut, avec une introduction et des notes* (Paris: Charpentier, 1851), xxvii.

16. Aeneas, Trojan hero and founder of Rome, was the son of Aphrodite, Greek goddess of love, and a human prince, Anchises. Romulus, the founder of Rome, was said to be the son of a human woman and the god of war, Mars.

17. An ancient region of central Italy.

18. Giovanni Boccaccio (1313–75), an early Italian Renaissance poet and author, wrote *Ameto*, or *Comedia delle ninfe fiorentine*, in 1341.

19. Étienne refers to the so-called Austrian lip (a thick under-lip), a prominent facial feature of the House of Hapsburgs.

20. A Persian monarch who assumed the throne under false pretences; his ears had been cut off as a punishment for heinous offenses, and when his deformity and true identity were discovered, he was slain by Darius.

21. Étienne Bonnot de Condillac (1715–80), a French Enlightenment philosopher; Georges-Louis Leclerc, Comte de Buffon (1707–88), a French naturalist and writer.

22. Italian pipes, similar to bagpipes, used to accompany traditional dances.

23. In recounting the legend of "The Silvery Veil," Zenobia refers to "a knot of visionary people, who were seeking for the better life" and then again to a "knot of visionary transcendentalists, who were still seeking for the better life" (Centenary Edition, vol. III, *The Blithedale Romance*, edited by Fredson Bowers et al., 114–15).

24. The last part of this quotation is from Spinoza's *Ethics*, Part 4, Proposition 67: "A free man thinks of death least of all things; and his wisdom is a meditation not of death but of life."

25. Gœthe's main character in *The Sorrows of Young Werther* (1774).

26. Lotte, a young girl engaged to another, who is Werther's love interest; despairing of Lotte, he commits suicide.

27. Étienne paraphrases from chapter 20 of *The Marble Faun* (Centenary Edition, vol. IV), 184.

28. Étienne's note: "Emerson, *Philosophie américaine*, p. 236 [From "Circles," *Collected Works* 2: 188]."

29. The statue in Perugia is actually of Julius III (1487–1555). Julius II (1443–1513) was known as "the Warrior Pope."

30. Both *Scenes of Clerical Life* (1858) and *Adam Bede* (1859) were written by George Eliot (Mary Ann Evans [1819–80]).

31. Étienne's note: "Miss [Mary Ann] Evans [George Eliot], as shown by other commentators."

32. First appearing in 1824, *The Westminster Review* continued publication through the beginning of World War I. George Eliot worked on its editorial staff.

33. Though not literally the last words of the novel, Hawthorne does summarize its meaning this way: "Among many morals which press upon us from the poor minister's miserable experience, we put only this into a sentence:—'Be true! Be true! Show freely to the world, if not your worst, yet some trait whereby the worst may be inferred!'" (Centenary Edition, vol. I, *The Scarlet Letter*, edited by Fredson Bowers and Matthew J. Bruccoli, 260).

XI

Émile Montégut

"Nathaniel Hawthorne" (1864)

I.

Death is without pity this year. He is reaping left and right, up and down, with a blind fury. Not content in a few months to have taken two men of great talent, Thackeray and Hippolyte Flandrin, the savage hunter, wanting even bigger prey, suddenly doubled his anger, and, in less than two weeks, has struck two men of genius: Meyerbeer and Nathaniel Hawthorne.

Not long ago, a distinguished writer spoke of the passing of Eugène Delacroix, remarking that men of letters are especially prone to feelings of isolation when they suffer the successive disappearances of the great artists and poets whom they have customarily admired.[1] Most of the time, we only know these celebrated people through their works or reputation. We have never been given the honor of their conversation; often we have never even seen their faces: some are separated from us by long distances, by oceans and tall mountains, others by rank and social class—and all by glory. None of this matters: they die and we feel a little more alone in the world than before. Their death hits us like a personal grief. And is it not a personal grief? For what we know about them is what is most precious. They have offered us not the banal hospitality of their salon, but the more privileged hospitality of their intelligence. They have given us access to their innermost recesses and shared their most intimate secrets. Their souls have combined with ours, their lives have been tied up in ours, their experiences have confirmed our experiences; even if they did not know or love us, *we* at least knew and loved them.

Among all these losses, however, still there are some that are particularly painful, some that wrench the heart more profoundly and evoke a special melancholy. These are the men who rose to fame at the same time we entered our youth, and who took possession of glory at the same time we took possession of life. Artists of great renown, already long established when we arrived at manhood, touch us less when they pass away because they are less our contemporaries; we did not see them born or growing up; we did not hear the first chorus of praise that greeted their arrival; we were not in the concert hall that night when a thousand other Christopher Columbuses were present at the discovery and could exclaim on the spot: a man of genius is among us! How different the deaths of the illustrious who had the same dawning as we did! They are associated not only with our intelligence, our admiration, our enthusiasm, but also with our dearest memories, our most ardent feelings, our most personal life. In a word, a link of mysterious sympathy attaches them to our heart.

Oh! The memory is vivid of the great literary success that marked our twentieth year. That success belongs to us as much as it does to the author, because from that moment we can date our own life, and when we find ourselves thinking about it, the incidents of our existence then come back unexpectedly, indissolubly peopled with the characters of the novelist and poet or brightened by the fantasies of the humorist. We see again the sun that shone the day when we bought our first number of *Vanity Fair,* the literary sensation at that time—the same hour that you entered your majority because I would love to assume that you are a contemporary of this novel.[2] Many years since have passed for you, and today, reflecting on it, don't you find that there was something in that title that you overlooked, something ironically emblematic? Aren't you now of the opinion that it is too bad that Thackeray's success cannot renew itself for each generation under the same title, offering as it does a natural preface to all human existence? It is astonishing how much at a distance you discover links between your own existence and those great literary triumphs of your youth. You perceive a thousand analogies between the sentiments they expressed and the state of mind you had when you read them. Indeed, reading was what pleased you when they came to find you, so that the good fortune that placed them in your hands was wiser than your own choice would have been. Not that you would have doubted it: each new book (like you, a child of the century) told you as much. Doesn't it touch you still, that autumn evening, when, in the silence of the countryside, *Jane Eyre* (for which you waited so impatiently) came to you as a resounding success, a book similar to a storm that breaks out in the wilderness or a happiness threatened by the very shadow that envelops it? How dear would that book be if you were to discover retrospectively that its character captured exactly that phase of your existence when it appeared! Its memory will always remain attached to your soul! And somber Hawthorne, did he not endear himself to you at just the right moment? Isn't it true that he came to you in the bosom of happiness to present his casket wreaths and his funereal perfumes? Oh! What favorable hours, those, of black melancholy and sinister dreams, to have conversations with Hawthorne's visions, to read *The Scarlet Letter, The House of the Seven Gables, Mosses from an Old Manse*! How the nascent celebrity of this lugubrious talent went hand in hand with melancholy preoccupations that were new, perhaps, for you as well! How the sentiments he expressed with so much depth—solitude, superstition, fear, despondency—lived and breathed in you! Thus, what sadness grips us when one of these men passes away who has been so intimately joined to our existence by mysterious osmosis. It seems as if a portion of us has disappeared with them. Leave it to a Chapelle[3] to cry over the death of Pindar with besotted tenderness; let your tears more genuinely mourn the deaths of the novelists and poets with whom you have grown up: rightly so, because they touch you more than the greatest genius of the past.

That is the sentiment that we have felt many times already, and especially so with the news of Hawthorne's death. But this time our regret is even better justified by that egoism of memory that we have just tried to describe, because Hawthorne was a veritable man of genius, because he was one of those rare persons to whom Nature gives birth in her hours of fantastic inspiration, of whom she makes but one copy, and whom she will never again bring to life once he has passed away. He was one of those original and unique talents like Heinrich Heine, like Thomas Carlyle, who, without equaling the very great geniuses, gives more than they do to those who read and study them: he gives a feeling of the new and unexpected. For minds already saturated with the familiar beauties of art and literature, such writers are the most energetic of stimulants, as well as the most amusing of surprises. In the greatest of geniuses there is almost always some fraction that we know, so to speak, in advance; and whatever really is new in such a man does not surprise us a bit either, because what he reveals to us is ordinarily so important, so essential to our existence, it seems impossible that we have not already come across it at some point or another. Genius speaks to us so simply that we are no more grateful to him than we would be to a messenger who faithfully transmits his words to us.[4] The genius of great writers is so impersonal that we barely feel the need to honor them for it. Moreover, they give us a certain feeling of security that, while increasing our respect for them, diminishes greatly our regret when they die: we feel that Nature, having taken them on as her interpreters, will preserve the molds in which they were cast, that she will use those molds for new creations, and that the forms of genius will not disappear with them. But those other rare persons in the group to which Nathaniel Hawthorne belongs are something else entirely. We have never seen them before, and we feel that once they are gone, we shall never see them again. What they say to us hits us like something that has never been said before and something that only they themselves can utter: whatever portion of truth—often very limited—that they have to reveal to us is intimately linked to their person. If they did not exist, a certain order of thought and feeling would have remained unknown to us, and we would still be unaware of the particular literary pleasures they have given us. In another sense, their disappearance is also more irreparable than that of the greatest men of genius. A Marivaux is more difficult to replace than a Lesage, a Diderot more than a Voltaire, a Wordsworth more than a Lord Byron.[5] There will always be Lesages, Voltaires, and Byrons because those forms of genius are too elementary, too simple or too great to disappear. But who after Marivaux will discover, with a hand that is at once so firm and so delicate, the secrets of the human heart? Where else will we encounter to the same degree that perfect harmony between delicacy and precision, between subtlety and sharpness? The sort of *plastic* incandescence of that volcano of eloquence that went by the name of Diderot, whose random spurts of lava became living figures, was extinguished forever. No one will ever again meet that mixture of the Ideal and the Real, of practical sentiment and mystical ecstasy that distinguished Wordsworth. No one again will bring to the simplest facets of life the same touching and austere tenderness, no one again will know how to fly heavenward on the wing of a butterfly or to bundle himself in a cocoon in order to penetrate the secrets of death and immortality.

In just this way the form of Hawthorne's genius has disappeared with him. No other writer will arrange those funereal bouquets he excelled at making, nor combine with the same art the everlasting flowers (devoid of scent or life)—the purple mallow (pale symbol of resignation and lassitude), the yellow marigold, the crazy columbine, and that violet, with its equivocal name, that made up the garlands of a dying Ophelia.[6] The cypress and the willows of that abandoned cemetery that he has made his literary domain will no longer have a caretaker. That somber and profound psychology lived only once.

There are few events in Hawthorne's biography; his life is entirely intellectual, and the little we do know of his history has been told by him in the prefaces to *Mosses from an Old Manse* and *The Scarlet Letter,* and in several chapters of his latest book, *Transformation.*[7] He was born in Salem, Massachusetts. We cannot give his date of birth with assurance. Some biographers have him born in 1809, others in 1804, but we lean toward an intermediate date, for we read that he was the fellow student of Longfellow at Bowdoin College and that he was graduated in the same year, 1825, which leads us to believe that he was almost the same age as the famous poet, born in 1807.[8] Hawthorne the democrat was not the first to arrive: he had ancestors and a genealogy; his lineage ties him to the very origins of the United States. He was a descendant of those emigrants, somber and zealous Puritans who made the vessel *Mayflower* famous, and who laid the cornerstone, as their descendant said, of the foundation of New England. You know them, these formidable personages, if only in having seen them pass (with a Bible in one hand, a sword in the other) in the novels of Walter Scott; if only to remind you, according to your synopsis of English history, of John Bradshaw's interrogation of Charles I.[9] The first person who carried the charming name of Hawthorne (Aubépine)—somewhat like the Furies who carried the name Eumenides, or "Kindly Ones"—established himself in the little town of Salem, so famous in the annals of American Puritanism for its witch trials and its obstinate fight against the Devil.[10] Satan had no enemy more formidable than this first Hawthorne—soldier, legislator, and judge all at once—and who, for better or worse, embodied, as his descendant has said, all the traits of the Puritan character. He was the persecutor of the poor Quakers, who have immortalized his name in their histories and are largely responsible for his terrible reputation. His son, who inherited his influence, made himself known for his severity during the witch trials. But everything will be accounted for in the here below, and the all-knowing wisdom that permitted the triumph of persecution will not let spilled blood go without vengeance. The pitiless justice and ferocious morality of these first Hawthornes were punished as soon as their supposed works of salvation were achieved. The family declined rapidly, its diminished fortunes represented by a long line of struggling seafarers and merchants, until at last its strong, yet long-hidden root gave rise to that lugubrious human flower with the name of Nathaniel Hawthorne—the culmination of a bloodline in which two centuries of Puritan doctrines, austere habits, bloody memories, melancholy thoughts and sorrows had run their course.

Without cherishing the memory of his ancestors, Hawthorne (ever the philosopher and skeptic) maintained for them a sort of timid respect; every time he speaks of them, he betrays the attitude, as it were, of a surprised child caught red-handed by severe parents. In the preface to his novel entitled *The Scarlet Letter,* he shows them speaking across the gulf of time:

> "What is he?" murmurs one grey shadow of my forefathers to the other. "A writer of story books! What kind of business in life—what mode of glorifying God, or being serviceable to mankind in his day and generation—may that be? Why, the degenerate fellow might as well have been a fiddler!" [*Such are the compliments bandied between my great grandsires and myself, across the gulf of time!*] And yet, let them scorn me as they will, strong traits of their nature have intertwined themselves with mine."
>
> (*SL* 10)

The author is right: the traits of the Puritan race are in him—indestructibly, indelibly—and from them he derives his singular originality. They persist in spite of his will, his philosophical opinions, his cool nature (even his religious agnosticism).

The qualities and peculiarities that distinguish him are the same that distinguished the English Puritans of the seventeenth century. That subtle and profound analytical ability to see beneath exterior and visible motives, to perceive the heart of the root of evil, descends in a straight line from the pitiless scrutiny that the Puritans exercised upon themselves, that rigorous examination of conscience (interrupted only for prayer), that saintly espionage to which their souls subjected every action and thought. The force of vision and hallucination by which Hawthorne transforms his thoughts into characters and his psychological hypotheses into realities is the same that acted so strongly upon his forebears, the irresistible consequence of their examinations of conscience. After long days of black reveries and painful interior confessions, those souls—starved for justice and vengeance, hardened by the persecution that they underwent and that likewise they inflicted—suddenly would see their solitude come alive and begin to converse with other strange characters: Sin, Death, Damnation, Grace, Salvation. These phantoms were not vain abstractions; they had recognizable human faces; they fated living creatures to death, to persecution, to hate, to love. Hallucination built a bridge between the abstract world of the soul and the concrete world of reality, and the Puritan passed from one to the other in a state of pious and terrifying somnambulism. For the Puritans, dream and reality formed a singularly close alliance, and from this came the tendency to express themselves through allegory. No one else but the Puritan writers, not even the greatest poets, has possessed so completely the aptitude that we admire incidentally in Milton and that has made Bunyan's name immortal. Even in the hands of the greatest poets and mystics, allegory gives us at best a superficial illusion, because it so baldly designates the symbol to be perceived and the dream to be discerned. But Puritan allegory obscures the symbol altogether and just barely permits us to unravel the dream. How difficult to recognize those abstractions in the familiar, intimate, domestic faces that look at us with the eyes of our neighbors, who speak to us with the sound of our parents' voices, who seduce or provoke us (as the case may be) with the physiognomies of our friends or enemies! This gift for allegory, an indispensable complement of his force of vision and psychological subtlety, Hawthorne possessed to the highest degree. He knew how to animate and shed merciless light upon the hidden desires of the soul and to make the shadows of guilty thoughts tremble; he conversed with the facts of conscience as easily as we converse with real people; he knew how to create a body for the formless, a language for the mute; interior and moral history is played out in his pages with a lucidity and a precision that more than one historian of the exterior and concrete world might envy. He was surely the son of the Puritans because it is fruitless to look for other faculties in him that would distinguish them. The subtle examination of conscience, the power of hallucination, the marvelous aptitude to express oneself through allegory—we find all of Hawthorne's talent in these three things. One can say, then, that this talent is an inheritance of flesh and blood, and that Hawthorne was particularly enriched by the legacy of his ancestors.

There is, however, a considerable difference between him and them, a difference that we will let our readers freely qualify as happy or sad according to the nature of their opinions. In his novels and above all in his short stories (several of which are admirable little works of art), we have nothing more than the material substance, the clay and the earth, of Puritanism in dissolution. The divine spirit, which was its essence, has completely disappeared. The phantoms that haunt the mind of Hawthorne are very much the same as those that haunted the minds of his ancestors, except that his wear the mantle of philosophy while theirs wore a Christian shroud. This descendant of the Puritans is, in a word, an unbeliever, a philosopher, and he belongs to that sect of literary and metaphysical types from Massachusetts familiarly classed as Transcendentalists. On this tuff of austere Calvinist gloom (that forms the base of his nature), the nineteenth century has thrown down successively its layers of liberalism, democracy, and German philosophy—indeed, socialism. Alas! These modern lights could not render Hawthorne's mind more joyous and were not able to let hope enter in. With his philosophical opinions, Hawthorne is even more somber than his Christian ancestors, because the lugubrious vision that the Puritans had of the world is worsened in him by the loss of religious faith. At least the radiance of divine grace spread its light on the visions of his ancestors and made beautiful Rembrandt paintings mixed with sun and shadow, rich with all the magnificence of chiaroscuro, while in Hawthorne we have only the illumination of a pale, cold metaphysical brightness that falls from stars without substance, and under which the poor human soul, shivering and shocked, goes off to search for the truth that darkness hides from it. The Puritans saw the world divided between two great powers, Jesus and Satan: one was a divine watchman always on his rounds in a wailing kingdom, with a lantern of grace in hand; the other, a sinister poacher, always hidden in the bushes of the law and the shrubbery of mundane interest, forever trying to take aim at those hapless souls. In Hawthorne, this vision, already somber, became completely black, because the Savior has disappeared, and with Him, all joy and tenderness, so that humanity seems even more damned under the reign of philosophical tolerance than it ever did under the reign of Calvinist predestination.

It was not just Hawthorne's talent that bore the imprint of Puritanism, but also his character. He had taciturn habits, and was inclined toward solitude without being unsociable, he was melancholy without being morose. His portrait is one of an intelligent and refined man, a little weak, in whom all joy was incessantly battered by an all-powerful sadness. A thin smile on his lips and a pale glimmer in his eyes confirm the existence of this melancholy struggle. Miss Frederica Bremer, the Swede who is well known for her beautiful novels, depicts him to us (in her curious *Journey to the United States*) sitting silent for long hours while in the company of his talkative friends—Emerson, Ellery Channing, and all the rest.[11] One evening, during one of those brief intervals of lassitude that athletes of the word indulge between their jousts of eloquence, Emerson saw Hawthorne (who had not yet uttered a syllable) daydreaming in a corner, and offered an assessment that picturesquely characterizes the other's taciturn nature: "Hawthorne rides well his horse of [the] night."[12] Would you care to hop on this horse and ride along with him? I warn you ahead of time that the journey will be heart-wrenching, and you are going to cross into that well-known country of Christian and Puritan geography, the Valley of the Shadow of Death.

II.

Philosophers have much discussed the question of knowing whether Man is born good or evil, and the debate has not yet been resolved satisfactorily.

Perhaps the question itself is poorly framed? Maybe it would be more judicious to ask if we are not born predisposed to believe in good more than in evil? If one fact is certain and constant, it is that (good or bad) we are all born optimists. Nature does not create pessimists. Pessimism is the sad fruit of experience and life; it is always possible to return to its root causes and to name the incident that engendered it in us. However, this is not the case for Hawthorne: pessimism for him is so much an inheritance of flesh and blood that we see it erupt in his very first stories, written in the full bloom of youth. With respect to psychological depth, life experience, and artistic form, his first collection of tales—or, rather, moral allegories (which he published under the title of *Twice-told Tales,* so named because they had appeared previously in newspapers and magazines)—is certainly much inferior to those collected in the volume entitled *Mosses from an Old Manse.* However, even in the earlier book there reigns a sort of naïve horror all the more affecting since experience plays a much lesser role. It is the spontaneous flowering of a soul melancholy by nature, already familiar for all eternity with sadness and terror. One feels that, almost without effort, he plays the lugubrious chords of misfortune, of old age, of sin, and of death, and that the somber melodies escaping from his lips are instinctive and involuntary. His imagination assumes physical form in the daughter of the scientist, Rappaccini (whose story he told), who grows up in a botanical garden composed of poisonous plants. To enter into this garden is death for anyone but her. But there alone, however, by the grace of her enforced acclimation, can she draw life, health, and beauty.

As soon as his literary vocation was pronounced, Hawthorne revealed a peculiar talent for expressing the melodies rendered by hearts when they are breaking, and for reproducing the beautiful iridescent colors exuded by souls that have been poisoned. Just as certain young people (exuberant and gay) have a knack for mimicking the voices of fashionable actors or the cries of different animals, Hawthorne perfectly captures the sound of funeral bells and that music (irregular and without rhythm, it is true, but undeniably expressive in its originality) composed by sobbing. *Twice-told Tales* was published in the fullness of youth: the first edition in 1837, the second in 1842. Oh! the singular distractions! What laughing images that young talent liked to surround himself with! When reading these tales, a sort of perfume of death—the stale aroma of box tree branches laid on the casket, of the burning candles, of the wreath of ever-lasting flowers—rises to one's nostrils and fills the brain with funereal visions. Death and sin appear in everything like natural productions of life and the world. All the work of life is to produce death; all the work of the world is to produce sin. Health and joy are only appearances and illusions: beneath the roses of youth lie the thorns of deformity and decrepitude. Youth, happiness, and beauty—all bend and collapse under the weight of a mortality that is in us from infancy, a little like the stones and soil that cave in from the efforts of a man who is trying to escape the grave. Funereal emblems are spread out everywhere—hearts gnawed by the worm that never dies, souls consumed by a fire that never burns out. How far removed we are—is it not so?—from the romantic allegories with which we are so familiar, from hearts pierced by Cupid's arrows and souls held captive by martyred paramours for whom they will never die! A long procession of people clothed in black, all mourning someone or something, come to tell us their invariably lugubrious stories, and, what is most poignant, perhaps, their eyes are dry as they confess. Hawthorne loves to speak for them when they have exhausted the wellspring of tears, when a surplus of misery has destroyed the magnetism of human sympathy. It has been a long time, a very long time, since they first became wedded to pain. Habit has blunted the sharpness of suffering in them. The vapors of their melancholy have solidified; their sorrow has petrified and condensed in the form of some mania or other eccentricity that makes one shiver.

What do you think of a gentleman who has the pleasant idea of ringing funeral bells on the day of his marriage? At the age of sixty, he marries the fiancée of his soul, the woman to whom his youth had given all his thoughts of love. Disdainful of all other affection, he has spent his whole life in expectation and solitude, and now, at the door of the tomb, she wishes to marry him. He obeys. But instead of appearing at the altar to the joyous peals of wedding bells, he arrives to the sound of a death knell, wearing a funeral shroud and accompanied by witnesses dressed in mourning. Eloquently he justifies his eccentricity: "After forty years," he tells his betrothed,

> "when I have built my tomb, and would not give up the thought of resting there—no, not for such a life as we once pictured—you call me to the altar. At your summons, I am here. But other husbands have enjoyed your youth, your beauty, your warmth of heart, and all that could be termed your life. What is there for me but your decay and death? And therefore I have bidden these funeral friends, and bespoken the sexton's deepest knell, and am come, in my shroud, to wed you, as with a burial service, that we may join our hands at the door of the sepulchre, and enter it together."

Still, one last accent of love surges forth in this old broken heart, like the last whiff of perfume escaping from the long-healed scar of an old myrrh tree:

"I have been wild. The despair of my whole lifetime had returned at once, and maddened me. Forgive; and be forgiven. Yes; it is evening with us now; and we have realized none of our morning dreams of happiness. But let us join our hands before the altar as lovers whom adverse circumstances have separated through life, yet who meet again as they are leaving it, and find their earthly affection changed into something holy as religion. And what is Time, to the married of Eternity?"

("The Wedding Knell," *TTT* 35, 36)

Here is another eccentricity that cedes nothing to the first. One Sunday, at the hour of worship, the Reverend Mr. Hooper, minister of Milford parish, stands before the flock whose care has been entrusted to him, with his face draped with a black veil. This black veil, as you might imagine, powerfully torments the imagination of his parishioners, who ask one another what it means and if their minister has lost his mind. Sunday after Sunday, however, the black veil never leaves the minister's face. Strange hypotheses circulate among the parishioners, whose veneration for their pastor now transforms into terror. Little by little, solitude engulfs Mr. Hooper. That simple morsel of black gauze suffices to put up a barrier between him and other men. Even the most tender and pious woman (who loves him) cannot resist the terror that this emblem of sadness engenders, and, after having vainly asked after his secret, decides to leave the congregation. Thus, gossiping opinion assumes that Mr. Hooper has committed a hidden crime, in punishment for which he has been condemned to wear the black veil; consequently, he grows old in the midst of general horror. Finally, the hour of deliverance arrives; Mr. Hooper's fellow churchmen surround him, beg him to reveal his secret, and finally to lift the black veil which for so long has hidden his face. Nevertheless, he still resists. "'Dark old man!'" exclaims one of these affrighted ministers, 'with what horrible crime upon your soul are you now passing to the judgment?'" Then, from the lips of the dying man, escapes this explanation of his lugubrious mania:

"Why do you tremble at me alone?" cried he, turning his veiled face round the circle of pale spectators. "Tremble also at each other! Have men avoided me, and women shown no pity, and children screamed and fled, only for my black veil? What, but the mystery which it obscurely typifies, has made this piece of crape so awful? When the friend shows his inmost heart to his friend; the lover to his best-beloved; when man does not vainly shrink from the eye of his Creator, loathsomely treasuring up the secret of his sin; then

deem me a monster, for the symbol beneath which I [*have lived, and*] die! I look around me, and, lo! on every visage a Black Veil!"
("The Minister's Black Veil," *TTT* 52)

How many other characters invite us to read the history of lingering agony on their faces? That sad old woman whom we see at the bedside of the dying man, and who presages death for all houses she enters, was long ago a beautiful girl. Unable to marry the one she loved, she accepted a union with the old man who left her a widow before her youth had expired. She could have remarried, but, alas!, at the bedside of this moribund man for whom she has cared for many years, she has contracted the infirmity of old age. Sadness has penetrated her soul as rheumatism penetrates the body, and she no longer finds herself at ease except when contemplating pain and death. She absolutely must have the spectacle of illness, the view of sad faces, the silences of shut-off rooms. This pale, wilted flower takes its life from the sap of the tomb.[13] That frenetic maniac whom we see lying at death's door had set off to travel the world in search an unpardonable sin, a sin that even God's clemency could not absolve. And, finally, after many voyages, he finishes by discovering that he, all the while, possessed that inestimable jewel, and that all he had to do was to give it up, as faithful trustee, to the father of all lies, to the one whom Dante saw chained below the hell of ice where frigid souls are punished.[14]

"The Shaker Bridal" is yet another somber story.[15] Two young people wait for years in vain for the hour when they are to be united. Both moved by a shared sadness, they come to find in a Shaker community the life of meditation and peace that suits tired hearts.[16] One day, one of the elders has the idea of placing them, according to the rites of the sect, at the head of the pious collective. Let them be united spiritually, at the very least, since a marriage of the flesh has been denied them, and let them preside in this way over the pacific destinies of the association! The patriarch, Ephraim, joins the hands of these two mystics and pronounces (on their heads) a speech full of all the consolations that religion can give to the afflicted. Upon hearing this speech, the fiancée collapses. The religious consolations that were supposed to give her force and courage instead are a deathly poison for her; these words of hope convey nothing but despair.

Such are the fantasies and caprices of this somber imagination. Do you not feel—you, children of the Latin race and of Catholic civilization—what a large gulf separates you from the society for which these tales were written? It is a very peculiar world to which you have almost no connection and in which your disoriented imagination strays like a foreigner in an unknown land. Obviously, in the same way that you have none of the preoccupations of the author, he has never known any of yours. This kind of originality—where, if you will, singularities of thought and feeling are marked by such excess—is such that our own European Protestant civilization can scarcely furnish us the means to understand it. We feel the presence of an incomparable moral element—exclusive and tyrannical, wholly unencumbered by the obstacles that restrained it in Europe—but there (in America) able to saturate the heart and soul of man. There is not a single one of those intersections of ideas, not a single one of those marriages of feeling that have given birth to modern European poetry. This race of feeling and thought has been so well preserved against all alloy that, even in England (the birthplace of Puritanism), we can hardly find it in such a state of purity.

Not only can the tales make you traverse space and take you far from the world familiar to you, they also make you go back in time and impose on you a sense of the past. Hawthorne has his literary origins, as well as his moral origins, in seventeenth-century England. By their character and outward form, his writings recall works from the Elizabethan and (even more so) the Jacobean periods: not, it is true, the poetic literature which was blossoming with such rich variety and under such magnificent light in Spenser, Shakespeare, Jonson, Beaumont, and Fletcher, but rather the other literary vegetation that grew up simultaneously and contributed its most somber flowers and prickliest branches: John Webster, John Ford, Robert Burton, Sir Thomas Browne, Bishop Jeremy Taylor, and, one of the first in talent, but last chronologically, the Puritan John Bunyan.[17] If Hawthorne resembles anyone, it is one of these old writers whose funereal and robust eccentricity he shares. Like Ford, he knows how to tell the progress of suffering in broken hearts. Like Webster, he knows how to make fools dance around heroes sworn to unhappiness. Like Burton, he knows how to classify different types of melancholic humors. Like Browne, he knows how to expound eloquently upon the nothingness of the world and the power of time which extends a shroud of loss over everything. Like Bunyan, he knows how to tell the anguish of the Christian who leaves home searching for deliverance from the burden of sin. Regarding Bishop Taylor, there is in a pious treatise of his a funereal anecdote that comes to mind every time I read one of Hawthorne's writings. A fair young German gentlewoman has long been asked in vain by her friends to have her portrait done. At last their relentless appeals exact from her a promise to have her likeness painted after she has spent a week in the tomb. They obey and, eight days after her death, they find her face half eaten by worms and a serpent lodged in her heart. "And so [s]he stands," writes Taylor, "pictured among [her] armed Ancestours."[18] Here we have a frontispiece for Hawthorne's works.

These are the real literary ancestors of Hawthorne, and I cannot help thinking that, if his talent resembles theirs, so too will his fate. He will live like them and in the same manner. Who today reads the dissertations of Sir Thomas Browne and Burton, the dramas of Webster, the sermons of Bishop Taylor? Gourmets of old literature and connoisseurs of good literature, lovers of rarities that are little more than curiosities of erudition, imaginations that, having exhausted the familiar pathways of classic literature, love to feel at ease in these asylums (closed to the profane) and there, united, can savor little-known and little-understood beauties. It will always be this way for Hawthorne. He will never be popular; but he will never be forgotten. If we cannot promise immortality to his memory, we at least can promise him longevity. Every fifty years, some admirer of beautiful things will reinvent him again, shed light on him and reprint him, and that will last a certain number of centuries—after which he will pass forever into the abysses of that eternity which throws its cold and austere shadow on his works.[19]

As for kindred in our time, he has none, even in America. I have looked high and low and have seen only two writers who bear a certain resemblance to him—the Englishman William Godwin, author of *Caleb Williams* (whose name often comes to mind when we peruse Hawthorne's writings), and the American Charles Brockden Brown, the author of *Wieland; or, the Mysterious Voice* and *Edgar Huntly*, who lived during the last years of the eighteenth century and the first of the nineteenth.[20] But Hawthorne is much too skeptical and not enough of a utopian idealist to be compared to Godwin. He loves too little and he hates too little to know the intensity of passion, the fever for justice that, in Godwin, becomes an overwhelming monomania. Between him and Brockden Brown, a more evident kinship exists. He loves to strike the same chords—remorse, superstition, fanaticism—but he supersedes his predecessor with all the superiority that a highly gifted artist has over an inept novice. He would never have jumbled up the elements that serve as the basis for *Wieland*—ventriloquistic deception (worthy of Ann Radcliffe) and brutal terror (worthy of Lewis)—with the deeper psychological themes of that novel.

Here I almost feel the need to make an aside and apologize to the reader for making him companionate with so many images of sadness and mourning. But what is to be done? My first obligation as a critic is to explain what gives life to Hawthorne's talent. Excuse me, then, as we move on to another section of the cemetery, abundantly planted with tombstones whose ingenious inscriptions give us pause for thought.

There are two other collections of Nathaniel Hawthorne's short stories and allegories, *Mosses from an Old Manse* and *The Snow-Image and Other Tales*. The first of these two collections, published in 1846, corresponds to the happiest and most smiling epoch of Hawthorne's life. After a short stay at the Fourierist association at Brook Farm, a brilliant and instructive escapade of youth that we shall speak of again, the already married Hawthorne came to establish himself in an old abandoned manse near the small village of Concord, Massachusetts, on the river of the same name. He stayed there for three years, from 1843 to 1846, three years that seem to have been full of peace and gentleness for him. What a charming description he traces for us, in the preface of this collection, of this peaceful abode, all steeped in the souls of pious clergymen who had lived there, ghosts in white collars and black robes who haunt him certain days, and of the indolent river Concord, which meanders so lazily toward its eternity, the ocean, and which must be observed for several weeks before discovering in which direction its waters flow. In this solitude full of sunshine, chosen friends come like bees drunk with nectar from all the beautiful metaphysical plants to make heard their melodious buzzing: his neighbor, the subtle and deep Emerson; the eloquent theologian Parker, who left us almost three years ago for the land of shadows; Ellery Channing, the nephew of the illustrious preacher, fantastic dreamer and brilliant speaker; Mr. Alcott, the eccentric pythagorician; Mr. Thoreau, curious erudite about all the debris of Indian relics; Mr. Hillard; the poet Longfellow. It was during these contemplative years that the collection *Mosses from an Old Manse* was composed, and, doubtless too, a part of *The Snow-Image:* strange books, much superior to *Twice-told Tales*.[21] Everything in these volumes, however, is not of equal worth; still it would be simple to excerpt one-hundred-fifty pages that might favorably compare with the best of English literature. To be sure, one-hundred-fifty pages is not very much, but it is enough to preserve a name. How many writers are there—in any era—who can assure themselves that they have written an equal number worthy of posterity's admiration?

The lingering but powerful influences of Puritanism, so perceptible in *Twice-told Tales*, are here effaced like the beliefs and superstitions of childhood, and the mature talent of the man appears in its definitive form in *Mosses from an Old Manse*. Psychological observation, previously enmeshed in Hawthorne's didactic manner and his piously eccentric anecdotes (as if in a sort of sinister glue!), now liberates itself and has free rein. His philosophical conversion is complete. Whereas in *Twice-told Tales* (in that charming piece of whimsy, "Sunday at Home") our daydreaming author pardons himself for no longer attending church, in *Mosses from an Old Manse* the lapse of faith is so radical and so violent (in the captivating short story, "Young Goodman Brown") that we can hardly hope to convey it.[22] Although he may disavow it, Hawthorne has not abandoned Puritanism completely. What has happened to him is typical of any older, traditional society that attempts to rejuvenate itself: the imagined renovation is at best incomplete. While new principles seem to govern rational intellect, the soul and that which makes up the foundation of our being and life remain captive to ancient doctrines (what theologians call "the habitual state").

I know more desperate books, but I know none that leaves the soul so completely sad and disenchanted, that makes it feel the chill of death to the same degree, as *Mosses from an Old Manse*. Hawthorne's melancholy is as much devastating as it is calm, and his pessimism is as cruel as it is irremediable. In the bursts of anger and the vivacity of loathing displayed by the most enraged misanthropes, we find compensations: the soul, reflexively, recuperates the ardor of belief in their blasphemous indignation and the gentleness of love in the bitterness of their hate. Hawthorne, to the contrary, leaves you incapable of any joy and of any love. With him there is no burst of anger, no sobbing, no tears, no despair—not one of these things that kill, but that also, paradoxically, save us. An imperturbable politeness governs the tone of his dolorous words; the implacable serenity of his sadness has no equal. One marvels at the tranquility with which he experiments with the soul's moral poisons—the poison of poverty, the poison of pride, the poison of regret—and the almost scientific precision with which he notes their progress. All the great sentiments—love, hope, friendship, faith—waste away and trudge under watch like those touched by consumption. The effect is overwhelming, like witnessing a murder that justice is powerless to prevent or a gradual suicide that we cannot arrest.

But these toxicological experiments are of the greatest beauty, and whoever is well-versed in the science of the soul will recognize the eminent merit of them. What a cruel theme is contained within "Rappaccini's Daughter"! That young woman's father has cultivated a garden made up entirely of venomous plants that differentiate themselves from their sisters, innocent flowers, by the richness and matted luster of their colors. The young girl has grown up in grace and beauty in the midst of these mortal flowers, never suspecting their dangerous power. One day, she opens the gates of the garden to a young student with whom she has exchanged many amorous glances. No sooner has he entered, however, than the fatal atmosphere does its work. The hideous hidden truth reveals itself suddenly to the young girl, and she falls inanimate on the body of her lover before the old savant has time to give her the preserving antidote that would have rendered her exposure innocuous.²³ What profound moral truths come out of this little story! There is, of course, the banal truth, though always good to remember, that the same thing that is harmless to some is fatal to others. Next, there is a more important truth: science has no secret antidotes to render certain poisons ineffective. Having grown accustomed to these toxins, we think we can escape from their influences. But the poisons we have nourished, seemingly harmless, nevertheless reach us through the ones we love in such a way that our blasé indifference (shockingly immoral) is only—after all—illusory. At last we discover another revelation of a higher order: all science that is not inspired by love is immoral and guilty; all research prompted merely by cold curiosity is perverse. The story of the chemist Alymer contains, in another form, the same high truth.²⁴ Aylmer has a wife of marvelous beauty who has not a single fault, except for a small mark on her cheek that resembles a tiny hand (which one might compare to a print left by the impress of a fairy). But is this birthmark a defect? Is it not simply a charming idiosyncrasy of nature that gives the young woman one more attractive quality? Nevertheless, this tiny blemish takes hold of Aylmer's imagination, besets his life with anxiety, paralyzes his love, and corrupts his happiness. To erase this mark, he uses all the resources of science. His wife, not wanting to be loved less, submits to his dangerous experiments. Little by little the hand disappears from her face: Aylmer's science has triumphed! Alas! Nature cannot be toyed with. That little hand is indissolubly part of the mysterious web of life; it disappears from her face only to clutch at her heart whose movements it stops.

In truth, Hawthorne could have turned the moral that comes from these two tales against himself, because the extremity of analysis, the extent to which he pushes it, is itself a sort of perversity. In the obstinate rummaging of the darkest corners of the soul and the labyrinth of the heart, strange things are discovered. Hidden treasures are not always found, neither diamonds nor pearls, but rather monsters and hibernating reptiles. Among them, surely one of the most dangerous is the serpent that torments the hypochondriac Elliston.²⁵ He goes everywhere complaining of a snake (coiled in his bosom!) whose bites make him suffer cruelly. Nothing can cure him of the funereal illusion. Friends cease their consolations, doctors abandon their science, and theologians their religious admonitions. However, Elliston is not mistaken. He truly has a serpent in his heart, the serpent of egotism that fattens itself on his essence. It is the same sickness that claims similar dominion over the unhappy Gervaise Hastings.²⁶ At the bequest of an old eccentric gentleman, an annual banquet is prepared for the ten most miserable persons to be found over the course of a year. At the first banquet, among a company of old maids, ferocious misanthropes, idiots who always complain of the cold by putting their hands up to their hearts, and anxious or taciturn hypochondriacs, there appears a handsome young man named Gervaise Hastings. What right has he to be there? No one can uncover the reasons for his invitation, yet they are so uncontestable that—year after year—Hastings never stops being one of the party. Youth slips away, then middle age, and Hastings is always chosen to be one of the ten guests. Hastings's unhappiness is profound indeed. He has spent his life loving nothing.

III.

Contemporary critics sometimes have included Hawthorne among the ranks of so-called humorists, but I believe that in this instance criticism has been duped by the form that the American writer loves to give to his thoughts. Like the humorists, Hawthorne is very fond of the short essay and the rapid sketch, which allow him to give substance to those fugitive essences of intelligence and those perfumes of the heart that would be lost and evaporate in longer treatises or novels. But there the resemblance stops. Hawthorne, to the contrary, is entirely without *humor* because, essentially, he has no joy, no cordiality. In him, there is none of that radiant gaiety that illuminates even the most somber states of the soul with moral sunshine, and that can restore the warmth of humanity to sentiments most shocked by cold or the most shivering affection. He has, here and there, some happy descriptions of nature, composed with a delicate and tranquil touch, some brilliant and cold caprices, akin to crystals of hoarfrost, a few amusing fantasies, like those chemical experiments—with their reflections of blue, pink, and green flames or unexpected combinations of color—that captivate the attention of children. But his snowflakes melt under your fingertips, and seldom do those beautiful flames not release some suffocating odor that brings us back to the peculiar atmosphere that Hawthorne's talent loves to breathe. Sometimes he tries to smile, but this smile is just like the adventures of his young, sleeping David Swan, who awakens without finding out that, one by one, Fortune, Love, and Death have come and leaned over his beautiful face in slumber.[27] He wakes from his dreams before imagination has the time to realize them. Yet Hawthorne often bears a great resemblance to a man who justly merits the name of humorist (though he does not belong to literature): the painter Hogarth. His psychology delights in explaining the same moral oddities that Hogarth loves to amuse himself with in his merciless way. Hawthorne takes great pleasure, for example, in enumerating for us the curious motives of Mr. Wakefield's conduct (the man who removes himself from his wife and friends for twenty years, living in a neighboring house, and who comes back home just as tranquilly as if he had left the night before).[28] Thus, in the entire tribe of humorists there is one to whom Hawthorne bears resemblance. Of course, this one is the most morose of all, the painter of Puritan morals and the preacher of Puritan principles on canvas.

Still, this pessimist has his hours of serenity where he sees human nature in an ideal and noble light. Besides his somber stories there is a whole series of philosophical allegories that are like Hawthorne's compliments to the human soul for the rich possibilities with which it is endowed and the brilliant future that could be its own. Hawthorne's opinion on the soul is, as it were, double: when he considers it in the here-and-now, his opinion is pessimistic and skeptical; when he projects it into the future, his opinion is more utopian. This fine, cold observer, who, while denying the doctrine of predestination demonstrates so well the doctrine of original sin, who knows so well which ambiguous shadows tarnish the purest souls, who gives himself the malicious pleasure (in one of his short stories) of making the phantoms of imaginary crimes walk past the conscience of a virtuous man, who only sees (when he looks to the future) Edenic perspectives, horizons of the promised land, and paradise regained.[29] Hawthorne's metaphysics and morals are as serene as his psychology is dismaying. There is a contradiction here, but a noble contradiction after all, where that obstinate hope that makes up the core of our nature is revealed. Hawthorne's moral philosophy is the same as that of his illustrious friends from Massachusetts. It is that German philosophy transformed by the Americans—that utilitarian idealism, that stoicism tinged with Benthamism—that casts its bright and piercing light in the writing of Emerson.[30] Two examples will suffice to give us an idea of these purely moral allegories. Perhaps you know Emerson's essay in which he asserts that every man's destiny is at his side (within his reach, so to speak), that it is chimerical to look for it in faraway regions or to dream about it in a world elsewhere?[31] The narrow boundaries of a village are enough to accomplish a vast destiny, and the most humble conditions are not an obstacle to the realization of our biggest dreams, provided that these dreams have their source in the moral life of the soul and not in the sensual life of the imagination. This doctrine has been expressed most dramatically by Hawthorne in two profound short stories: "The Threefold Destiny" and "The Great Stone Face."[32] A young man dreams of three things: that he will discover treasure at the foot of a tree; that the most beautiful woman in the world will love him; that he will be greeted as a king by three old men he meets at the gates to a city. He leaves to seek fulfillment of these prophetic visions, but, after many long years of sojourning, returns without finding anything, weary and sad. Upon his return, he meets the beautiful Faith, a companion from childhood, who accepts with love the offer he makes her with his tired heart, and three old men, municipal officers of the town, greet him and offer him the responsibilities of a village schoolmaster. With regard to the treasure, after having searched in vain in his garden, he discovers it in his harvest: the soil, tilled by his own hands, is more fruitful.

"The Great Stone Face" is the most noble page ever penned by Hawthorne. Somewhere in New England, there lies an outcropping of rocks arranged in such a way that, from a distance, it offers the viewer a profile of a gigantic human face.[33] A prophetic tradition, which embodies American pride (and which recalls the legend of the severed head found beneath Rome's Capitol),[34] says that there will appear in America a man whose traits will resemble those of the Great Stone Face. This man will be the greatest figure on earth, he will dominate America, and through him America will dominate the universe. From childhood, a young American who has heard this legend looks everywhere for the man whose visage is similar to the Stone Face; others around him do the same and think they have found him: first they gather around a rich merchant whose vessels are sailing the seas, a Medici of the New World, and who holds in his hands tremendous capital, whose credit rules the Exchange; next they flock to a general who has won many battles; then they cleave to an eloquent orator. "He is the very image of the Great Stone Face!" they cry, but they are always let down and the great man never appears. Meanwhile, the young child becomes an innocent, devoted man. With quiet modesty, he accomplishes the work that, little by little, is put before him by obligation or necessity. He earns his keep, helps his neighbors—even with the smallest of jobs—and over time he finds that by excelling in life he has earned a fine reputation without even thinking about it. His neighbors, his city, then the state, and then the entire Nation, perceive that they have among them a man who grew up inconspicuously, like a solitary oak in the forest, simple, but full of strength all at once. And the traits of this man resemble those of the Great Stone Face. The great man of America existed as an unknown to his compatriots and to himself. He was not announced by thunderous rounds of applause, military fanfare, or by the metallic clinking of riches. Yet again, Hawthorne has no page more beautiful or noble than this.

Every young nation has its age of generous hopes and radiant dreams. This series of philosophical allegories brings us back to those happy days, the happiest the American republic has ever known (*Halcyon Days,* in poetical English) the period between the liberation of Texas and the 1847 [1846–48] Mexican-American War. Ten quick years, full of confidence, hope, brilliant dreams, and generous chimeras never to return again! So great was the confidence of the American republic in its destinies then, so candid was its pride, that its illusions won other peoples who turned their attention to it as they would to a promised land where the redemption of humanity would be fulfilled. It was a time when universal joy seemed within reach, when we could see humanity's poorest children harvesting the wheat from their own fields, pressing the grapes of their own vines, and, at night, sitting next to their fig trees, teaching the morals of happiness and wisdom of the "good times to come" to new generations. *Les bons temps à venir*—"good times to come"—was an expression often used then by the prophetic voices of the Massachusetts savants. Alas! Is it true, as we were told the other day by one of the most illustrious men in France, that really to understand our dreams we must always reverse their implied meanings: that we must read chagrin when they say joy, and find suffering when they promise happiness? By what malice of nature is it that man, of all beings given life, is the only one for whom prophecies are uncertain and deceiving? The seagull surely prophesies the arrival of a storm, and the swallow the return of spring; the melodies of the nightingale promise warm and luminous nights; but the phenomena of the moral world do not obey the instincts of the human soul as the phenomena of nature do the instincts of the birds and the beasts. The hopeful words of sages too often are answered by grief. How many times, during the course of a life, have we had occasion to remember Juliet's words damning the morning bird ("Some say the lark and loathed toad change eyes"),[35] thinking that the funereal raven, in a similar exchange, would appropriate the nightingale's melodious voice, and would be the surest emblem of the soul's fond wishes. It is this epoch of chimerical hope, this springtime of the American soul, that often revives Hawthorne's moral allegories for us, that revives in particular the beautiful legend of "The Great Stone Face."

These hopes alone would be enough to explain why the wisest and most enlightened minds of the American Union lent such credence to the socialist dreams of that era. The barrier that separated humanity from happiness seemed so frail that the hand of a child could knock it down. Plans for utopian states, harmoniously constructed societies built upon a new moral architecture, sprang up everywhere, convinced that their designs were more enlightened than the old instinctual architecture that had produced an imperfect social order, no better than those ancient, asymmetrical cities where palaces were surrounded by market stalls and where more humble dwellings were a shambles. Some of these plans even began to take shape. One of the most famous attempts was one in which Hawthorne took part around 1840. A Fourierist association made up of a crowd of young enthusiasts (among whom we find the poet Dana, Ellery Channing, and so forth) established Brook Farm in Roxbury, Massachusetts, under the direction of George Ripley. The Association did not live up to all the promises that it made, and it broke apart with no other consequence than having enhanced the experience and practical wisdom of its members, and having kept them apart, momentarily, from the harsh realities of the "old world," as they preferred to call all other societies, including their own young American democracy. However, the stay at Brook Farm was not lost upon Hawthorne. Ten years later, having collected his memories, he realized that this utopia through which he had passed was connected more or less directly to the imaginary land dear to all poets, and that he was at least able to claim a stake there. He tried to reconstitute the daydream from which he was awakened years before, and he wrote the remarkable account entitled *The Blithedale Romance*. But it was not easy: the unreal chimera of utopia cannot compete with the more substantial Idealism that blooms in the true kingdom of Fairyland, and the novel remains the least well-known and the least popular of Hawthorne's works.

One must not conclude that this half-obscurity is owing to the inferiority of the book. *The Blithedale Romance* is worth just as much as Hawthorne's other writings, but the vast public (happily enough) cannot appreciate characters and passions that are foreign to itself. This is a novel made to be understood only by those rare, unfortunate souls who have had the misfortune to live among dangerous brethren, whom, for lack of a better expression, we might call *alexandrine* types. Such readers will recognize the truth in the portraits traced by Hawthorne of Hollingsworth (the philanthropist), Westervelt (the charlatan), Priscilla (the sleepwalker), and, Zenobia (the emancipated prophetess of the weaker sex). For the honor and happiness of those unfortunate readers, I hope they share the sentiments of the skeptic Miles Coverdale (pseudonym of Hawthorne himself) with regard to these characters, and (like him) will discover the difficult struggle they have to wage in order to defend themselves against the obsessions of their companions' disquieting wills, to silence the insolent babbling of their compromising imaginations, and to elude the artifices of their ambiguous casuistry. They will find here above all an inexplicable anxiety and obscure melancholy that takes hold of them from the very first page. There they are, this cast of characters, delineated by the hand of a master, with their dryness of heart, their intractable pride, their poverty of imagination, their insubstantial affections, their principles of conduct drawn from other motives than those that govern the common behavior of men. Ambiguous beings for whom the adjective "eccentric" seems to have been invented: we do not know how exactly to define them. Are they virtuous or perverse, innocent or guilty? They escape the laws of humanity and cannot be judged by them. They are eloquent (if the gusts of wind on a bare steppe are eloquent), poetic (if that voice of nothingness that comes from the shadows during the slumber of creation is poetic), profound (as nothingness and the three dimensions of space are deep). Such, in particular, is that singular character Hollingsworth, who gallops toward the absurd with such heroic intrepidity, and who resists so bravely all common sense and evidence. Do not covet Hollingsworth's friendship: it is dangerous, and, furthermore, you would not be sure of obtaining it. In order to be loved by him, one must be a little poisonous or a little patricidal. Hollingsworth is possessed by a philosophical hobbyhorse called the "moral regeneration of criminals." He believes himself to be generous and devout because he lives in service to this idea; he cannot see that this idea is nothing more than an extension of himself, and he commits an act of fetishism and pride worse than that of Pygmalion. Woe to those in whom he discovers some virtue or some talent that might serve to realize his philanthropic obsessions! He will break your heart, he will trample you underfoot for the greater glory of his chimeras. And do not believe that it is easy to escape Hollingsworth once he has decided that you might help him in his designs. Ask Miles Coverdale instead what resolve he had to muster in order to say "No!" to the importunities of this tyrannical stubbornness! What a beautiful scene it is in which Hollingsworth and Coverdale part ways. It admirably gauges the threat that these chimerical characters represent. The lesson is instructive and can be useful for everyone. So, although *The Blithedale Romance* was intended mostly for readers who have known utopian idealists, we would not hesitate to recommend it as well to those who have not yet had this sad honor. We never know whom we might meet in life.

In truth, it seems that Hawthorne was predestined to run through the entire gamut of sad emotions. Among these sentiments, infinite in their variety, there is none more irritating and more bothersome than that unspeakable anxiety we experience whenever we try to read another's face but find that his true nature is indecipherable, even though we earnestly need to get to the heart of things. It is the cruelest form of indecision: the pressure of a thousand conflicting emotions makes us tread on pins and needles, and paralyzes our mind, which must both quell an anger that dares not explode (for fear of being mistaken) and avoid a prudence that would convict us of pusillanimity. This paranoia is marvelously expressed by *The Blithedale Romance,* which, one might say, was written altogether under the influence of *jettatura,* or the Italian "evil eye." It seems as if we see shadows pass and hear the noise of the flight of timid ghosts who, having approached us in order to be noticed, are fleeing in order to escape recognition. And above all these characters, before whom conscience trembles, glides the demon of Ambiguity on extended wings.

Let us leave *The Blithedale Romance* and return to clearer, if not less somber, perceptions. One that Hawthorne admirably expressed (and that we are shocked to encounter in young, democratic America) is a perception of decline. It would seem that such a sentiment ought properly to belong to our own older civilization—much as ivy inseparably clings to ruins—and that it should be particularly painful in countries where gross inequities of condition transform all reversals of fortune into catastrophes, and where feudal family traditions implicate everyone in their consequences. In America, where that strict solidarity of the family and where inequities of condition do not exist, we have trouble understanding how such a sentiment has seen the light of day. Alas! The human heart is the same everywhere, and our psychological anatomy discovers in itself the roots of good and evil, a double harvest together, where hereditary virtues and the spirits of caste and inequality also sprout. In America, no more so than elsewhere, man cannot escape this fate of his nature, both happy and sad at once, that pushes him to find stability in a world where all is fleeting, and to yearn for immortality in a world where nothing lasts. There, as elsewhere, memories of the nation's origins, participation in its great events, and the blinding adherence to doctrine have sufficed to separate certain families from the mass of society. The rich plantation owner in Virginia or the Carolinas, with aristocratic mores, descendant of English gentlemen and adventurers from the time of Queen Elizabeth and King James, would have some difficulty recognizing as his equal the modest Yankee farmer of the North. In this New England itself, so strongly democratic, the families of Puritan origin distinguish themselves (to a certain degree) from the majority of the population: to be descended from a *Mayflower* emigrant, from a zealous preacher who was a disciple of Increase Mather, or from an ally of Governor Endicott conveys a sort of title. Finally, we know particular deference is given to families who helped in achieving the revolution that would separate the United States from England.

Do not believe that declension weighs less heavily in a democratic country than it does in an aristocratic one. It is a very interesting fact that equality renders all decline more painful because it leaves no resources to pride. Effectively, in aristocratic countries, condition is determined by moral realities that nothing can alter; it accompanies their possessor in ruin and unhappiness, is inseparable from that person and cannot even be undone by death. A ruined gentleman himself stays intact, and, except in the case of dishonor, decline affects only those circumstances external and contingent to his existence. But it is not so in democratic countries, because there rank and condition are determined only by riches. There, whoever loses his fortune loses his rank and condition, even his honor. It is this type of decline that Hawthorne admirably describes in the longest of his novels, *The House of the Seven Gables*.

If the reader is curious to know the differences of form the same feeling might assume in the context of different civilizations, he might compare *The House of the Seven Gables* to *The Bride of Lammermoor,* and the decadence of the Ravenswoods to that of the Pyncheons.[36] How much easier it would appear to him to die of starvation with Ravenswood and Caleb Balderstone than to get by in tidy misery with Miss Hepzibah, Clifford Pyncheon, and Uncle Venner in the House of the Seven Gables. In Scott's romance, the decadence of nobility gives rise to nothing but savage despair and a proud taciturnity. But bourgeois decadence engenders the worst infirmity that can afflict the human soul: timidity. Nothing is more lamentable than the spectacle of Miss Hepzibah Pyncheon, obliged to open a cent shop in order to survive. She, the descendant of Puritans, the gentlewoman from the land of the Yankees, deprived of her fortune—there she is, now suddenly the inferior of the middling gossiping townsfolk who come to frequent her counter! The quality of the cloth, give or take a single ornament, determines deference or respect. Hawthorne, with lacerating delicacy, has noted all the flinchings, all the apprehensions, all the nervous timidities that torture poor Hepzibah's soul on the day when she decides upon this enormous act: opening a humble storefront in her ancestral home. It is a unique painting of suffering that the sentiment of human respect can inflict upon one forsaken. No less admirable is the portrait of Hepzibah's brother, Clifford Pyncheon, a tortured soul in the manner of Torquato Tasso—a Torquato Tasso of the American middle class—a Tasso minus the gift of the poetic word, a being born for his unhappiness with all of his susceptible and exquisite senses and innate taste for beauty.[37] The delicacy of his nature demands a happiness that the weakness of his nature renders impossible: Clifford wilts and languishes between an imperious exigency and a radical impossibility! Rarely has psychological penetration gone so far.

IV.

The House of the Seven Gables is perhaps of all of Hawthorne's books the one by which we can best judge the qualities—and lacunae—of his talent. All the funereal images and the poignant ideas that we have laid before the reader's eyes might make him think that Hawthorne's talent approaches the melodramatic. Nothing could be farther from the truth. Hawthorne is loath to leave the domain of psychology; the terrors and sinister sentiments (which he paints masterfully) rarely extend beyond the threshold of the soul, and hardly ever end up presenting themselves through some sort of melodramatic exterior combination, but instead have the advantage of being pure, strong, and gripping. He takes extraordinary pains to people his novels with characters and events, to invent a fable, to knit a drama. His long-winded works resemble those desolate places where crimes might take place without any witness save the birds in the sky, the reptiles on the ground, and the wide-open, yet invisible eye of the characters' conscience. *The House of the Seven Gables,* running to four-hundred compactly printed pages, is nothing more than a long analysis of two abandoned and solitary souls. The reader must wait for the drama until the end of the book, but, when it arrives, he finds it to be insufficient—or, rather, adequate for a work half as long. *The House of the Seven Gables* is an admirable psychological study but only a would-be novel.

Once, and only once, did Hawthorne achieve the great dramatic effects of terror and pity that make for popularity without leaving his psychological domain, carried only by the strength of his subject. In his youth, before he had become a well-known name, Hawthorne held a modest position as a custom's house officer in Boston, a place for which he was indebted to Mr. Bancroft, the historian of the United States.[38] After turning his psychological gaze upon all his fellow customs house employees (whose portraits he traces for us so vividly in the preface to *The Scarlet Letter*), Hawthorne looked for a way to end office boredom much as a lazy army officer tries to escape the fatigue of garrison life. He began rummaging through the papers and documents of the customs house; and it was in these papers, many of which dated back to the time of the Puritans, that he found the elements that he would later compose into the most peculiar work in the annals of literature: *The Scarlet Letter.*

It is the story of an adulterous woman, condemned by the Puritan tribunal to wear on her breast a capital A, embroidered of red wool—a judgment that puts her to shame and earns scorn from all. Her accomplice is a young minister, who, as fate would have it, is forced to sit among her judges. Only a lyric drama could furnish appropriate comparisons to express the intensity of pain contained within this book; it would even be right to say that, despite the resources of musical art, the most dramatic opera could not match the lugubrious trio that Hawthorne makes us hear. We attend to the slow destruction of three hearts, all differently but all equally wounded—

mortally wounded all three—that shroud themselves in silence and hide the secret eating away at them, like the little fox who gnawed at the young Spartan's entrails.[39] Every line of the book delivers Death's first blow, a Death neither fantastic nor macabre, but rather grimly determined, ready for the job at hand, utterly Puritan, whose concealed, slow, and sustained work we follow. To brighten this somber tableau and give it light, the author uses a technique that only makes it more painful. The beam that lights up his drama like Rembrandt's chiaroscuros is Pearl, the child born of the adultery, a little, doubting, bizarre flame, who makes us want to ask her if she is some heavenly light sent down to call back the broken hearts to love, or if she is a will-o'-the-wisp made to dance over their tombs. Two scenes stand out in the middle of this story: their pathetic force can scarcely be equaled, and one can hardly forget having read them. The first is the scene where Hester Prynne pleads with the Puritan council to keep her child (who want to take Pearl away), and betrays the secret to the reader through the intimate manner in which, in a paroxysm of anguish, she addresses the young minister sitting amidst the judges. The second is the one in which the young minister, gasping under remorse, faints and is revived by the outraged husband, still unaware of the offender's name, in the same public square where Hester stood in shackles.

I previously named the old dramatist John Ford among Hawthorne's literary ancestors. If the reader has admired the wrenching scenes in *Broken Heart* in which Ford has us attend Penthea's agony, he will also admire Hawthorne's depiction of Hester Prynne's sorrows and Dimmesdale's anguish.[40] They are the same types of feelings, and the modern author cedes nothing to the older playwright.

Hawthorne's political opinions placed him in the Democratic Party, a fairly strange circumstance if we reflect upon the philosophical society in which he lived and the power of the Republican Party—a recent transformation of the old Whig and Free-Soiler parties—in the state in which he was born. Perhaps this can be explained by the same skepticism that had estranged him from Brook Farm after his few months' residence there, his limited taste for the extreme views, gruff philanthropy, and resolute politics of the Republican Party. Be that as it may, when Franklin Pierce replaced Millard Fillmore as president of the United States, Hawthorne celebrated his election as a personal triumph, and wrote a dithyrambic biography of this honest but weak man to whom we can trace the origins of the war which not long ago destroyed the United States, because of the laxity he demonstrated in the execution of the Clay compromise and his injudicious tolerance for revoking the old Missouri Compromise.[41] In recompense, Pierce named Hawthorne consul to Liverpool, where he lived, one might easily believe, less concerned with his administrative duties than with literature, psychology, and travels to Italy and other countries of the Old World. We owe his last great work, *Transformation; or, the Romance of Monte-Beni*, to this stay in Europe.

I owe a reparation to the author's memory. When this novel appeared, after a first reading (and just appreciation of its superior beauties and the singular depth of its theme), I ranked it a little above Hawthorne's other works. A second reading has slightly modified this judgment. Doubtless, there are faults. The work does not have the powerful unity of *The Scarlet Letter* or the energetic concentration of the short stories; the story line is not tight enough; the descriptions of the countryside, museums, and churches impinge perhaps too much on the fable; but the beauty of the subject and the depth of psychological analysis erase all these defects. We cannot say too much in praise of this novel; it is worthy of all the meditations of a philosopher.

In one of his visions, the Puritan John Bunyan discovered that there were roads that began in Heaven and went straight to Hell; for his part, Hawthorne recognized that there are roads that originate in Hell and ascend to Heaven. Evil, for example, may be not only the occasion or the auxiliary, but also the very generative cause of Good. Innocence without blemish, on the other hand, and unclouded happiness imply a certain perfection, but a perfection that depends on the absence of a moral life. Which one is happier—the man descended from the fauns of pagan antiquity (innocently free, lightheartedly candid, naïvely sensual) or the man formed on the model of modern Christian life—disquieted, meditative, melancholic, incapable of tranquil delight, effortless freedom, or confident exhilaration, knowing that all joys reveal grief and all pleasures corruption? The faun is surely the happier, and he is the happier precisely because he is the more immature. The faun can transform himself, the instinctive man can become a moral man, but he will pay for that transformation with his happiness and his innocence, because only one power can effect his metamorphosis—that of sin, crime, and remorse. The faun must be chased from his Eden in order to lose innocence and primitive purity and to acquire the life of the soul. If Nature wants him to be happy, she will leave him in the company of the beasts of the forest; if she wants him to be noble, she will call Sin to his aid and will give him the company of Misfortune and Remorse. With the same admonition that she gave to one of the most unfortunate and famous sons of Italy (whom she so strangely greeted upon his first entrance to the world), Nature will say to him, "Go, my beloved child. You shall be regarded as my favored one for many centuries: live—be great and unhappy."[42]

Among all the children of Italy, the old country of fauns and nymphs, there is none more cheerful and light of heart than Donatello, the count of Monte-Beni. His life passes by innocently and voluptuously, as candid and wild as the life of the beautiful creatures of the woods and the melodious children of the air. For him, the world of the soul and the world of the body are not separate and hostile. Instead, there is but one, one that his dormant conscience has not even taken pains to name, whose laws he follows without knowing them, with an obedience that costs him nothing but the sweetness of pleasure. Fed in such a way by the nourishing saps of instinct, his being flourishes with gracious liberty and harmonious unity. So close are his ties to Nature that he rediscovers her primitive language, the one that Adam spoke to the animals in earthly paradise. When he goes into the forest and he wants to talk to his brothers, he sits at the breast of his mother, Earth, and begins to sing a melody of his own invention, a melody that in every note sounds tender, plaintive, passionate, and joyous. After a few moments, the foxes come out of their dens and venomous reptiles poke their heads out of their lairs to hear him. The animals are not afraid of him. All feel as if they are children of a common mother.

Miriam, a young English girl[43] he loves and who tries to provoke him (as one tries to goad a greyhound or a spaniel), at last discovers that he bears a certain resemblance to the *Faun* of Praxiteles. This circumstance, which at first seems strange to him, is quite naturally explained, because, without keeping in mind the mythological origin that the nobility of Monte-Beni have given themselves (they are descendants, so they claim, of the offspring of a faun and a mortal, and their lineage includes a knight who had been loved by a naiad), it is not even remotely possible to imagine for Praxiteles's faun an existence more elementary—more naive, closer to instinct—than that of Donatello. Donatello is unaware of Evil, but one day Fate obliges him to it in a way that imperils his happiness. In their walks through the environs of Rome, Donatello and Miriam are constantly harassed by a type of maniac in monk's robes, who follows Miriam everywhere and whose enigmatic gestures seem to imply a secret. One night an agitated Donatello throws him from the top of the Tarpeian Rock, the same torture that the Ancients inflicted, at the same site, upon cowards and traitors. With a ghastly scream, the detestable spirit of Fra Antonio returns to the underworld, but, at the same moment, happiness departs forever from Donatello's soul. The happy faun is no more: never again will he jump like a gazelle or betray the innocent audacity and impish frolic of an undomesticated pet. Melancholy sits fixedly in a soul where everything had been fluid; Remorse spreads out its shadows where everything had been light. Several months after this incident, the sculptor Kenyon tries to resume work on a bust of Donatello but discovers that he is impeded by a singular difficulty: not one of the traits that he had sketched even so recently now matches the pensive, serious, dolorous face upon which he gazes. A new man is born, but this new man does not inherit the privileges of the old. Nature turns away her maternal face, and the animals retreat from his approach. One day when Donatello goes to walk away his troubles deep in the woods, he tries to sing as he did before that primitive melody through which he made himself understood to the denizens of the forest. The bushes move and leaves scatter, but not one bird, not one creature shows itself. In losing his innocence, he has lost the powers he held from Nature, and he breaks down in tears. From then on, he will live only for the moral good to which he was initiated by involuntary crime and remorse.

Transformation, which dates from 1860, is the last great work by Hawthorne. From then on, with the exception of one volume entitled *Our Old Home* (in which he summarized his impressions of his stay in Europe)[44] Hawthorne kept silent. He died just at the moment, they say, when his Roman friends again were expecting him in the city about which he spoke with such eloquence and respect in that very novel, *Transformation*.

What is the moral scope of Hawthorne's works, and what is the nature of the impressions they leave us? Are those impressions salutary or dangerous, designed to elevate the soul or batter it down? To this question, we will make a double answer. No, without a doubt, one must not look to Hawthorne for words of consolation and hope; and yet, no matter how sad and disenchanting they might be, his writings do not lead us to denigrate human nature. No misanthrope, no pessimist has had such a high opinion of the soul. Hawthorne made a psychological discovery of the highest importance: the human soul is the most delicate substance and its real temperament is a nervous temperament, and that sensibility is the basis for all its acts. The most perfect barometer cannot register the smallest of variations in the external atmosphere with as much precision as the soul responds to variations in the moral atmosphere. One atom will suffice to destroy its health, a wisp of wind to tarnish its candor. The soul is corruptible, true, to the last degree, but this vulnerability stems from the same cause as its delicacy, and its depravations, like its virtues, bear witness in the same way to its sensibility. Happy, then, is our soul even with its sicknesses and vices, since these maladies and vices are, for those who look carefully, just as much proof of its nobility and indications of its supreme value. In his own way, Hawthorne applies the revelation of truth that Christianity brought to the world: that the price of the soul is infinite and that, even in the sorriest conditions of existence, it cannot be bought with all the treasures of the earth.

I will close with advice that summarizes in concise form all the morality we can take from Hawthorne's writings and the type of *spiritual* service we can ask of them. Carefully refrain from picking up his books in days of mourning or sadness, when you need consolation and hope; but take them from your library shelf, where you left them, on the days when life seems sweet or whenever happiness has smiled upon you, and read a few pages in order to remind yourself of your true condition: one of suffering and sorrow. For you, this reading will be like donning one of those hair shirts that the pious employ to remind their flesh, avid for pleasure, of the necessity of penitence and the terrible reality of death.

Le moniteur universel (27 Jun., 11 Jul., 11 and 27 Aug. 1864)

Notes

1. Montégut refers to Charles Baudelaire's eulogistic overview, "L'œuvre et la vie d'Eugène Delacroix," *L'opinion nationale* (2 and 14 Sept.; 23 Nov. 1863); rpt. in *Œuvres complètes* ([Paris]: Bibliothèque de la Pléiade, 1961), 1114–41.

2. Thackeray's masterpiece was issued in illustrated monthly parts from 1847 to 1848.

3. Chapelle was the name by which Claude Emmanuel Lhuillier (1626–86), a French libertine poet, was familiarly known.

4. Montégut would seem to be redacting Emerson's famous dictum (from "Self-Reliance") that "in every work of genius we find our own rejected thoughts: they come back to us with a certain alienated majesty."

5. Pierre Carlet de Chambelain de Marivaux (1688–1763), French author and playwright, is recognized for the playful language of flirtation (*marivaudage*) in such plays as *Le jeu de l'amour et le hasard* (1730). Alain René Lesage (1668–1747), a contemporary of Marivaux, authored satires and realistic novels such as *Le diable boiteux* (1707) and *Gil Blas de Santillane* (1715–35), as well as comedies such as *Turcaret* (1709). Denis Diderot (1713–84) and Voltaire, a.k.a. François Marie Arouet (1694–1778), were two of the most prolific philosophers of the French Enlightenment. William Wordsworth (1770–1850) is considered the leading poet of English Romanticism; his seminal work, *Lyrical Ballads* (1798), was written with Samuel Taylor Coleridge. George Gordon (Lord) Byron (1788–1824), one of the most well known British Romantics, led an unconventional life that seemed to embody the characteristics of the heroes of his own works.

6. In Act 4, Scene 7, of *Hamlet,* Queen Gertrude reports the drowning of Ophelia, whose corpse is adorned with "fantastic garlands" made up of "crow-flowers, nettles, daisies, and long purples," called "dead men's fingers." Not really a flower, the latter are actually coral polyps commonly found in the coastal waters of the North Atlantic.

7. The British publisher's title for *The Marble Faun* (1860).

8. Hawthorne was born 4 Jul. 1804 in Salem, Massachusetts.

9. In December 1649, John Bradshaw (1602–59) served as the Chief Judge in the trial of Charles I, accusing the British monarch of "a wicked design to erect and uphold in himself an unlimited and tyrannical power to rule according to his will, and to overthrow the rights and liberties of the people of England." The king, who refused to recognize Parliament's power to try him, was executed in January 1650.

10. For Hawthorne's genealogy, see chapter VI, note 1.

11. Fredrika Bremer (1801–65), Swedish novelist, traveled extensively in the United States between 1849 and 1861 and published an account of her visit, *The Homes of the New World: Impressions of America*, 2 vols., translated by Mary Howatt (New York: Harper & Brothers, 1853). Montégut may be conflating his sources, as Bremer's epistles do not repeat this anecdote. The one direct encounter with Hawthorne that she describes conveys a similar impression, however, as she recounts an evening spent "in an endeavor [to] converse. But, whether it was his fault or mine, I can not say, but it did not succeed. I had to talk by myself, and at length became quite dejected, and felt I know not how. Nevertheless, Hawthorne was evidently kind, and wished to make me comfortable—but we could not get on together in conversation" (2: 597). Montégut wrote a brief notice of Bremer's work ("Divers auteurs américains") for *the Revue des Deux Mondes* (15 Oct. 1853): 399–403.

12. George W. Curtis recorded Emerson's remark in the sketch of Hawthorne that he included in *Homes of American Authors*, a miscellany compiled by various hands (New York: G. P. Putnam & Company, 1853), 300. Montégut wrote a brief notice of this volume for the *Revue des Deux Mondes* (1 Aug. 1853): 632.

13. "Edward Fane's Rosebud," first published in *Twice-told Tales* (1837).

14. "Ethan Brand," first published in *The Snow-Image, and Other Twice-told Tales* (1852).

15. First published *in Twice-told Tales,* 2nd ed. (1842).

16. Formally known as the United Society of Believers in Christ's Second Coming, this Christian body was first inspired in England in 1758 by Sister Ann Lee, who later removed to America with a small group of believers in 1774. The Shakers, as they commonly came to be known, developed an idiosyncratic mode of religious expression which included communal living, productive labor, celibacy, and a ritual noted for its dancing and bodily quivering.

17. Montégut adduces a canonical roll call of late-sixteenth- and early-seventeenth-century literary masters. Edmund Spenser (ca. 1552–99) celebrated the greatness of Elizabeth and her realm in *The Faerie Queene*. Montégut was well acquainted with the works of William Shakespeare (1564–1616), whose plays and poems he soon would translate into French (10 vols, 1868–73). Shakespeare's near-contemporaries, Ben Jonson (1572/73–1637), Francis Beaumont (1584–1616), and John Fletcher (ca. 1579–ca. 1625), wrote numerous stage plays, court masques, and poetic works. John Webster (ca. 1578– ca. 1632) is best known today for his revenge-tragedies, *The White Devil* and *The Duchess of Malfi*. John Ford (1586–1639?) wrote dramas that explored melancholy, torture, incest, and other psychological themes. Robert Burton (1577–1640) took a heroically encyclopedic view of his subject in *The Anatomy of Melancholy,* first published in 1621 and enlarged through successive editions. Sir Thomas Browne (1605–82) wrote numerous learned tracts on religion, medicine, and natural history. John Bunyan (1628–88), a lay Puritan preacher, wrote *The Pilgrim's Progress* (1678–84), perhaps the most

famous English allegory. Bishop Jeremy Taylor (1613–67) survived the Puritan commonwealth despite his Royalist sentiments and wrote movingly about religious toleration and cases of conscience.

18. Jeremy Taylor, *Holy Living and Holy Dying*, 2 vols., edited by P. G. Stanwood (1650–51; rpt. Oxford: Clarendon Press, 1989), vol. 2, 25–26. In the original text, Taylor's example is a gentleman, not a woman.

19. Montégut anticipates the judgment of William Dean Howells, who wrote in *Literary Friends and Acquaintance* (New York: Harper & Brothers, 1900) that "we are always finding new Hawthornes, but the illusion soon wears away, and then we perceive that they were not Hawthorne's at all; that he had some peculiar difference from them, which, by and-by, we shall no doubt consent must be his difference from all men evermore" (56–57).

20. Besides writing novels such as *Caleb Williams* (1794), William Godwin (1756–1836) endorsed a radical theory of political justice and human perfectibility. Charles Brockden Brown (1771–1810) was one of the first Americans to attempt a career as a writer of prose fiction, producing a series of Gothic romances at breakneck speed: *Wieland; or, The Transformation* (1798), *Arthur Mervyn* (1799), *Ormond* (1799), *Edgar Huntly* (1799), *Clara Howard* (1801), and *Jane Talbot* (1801). One of the principal figures in *Wieland* is a shape-shifter, Carwin, whose talent as a ventriloquist (or biloquist, as Brown prefers to denominate him) confuses the other characters and helps to precipitate the novel's catastrophe.

21. After leaving Brook Farm, Hawthorne married Sophia Peabody (1809–71) in July 1842. The couple immediately took up residence at the Old Manse in Concord, where they lived for three and a half years. The Hawthornes moved back to Salem in 1845; many of the stories collected in *The Snow-Image* probably were written there.

22. Montégut would have had no way of knowing that Hawthorne first published "Young Goodman Brown" in the *New-England Magazine* in 1835 and only later collected it in *Mosses from an Old Manse* (1846).

23. Significantly, Giovanni's entrance to the garden is prompted as much by his curiosity about Dr. Rappaccini's experiments as by the presence of Beatrice; he is admitted not by Rappaccini's daughter but by a servant woman who knows of a private gateway and whom he bribes. Beatrice collapses, moreover, after she imbibes a (too-powerful) antidote brought by her admirer, who now holds her responsible for his having contracted the garden's fatal contagion. Perhaps because he later recognized the error of his paraphrase, Montégut omitted this passage when he reprinted this essay as an Introduction to a French edition of Hawthorne's stories, *Contes étranges*, published in Paris in 1866.

24. "The Birth-Mark," first published in *Mosses from an Old Manse* (1846).

25. "Egotism; or, The Bosom-Serpent," first published in *Mosses from an Old Manse* (1846).

26. "The Christmas Banquet," first published in *Mosses from an Old Manse* (1846).

27. "David Swan," first published in *Twice-told Tales* (1837).

28. "Wakefield," first published in *Twice-told Tales* (1837).

29. "The Haunted Mind," first published in *Twice-told Tales*, 2nd ed. (1842).

30. The Utilitarian philosophy of Jeremy Bentham (1748–1832), an English jurist, advocates the moral principle of the greatest good for the greatest number.

31. Emerson expresses variants of this idea in different essays, but his most sustained critique of the "superstition" of travel is found in "Self-Reliance":

It is for want of self-culture that the superstition of Travelling, whose idols are Italy, England, Egypt, retains its fascination for all educated Americans. They who made England, Italy, or Greece venerable in the imagination did so by sticking fast where they were, like an axis of the earth. In manly hours we feel that duty is our place. The soul is no traveller; the wise man stays at home, and when his necessities, his duties, on any occasion call him from his house, or into foreign lands, he is at home still and shall make men sensible by the expression of his countenance that he goes, the missionary of wisdom and virtue, and visits cities and men like a sovereign and not like an interloper or a valet.

(*Collected Works* 2: 46)

32. First published, respectively, in *Twice-told Tales,* 2nd ed. (1842), and *The Snow-Image and Other Twice-told Tales* (1852).

33. Montégut refers, of course, to the monumental granite outcropping known as the "Old Man of the Mountains," which has long been the state symbol of New Hampshire, but which collapsed in May 2003 owing to the eroding powers of snow, wind, and rain.

34. The ancient historian Livy recounts this legend in *The Early History of Rome: Books I–V of the History of Rome from Its Foundations,* translated by Aubrey de Sélincourt (Baltimore: Penguin, 1960), book 1:55.79.

35. From William Shakespeare's *Romeo and Juliet,* Act 3, Scene 5.

36. Montégut invites comparison with the 1819 historical romance by Sir Walter Scott (1771–1832), which chronicles the dispossession of the Ravenswood family after the Glorious Revolution and the revenge-tragedy that ensues. Caleb Balderstone is the faithful retainer of the Ravenswood clan, determined to maintain the fallen dignity of the family in the eyes of the world.

37. Torquato Tasso (1544–95), Italian poet best remembered for his epic of the First Crusade, *Gerusalemme liberata* (1581).

38. George Bancroft (1800–1891) published his monumental—and nationalistic—*History of the United States* in ten volumes from 1834 to 1876. Himself the recipient of numerous patronage appointments to government posts, Bancroft helped secure Hawthorne his job at the Boston Custom House in 1839, which he kept until 1841. Hawthorne's later patronage appointment as Surveyor of the Port of Salem (1846–49) owed more to the intervention of other friends in the Democratic Party. His dismissal from the latter post occasioned the writing of "The Custom-House" Introduction to *The Scarlet Letter.* Montégut has innocently conflated the two events.

39. In his account of the rigors of Spartan discipline inspired by Lycurgus, Plutarch cites the example of a young boy who has stolen a fox and hidden it under his garments: ashamed of the theft, he prefers to have the animal gnaw on his entrails until he dies from the wounds rather than reveal his secret.

40. John Ford (1586–1639), English dramatist, whose play, *Broken Heart,* was published in 1633.

41. Despite initial reservation, in 1854 Pierce signed the notorious Kansas-Nebraska Act, which repealed the ban on slavery in the western territories that had been in place since the admission of Missouri to the Union in 1820. In the wake of this legislation—and the bitter debate preceding its passage—the old party system disintegrated, and mounting tensions between North and South propelled the country toward civil war.

Montégut wrote an essay on Pierce based largely on Hawthorne's campaign biography; see "Le général Franklin Pierce," *Revue des Deux Mondes* (1 Feb. 1852): 605–16.

42. Montégut quotes the opening lines of a "Dialogue between Nature and a Soul" by Giacomo Leopardi (1798–1837), Italian poet and essayist. The dialogue was first published in *Operette morali* (1835).

43. In Hawthorne's novel, Miriam's precise ancestry is never disclosed.

44. Published by Ticknor & Fields in 1863.

Biographical Register

Addison, Joseph (1672–1719)—British politician, writer, and founder of *The Spectator*, an influential periodical of the Augustan period.

Alcott, Amos Bronson (1799–1888)—American Transcendentalist author and reformer-at-large.

Andros, Edmund (1637–1714)—Royal Governor of the short-lived Dominion of New England (1686–89). He was expelled by the Massachusetts colonists after the accession of William and Mary.

Baudelaire, Charles (1821–67)—Influential French poet, critic, and acclaimed translator of Edgar Allan Poe; achieved fame and notoriety through the publication of *Les fleurs du mal* in 1857.

Bellamont, Richard Coote (1636–1701)—Another unpopular Royal Governor of colonial Massachusetts (1699–1700).

Bellingham, Richard (1592–1672)—Governor of the Massachusetts Bay Colony for various terms; renowned for the severity of his punishments against Quakers and other heretics.

Bradstreet, Simon (1603–97)—Last governor of the Massachusetts Bay Colony under the original charter granted by James I; succeeded by Edmund Andros.

Brown, Charles Brockden (1771–1810)—One of the first novelists of the new republic; pioneered the exploration of Gothic themes in American settings.

Bunyan, John (1628–88)—British preacher and writer most noted for his allegory *The Pilgrim's Progress* (1678).

Bryant, William Cullen (1794–1878)—American Romantic poet and editor, best remembered for "Thanatopsis" (1817) and his verses on nature.

Calvin, John (1509–64)—French theologian instrumental in drafting key doctrines of the Protestant Reformation.

Carlyle, Thomas (1795–1881)—Scottish essayist and historian whose two-volume work, *The French Revolution: A History* (1837), was a major contribution to nineteenth-century thought about the end of France's Old Regime.

Channing, William Ellery (1818–1901)—American Transcendentalist poet and ardent disciple of Emerson.

Channing, William Henry (1810–84)—Unitarian minister and Transcendentalist; co-edited the *Memoirs of Margaret Fuller Ossoli* (1860) with Emerson and James Freeman Clarke.

Clay, Henry (1777–1852)—American statesman and legislator, famous for his willingness to forge alliances across party and sectional lines, most notably in the Compromise of 1850, which attempted to resolve the vexing issue of slavery in the territories newly acquired after the Mexican War (1846–48), but which, largely because of its provision mandating the return of fugitive slaves, further propelled the nation toward civil war.

Cooper, James Fenimore (1789–1851)—Often referred to as "the American Scott" because of his interest in historical romance, Cooper is best known for his "Leather-stocking Tales," a series of novels written from 1823 to 1841.

Cowper, William (1731–1800)—Sensitive and hypochondriacal from birth, the British poet and satirist suffered from severe bouts of depression throughout his life.

Curtis, George William (1824–92)—American author and editor; an early convert to Transcendentalism and resident at Brook Farm.

Dana, Richard Henry, Jr. (1815–82)—American author best known for his sea narrative, *Two Years before the Mast* (1840), but also for his involvement in Free Soil politics and the defense of escaped blacks prosecuted under the Fugitive Slave Act.

Delacroix, Eugène (1798–1863)—Often considered the greatest French Romantic painter, he depicted historical and contemporary events as well as subjects drawn from literature.

Emerson, Ralph Waldo (1803–82)—Trained at Harvard for the Unitarian ministry, Emerson famously left his pulpit to rediscover his vocation as a philosopher, poet, and essayist whose work inspired Transcendentalism.

Endicott, John (1558–1665)—Served occasional terms as Governor of the Province of New England and was greatly feared as a stern enforcer of Puritan codes. Under his administration, four Quakers were hanged for violating the laws of theocratic Orthodoxy.

Fillmore, Millard (1800–1874)—Thirteenth President of the United States (1850–53), succeeding Zachary Taylor who died in office.

Flandrin, Hippolyte (1809–64)—French Neoclassical painter, known for his portraits and religious murals in the Saint-Germain-des-Prés church in Paris.

Fourier, François Marie Charles (1772–1837)—French utopian socialist and philosopher who advocated that society be reorganized into cooperative communities or phalanxes. In the United States, Fourier's ideas were popularized by Albert Brisbane (1809–90) through his 1840 treatise, *The Social Destiny of Man*, and his journal, *The Phalanx*.

Freneau, Philip (1752–1832)—Known as "the poet of the American Revolution" by virtue of work such as *The Rising Glory of America* (1771).

Fuller, Sarah Margaret (1810–50)—American journalist and Romantic critic. An occasional visitor at Brook Farm, she is often taken as the figure after whom Hawthorne modeled the character of Zenobia in *The Blithedale Romance*. She drowned off Fire Island, returning from Italy with her (probable) husband, Count Giovanni Ossoli, and infant child.

Gage, Thomas (1719–87)—Commander-in-Chief of British forces during the American Revolution (1763–75).

Godwin, William (1756–1836)—English novelist and political writer who endorsed a radical theory of political justice and human perfectibility; his best-known work of fiction is *Caleb Williams* (1794).

Gœthe, Johann Wolfgang von (1749–1832)—Germany's greatest man of letters (in the words of George Eliot), author of the great dramatic poem *Faust* (1808/1832) and the influential Romantic novel, *The Sorrows of Young Werther* (1774).

Hegel, George Wilhelm Friedrich (1770–1831)—German philosopher of Idealism, who proposed that rational unity evolved from a dialectical process of contradiction and negation.

Heine, Heinrich (1797–1856)—Major German poet and writer known especially for his lyric verse.

Hillard, George S. (1808–79)—Harvard-trained lawyer who devoted much of his life to the cause of literature.

Hoffmann, Ernst Theodor Wilhelm (1776–1822)—Better known by his pen name E. T. A. Hoffmann (Ernst Theodor Amadeus Hoffmann), a German author of fantasy and horror influential in the Romantic movement.

Hogarth, William (1697–1764)—British painter, engraver, and satirist, celebrated for his grotesque representations of vice and folly and for didactic canvas series—such as *The Rake's Progress* (1733–35) and *Industry and Idleness* (1747)—that conveyed moral lessons.

Howe, William (1729–1814)—Succeeded Thomas Gage as Commander-in-Chief of British forces during the American Revolution (1775–78).

Irving, Washington (1783–1859)—American author of the much-beloved *Sketchbook* (1820) and many volumes of history and biography.

Kant, Immanuel (1724–1804)—German philosopher of the Enlightenment; intellectual father of German Idealism and Transcendentalism.

Kuyp, Aelbert Jacobsz (1620–91)—Dutch landscape painter. His surname is more often spelled Cuyp.

Lamb, Charles (1775–1834)—English essayist who often worked in collaboration with his sister Mary; most celebrated for his collection of humorous works, *Essays of Elia* (1823), and his children's book, *Tales from Shakespeare* (1807).

Lewis, Matthew Gregory ("Monk") (1775–1818)—British author of a staple of Gothic literature, *The Monk* (1796), from which his familiar literary nickname was derived.

Lowell, James Russell (1819–91)—American poet, critic, satirist, and diplomat.

Longfellow, Henry Wadsworth (1807–82)—Most beloved of the "Fireside" poets and Bowdoin classmate of Hawthorne.

Mackenzie, Henry (1745–1831)—The "Addison of the North," a Scottish essayist from Edinburgh.

Mather, Increase (1639–1723)—A major figure in the early history of the Massachusetts Bay Colony, Mather was involved with the government of the colony, the administration of Harvard College, and most notoriously the Salem witch trials. He was the son of Richard Mather and father of Cotton Mather, both influential Puritan ministers.

Maturin, Charles Robert (1782–1824)—Anglo-Irish Protestant clergyman who authored numerous Gothic novels and plays, notably *Melmoth the Wanderer* (1820).

Mérimée, Prosper (1803–70)—Prolific French author of fiction and drama, best known for his novella *Carmen* (1845), adapted by George Bizet for his much-loved opera.

Meyerbeer, Giacomo (1791–1864)—German composer whose works, for much of the nineteenth century at least, were standard features of the operatic repertoire.

Nodier, Charles (1780–1844)—French author best known for his short tales.

Parker, Theodore (1810–60)—Unitarian minister who resigned his pulpit to become a spokesman for the Abolitionist crusade.

Peabody, Elizabeth (1804–94)—A pioneer in children's education and many other reform movements, she became Hawthorne's sister-in-law when he married Sophia Peabody (1809–71) in 1842.

Pierce, Franklin (1804–69)—Fourteenth President of the United States; a Bowdoin classmate of Hawthorne, he nominated the author as American consul to Liverpool in 1853.

Poe, Edgar Allan (1809–49)—American poet, critic, and author of Gothic tales and novels. His career in France was championed by Charles Baudelaire, who devoted much of his life to translating his works.

Radcliffe, Ann (1764–1823)—A leading exponent of the Gothic novel, best known for *The Mysteries of Udolpho* (1794).

Randolph, Edward (ca. 1632–1703)—British agent for Massachusetts and customs collector during the period prior to the annulment of the first colonial charter in 1684, an act for which he was principally responsible, earning him the contempt of those he governed.

Ripley, George (1802–80)—Unitarian clergyman and principal founder of the Brook Farm Association at Roxbury, Massachusetts.

Sand, George (1804–76)—pseudonym of Amantine Aurore Lucile Dupin, Baronne Dudevant, French novelist and feminist, whose behavior (and writing) defied conventional moral standards.

Schelling, Friedrich Wilhelm Joseph (1775–1854)—German author of *Naturphilosophie*, the Idealist principles of which form the basis for American Transcendentalism.

Scott, Sir Walter (1771–1832)—British novelist whose historical romances achieved great success with nineteenth-century audiences.

Sterne, Laurence (1713–68)—Anglo-Irish writer who penned *Tristam Shandy* (1761–65).

Tasso, Torquato (1544–95)—Italian poet of the sixteenth century; author of *La Gerusalemme Liberata* (1580), an epic chronicle of the First Crusade to liberate Jerusalem from Muslim occupation.

Taylor, Zachary (1784–1850)—Twelfth President of the United States (1849–50); the Whig Party's victory in 1848 prompted Hawthorne's dismissal from his position as customs inspector at Salem.

Thoreau, Henry David (1817–62)—American author and Transcendentalist, most famous for his active pursuit of self-reliance at Walden Pond.

Töpffer, Rodolphe (1799–1846)—Swiss satirist and caricaturist.

Vane, Henry, Sir (1613–62)—Puritan statesman and member of Parliament; governor of Massachusetts Bay Colony (1636–37).

van der Velde, Esaias (ca. 1587–1630)—Dutch landscape painter.

Winthrop, John (1588–1649)—Leader of the Puritans in England and first governor of the Massachusetts Bay Colony (1629–49), his term briefly interrupted by that of Henry Vane.

Works Cited

Alexander, Jean. *Affidavits of Genius: Edgar Allan Poe and the French Critics, 1847–1924.* Port Washington, NY: Kennikat Press, 1971. Print.
Anesko, Michael. *Letters, Fictions, Lives: Henry James and William Dean Howells.* New York: Oxford University Press, 1997. Print.
Anon. "Contemporary French Literature." Rev. of *Essais morales et historiques,* by Émile Montégut. *North American Review* 88 (1859): 210–27. Print.
Anon. Rev. of *Hawthorne,* by Henry James. *The Nation* 30 (29 Jan. 1880): 80–81. Print.
Anon. "Sketchings: Hawthorne in Relation to Art." *The Crayon* 7 (Oct. 1860): 298–301. Print.
Antoniazzi, Barbara. "The American Canon and the 'Revue des Deux Mondes.'" *Il bianco e il nero.* Udine [IT]: Campanotto editore, 1998. 107–21. Print.
Arac, Jonathan. "The Politics of *The Scarlet Letter.*" *Ideology and Classic American Literature,* edited by Sacvan Bercovitch and Myra Jehlen. New York: Cambridge University Press, 1986. 247–66. Print.
Asselineau, Roger. "Hawthorne Abroad." *Hawthorne Centenary Essays,* edited by Roy Harvey Pearce. [Columbus]: The Ohio State University Press, 1964. 367–85; 470–76. Print.
Bach, Max. "A Review of Second-Empire Reviews." *French Review* 35 (Jan. 1962): 295–301. Print.
Barine, Arvède. "Un critique contemporain: Émile Montégut." *Revue bleue* [*La revue politique et littéraire*] 37 (15 May 1886): 617–23. Print.
———. "Puritan ou pessimiste." *Revue bleue* [*La revue politique et littéraire*] 19 (31 Jul. 1880): 99–106. Print.
Baudelaire, Charles. "L'œuvre et la vie d'Eugène Delacroix." *L'opinion nationale* (2 and 14 Sept.; 23 Nov. 1863. *Œuvres complètes.* [Paris]: Bibliothèque de la Pléiade, 1961. 1114–41. Print.

Bercovitch, Sacvan. *The Office of the Scarlet Letter.* Baltimore: Johns Hopkins University Press, 1991. Print.

——— and Myra Jehlen, eds. *Ideology and Classic American Literature.* New York: Cambridge University Press, 1986. Print.

Brown, Ruth. "A French Interpreter of New England's Literature 1846–1865." *New England Quarterly* 13 (1940): 305–21. Print.

Browne, Nina E. *A Bibliography of Nathaniel Hawthorne.* Boston: Houghton, Mifflin & Co., 1905. Print.

Cambiaire, Célestin Pierre. *The Influence of Edgar Allan Poe in France.* New York: G. E. Stechert & Co., 1927. Print.

Caramello, Charles. *Henry James, Gertrude Stein, and the Biographical Act.* Chapel Hill: University of North Carolina Press, 1996. Print.

Caro, Elme Marie. Letter to Émile Montégut, 18 Apr. 1878. *Bibliographie méthodique et critique des œuvres d'Émile Montégut.* Pierre-Alexis Muenier. Paris: Librairie Garnier Frères, 1925. 142–43. Print.

Carpenter, Frederic. "Puritans Preferred Blondes: The Heroines of Melville and Hawthorne." *New England Quarterly* 9 (1936): 253–72. Print.

Chadbourne, Richard M. "The Essay World of Émile Montégut." *PMLA* 76.1 (Mar. 1961): 98–120. Print.

Chartier, Roger and Henri-Jean Martin, eds. *Histoire de l'édition française.* Vol. 3. Paris: Promodis, 1985. Print. 4 vols.

Chasles, Philarète. *Anglo-American Literature and Manners,* translated by Donald MacLeod. New York: C. Scribner, 1852. Print.

———. "De la littérature dans l'Amérique du nord." *Revue des Deux Mondes* (1 Jul. 1835): 169–202. Print.

Colacurcio, Michael. *The Province of Piety: Moral History in Hawthorne's Early Tales.* Cambridge, MA: Harvard University Press, 1984. Print.

Conway, Moncure Daniel. *Life of Nathaniel Hawthorne.* New York: Scribner & Welford, 1890. Print.

Copans, Simon. "French Opinion of American Democracy, 1852–1860." Dissertation Brown, 1942. Print.

Crowley, J. Donald, ed. *Hawthorne: The Critical Heritage.* New York: Barnes & Noble, 1970. Print.

Curtis, George W. et al., eds. *Homes of American Authors: Comprising Anecdotical, Personal, and Descriptive Sketches by Various Writers.* New York: G. P. Putnam & Co., 1853. Print.

Dawson, Hugh J. "Discovered in Paris: An Earlier First Illustrated Edition of *The Scarlet Letter.*" *Studies in the American Renaissance* (1988): 271–80. Print.

DeMarco, Eileen S. *Reading and Riding: Hachette's Railroad Bookstore Network in Nineteenth-Century France.* Bethlehem, PA: Lehigh University Press, 2006. Print.

Douglas, Ann. *The Feminization of American Culture.* New York: Knopf, 1977. Print.

Eliot, T. S. "The Hawthorne Aspect." *The Little Review* 5 (1918): 48–49. Print.

———. "Les lettres anglaises: le roman anglais contemporain." *La nouvelle revue française* 28 (1 May 1927): 669–75. Print.

Emerson, Ralph Waldo. *The Collected Works of Ralph Waldo Emerson,* edited by Alfred R. Ferguson et al. 7 vols. to date. Cambridge, MA: Belknap Press of Harvard University Press, 1971–. Print.

———. *Essais de philosophie américaine, de R. W. Emerson, traduits de l'anglais par É. Montégut, avec une introduction et des notes*, translated by Émile Montégut. Paris: Charpentier, 1851. Print.
Étienne, Louis. "Les conteurs américains: Edgar Allan Poe." *Revue contemporaine* 32 (15 Jul. 1857): 492–524. Print.
———. "Les conteurs américains: Nathaniel Hawthorne." *Revue contemporaine* 31 (30 May 1857): 633–63. Print.
———. "Le roman transcendentaliste en Amérique." *Revue européenne* (Nov. 1860): 46–68. Print.
Faust, Bertha. *Hawthorne's Contemporaneous Reputation: A Study of Literary Opinion in America and England 1828–1864*. 1939. New York: Octagon Books, 1968. Print.
Fields, James T. *Yesterdays with Authors*. Boston: J. R. Osgood & Co., 1871. Print.
Finney, Gail. Rev. of *Die Literatur des 19. Jahrhunderts im Urteil von Emile Montégut*, by Burkhart Küster. *Nineteenth-Century French Studies* 13 (Winter–Spring 1985): 175–77. Print.
Fogle, Richard Harter. *Hawthorne's Fiction: The Light & the Dark*. Norman: University of Oklahoma Press, 1952. Print.
Forgues, [Paul] É[mile]-D[aurand]. "Études sur le roman anglais et américain: les contes d'Edgar A. Poe." *Revue des Deux Mondes* (15 Oct. 1846): 341–66. *Affidavits of Genius: Edgar Allan Poe and the French Critics, 1847–1924*, translated by Jean Alexander. Port Washington, NY: Kennikat Press, 1971. Print.
———. "Poètes et romanciers américains: Nathaniel Hawthorne." *Revue des Deux Mondes* (15 Apr. 1852): 337–65. Print.
Foxcroft, Frank. Rev. of *Hawthorne*, by Henry James. *Literary World* 11 (14 Feb. 1880): 51–53. Print.
Fuller, Margaret. *Memoirs of Margaret Fuller Ossoli*. 2 vols. Edited by Ralph Waldo Emerson, James Freeman Clarke, and William Henry Channing. Boston: Phillips, Sampson and Co., 1852. Print.
Gohdes, Clarence. *American Literature in Nineteenth-Century England*. Carbondale: Southern Illinois University Press, 1944. Print.
Gonnaud, Maurice. "Democratic Aesthetics," *Transatlantica* 1 (2007). Internet. 5 Nov. 2007.
Goodrich, Frank B. [Dick Tinto]. "France." *New York Times* (11 Sept. 1854): 2.2. Print.
Habegger, Alfred. "Henry James's Rewriting of Minny Temple's Letters." *American Literature* 58.2 (May 1986): 159–80. Print.
Hawthorne, Nathaniel. *Contes racontés deux fois* [*Twice-told Tales*]. Nouvelle bibliotheque populaire, translated by Charles Simond. Paris: Henri Gautier, 1888. Print.
———. *Le livre des merveilles*. [*A Wonderbook for Boys and Girls*], translated by Léonce Rabillon. Paris: Hachette, 1858. Print.
Helgesen, Moira Anne (Curr). "Forgues: Nineteenth Century Anglophile." Dissertation University of Colorado, 1955. Print.
Holder, Alan. "T. S. Eliot on Henry James." *PMLA* 79.4 (Sept. 1964): 490–97. Print.
Howells, William Dean. Rev. of *Hawthorne*, by Henry James. 1880. *Letters, Fictions, Lives: Henry James and William Dean Howells*, by Michael Anesko. New York: Oxford University Press, 1997. 143–46. Print.
James, Henry. *Autobiography*, edited by F. W. Dupee. New York: Criterion Books, 1956. Print.

———. "Charles Baudelaire." 1876. *Literary Criticism: French Writers; Other European Writers; The Prefaces to the New York Edition*, edited by Leon Edel. New York: Library of America, 1984. 152–58. Print.

———. *Hawthorne. Literary Criticism: Essays on Literature; American Writers; English Writers*, edited by Leon Edel. New York: Library of America, 1984. 315–457. Print.

———. Letter to Alice James, 22 Feb. [1876], *Henry James Letters*. Vol. 2. Edited by Leon Edel. Cambridge, MA: Belknap Press of Harvard University Press, 1974–84. 28–31. Print. 4 vols.

———. Letter to Frederick Macmillan, 11 Oct. [1878]. *The Correspondence of Henry James and the House of Macmillan, 1877–1914: "All the Links in the Chain,"* edited by Rayburn S. Moore. Baton Rouge: Louisiana State University Press, 1993. 18–19. Print.

———. Letter to Frederick Macmillan, 28 Sept. [1879], *Henry James Letters*. Vol. 2. Edited by Leon Edel. Cambridge, MA: Belknap Press of Harvard University Press, 1974–84. 255–57. Print. 4 vols.

———. Letter to Henry James, Sr., 11 Apr. [1876]. *Henry James Letters*. Vol. 2. Edited by Leon Edel. Cambridge, MA: Belknap Press of Harvard University Press, 1974–84. 36–40. Print. 4 vols.

———. Letter to Henry James, Sr., 18 Oct. [1878]. bMS Am 1094 (1873). Houghton Library, Harvard.

———. Letter to Henry James Sr., 24 Feb. 1881. *Henry James Letters*. Vol. 2. Edited by Leon Edel. Cambridge, MA: Belknap Press of Harvard University Press, 1974–84. 344–46. Print. 4 vols.

———. Letter to the James family, 1 Nov. [1875]. *Henry James Letters*. Vol. 1. Edited by Leon Edel. Cambridge, MA: Belknap Press of Harvard University Press, 1974–84. 484–87. Print. 4 vols.

———. Letter to Thomas Sergeant Perry, 14 Sept. 1879. *Henry James Letters*. Vol. 2. Edited by Leon Edel. Cambridge, MA: Belknap Press of Harvard University Press, 1974–84. 254–56. Print. 4 vols.

———. Rev. of *Passages from the French and Italian Note-Books of Nathaniel Hawthorne*. 1872. *Literary Criticism: Essays on Literature; American Writers; English Writers*. Edited by Leon Edel. New York: Library of America, 1984. 307–14. Print.

———. Rev. of *Souvenirs de Bourgogne*, by Émile Montégut. 1874. *Literary Criticism: French Writers; Other European Writers; The Prefaces to the New York Edition*. Edited by Leon Edel. New York: Library of America, 1984. 588–91. Print.

Keller, Hans. "Emerson in Frankreich: Wirkungen und Parallelen." Dissertation Hessischen Ludwigs-Universität zu Giessen, 1932. Print.

Kijinski, John J. "Professionalism, Authority, and the Late-Victorian Man of Letters: A View from the Macmillan Archive." *Victorian Literature and Culture* 24 (1996): 229–47. Print.

Küster, Burkhart. *Die Literatur des 19. Jahrhunderts im Urteil von Emile Montégut*. Tübingen: G. Narr, 1982. Print.

Laborde-Milaà, A[uguste]. *Un essayiste, Émile Montégut, 1825–1895*. Paris: M. Escoffier, 1922. Print.

Lathrop, George Parsons. *A Study of Hawthorne*. 1876. New York: AMS Press, 1969. Print.

Lawrence, D. H. *Studies in Classic American Literature*. 1923. New York: Viking Press, 1964. Print.

Levin, A[braham]. *The Legacy of Philarète Chasles.* Chapel Hill: Studies in Comparative Literature, University of North Carolina, 1957. Print.

Levin, Harry. *The Power of Blackness: Hawthorne, Poe, Melville.* 1958. New York: Vintage Books, 1960. Print.

Livy. *The Early History of Rome: Books I–V of the History of Rome from Its Foundations,* translated by Aubrey de Sélincourt. Baltimore: Penguin, 1960.

Lyons, Martyn. *Le triomphe du livre: histoire sociologique de la lecture dans la France du XIXe siècle.* Paris: Promodis, 1987. Print.

MacClintock, Lander. "Sainte-Beuve and America." *PMLA* 60.2 (Jun. 1945): 427–36. Print.

Male, Roy R. *Hawthorne's Tragic Vision.* Austin: University of Texas Press, 1957. Print.

Mantz, Harold Elmer. *French Criticism of American Literature before 1850.* New York: Columbia University Press, 1917. Print.

Masson, Paul. Introduction and translation of "*La fiancée du shaker.*" *Revue bleue* [*La revue politique et littéraire*] (16 Nov. 1889): 627–30. Print.

Matthiessen, F. O. *American Renaissance: Art and Expression in the Age of Emerson and Whitman.* New York: Oxford University Press, 1941. Print.

McCall, Dan. *Citizens of Somewhere Else: Nathaniel Hawthorne and Henry James.* Ithaca, NY: Cornell University Press, 1999. Print.

McGee, Sidney Lamont. *La littérature américaine dans la "Revue des Deux Mondes," 1831–1900.* Montpellier: Imprimerie de la Manufacture de la Charité, 1927. Print.

Melville, Herman. "Hawthorne and His *Mosses.*" *The Writings of Herman Melville.* Vol. 9: *The Piazza Tales and Other Prose Pieces 1839–1860,* edited by Harrison Hayford et al. Evanston and Chicago: Northwestern University Press and The Newberry Library, 1987. 239–53. Print. 15 vols. to date.

Miller, Perry. *Errand into the Wilderness.* Cambridge, MA: Harvard University Press, 1956. Print.

———. *The New England Mind: The Seventeenth Century.* New York: Macmillan, 1939. Print.

Mollier, Jean-Yves. *Louis Hachette, 1800–1864: fondateur d'un empire.* Paris: Fayard, 1999. Print.

Montégut, Émile. "Carlyle et Emerson." [Rev. of *Representative Men,* by Ralph Waldo Emerson.] *Revue des Deux Mondes* (15 Aug. 1850): 722–37. Print.

———. *Écrivains modernes de l'Angleterre.* 2 vols. Paris: [n.p.], 1885–89. Print.

———. *Essais de philosophie américaine, de R. W. Emerson, traduits de l'anglais par É. Montégut, avec une introduction et des notes.* Paris: Charpentier, 1851. Print.

———. "Le général Franklin Pierce." *Revue des Deux Mondes* (1 Feb. 1852): 605–16. Print.

———. Letter to Elme Marie Caro. 3 May 1878. *Bibliographie méthodique et critique des œuvres d'Émile Montégut.* Pierre-Alexis Muenier. Paris: Librairie Garnier Frères, 1925. 157. Print.

———. "Marguerite Fuller." [Rev. of *Memoirs of Margaret Fuller Ossoli,* edited by Ralph Waldo Emerson and W. H. Channing.] *Revue des Deux Mondes* (1 Apr. 1852): 37–73. Print.

———. "Nathaniel Hawthorne." *Le moniteur universel.* (27 Jun.; 11 Jul.; 11 and 27 Aug. 1864): 886; 935; 1033–34; 1083–84. Rpt. *Nathaniel Hawthorne.* Paris: J. Laisné, 1866; and as "Introduction" to *Contes étranges imités d'Hawthorne,* translated by E. A. Spoll. Paris: Librairie Contemporaine, 1866. 5–50. Print.

———. "Un penseur et poète américain: Ralph Waldo Emerson." *Revue des Deux Mondes* (1 Aug. 1847): 462–93. Print.

———. "Revue littéraire américaine: divers auteurs américains." *Revue des Deux Mondes* (15 Oct. 1853): 399–403. Print.

———. "Le roman abolitioniste en Amérique." [Rev. of *Uncle Tom's Cabin* by Harriet Beecher Stowe.] *Revue des Deux Mondes* (1 Oct. 1852): 155–85. Print.

———. "Le roman populaire et le rôle du romanesque en Amérique." [Rev. of *Ruth Hall*, by Fanny Fern]. *Revue de Deux Mondes* (1 Jul. 1856): 181–200. Print.

———. "Un roman socialiste en Amérique." *Revue des Deux Mondes* (1 Dec. 1852): 809–41. Print.

———. "Un romancier pessimiste en Amérique: Nathaniel Hawthorne." *Revue des Deux Mondes* (1 Aug. 1860): 668–703. Print.

———. "Scènes de la vie et de la littérature américaine." *Revue des Deux Mondes* (1 Dec. 1854): 876–911. Print.

Monteiro, George. "'The Items of High Civilization': Hawthorne, Henry James, and George Parsons Lathrop." *The Nathaniel Hawthorne Journal 1975*, edited by C. E. Frazer Clark. Englewood, CO: Microcard Edition Books, 1975. 146–55. Print.

Moore, Rayburn S., ed. *The Correspondence of Henry James and the House of Macmillan, 1877–1914: "All the Links in the Chain."* Baton Rouge: Louisiana State University Press, 1993. Print.

Morley, John. Letter to Henry James, 9 Oct. 1878. *The Correspondence of Henry James and the House of Macmillan, 1877–1914: "All the Links in the Chain,"* edited by Rayburn S. Moore. Baton Rouge: Louisiana State University Press, 1993. 17–18. Print.

Muenier, Pierre-Alexis. *Bibliographie méthodique et critique des œuvres d'Émile Montégut*. Paris: Librairie Garnier Frères, 1925. Print.

Nadel, Ira B. *Biography: Fiction, Fact and Form*. London: Macmillan, 1984. Print.

Nettels, Elsa. "Henry James and the Art of Biography." *South Atlantic Bulletin* 43 (1978): 107–24. Print.

Nordmann, Jean-Thomas. *La critique littéraire au XIXe siècle, 1800–1914*. Paris: Librairie générale française, 2001. Print.

Pancost, David W. "Henry James and Julian Hawthorne." *American Literature* 50.3 (Nov. 1978): 461–65. Print.

Poe, Edgar Allan. Rev. of *Twice-told Tales*, by Nathaniel Hawthorne. 1842. *Essays and Reviews*, edited by G. R. Thompson. New York: Library of America, 1984. 568–77. Print.

———. Rev. of *Twice-told Tales* [2nd ed.] and *Mosses from an Old Manse*, by Nathaniel Hawthorne. 1847. *Essays and Reviews*, edited by G. R. Thompson. New York: Library of America, 1984. 577–88. Print.

Quinn, Patrick F. *The French Face of Edgar Poe*. Carbondale: Southern Illinois University Press, 1957. Print.

Reynolds, Larry J. *European Revolutions and the American Literary Renaissance*. New Haven, CT: Yale University Press, 1988. Print.

Rocks, James E. "Hawthorne and France: In Search of American Literary Realism." *Tulane Studies in English* 17 (1969): 145–57. Print.

Saintsbury, George. *A History of Criticism and Literary Taste in Europe from the Earliest Texts to the Present Day*. 3 vols. Edinburgh: W. Blackwood and Sons, 1900–1904. Print.

Simpson, Claude M. *Centenary Edition of the Works of Nathaniel Hawthorne*. 23 vols. "Historical Commentary," *The American Notebooks*, vol. VIII, edited by Claude M. Simpson. Columbus: The Ohio State University Press, 1972. 677–98. Print.

Skard, Sigmund. *American Studies in Europe: Their History and Present Organization*. 2 vols. Philadelphia: University of Pennsylvania Press, 1958. Print.

Skinner, J. W. "Some Aspects of Émile Montégut." *Revue de littérature comparée* 3 (1923): 283–88. Print.

Stewart, Randall. "Editing Hawthorne's Notebooks: Selections from Mrs. Hawthorne's Letters to Mr. and Mrs. Fields, 1864–1868." *More Books, Being the Bulletin of the Boston Public Library* 20 (1945): 299–315. Print.

Taine, Hippolyte. Letter to Émile Montégut. 9 Apr. 1878. *Bibliographie méthodique et critique des œuvres d'Émile Montégut*. Pierre-Alexis Muenier. Paris: Librairie Garnier Frères, 1925. 142–43. Print.

———. *Histoire de la littérature anglaise*. 4 vols. Paris: Hachette, 1863–64. Print.

Tocqueville, Alexis de. *Democracy in America*, translated by Arthur Goldhammer. New York: Library of America, 2004. Print.

Tolliver, Willie. *Henry James as a Biographer: A Self among Others*. New York: Garland, 2000. Print.

Trilling, Lionel. *The Liberal Imagination: Essays on Literature and Society*. 1950. New York: Anchor Books, 1953. Print.

Virtanen, Reino. "Émile Montégut as a Critic of American Literature." *PMLA* 63.4 (Dec. 1948): 1265–75. Print.

Wagenkknecht, Edward. *Nathaniel Hawthorne: Man and Writer*. New York: Oxford University Press, 1961. Print.

Wagonner, Hyatt. *Hawthorne: A Critical Study*. Cambridge, MA: Harvard University Press, 1955. Print.

Ward, F. O. Letter to Paul Émile-Daurand Forgues. 9 Feb. 1852. "Forgues: Nineteenth Century Anglophile." Moira Anne (Curr) Helgesen. Dissertation University of Colorado, 1955. 113–14. Print.

Wellek, René. *A History of Modern Criticism, 1750–1950*. 8 vols. New Haven, CT: Yale University Press, 1955–92. Print.

Whipple, Edwin P. "Nathaniel Hawthorne." *Character and Characteristic Men*. Boston: Ticknor & Fields, 1867. 218–42. Print.

Winters, Yvor. "Maule's Curse, or Hawthorne and the Problem of Allegory." *American Review* 9 (Sept. 1937): 339–61. Rpt. *In Defense of Reason*. Chicago: Swallow Press, 1947. 157–75. Print.

Zimmerman, Melvin. "Baudelaire, Poe and Hawthorne." *Revue de littérature comparée* 39 (Jul./Sept. 1965): 448–50. Print.

Index

Académie française, 15–16
Addison, Joseph, 100
Albert the Great, 89, 221
Alcott, Amos Bronson, 36, 132, 270
Arac, Jonathan, 55, 69nn39–40
Aubigné, Théodore Agrippa d', 229n5

Bacon, Roger, 89, 221
Bancroft, George, 281, 289n38
Barine, Arvède, 19, 84
Barnum, Phineas T., 10
Baudelaire, Charles, 3, 10, 15, 21, 30–31, 91, 67n17, 194, 194n1, 286
Baudrillard, Jean, 19
Beaumont, Francis, 268
Bellingham, Richard, 57, 113, 171
Bentham, Jeremy, 274, 288n30
Bercovitch, Sacvan, 69n39
Bersot, Ernest, 16
Boccaccio, Giovanni, 239
Boileau, Nicolas, 138, 162n24
Boston (MA), 100, 105–6, 127, 161, 235, 249, 281

Bowdoin College (Brunswick, ME), 100, 128n8, 260
Bradshaw, John, 260
Bradstreet, Simon, 113
Bremer, Fredrika, 265, 287n11
Bridge, Horatio, 128n8
Brisbane, Albert, 44
Brockden Brown, Charles, 21, 99–100, 175, 269
Brodhead, Richard, 77
Brontë, Charlotte, 17, 258
Brontë, Emily, 17
Brook Farm (Roxbury, MA), 44, 47, 55–56, 75, 77, 100, 102, 130, 132, 137, 139–40, 176, 178–80, 182, 215, 270, 277, 282
Brooks, Van Wyck, 19
Browne, Sir Thomas, 268–69
Bryant, William Cullen, 100
Buffon, Comte de (Georges-Louis Leclerc), 242
Buloz, François, 9, 14–15, 18
Bunyan, John, 57, 125, 131, 170, 249, 262, 268, 283

303

Burton, Robert, 101, 200, 229n5, 268–69
Bushman, Richard, 19
Byron, George Gordon, Lord, 201, 259, 286n5

Calderón, Pedro, 24, 60, 65n6, 76, 131, 229n1
Calvin, John, 249
Cambridge (MA), 48, 77, 152, 163n30
Carlyle, Thomas, 16, 100, 127, 160, 163n36, 258
Caro, Elme Marie, 16
Carpenter, Frederic, 50, 68n34
Channing, William Ellery, 57, 132, 137, 170, 175–76, 263, 270
Channing, William Henry, 215
Chapelle (Claude Emmanuel Lhuillier), 258, 286n5
Charivari, 13
Charles I, King, 260
Chasles, Philarète, 8, 11, 21, 68n33
Chateaubriand, François-René de, 171, 194n6
Colacurcio, Michael, 24
Coleridge, Samuel Taylor, 286n5
Concord (MA), 36, 43, 57, 77, 100, 103–4, 106, 128n3, 132, 170, 176, 270
Condillac, Étienne Bonnot de, 242
Conway, Moncure D., 68n27
Cooper, James Fenimore, 21, 99–100
Corneille, Pierre, 174, 194n8
Cowper, William, 189
Cromwell, Oliver, 130
culture, American
abolitionism, 55, 138, 193
as post-colonial, 7–9, 21, 100–101, 133–34, 138–40, 234–35
Civil War, 73
class divisions, 50–53, 125–26, 137–39, 213
Compromise of 1850, 55, 138, 193, 282
democracy, 55–57
election of 1848, 128n4
election of 1852, 193, 282
Homestead Act, 138
journalism, 108–9, 138, 175, 180

literature, 165–66, 183–84
manners, 174–76, 180–81, 183–84
materialism, 126, 139, 166, 174–77
Mexican-American War, 44, 275
political parties, 100, 106–8, 138, 162n22, 193, 282
Puritanism, 23–24, 84, 164–74, 206–7, 260–63
Salem witch trials, 130, 161n7, 260
Second Great Awakening, 44
Shakerism, 34, 114–17, 267, 287n16
slavery, 55, 129, 193
socialism (*see also* Brook Farm), 44–45, 102, 129, 132, 137–40, 176–79, 215, 276–77
Transcendentalism, 36–37, 43, 47, 49, 56–57, 60–62, 166, 175, 180, 186, 188, 192–93, 232–52, 262–63
War for Independence, 99–100, 113–14, 127n1
women, 45, 49, 141, 143–44, 162n22, 180–82, 194n12
culture, French
appreciation of Hawthorne, 32, 67n26
attitudes toward the United States, 7–11
Bibliothèque des chemins de fer, 32
class divisions, 178
Collège de France, 15
democracy, 9–10
interest in American literature, 7–11, 18, 21–22
The July Monarchy, 16–17
literature, 171–72, 174, 267–68
literary criticism, 8–9
literary market, 3–4, 32, 79
reading public, 3–4
The Restoration, 15
Revolution of 1789, 56, 58–59, 84–85, 202, 229n8
Revolution of 1848, 4, 7, 9, 15, 18, 44, 46, 77, 194, 275
The Second Empire, 9–10, 16–17, 18, 22, 43, 49
The Second Republic, 9, 17, 18, 44
Cummins, Maria, 10
Curtis, George William, 175, 229n10

Dana, Richard Henry, Jr., 137, 277
Dante, 16, 54, 160, 187, 195n19, 267
Delacroix, Eugène, 256, 286n1
Delangle, Claude Alphonse, 13
Descartes, René, 141
Dickens, Charles, 32
Diderot, Denis, 259, 286n5
Douglas, Ann, 57

Eliot, George, 251
Eliot, T. S., 77–78, 83, 86
Emerson, Ralph Waldo, 8, 10, 15–16, 18, 21, 35, 43–44, 57, 60–61, 74–75, 77, 100, 102–3, 125, 127, 132–33, 136, 161, 162n16, 170, 175–76, 188, 205, 229, 233, 235, 242–44, 251, 263, 270, 274, 286n4, 287n12, 288n31
Endicott, John, 113–14, 157, 171, 279
ÉTIENNE, LOUIS
life and career, 17–18
social and political views, 17–19, 44–46, 49, 52–54, 56–57, 60–61, 164–66
style, 17–19, 23–24, 56–57, 61
as translator, 38–43

Faust, Bertha, 4–5
Fields, James T., 28, 52, 93
Fillmore, Millard, 282
Flandrin, Hippolyte, 256
Flaubert, Gustave, 15
Fletcher, John, 268
Fontaine, Jean de la, 121, 128n13
Ford, John, 268, 282, 287n17
FORGUES, PAUL ÉMILE-DAURAND
life and career, 13–14
"Old Nick," 13
social and political views, 13, 22–23, 49, 55
as translator, 14, 31, 33–34
Fourier, Charles, 37, 44, 129, 132, 215, 270
Foxe, John, 57, 170–71, 194
Franklin, Benjamin, 59, 166
Freneau, Philip, 175

Fuller, Margaret, 10, 15, 45, 73, 161, 175, 180, 182, 194n13, 215

Gazette des Tribunaux, 155, 163n32
George III, King, 189
Girardin, Delphine de, 185, 195n16
Godwin, William, 100, 133, 269
Gœthe, Johann Wolfgang von, 16, 229n3, 233, 243–44, 253n3, 254n10, 254n25
Gonnaud, Maurice, 8
Griswold, Rufus, 99–100, 127n1
Guido, 219, 230n22, 249

Hachette (Publisher), 32
Hale, John Parker, 138, 162n22
Hawthorne, Julian, 91, 194n13
HAWTHORNE, NATHANIEL
biography, 99–100, 102–3, 106, 130–32, 166–67, 260–62, 270–71
European travel, 217–21, 234–35, 285
politics, 49, 55, 102–3, 106–14, 130, 175, 182, 193, 206, 282–83
Works:
NOVELS
—*The Blithedale Romance,* 28, 31, 34–41, 44–49, 129–61, 177–82, 198, 215–16, 243, 246, 277–79
—*The House of the Seven Gables,* 14, 28, 31, 42, 49–54, 61, 74, 113, 118–19, 26–27, 168–69, 183–93, 213, 242, 249, 258, 279–81
—*The Marble Faun* (*Transformation*), 32, 42–43, 60–63, 65, 73, 87–91, 217–29, 230n25, 232–52, 283–85
—*The Scarlet Letter,* 14, 22, 31, 33–34, 36, 41–42, 52, 57–59, 113, 118, 130–31, 161n6, 172–74, 213–15, 242, 249, 251, 255n33, 258, 281–82
PREFACES, 99–100
—"The Custom-House" Introduction to *The Scarlet Letter,* 22, 31, 33–35, 37–38, 59, 106–9, 131–33, 261, 281

PREFACES (*Continued*)
—Preface to *The Blithedale Romance*, 137
—Preface to *The Snow-Image*, 33, 102
—Preface to *Twice-told Tales*, 28, 34, 67n16, 119

SHORT STORIES AND SKETCHES, 216–17
—"The Artist of the Beautiful," 217
—"The Birth-mark," 31–32, 120–21, 217, 272
—"Buds and Bird-Voices," 125
—"Mrs. Bullfrog," 167–68
—"The Celestial Railroad," 57, 125, 170–71
—"The Christmas Banquet," 217, 272–73
—"David Swan," 32, 205, 273
—"Dr. Higginbotham's Catastrophe," 32
—"Earth's Holocaust," 56–57, 84–85, 202–3
—"Edward Fane's Rosebud," 267
—"Egotism; or the Bosom-Serpent," 217, 224, 272
—"Endicott and the Red Cross," 114
—"Ethan Brand," 28, 112–13, 161, 267
—"The Great Stone Face," 43–44, 136, 274–76
—"The Haunted Mind," 274
—"Legends of the Province-House," 55, 113
—*Mosses from an Old Manse*, 14, 32, 74, 132, 200, 217, 258, 260, 264, 270–73
—"The Old Manse," 22, 103–6, 167, 270
—"The Minister's Black Veil," 31, 120–22, 266–67
—"The Procession of Life," 125–26
—"Rappaccini's Daughter," 29–30, 32, 128n2, 217, 224, 264, 271–72, 288n23
—"A Rill from the Town-Pump," 125
—"The Shaker Bridal," 34, 114–17, 267

—"Sights from a Steeple," 125
—"Snow-Flakes," 125
—"The Snow-Image," 23, 33, 109–12, 161, 167, 194, 217, 270
—*The Snow-Image and Other Twice-told Tales*, 270–73, 288n21
—"Sunday at Home," 26, 125, 270
—"Sylph Etherege," 112
—"The Threefold Destiny," 43, 137, 274–75
—*Twice-told Tales*, 31–32, 100, 217, 264, 270–71
—"The Vision of the Fountain," 125
—"Wakefield," 120, 122–24, 273–74
—"The Wedding Knell," 31, 161, 265–66
—"Young Goodman Brown," 31, 217, 271, 288n22

OTHER
—*The French and Italian Notebooks*, 64
—*The Life of Franklin Pierce*, 55, 193, 195n22
—*Our Old Home*, 285
—*A Wonderbook for Boys and Girls*, 32

TRANSLATIONS, 31–32
—*Contes étranges*, 32
—*Contes racontés deux fois*, 32, 67n26
—"*La fiancée du Shaker*," 68n27
—*La lettre rouge A*, 14, 31
—*Le livre des merveilles*, 32, 68n27
—*La maison aux sept pignons*, 14, 31
—*Miriam* [*The Marble Faun*], 32
—*Trois contes*, 32

WRITING
—allegory, 26–27, 113, 207–8, 212–13, 261–62
—Catholicism, attitude toward, 225–27, 250–51
—defects of artistry, 28–29, 53, 62–63, 66n15, 118, 135, 134–35, 158, 184, 186–87, 204–5, 212–13, 217, 224–25, 283
—detachment, 28, 53, 133, 135, 158–59, 184–85, 197–98, 200–205, 208–9, 273–74
—evil, problem of, 58–59, 164–66, 171, 263–64

WRITING (Continued)
—gothicism, 118, 134, 187, 264–65
—governed by ideas, 22–23, 242–43, 250, 262–63, 274
—humor, 23–24, 100, 103–4, 205–6, 273–74
—history, as subject, 21, 207–8, 281
—(im)morality, 101–2, 109, 133, 135–36, 142, 209–212, 249, 277–78, 285–86
—psychology, 25–26, 53–54, 58, 101, 118–19, 131–32, 134–35, 186–89, 264–65, 270–71, 284–85
—Puritanism, genealogy of, 23–26, 30–31, 58–59, 75–76, 130–32, 166–67, 206–8, 233, 250, 260–63, 270–71
—style, 100–101, 118–19, 126–27, 158–59, 208–9
Hegel, Georg Wilhelm Friedrich, 203, 242
Heine, Heinrich, 258
Hetzel, Pierre-Jules, 15, 32, 252
Hillard, George, 36, 103, 132, 270
Hoffmann, E. T. A., 118, 122, 168, 218, 230n20
Holmes, Oliver Wendell, 14
Homer, 242
Horace, 233, 252n2
Howells, William Dean, 90, 288n19
Hugo, Victor, 252n1

Irving, Washington, 21, 72, 99–100, 108, 118

JAMES, HENRY
 appropriation of French insights, 71–73, 81–90
 on American provincialism, 87–90
 enduring significance of critical views, 73, 78–79, 83, 93n12
 Hawthorne, 5, 25, 53, 58, 63, 71–91
 opinion of Montégut, 78–79, 93n12
Jonson, Ben, 268
Journal du Commerce, 13
Julius II, Pope, 250

Kant, Immanuel, 242
Knox, John, 199, 229n4

Lamb, Charles, 9, 100–101, 133
Lathrop, George Parsons, 72–73, 80, 84, 92n5
Laugel, Auguste, 79
Lawrence, D. H., 58–59
Legouvé, Ernest, 16
Leopardi, Giacomo, 283, 290n42
Lesage, Alain-René, 195n21, 259, 286n5
Levin, Harry, 11, 19, 69n50
Lewis, Matthew ("Monk"), 118, 269
Lincoln, Abraham, 73
Livy, 162n19, 275, 289n34
Longfellow, Henry Wadsworth, 10, 15, 100, 132, 260, 270
Louis XIV, King, 113
Louis-Philippe, King, 15–16
Lowell, James Russell, 77, 92n3, 105

Mackenzie, Henry, 100
Mallarmé, Stéphane, 3
Marivaux, Pierre Carlet de Chambelain de, 259, 286n5
Mather, Increase, 279
Matthiessen, F. O., 25, 77
Maturin, Charles Robert, 118
Melville, Herman, 10, 13, 18–19, 23–24, 31, 66n14
Merimée, Prosper, 125
Meyerbeer, Giacomo, 256
Michelet, Jules, 15
Miller, Perry, 24–25, 27
Milton, John, 262
Molière, 129, 161
Montaigne, 9, 134, 188
Montalbán, Juan Pérez de, 65n6
MONTÉGUT, ÉMILE
 aesthetic values, 16, 129, 133, 158–59, 216–17, 227–29
 life and career, 13–17
 range of critical interest, 10–11
 social and political views, 16–17, 23, 43–44, 46–48, 55–56, 132

308   Index

MONTÉGUT, ÉMILE (*Continued*)
    style, 47, 63–64
    theory of genius, 256–59
    as translator, 15, 37–42, 44–49
Morley, John, 71, 93

Napoleon I, Emperor, 188
Napoleon III, Emperor, 9, 18, 43
Nettels, Elsa, 71
New York Tribune, 79, 138
Nodier, Charles, 99–100, 126
North American Review, 206, 163n30
Novalis (Georg Philipp Friedrich Freiherr von Hardenberg), 235, 253n8

Paris, Gaston, 16
Parker, Theodore, 137, 270
Peabody, Elizabeth, 66n9, 162n21
Peabody, Sophia, 80, 93n17, 132
Pepys, Samuel, 101
Pérez, Juan, de Montalbán, 65n6
Pierce, Franklin, 15, 55, 193, 282
Plato, 176–77, 188
Plutarch, 235
Poe, Edgar Allan, 3–4, 6, 10, 13, 17–18, 21, 30–31, 66n15, 67n17, 83, 91, 101, 139
Praxiteles, 64, 222–23, 233–34, 236–37, 244, 249, 284

Quinn, Patrick, 6, 31

Radcliffe, Ann, 118, 168, 269
Raleigh, Sir Walter, 139
Ramus, Petrus, 27
Randolph, Edward, 113–14
Renan, Ernest, 15–16
Revue britannique, 13
Revue contemporaine, 17–18, 32, 63
Revue des Deux Mondes, 2, 4, 9, 14–16, 18, 34, 39, 53, 63, 79
Revue de Paris, 13
Reynolds, Larry J., 4, 6

Ripley, George, 137, 175, 215, 277
Rocks, James E., 5, 65
Rojas Zorrilla, Francisco de, 65n6
Rome, 136, 221, 226, 235–36, 241, 275, 284
Rousseau, Jean Jacques, 13, 201
Roxbury (MA). *See* Brook Farm
Ruskin, John, 230n22

Sainte-Beuve, Charles Augustin, 10–11, 13–16, 79
Saintsbury, George, 11, 79, 93n12
Salem (MA), 77, 94n23, 99, 127n1, 130, 166, 260
Sand, George, 58, 118, 194
Schelling, Friedrich Wilhelm Joseph von, 242
Scott, Sir Walter, 99–100, 118, 130, 260, 280, 289n36
Seward, William, 138, 162n22
Shakespeare, William, 15–16, 35, 41, 66n14, 101, 139, 157, 168, 188, 220, 268
Shelley, Percy Bysshe, 201
Sidney, Sir Philip, 139
Smith, Gerrit, 138, 162n22
Spenser, Edmund, 268
Spinoza, Baruch, 235, 243, 252
de Staël, Madame, 182, 217
Sterne, Laurence, 100
Stowe, Harriet Beecher, 129
Stuart, Mary, Queen, 199, 229n4
Swedenborg, Emmanuel, 140, 188
Swift, Jonathan, 205, 220

Taine, Hippolyte, 10–11, 15–16, 60, 79
Tasso, Torquato, 51, 280
Taylor, Bishop Jeremy, 220, 268–69
Taylor, Zachary, 100, 107, 128n4
Tennyson, Alfred, Lord, 17
Thackeray, William Makepeace, 17, 256–57, 286
Thoreau, Henry David, 77, 132, 270
Titles by Other Authors
    Adam Bede (G. Eliot), 251

Titles by Other Authors (*Continued*)
Los amantes de Teruel (Pérez), 65n6
Ameto (Boccaccio), 239
The Anatomy of Melancholy (Burton), 229n5, 287n17
The Arabian Nights, 139
Ars Poetica (Horace), 252
"Art" (Emerson), 61, 234–35, 253n7
Les aventures du baron de Faeneste (Aubigné), 229n5
The Book of Martyrs (Foxe), 57, 170
The Bride of Lammermoor (Scott), 51, 280, 289n36
Broken Heart (Ford), 282
Caleb Williams (Godwin), 269
Childe Harold's Pilgrimage (Byron), 19, 171, 194n7
"Circles" (Emerson), 61, 250, 255n28
"Compensation" (Emerson), 61, 235
Corinne (de Staël), 217, 230n19
The Decameron (Boccaccio), 157
Democracy in America (Tocqueville), 7–9, 11, 46
"The Descent into the Maelström" (Poe), 139
"Dialogue Between Nature and a Soul" (Leopardi), 283, 290n42
Don Juan (Hoffmann), 218, 230n20
Edgar Huntly (Brockden Brown), 269
El más impropio verdugo (Rojas Zorilla), 65n6
Émile (Rousseau), 13
Errand into the Wilderness (Miller), 24–25
Essays: First Series (Emerson), 43, 60, 235, 253n7
Ethics (Spinoza), 254n24
Fables (La Fontaine), 121
Faust (Gœthe), 210, 235, 254n10
Female Life among the Mormons (Ward), 10
The Feminization of American Culture (Douglas), 57
Les fleurs du mal (Baudelaire), 17, 30, 91, 164, 194n1
French Poets and Novelists (James), 72
From Puritan to Yankee (Bushman), 19
"Ganymede" (Gœthe), 233, 253n3

"The Gold-Bug" (Poe), 139
Hamlet (Shakespeare), 241, 259, 286n6
"Hawthorne and His *Mosses*" (Melville), 23, 31, 66n14
"The Hawthorne Aspect" (T. S. Eliot), 77–78
Histoire de Gil Blas de Santillane (Lesage), 54, 69n38, 189–90, 195n21, 286n5
Holy Living and Holy Dying (Taylor), 268–69, 288n18
Homes of American Authors (Curtis), 229n10, 287n12
Homes of the New World (Bremer), 287n11
Indiana (Sand), 58, 174, 194n9
Jane Eyre (C. Brontë), 258
The Lamplighter (Cummins), 10
Légende des siècles (Hugo), 232, 252
Lélia (Sand), 58, 118, 128n12, 174, 194n9
Le lutrin (Boileau), 138, 162n24
Libres opinions morales et historiques (Montégut), 15
The Life of P. T. Barnum, Written by Himself (Barnum), 10
Literary Friends and Acquaintance (Howells), 288n19
"*Le lorgnon*" (Girardin), 185, 195n16
"Love" (Emerson), 128n7
Maule's Curse (Winters), 26–27
Le médecin malgré lui (Molière), 130
Memoirs of Margaret Fuller Ossoli (ed. Emerson et al.), 73, 161
The Merry Wives of Windsor (Shakespeare), 157
Moby-Dick; or, The Whale (Melville), 10
Nathaniel Hawthorne and His Wife (Julian Hawthorne), 194n13
Notes of a Son and Brother (James), 73, 92n8
Old Mortality (Scott), 161n5
The Pilgrim's Progress (Bunyan), 57, 125, 161n9, 170
Polyeucte (Corneille), 174
Prose Writers of America (Griswold), 100, 127n1

Titles by Other Authors (*Continued*)
René (Chateaubriand), 171
Representative Men (Emerson), 188
Romeo and Juliet (Shakespeare), 276
Ruth Hall (Fern), 10
Scenes of Clerical Life (G. Eliot), 251
"Self-Reliance" (Emerson), 43, 136, 162n16, 258, 286n4, 288n31
The Social Destiny of Man (Brisbane), 44
The Sorrows of Young Werther (Gœthe), 243
Souvenirs de Bourgogne (Montégut), 93n12
Studies in Classic American Literature (Lawrence), 58
A Study of Hawthorne (Lathrop), 66n9, 72, 80, 92n5
Uncle Tom's Cabin (Stowe), 10, 129, 161
"The Unparalleled Adventures of One Hans Pfaall" (Poe), 139
Vanity Fair (Thackeray), 257
Wieland (Brockden Brown), 269
"Woodnotes I" (Emerson), 61, 238, 254n15

Tocqueville, Alexis de, 4, 7–8, 11, 21, 45–46, 50–51, 53, 56, 75
Töpffer, Rodolphe, 126
Trilling, Lionel, 45, 68n32
Turgenev, Ivan, 32

Valéry, Paul, 3
Vane, Sir Henry, 113
Verne, Jules, 32
Virtanen, Reino, 5
Voltaire (François-Marie Arouet), 205, 259, 286n5

Wagonner, Hyatt, 65
Ward, Maria (pseud.), 10
Warner, Susan B., 13
Webster, John, 200, 220, 229n5, 268–69
Wellek, René, 79, 93n12
Whipple, Edwin P., 66n15
Winters, Yvor, 26–27
Winthrop, John, 113, 127n1
Wordsworth, William, 17, 220, 259, 286n5

www.ingramcontent.com/pod-product-compliance
Lightning Source LLC
Chambersburg PA
CBHW021833220426
43663CB00005B/223